Exploring the Essentials of Healthy Personality

Exploring the Essentials of Healthy Personality

What Is Normal?

Camay Woodall, PhD

 PRAEGER

AN IMPRINT OF ABC-CLIO, LLC
Santa Barbara, California • Denver, Colorado • Oxford, England

Library of Congress Cataloging-in-Publication Data

Woodall, Camay.
  Exploring the essentials of healthy personality : what is normal? / Camay Woodall.
     pages   cm
  Includes index.
  ISBN 978-1-4408-3194-2 (hardcover : alk. paper) — ISBN 978-1-4408-3195-9 (ebook)
 1. Personality. 2. Mental health. 3. Self-esteem. 4. Self-reliance. 5. Self-confidence.
I. Title.
  BF698.W66   2014
  155.2—dc23   2014007249

ISBN: 978-1-4408-3194-2
EISBN: 978-1-4408-3195-9

18 17 16 15 14   1 2 3 4 5

This book is also available on the World Wide Web as an eBook.
Visit www.abc-clio.com for details.

Praeger
An Imprint of ABC-CLIO, LLC

ABC-CLIO, LLC
130 Cremona Drive, P.O. Box 1911
Santa Barbara, California 93116-1911

This book is printed on acid-free paper ∞

Manufactured in the United States of America

For Mary: Whose love and support, courage and sense of fun inspire me to this day.

For Ralph: The best father a girl ever had.

And for Will . . .

Contents

Acknowledgments

My greatest appreciation goes to my son, Jeff Woodall, whose amazing technical skill guided me through all my ineptness. Thanks also to Kate Krupey for further technical and editorial assistance. Barbara Lamb of The Johns Hopkins University Press provided formal editorial help as well as many good suggestions for improving clarity. Bryan Miller provided essential help with formatting. Debbie Carvalko, my editor at Praeger, has been the voice of reason, restraint, and pragmatism. Everything she required made the book better. Charlotte and Mike Gordon helped scrutinize the page proofs for scanning errors.

Arnold Andersen's tutelage at the Johns Hopkins Hospital Eating Disorders Unit taught me much about the physical sequellae of anorexia nervosa and bulimia. He encouraged my innovative ideas on "professional anorexia," as well as the therapeutic approach I developed in my doctoral dissertation and used successfully with our patients.

Deep appreciation and gratitude to my peer supervision group, Liza Frank, Judith Sheagren, and George Strutt, for many illuminating discussions. And in loving memory of Eileen Higham, whose unique observations and incisive wit enriched our meetings.

Special thanks to physicians Randolph Whipps and Ariane Cometa for helpful discussions about women's need for bio-identical (human) hormone replacement, proper nutrition, and other health issues.

Much gratitude to my professor, Dorothy Dinnerstein, who transformed my understanding of male–female dilemmas and their necessary solutions. Her book *The Mermaid and the Minotaur: Sexual Arrangements and Human Malaise* illustrated that since women and men have lived such different histories, the view from a woman's place does provide new knowledge.

Thanks also to many friends and colleagues at the Roche Institute of Molecular Biology, from whom I learned so much. Particularly to friend and colleague John Williams, professor of biochemistry at the Australian National University, who singularly understood my wish to switch from cell biology to psychology for my doctoral degree. Thanks also to distinguished professor of psychology Barry R. Komisaruk for having recommended me to the Johns Hopkins Department of Psychiatry and Behavioral Sciences for a postdoctoral position.

One of the most inspiring persons in my life has been my friend and mentor Jerome Frank, professor of psychiatry at Hopkins, whose book *Persuasion and Healing* is essential reading for anyone learning psychotherapy. Professor Frank helped me rehearse my talks and presentations, stressing the difference between creativity and speculation.

Thanks also to my readers—Lorraine and Larry Miller, Ronda and Phil Pinton, Kate and Mike Krupey, Charlotte and Mike Gordon, and Jill Bloom—for their careful perusal and criticism of parts of the manuscript. Their questions and feedback helped me reorganize many of the original arguments in the book.

Heartfelt gratitude to my daughter, Dominique Battles, for her irreplaceable support. She is proof of all we can learn from our children. Scholar, author, and exemplary wife and mother, I thank her for years of insightful discussions on a number of the topics that ended up in these pages.

I treasure the memory of my childhood friend, Lil, who died too young from one of the diseases I write about in this book. She may have benefited from reading it.

Finally, appreciation and thanks to all my patients over the span of 30 years, both at the Johns Hopkins Hospital and in my private practice, for their personal contributions to my understanding of "the essentials of healthy personality." Their poignant stories remain the heart and soul of this book.

Introduction

Someone was calling my name. I'd just returned to my car after a day of giving talks at a high school about the dangers of eating disorders. I turned and saw one of the students running toward me, a girl of about 17. I held out my hand to her, and as she grasped it, she said breathlessly, "Doctor Woodall, I couldn't ask you this in front of the whole class." She hesitated. I smiled, and she continued, "Why does my mother sleep eighteen hours a day, and has for my whole life? Is that normal?"

I looked at her. This was no carefree teen. She looked tired, and her eyes were brimming with tears. "No, it's not normal," I said. "Sleeping eighteen hours a day, every day, is a serious symptom. Has your mother ever been examined by a physician?" She shook her head no. "Well then," I continued, "we could look at this as psychological—perhaps severe depression. No psychological exam either?"

"No," she said. "My father would never permit it."

She described her father's expectation—barely verbalized—that she, the eldest child, take care of the two younger ones. From the age of nine, she had had the responsibility of her two younger siblings after her father went to work at three in the afternoon. This situation had all but canceled her childhood and separated her from her age group.

I explained to her that her mother's excessive sleeping would require a thorough evaluation to rule out medical conditions, but that sleep *can* be used as a drug. Excessive sleeping can be a sign of severe depression or perhaps a case of narcolepsy. It would take a good workup to be certain. Clearly, this girl knew this was not going to happen. She was certain of only one thing; her mother's condition was not due to alcohol. I asked if she might reach out to others—relatives or someone at her church. She shook her head. Her father would not permit this, she said. Then she walked away. I called her back and gave her my card, saying she could call me at any time. She never did.

What will happen to this girl? At the very least, she had developed a sense of her self-worth that was defined by service to others. She was already overly compliant—perhaps compulsively so—doing too much for a demanding parent out of a sense of duty and perhaps guilt. She will likely grow up feeling profoundly cheated, which in turn can engender feelings of anger toward her father. This anger will doubtless be unacceptable to such a "good girl," so it will be repressed, and her conscious feeling will be "I am only valued for what I do. So to be loved, I have to do more."

She may grow up resenting her siblings and perhaps not wanting children.

Or she may have children and spoil one of them while pushing the others away.

She may expect her children to take care of her.

She may indeed seek a husband who needs her caretaking and then resent him. Or she may only choose men who indulge her whims.

Any of these outcomes would represent this girl's adaptation to her family's current expectations. She could not do otherwise and stay in this family. Because of her acceptance of these expectations, she was not going to grow up without some kind of symptom. Her inner conflict and ambivalence were significant. How different her life could have been if her mother had been evaluated and treated, or if she had had an emotionally healthy mother who took good care of all three children and let her have a happy, protected childhood.

ARE HAPPINESS AND EMOTIONAL HEALTH RELATED?

The "essentials of emotional health" and expressions of happiness can overlap. We may not always recognize how closely related happiness and emotional health are. To quote psychology professor Sonja Lyubomirsky:

> A recent review of all the available literature has revealed that happiness does indeed have numerous positive byproducts, which appear to benefit not only individuals, but families, communities and the society at large. The benefits of happiness include higher income and superior work outcomes (e.g., greater productivity and higher quality of

work); larger social rewards (e.g., more satisfying and longer marriages, more friends, stronger social support, and richer social interactions); more activity, energy and flow; better physical health (e.g., a bolstered immune system, lowered stress levels, and less pain); and even longer life. The literature, my colleagues and I have found, also suggests that happy individuals are more creative, helpful, charitable and self-confident; have better self-control; and show greater self-regulatory and coping abilities. (Lyubormirsky, as quoted in D. Buettner 2010, 19)

It can be argued that these categories of happiness are linked to or are effects of a person's mental and emotional health. For example, people who show high levels of self-esteem, patience, and responsibility—all features of healthy personalities—have a good work ethic, greater work satisfaction, and happier relationships. Developmental psychologists have shown that this emotional health in turn is the result of adequate care and protection during a person's early years. It may well be that when families, communities, and then governments can provide these basics to their children and citizens, the result is a high level of this complex phenomenon: happiness.

We should note that overall happiness is affected by the level of "happiness" a person starts with, an interesting phenomenon. Certain older generations, in particular those who experienced the Great Depression, started out much less happy than did later generations. It may have been more difficult for them to transcend their early deprivation to experience their happiness as increasing with age, as happens with other cohorts (Urry & Gross 2010).

My professional experience has shown me that people are happy when they feel lucky. They feel fortunate to have found a wonderful partner, to finally be pregnant, or to have found a house that finally they both like. They feel lucky to have finished their degree or to be visiting a country they had dreamed about. In other cases, happiness may be an outcome of the confluence of certain circumstances, even chance.

Hold on, you may be saying. Some people are only happy when they have power over others. And lots of people would be very happy if they won a million dollars. Yes, having money does make people happier. But the finding is that, after a certain amount of money has been acquired, there is no further increase in happiness. And the lottery winners soon go back to their previous level of happiness, before they won the money. In fact, a study in the *Journal of Personality and Social Psychology*, a meta-analysis of 638 studies in 63 countries, found that feelings of well-being were correlated more with the freedom to do what one wants than with wealth (Fischer & Boer 2011, 164–84). As for people seeking power over others, that is often motivated by revenge and sadism (enjoying another person's pain), and it is very abnormal. Such power has to be maintained by force, and sooner or later, tyrants fall to other power seekers.

It is a premise of this book that ongoing happiness and contentment may be linked to emotional health. Not glee, not the excitement of watching a game, but the quiet, day-to-day contentment that is the result of freedom from tension, anxiety, and depression. This kind of happiness nurtures you from dawn to dusk. It comes from your own efforts—efforts to work toward your goals, to be a more patient parent, to understand the people around you, to strive for answers to your own good questions. It comes from the confidence that each day you try to be fair, and you cultivate gratitude for all you have.

DEFINING "NORMAL"

If emotional health is linked to happiness, how do we get it? The ensuing chapters attempt to examine this question. But we should first consider that many people do not believe emotional health is real or achievable. Their stance is that "Nothing is normal and everything is normal"—and to be fair, these distinctions are not always clear. We are certain that a gunman killing eight hostages is "sick," but we may not be able to understand where our own rage comes from. We may be vaguely aware we are eating "emotionally" but be surprised to find we have gained 20 pounds. Is suicide always a "disturbed" behavior, or can it be a reasonable, responsible act? A physician who was herself diagnosed with advanced cancer wanted to take her own life. Is that normal? (It can be.) Is it normal to peer at one's naked neighbor through binoculars? That's harmless, isn't it? (No, for several reasons.) Is it normal to love and resent the same person? (Yes. You might love him for one set of reasons, and you might resent him for a very different set of reasons). Defining "normal" is complex.

A BIT OF HISTORY

Attempts to suggest what is normal and what is not are philosophical staples. In the history of psychology, these concerns predate Sigmund Freud. Philippe Pinel, working in Paris in the early 1800s, was among the first doctors to champion the humane treatment of mental patients. He was disillusioned with the medical treatments of his day, which included opium, camphor, and bloodletting. He recognized that the way people are valued or devalued affects the way they feel about themselves. In dramatic contrast to the beliefs of his time—and anticipating Freud's observations—Pinel held that depression could be the result of serious losses—for example, financial problems or a failed love affair, that overwhelm a person's adaptive capacities.

More recently, the conditions leading to healthy (normal) personality were described by two child development experts, T. Berry Brazelton and Stanley I. Greenspan (2000) in their book *The Irreducible Needs of Children*. There are no surprises in their recommendations; normal human needs persist. Children must have "on-going nurturing relationships" (1); "physical protection" (53); "limit-setting, structure and expectations" (145); and "experiences tailored to individual differences" (79).

Not that parents need to be perfect. D. W. Winnicott, the famous English psychoanalyst who was also a pediatrician, talked about "good-enough mothering." A certain amount of frustration—but not abuse—teaches children delay of gratification (patience for a reward down the road), which makes them stronger and correlates with all kinds of success in adulthood. Even child neglect is not always deliberate. Sometimes parents have been depressed for years. Never having had their own needs met adequately in their childhood, they cannot then nurture their own children. They do not know this when they decide to have children; it is the strain of raising children that tips them over into depression.

This book's cases and discussions examine these important issues—how mothers and small children can be dangerously isolated and frightened. How society can marshal resources for them well before Social Services need step in. Programs like Early Head Start and the Nurse-Mother program, which are now available (in some states) from birth on, address problems of mental health and nutrition at the moment these interventions are most needed. Comforting and encouraging young mothers who may be feeling overwhelmed starts a very auspicious pattern; mothers can then give that nurturance to their babies. We nurture ourselves when we nurture our children. We can share the warmth we give to our own child. *Every emotionally healthy adult is a good parent to herself or himself.*

One of the first psychologists to examine mother–child interactions, Margaret Mahler, observed that children work very hard to get the nurturance they need. If their parents cannot do it, children reach out to grandparents or, failing that, in desperation to neighbors, visiting relatives, and even to older siblings and cousins. Some of my own patients report having been very much helped as children by their friends and their friends' parents. One woman told me that as a three-year-old, she would take the elevator up to visit a couple who had befriended her in that elevator. She had watched to see where they got off. When I asked if her mother had ever missed her, she said her mother would often pass out from drinking, and that's when she became so frightened she sought out the kind couple from the elevator. It worked. The couple realized what was happening and took care of the little girl for a long time. What is amazing is that this three-year-old knew how to get the help she desperately needed and went looking for it.

THE ROLE OF THERAPY

One of the most effective and enduring ways of understanding one's early history and its ongoing effects is psychotherapy. Think of therapy as a respectful, sustained examination of what is bothering you: the questions that do not go away, the sadness that does not lift, the anxiety that grips you—all this is the stuff of therapy. We get a "second chance" in therapy to work through our life's unresolved problems.

Freud called the process of therapy "the talking cure," but in recent years, scientists have discovered that it is much more. Psychotherapy actually changes the brain (Doidge 2007). Neurons change shape and increase in number when long-term memory is formed. Eric Kandel won the Nobel Prize in 2000 for this discovery, which was the first evidence that learning leads to neuroplastic changes—that is, it creates more and stronger synapses. Extending Kandel's work, researchers could show that each time a memory was evoked, it became *labile* and subject to influence. Before the memory could be put back into storage, new proteins must be made. Thus neuronal connections are *altered* by remembering something, again and again, while it is being discussed and analyzed. If we can better understand what happened in the past, with all the reasoning and nuances available to the adult mind, we can change our *experience of the past*. And that *changes the past*. Looking back as adults gives us perspective. It is a life-changing perspective to consider the events of our lives with regard to the period in which they happened. We really begin to understand our motives, the motives of those around us at that time, and the pressures with which people in our past may have lived with.

This process is eminently useful, both in therapy and in life in general. We are not responsible for the family we are born into and to which we must adapt. We must bond to our original family because human infants are born in such a helpless state. That bond is life-saving. If the bond is mutually satisfying, it is a life-long blessing. But if there were serious deficits—neglect, a lack of "good-enough mothering," or outright abuse—neurotic problems will develop. Then as adults we have the responsibility to ask ourselves, "What happened in my early life that now can make me unhappy and unfair to myself and to others around me?" We owe it to ourselves especially, and to those we say we love, to examine any recurrent problem or "hang-up," that gets in the way of genuine happiness.

It helps to understand what psychologists mean by the concept of "neurosis." It is a pattern of behavior that develops early in life as a reaction to some noxious influence or pressure, like an erratic feeding schedule or a family that has screaming fights. The child reacts with fear or with anger and sometimes with withdrawal from the actions that frighten him. His reaction can become a pattern. He reacts in the same way—for example, withdrawing each time the threatening action happens, and this response interferes with his learning and development. The pattern becomes more rigid as the child gets older. By adulthood, it has become so rigid that it does not change, even with the passage of time or when new information indicates that the neurotic response is no longer needed. Neurosis is like a superstition, a false belief that regulates a person's behavior despite being illogical.

People will sometimes see that their fears are irrational but not be able to give them up. Try to think of neurosis as a person's effort to defend herself or himself against *anxiety*. Most symptoms are defenses against anxiety. For example, a phobia is an avoidance of certain fear-inducing places like elevators or bridges. Depression is a defense against the sadness and anxiety caused by a loss. Substance abuse may be a defense against the anxiety caused by certain existential challenges—an overwhelming job or relationship, a dramatic change in income, or the collapse of a narcissistic sense of self.

How are we to understand the concept of neurosis in a simple, descriptive way? Consider an example. It is normal and healthy to reach out for friends as we are growing up—classmates, teammates, and later, romantic interests. It would be unhealthy, indeed worrisome, for a child *not* to reach out for friends of any type. The reasons why this might happen to a child would be different for each person. But the normal need for affiliation—the element of affiliation—is a normal human need we can depend on. So we already have one answer to the question "What is normal?" It is our need for people. We are social beings from the very beginning of life and throughout our lives (Lieberman 2013).

To be sure, "normal" refers to a *wide range of behavior that is both adaptive and expressive.* Yet self-expression—doing what we want when we want—must take into account the right of other people to do the same. Others have the same rights and privileges we want for ourselves. *Ab*normal behavior, on the other hand, is narrow and specific and is judged by its effects. For example, staying in an abusive relationship is usually an abnormal behavior and deserves to be examined by a professional. In a word, a behavior becomes abnormal when it begins to hurt someone else, or indeed, oneself.

I am aware that what is considered normal in one culture may not be accepted as such in another culture. Nor am I forgetting that what was accepted as normal in one era of our history is unacceptable in another. A good example of this is the child labor laws. In the 1920s and 1930s, a limit had to be imposed by law on the number of hours a child could work in the sweatshops. Yet even today, in some cultures, child labor is deemed acceptable and necessary. Throughout world history, children were not as valued as they are now, as Edward Shorter (1982) graphically describes in his book, *A History of Women's Bodies.*

The notions of what is healthy and normal in the lives examined in this book reflect recent and ongoing developments in concepts of fairness and justice. What I have followed in the main is my training in clinical psychology and the rigorous diagnostic evaluations I learned while working at the Johns Hopkins Hospital. But diagnoses can be rigid and narrow. Real people are complex and unique; their personality parameters can overlap the diagnostic labels that insurance companies require.

In addition, the *Diagnostic and Statistical Manual,* Fifth Edition (DSM-5) is, at this writing, the subject of much controversy (Bradshaw 2012; Caccavale 2012; Clay 2014). The major criticism is the "medicalization" of mental illness with the first line of treatment being drugs. What is worse, research findings have expanded the criteria for mental illness such that more than 50 percent of the population can now be diagnosed with a disorder. This excess has now been documented in a new book by Allen Frances, one of the framers of the DSM-4. Frances's (2013) survey, *Saving Normal: An Insider's Revolt against Out-of-Control Psychiatric Diagnosis, DSM-5, Big Pharma, and the Medicalization of Ordinary Life* delivers a wealth of evidence on how "diagnostic inflation" has produced "fake epidemics" of autism, attention deficit disorder, and childhood bipolar disorder. This book may powerfully diminish the influence of American psychiatry on the diagnosis of mental illness. The solution is to switch to the International Classification of Disease. As of October 1, 2014, all psychologists will be using this code, devised by the World Health Organization, used throughout the world, the ICD-10-CM. Psychologist Carol D. Goodheart (2014) has produced an ICD "primer" specifically for psychological and behavioral conditions.

I have also drawn on extensive training with psychoanalytic teachers, as well as a lifetime of reading, but there is much original thought in the book, in both concepts and interpretations. A major resource is my 30-year experience with therapy patients and their poignant stories. The conclusions I come to and the recommendations I make are drawn from this irreplaceable source.

It is striking that the people who take their therapy most seriously and care about their progress *have essentially normal personalities,* although they struggle with a variety of false beliefs and often feel emotionally overwhelmed. The truth is, we never get the "sickest"—that is, the most rigidly defended people, in therapy. We get their children, their spouses, and their employees. The "sickest" people usually do not accept therapy. So their wives, husbands, children, and employees come for therapy, confused, angry, suffering, and not knowing what is right and fair.

My categories are not exhaustive, of course, but they do provide a good overview, another way of thinking about *mens sana in corpore sano* (a sound mind in a sound body). The overriding purpose of this book is to stimulate a more nuanced, practical, and humane discussion. I hope that my patients' stories can edify and illuminate others' lives who may suffer some of the same dilemmas. Listening to people in emotional distress over the years, I have learned much about emotional health and about my own inadequacies as a person and as a parent. We cannot live our lives over, but we can share what we have learned about human quandaries and the vision and hope that survive them.

REFERENCES

Bradshaw, J. (2012, July–August). "Amended DSM 5 Draft Still Criticized." *National Psychologist*, 8.

Brazelton, T. B. & Greenspan, S. I. (2000). *The Irreducible Needs of Children.* Cambridge: Perseus Publishing.

Caccavale, J. (2012, March–April). "Is APA Really Leading the Charge against Medicalization of Mental Health?" *National Psychologist*, 12.

Clay, R. (2014, January). "Your Diagnostic Codes Are Changing." *Monitor on Psychology* 45(1): 42–44.

Doidge, N. (2007). *The Brain That Changes Itself.* New York: Penguin Books.

Fischer, R. & Boer, D. (2011). "What Is More Important for National Well-Being: Money or Autonomy? A Meta-Analysis of Well-Being, Burnout, and Anxiety across 63 Societies." *Journal of Personality and Social Psychology* 101(1): 164–184.

Frances, A. (2013). *Saving Normal: An Insider's Revolt against Out-of-Control Psychiatric Diagnosis, DSM-5, Big Pharma, and the Medicalization of Ordinary Life.* New York: HarperCollins.

Goodheart, C. D. (2014). *A Primer for ICD-10-CM Users: Psychological and Behavioral Conditions.* Washington, DC: American Psychological Association Books.

Lieberman, M. D. (2013). *Social: Why Our Brains Are Wired to Connect.* New York: Crown.

Lyubomirsky, S. (2010). In D. Buettner (Ed.), *Thrive: Finding Happiness the Blue Zone Way*, 19. Washington, DC: National Geographic Society.

Mahler, M. (1979). *Selected Papers of Margaret Mahler, Volume 1. Infantile Psychosis and Early Contributions.* New York: Jason Aronson.

Shorter, E. (1982). *A History of Women's Bodies.* New York: Basic Books.

Urry, H. L. & Gross, J. J. (2010). Emotion Regulation in Older Age. *Current Directions in Psychological Science*, 19, 352–57.

Winnicott, D. W. (1971). *Therapeutic Consultations in Child Psychiatry.* New York: Basic Books, Inc.

Chapter 1

Realism and the Struggle with Self-Deception

The trouble is, we cannot see reality steadily, nor see it whole.
—Dorothy Dinnerstein

Perhaps the single most important criterion of healthy personalities, "realism" refers to the effort to see things as they are: to look outward and know what is actually happening around us and to look inward and bravely admit how we feel about it. We also need to accurately assess how our actions and failings fit with those around us—family, co-workers, friends, and community. Realism enables us to recognize the willfulness in our own behavior. Just as importantly, we can recognize and appreciate what is right and good about ourselves and our behavior. *Realism struggles for objectivity, for the big picture.* We know we are not perfect, and we strive to be better—to work on our personal problems, to improve our marriages, to be more fair and helpful to our children, and to give our best in our work. Relationships—with others and with ourselves—are always evolving, always in a state of becoming.

"Realistic" is another word for "adaptive," what is helpful and appropriate for any given situation. Being realistic means we will stop making excuses for, or covering up, the frank, abusive behavior of a spouse, teenager, supervisor, co-worker or "friend." An example may clarify: Suppose a son has suffered "put-downs" from his father and that it started very early, perhaps at age eight or nine. As an adult, the son has a difficult decision to make. It is not healthy to allow himself to continually be humiliated. The son complains to his father, refusing the criticism and letting his father know that their relationship is threatened. If the father responds with more "put-downs," realism requires that the son distance himself from his father and limit his visits. If the father does not begin to understand and reform his behavior, then the son limits visits even further. This decision represents a claim for the son's self-respect, despite the loss. The son will suffer, giving up the dream that his father will change and give him the respect he deserves. But he will have done the brave and right thing, and he will know how to treat his own son. Thus, developing insight, which informs realism, requires at least four maturational skills: *intelligence, patience, courage,* and *commitment.*

"Intelligence" here means the cognitive capacity to grasp the total situation, the big picture. Before we can change a situation, we have to be able to assess it, with all its nuances, and understand their meanings. For this reason, normal personality functioning probably requires normal IQ, in the sense that a person can perceive and evaluate many disparate data almost simultaneously. Findings from the work of IQ researcher James Flynn (1998) show that populations increase in IQ by about six points a decade when tested on "culturally reduced" tests. This means that we are becoming "smarter" because children from many cultures are adapting to a more complex, electronic world.

Patience is also necessary since personal growth takes time—from the beginning of understanding to actually putting insights into practice. Growth is incremental, and there are often setbacks. These setbacks are resistances that often come from events that happened during childhood. Facing the connections between what is happening now and what happened years ago takes not only intelligence and patience but also *courage.* Why? Because this is the part that may hurt our feelings.

It is so hard to acknowledge that we may have "problems," "issues," or whatever the current popular word is for "baggage." It takes courage to recognize sadness or anger, to stay with it long enough to understand it, and to learn how to change it. All three skills are needed in order to reach the fourth: commitment. Commitment is a fierce dedication to the truth, whatever it may be and however uncomfortable it may make us feel. We are studying and discussing our own lives: we *want* to know what is real and what is actually happening. How different this attitude is from that of a person who fears and hates what is real, who avoids any discussion that might clarify it, or who simply has no energy to find out what is true (a feature of depression).

One effective method to achieve realism is psychotherapy. What therapy often contributes is an important realization: *I did not cause this situation that now makes me unhappy, and I do not want it to continue.* Taking an interest in your own psychological growth and looking at it clinically will give you objectivity and some relief from wounded self-esteem. Therapy is a course whose subject is *you*. The teacher, your therapist, can get at the answers by asking the right questions. Do you want the answers? Sometimes they will be unwelcome or sound unwarranted. With patience, a well-trained therapist will show you the connections. This is the road to *insight*—realism about your inner self.

The more rigidly resistant to developing insight (the "sicker" people are), the less they show the necessary patience, courage, and commitment. People can be very intelligent and yet remain emotionally "stuck." They will vigorously reject your complaints and assertions. You are wrong, no matter how logical and compassionate your plea. Besides, you are hurting their feelings; you're being mean. They refuse to learn anything from the discussion or change their behavior to accommodate your complaint. This rigidity in spouses, bosses, and parents (and politicians) makes them unreachable and leaves the rest of us struggling. That is why I say that we never get the "sickest," most resistant people in therapy. We get their spouses, children, and employees, who are struggling to communicate with significant, respected, often loved persons who cannot or will not reciprocate.

The difference between your efforts and those of your adamant spouse, parent, or employer is one of openness and flexibility. Emotionally healthy people can grieve instead of denying; can suffer instead of attacking. They realize their own vulnerabilities, and they accept them. What is missing in your loved one is the ability to see another person's point of view; to feel hurt and to stay with that discomfort; to seek alternatives that are acceptable to both; to give up their rigidity and be receptive and caring throughout the discussion.

HOW DO PEOPLE BECOME "RIGID"?

Let's consider the definition of the classic term "neurosis." It is what we mean when we say "hang-up" or "baggage." It is a developmental pressure or event that distorts some, but not all, of a person's behavior. It can become a lifelong motivation—a preference for relationships that are not very good for us, for example. A neurosis represents our reaction to something that did not happen for us in a supportive way

while we were growing up. There may have been parental requirements that were too harsh and unsympathetic or tasks that were
beyond our ability at a particular stage of development. Some children
have remarkable stamina and actually meet such requirements, but the
struggle often leads them to develop their self-esteem around being a
"survivor." There is an angry edge to their personality, and they often
look down on others who "can't take it." As adults, these persons
have great difficulty feeling vulnerable. But vulnerability has many
benefits, and it is a requirement for experiencing love.

Rigidity is one of the primary personality traits clinicians identify
as neurotic:

> The measure of health is flexibility, the freedom to learn through experi-
> ence, . . . to be influenced by reasonable argument, admonitions, exhorta-
> tion, and the appeal to emotions; . . . and especially the freedom to cease
> when sated. . . . The essence of illness is the *freezing* of behavior into
> unalterable and insatiable patterns. It is this which characterizes every
> manifestation of psychopathology. (Kubie 1969, 20–21, emphasis added)

If a person has felt chronically threatened from early on, he or she
may respond with a rigid hypervigilance. Some people, for example,
do not remember ever having been put to bed as children. Their rec-
ollections are of the parents drinking and fighting long into the night.
The children simply crawled up the stairs and fell asleep where they
could. ("Dickensian" is a fair term for many of the experiences we
hear about in therapy.) Neurosis can also result from a trauma: beat-
ings, starvation, humiliation, sexual abuse, etc. Such treatment does
not make us bad or crazy, but it means that whatever deficiency or
abuse we suffered during childhood *will* have an effect on our lives as
growing children, and then as adults. If the wound is serious enough
to compromise our work or our relationships, we will likely develop
methods to try to keep it from disorganizing us and making us anxious. We will develop *defense patterns.*

Living the Past

Our need for defenses begins in our past—all the situations we had
to adapt to when we were most vulnerable. And yet the past is precious. Our nostalgia for the past contains all our wishes and dreams,
our identifications and fears that are also born there. How do defense
patterns develop? And how do they compromise our hold on reality?

Defense patterns develop in the very early interactions with the people around us, usually our mother and father. Some little children can take a lot of overstimulation in the form of loud noises, people shouting, and outright neglect—cold, hunger, and the like. But most children will react with anxiety to such experiences, and *that* is the reason for defense patterns: they stem from our need to protect ourselves from *anxiety*. Thus, a child may scream with terror at frightening events or even the anticipation of them, which may set the stage for panic attacks. A child may withdraw and hide when he or she feels frightened. . . . Or a child may strike out defensively each time he feels anxious. . . . If the people in a child's life are cold and unresponsive to his or her emotional needs, that child can give up on emotions and value only the intellectual life. He or she can then excel in school, and later in academic life, but have serious deficits in emotions—in recognizing, feeling, and expressing them. We can see that the defense a child erects against a particular stressor will contain, and be affected by, that child's particular skills. In a word, defenses are *creative.*

Our lives can thus become complicated by our varied efforts to adapt to the excessive pressures we suffered as children—a good definition of neurosis. Defense patterns develop autonomously as our bodies and brains adjust to varying amounts and types of stress. For example, a girl who grew up with a jealous mother and a detached father may find herself marrying a detached husband whose mother is jealous of *her*. And she herself may have trouble trusting at all. Do we know we are doing this? Don't we see the similarities? No. All we know is that we feel a strong pull toward this person. It feels right. And the euphoria of sexual attraction convinces us. Freud called this the "repetition compulsion," the attempt to restage in our adulthood any unresolved patterns from our early life in an effort to master them, to change the outcome.

Does that mean that these marriages will be unhappy? They could well be, but not if both spouses can *learn*, in life or in therapy, to see the connections, to see the other clearly; no lying or deception, no coercion or unfair claims, loving the other for the person he or she is, accepting each other's personal preferences with love and humor. In a word, insight.

My bias is that I know of no other way besides dynamic psychotherapy to correct developmental difficulties and offer individuals relief, a happier life, and the recognition that their suffering is a fate to which they silently consent.

Psychoanalysis offers a theoretical framework for exploring the possibility of a way out of the nightmare of endless "progress" and endless Faustian discontent, a way out of the human neurosis. . . . In the case of the neurotic individual, the goal of psychoanalytical therapy is to free him from the burden of his past, from the burden of his history, the burden which compels him to go on having (and being) a case history. And the method of psychoanalytical therapy is to deepen the historical consciousness of the individual . . . til he awakens from his own history as from a nightmare. (Brown 1959, 19)

DEFENSE PATTERNS AND HOW PEOPLE USE THEM

We struggle with reality in so many ways. These uniquely human defenses against anxiety have been well studied by psychologists and psychoanalysts, whose task it is to identify how defenses operate in the lives of the people they work with. We have to first give credit to the originator of these insights. Sigmund Freud's formulations about defense patterns are, to this day, informally referred to as "Freudian" defenses. They have never been surpassed for their explanatory value and are an inexhaustible resource for research. The defense concepts are retained in later versions of psychoanalysis that are more relational, especially in the work of W. R. D. Fairbairn and Donald Winnicott. Psychoanalysis has given researchers and clinicians a powerful method for understanding motivation and behavior. While psychoanalysis is more time intensive, the outcomes can be shown to be measurably superior to short-term and more superficial approaches. Jonathan Shedler examined 8 meta-analyses, covering 160 studies, and concluded:

Empirical evidence supports the efficacy of psychodynamic therapy. Effect sizes for psychodynamic therapy are as large as those reported for other therapies that have been actively promoted as "empirically supported" and "evidenced based." In addition, patients who receive psychodynamic therapy maintain therapeutic gains and appear to continue to improve after treatment ends. Finally, non-psychodynamic therapies may be effective in part because the more skilled practitioners utilize techniques that have long been central to psychodynamic theory and practice. The perception that psychodynamic *approaches* lack empirical support does not accord with available scientific evidence and may reflect selective dissemination of research findings. (Shedler 2010, 98)

Psychoanalysis has evolved since Freud first developed his notions of intrapsychic functioning. For me, the growing edge of psychoanalysis is Object Relations Theory, which begins with the work of Melanie Klein. Her postulates of "projective identification" and "splitting" were expanded upon by W. R. D. Fairbairn, Harry Guntrip, and the innovative Donald Winnicott. Through all of this, the classic Freudian defenses retain their explanatory power. Anna Freud (1966), in her classic book *The Ego and the Mechanisms of Defense*, applied her father's ideas about defense patterns to early childhood development. She described the fundamental problem of anxiety—how we use psychological defenses to distort reality for the purpose of protecting ourselves from that anxiety: "The crucial point is that whether it be dread of the outside world [parental punishment] or dread of the superego [conscience] it is the anxiety which sets the defensive process going" (p. 57).

Notably, Freud's cases dealt with inhibited people. This was still the early 1900s. People were taught to be reserved and to develop strong control of their normal impulses, especially sexual feelings and wishes. Today, many of the people we see in therapy are the opposite: uninhibited and impulsive. They suffer from such addictions as compulsive gambling, drugs, alcoholism, and sexual impulsivity. Internet addictions are the latest addition to this list, and recent evidence shows that these can actually change the wiring of the brain (Lin et al. 2012).

In reading the case studies, you may feel convinced that I am writing about someone you know or grew up with. That is because the defense patterns are so common that we have all used them at one point or another to manage tension. If we can recognize ourselves in the case studies and laugh, we are sufficiently realistic. Others we will read about have clearly created their "own little world" and resist any redirection. But they are all instructive.

Denial

The most familiar mental defense mechanism is denial, which is the frank refusal to see the truth. In childhood, denial can protect children from overwhelming anxiety by literally cutting them off from what is actually happening. Denial can be *adaptive*. For example, we all know we are going to die, but it is not helpful to dwell on death. Or, if we are involved in a difficult task, like taking an important test, it is not helpful to worry about the argument we may have had that morning with our parent or spouse. Denial provides a calming division of our energy so that we can make the best use of our time—and ace that test. Denial is adaptive when we know we are denying and why.

Without that insight, denial can damage our lives precisely because it distorts reality. A dramatic example is shown in the case of a bright, energetic woman, an executive, who came to therapy for help concerning her sister, who was a drug addict. This woman, Beverly, was very overweight, but she never mentioned her weight. Her sister, she said, was now living with her, and they fought all the time. Beverly always gave in and was even providing money, which her sister used consistently for drugs. Beverly knew the term that described what she was doing and called herself an enabler. She wept, saying that her parents had died and that this sister was her only family. Her father had given her sister money to move to California, and she had returned addicted to various street narcotics. Beverly knew she was continuing her father's mistake in supporting her sister's way of life.

What Beverly did not know was that she was denying her own weight problem. I guessed her weight to be about 260 pounds, but she never mentioned weight as one of her therapy concerns and ignored my questions during the history taking. I knew there would be a day of reckoning. One day Beverly came to therapy in tears. A co-worker had taken a group picture that showed Beverly's full body. She felt mortified. I was puzzled as to what she meant. Surely she knew that her co-workers saw her coming and going each day. I asked, very gently, "Was that picture a surprise to you?" She glared at me with anger. "When I think of myself it is from here up," she said, placing her flat hand emphatically across her neck. She actually experienced herself as a disembodied head. As long as she avoided any visual evidence about her body, her denial was intact. She had developed tactics to avoid encountering mirrors or glass walls that reflected her whole body. She had arranged her apartment in a similar way—no surprise reflections from pictures on the walls. She owned only one mirror, in her bathroom. Certain essential tasks, like buying clothes, were done online. She was brilliant, and she knew it. She valued herself and wanted others to value her *only* for her innovations and management skills. Her anxiety and shame about her weight were formidable, as evidenced by the ferocity of her denial.

With much difficulty, she related an incident that had occurred when her father was still alive. Seemingly out of the blue, he blurted out how aggrieved he was that she had gained so much weight. She had been such a thin and beautiful girl, but she came back from college very overweight. Her father was very distressed because he knew he was ill. He pleaded with Beverly to take him seriously and lose weight while he was still alive. Beverly's reaction was one of dramatic embarrassment. She felt her father was being cruel to her. She spoke as if she really wanted and expected her father—and indeed all others—to *share* her denial and act as if her illusion about herself were true: she existed only from the neck up. This extraordinary denial was complicated by anger. Beverly felt that her co-workers were deliberately offending her by referring to the body she could not accept. The strength of this denial would not allow her, even in therapy, to face the reality of her weight. She would allow no discussion of food and eating. We spent many sessions working on her relationship with her sister, who finally went into rehab.

Then, as it eventually will for us all, reality forced itself on Beverly. A big promotion she had interviewed for was awarded to another person outside her department. It was widely rumored that she had not been chosen because of her weight. (Yes, this happens, although it is immoral and probably illegal.) Beverly was shocked, almost immobilized. This brilliant, creative, and verbally effusive lady now sat before me silent and emotionally desolate. The look in her eyes was different. It was as if she knew that when she had cut her head off with her hand, she then buried it in the sand. When she finally did speak, her voice was different, less pressured and lower in tone. She had *deserved* that promotion. No one was saying she did not. Slowly, she began to analyze the situation. The requirement for frequent international travel, the expected appearances on television—that was it. Those were the factors that had swayed the decision.

Her therapist had said almost nothing. It was not necessary. Weeping, Beverly described what the promotion would have meant to her. A chance for fancier problems to solve, travel abroad, more authority in the company. Her father's plea now haunted her. Why could she not give him his wish while he was still well enough to celebrate with her? Then, all by herself, Beverly found a Weight Watchers facility. For the first time in her life, she allowed herself to be weighed. She began referring to her propensity for massive denial as "my blinder mind." She and her therapist then made the following connections. Her father had been alcoholic. Her sister was addicted to narcotics.

Her own addiction was to *food*. With these connections, her militant denial was dissolving. The biblical metaphor would apply: the scales had fallen from her eyes.

Introjection

"Introjection" refers to the action of taking into the self, through identification, the partial personality aspects of the people around us, usually a parent, grandparent, or sibling. A child introjects parental standards, and this becomes his conscience or, in psychoanalytic terminology, his superego. Introjection can be painful and damaging, as when a person identifies with a hated part of his parent and then hates that part in himself. Suppose a man's father always talked down to him when he was a child. The father would ask the son a difficult question to set him up. Then he would discount the son's naïve answer and launch into a lecture beyond the son's understanding and in a tone intended to humiliate. The son hates these episodes but loves his father, who behaves this way in order to feel superior.

When the son grows up, he will tend to treat his friends as he was treated. That is, he will choose friends who lack self-confidence and then criticize their opinions and lecture to them about his own superior notions. The problem will not improve when he is old enough to date. Within a short time of meeting a girl, he will begin lecturing her. Because this process is subconscious, this man will not realize what he is doing, although he will consciously feel superior to others. Only when he loses relationship after relationship by being an insufferable know-it-all might he finally realize the way he has become very like his father. He will first need to accept that he hated his father's behavior while he was growing up—often the most difficult step. This does not mean that he should go home and scream at his father. It does mean that he, perhaps with the help of a therapist, must separate the hated behavior from all the rest of the father that he loves. He must recognize that he took in—introjected—the father's arrogance with the very air he breathed as a child. And he must consciously reject that arrogance in himself. Not an easy task. This requires vigilance. Most helpful at this point would be routinely consulting others as to the quality of his message: "How did that sound? Was I being bossy?" When met with a resounding "yes," he should reformulate his statements with patience and humor. The ability to do this would show striking growth in this man, to the relief of all those around him.

Repression

"Repression" refers to the expulsion from consciousness of devastating events from our past. It is thought to be more drastic than denial because a person cannot willfully recall the repressed event (Anderson et al., 2004). Sometimes people seek hypnosis to get at scary memories, but these may not always be accessible.

The actual neural mechanisms that subserve repression may have been described by Norman Doidge (2007). Doidge, a psychiatrist, psychoanalyst, and researcher, says that "early childhood trauma causes massive plastic change in the hippocampus [the part of the brain involved with memory], shrinking it so that new, long-term explicit memories cannot form" (240). Further, the actual damage is caused by a stress hormone known as a glucocorticoid. "Glucocorticoids kill cells in the hippocampus so that it cannot make the synaptic connections in neural networks that make learning and explicit long-term memory possible" (240). Thus, if this mechanism for repression is correct, it protects a person from terrifying experience by shutting down brain processes that *form* memories. The person does not remember the event because no memory of it was ever formed.

Yet there is evidence that repressions are not total, that they can cause ongoing effects such as phobias. Perhaps repressed memories go into a "trash bin," where they still can cause anxiety, even fearful flashbacks. This is illustrated by the case of a very tense woman, Terry, who came to therapy after college to discuss an incident that had occurred when she was 20 years old. She had been dating a man who had seemed just wonderful, she said. They loved the same music, so one night he suggested she go home with him to look over his collection. She had an idea this might lead to sex, but that idea was beginning to appeal to her. The boyfriend did indeed take her up to his bedroom, where she encountered a frightening complication. There was another older man—who greeted her with a kiss. She turned with alarm to her boyfriend, who was smiling. She has no memory of what happened after this (there had been no drinking or drugging). She also does not remember how she got home. But within weeks, she discovered that she was pregnant. With much apprehension, and without telling her parents, she elected to have an abortion. She then left her college program, moved to another state, and enrolled at another college. She said she did not suffer any emotional symptoms at this point and kept in contact with her friends and family.

For a few years, Terry kept what she did remember to herself. What frightened her most was that she had no memory for *most* of what had happened in that bedroom. Actually, it may have been a reaction to intense fear itself—a subconscious adaptation:

[F]ear emotions (anxiety, terror, worry, horror) and the enhanced memory of frightening events may take place in the amygdala *below* the conscious level, which makes sense because the amygdala must detect danger rapidly. Thinking involves coordinated interactions among huge numbers of neurons and synapses which, in turn, take precious time. This is why we have reflexes in the lower parts of our brain, below the thinking cortex. (Nelson 2011, 174–175, italics his)

Thus, Terry's *body* may have reacted to the threat before her mind could process it. Thinking takes time. All she *knew* was that she was trapped. Perhaps she *had* been drugged. Alternatively, it may have been what is called a dissociative experience, wherein a person involuntarily separates herself from the reality of an unbearably stressful event (Herman 1992; Ferentz 2012.) She does not remember it because the event was not processed by her brain in the usual ways. People who have dissociative experiences report lost chunks of time they cannot account for.

A perhaps more plausible explanation of this phenomenon comes from the Polyvagal Theory of Stephen Porges. The autonomic nervous sytem, Porges says, has a third alternative to fight or flight. Recall that the sympathetic branch of the autonomic supports action against a threat, while the parasympathetic allows for relaxation of that effort and restoration. The third capacity is immobilization and loss of consciousness. Porges teaches that this defense system is

dependent on the parasympathetic nervous system. . . . The root of the Polyvagal Theory is the recognition that in the absence of the ability to fight or flee, the body's only effective defense is to immobilize and shut down. This can be observed as fainting or nausea, both features of an ancient vagal circuit. . . . However, unlike the uniquely mammalian vagal pathway, these vagal pathways are unmyelinated, and are only effective as a defense system when the newer circuits, including the sympathetic nervous system, are no longer available. (Porges, as quoted in Howes, 2013, 67)

The example Porges gives is that of a child being forcefully held down and abused—what he calls "immobilization with fear." I think this explains graphically what Terry experienced when her boyfriend's "friend/father" kissed her and she realized she was trapped.

What was her reason for eventually seeking therapy? It was increasing anxiety. Anxiety disorders are often delayed reactions, and Terry began to feel intense fear of any enclosed space. Elevators were impossible, and even turning a corner frightened her. She would not go into an empty room alone. The fears increased until they were limiting all her activities. In therapy, we discussed the evolution of these fears. I commended her for being able to tell me the story of the abortion and its antecedents. How difficult it had been for her to endure all this by herself. For three years, she had not shared it with anyone. Then two of her friends related their own stories of sexual harassment and forced sex. Terry began to feel more and more uncomfortable. She said she would stay at home for days at a time. Her anxiety was beginning to control her whole life. Therapy and some work with a hypnotherapist helped her with her phobias. Eventually, she did begin to date again, but she did not want to pursue the "repressed" memory. She had been raped, perhaps twice. She did not care to know more.

But problems like this do not disappear. Unresolved issues with significant subconscious content can surface again as one's life unfolds. I worried that Terry may have intrusive memories of that terrible night when, for instance, her own daughter turned 18 or 19. At that point, I hope that Terry would consider returning to treatment. She knows now that anxiety can be an important signal.

Identification with the Aggressor

The defense with the dramatic name of "identification with the aggressor" is actually dramatic in its effects. One oft-quoted example is what happened in the Nazi concentration camps. Inmates were regularly pushed around and mistreated by the camp guards. At certain points, the guards would designate an inmate to help with controlling the others. Often, those designated could be just as cruel as the camp guards themselves. They had identified with their aggressors. It gave them power in a situation in which they were powerless by definition.

A similar thing can happen in families. A child or teenager who has a harsh, controlling parent can cope by becoming like that parent. The child or teen can adopt the tactics of the parent and use them against that parent or others. If a girl is consistently criticized, she will become critical toward others, especially those she has some power with, like siblings and friends. If she is often humiliated, she will learn to humiliate others. This tendency can develop even when we don't want it. A young woman came to therapy complaining that she had developed the habit of screaming at her three-year-old daughter. This woman wept, saying her own mother had screamed at her constantly when she was growing up. "I always said I would never be like my mother," she said. "But when I get angry, I sound just like her."

The lesson here, as the adage says, is that children learn what they live. Happy, healthy parents raise happy, healthy children, who in their turn can love their own children. Not-so-happy, neurotic parents unwittingly put pressures on their children, pressures that will be transformed in some way as the children struggle to adapt, then expressed as symptoms by those children as they become adults. The past, it has been observed, is written on our nervous system.

Intellectualization

Freud called this "flight to the head." It refers to the overvaluation of the mind that can occur as children grow to adulthood, especially when they find that emotions cause them confusion and pain. If emotions are felt to be unreliable or conflicted, a child can give up on them and put all his or her efforts into reading, learning, concepts, and ideas.

A poignant example: Alan, 41 years old, came to therapy at the request of the woman he planned to marry. His work was in IT, and he had won many awards for his innovations. He seemed ill at ease in the therapy session, glancing around and saying he was not sure what the therapist wanted him to do. He confessed that he was more comfortable working with men. It became clear that he had no vocabulary for expressing emotions. This is an identified personality trait called alexithymia (Sifneos 1996). It represents a paucity of emotional expression and possibly the disconnection of the verbal expression from the emotion itself. Such individuals also show an impoverishment of imagination and fantasy.

Alexithymia correlates with many emotional problems—for example Asperger's syndrome, depression, and anxiety disorders. Persons with alexithymia can feel strong emotional pain and rage but lack the ability to explain these feelings to others or to relate to the suffering of others. Causes for the genesis of alexithymia are still being argued, but what makes most sense to therapists is the connection between the symptoms of the condition and early deprivation or trauma. Arguments for a decreased corpus callosum (the neural bridge between the two brain hemispheres) in persons with alexithymia are reasonable. We know the brain of an infant is shaped by the responses received from the mother or other caretaker. If the baby's reaching out is not met with a caring, sympathetic response, the baby discounts his own needs. His frightened withdrawal from that interaction would erase the psychological representation of the emotional need. Without vital feedback from the mother—reactions to her baby's facial expressions—an infant cannot form an organized sense of self.

Alan described his early experience. His parents, he said, were completely focused on each other and had little time for him. When he was small, they would go away for weeks at a time, leaving him with neighbors. When the therapist asked him how he had felt about being left, he became quiet. He didn't know how to express his feelings, but he mentioned a memory. When he was about 7, his mother was complaining loudly about something in the kitchen. In his presence, she said emphatically that she should never have become a mother. (Imagine how a 7-year-old would feel on hearing this.) Early on, he said, he had learned to tinker with machines. By the age of 10, he was taking apart radios and reassembling them. He had already given up on feelings; they were too painful, confusing, and unreliable.

What he *could* rely on was his marvelous mind, which is why this defense is called intellectualization. Alan passionately enjoyed math and science and began winning contests in middle school. Computers became his life. He married and had a daughter, but within a few years, his wife left, and his time with his daughter was cut short. It seems he could not express love, which requires openness and vulnerability.

The woman he now wanted to marry was a colleague, brilliant but also fun to be with, and very loving. She was wonderfully patient with him, coaching him every step of the way. For the first time in his adult life, he felt vulnerable, and he reacted by saying almost nothing. But his new lover was not daunted. She told him he was in love with her (he was), that they were good for each other (they were), and that he needed to learn to talk about his feelings.

In therapy, Alan floundered in a semicomical way. He was like a fish out of water. His place was in the electronics world. What was he doing in a nice office talking to a female therapist? We talked about his fiancée's complaints, and he squirmed. At one point, struggling for a way to reach him, I asked him if he indeed loved this fine woman who had referred him to me. He looked at me with indignation. "Of course

I do!" he exclaimed. I saw my opportunity and went for it: "Well," I asked, *how is she to know that?* She cannot read your mind." He looked at me, alarmed. He was beginning to understand that the reason for his isolation was, at least in part, his inability—or unwillingness—to reach out. What good was loving this woman if he could not tell her how he felt? We had to make the connection between feeling something and saying it *in words*.

From that point, he became like Liza Doolittle in *My Fair Lady*. In every session, I reviewed the week's events and asked how he felt about them. We talked about ways to say how he felt, because others could not read his mind. In each instance, I asked when he had first felt a particular feeling. He agreed that, as a child, he had felt much that could not be communicated. The therapist was restating those things he had felt as a child but had never learned to express. (Indeed, if he had expressed his needs to his parents, would they have responded? How do you talk to a mother who has told you she didn't want you?) I stated how pained I felt for him as a child. How lonely he must have been. Alan's eyes softened. He responded, yes, he had been lonely, but pushed it away when he would start to cry . He still would not allow himself to cry.

But he was on a new mission; he did not miss a therapy session. He practiced saying out loud how he felt. His assertion increased: "I want this"; "I don't want that"; "I feel happy"; "I feel annoyed"; "I would rather not." Much like Liza Doolittle, he was learning a new language. And finally, like her, he got it. He and his "fair lady" are happily married. His daughter was in their wedding. He can laugh. He can say how he feels about most things. He can express appreciation and love. Most significantly, he can cry. And now, when he does cry, he is comforted.

Resistance

One of the most common and easily recognized defenses, "resistance," describes the simple refusal to take in what the other person is saying. It represents a *refusal* to be influenced by the other. And when it is the therapist's words that are being resisted, a person's therapy encounters a major impediment. A therapist's statement may be sensitive and focused, but the patient will deflect it, saying his behavior means something entirely different. Usually it is because the person in therapy does not want to think of himself as having the motivation described by the therapist. For example, a man who thinks of himself as a "people pleaser" will not be able to "own" the angry, even mean behavior attributed to him by his wife. And as long as he "resists" that reality, their marital therapy will not progress.

Resistance is, again, the refusal to be influenced, often because it challenges a person's image of himself. For example, Nora complained in therapy that her husband would not discuss their joint session with her during the week. In therapy, the following week, her husband, Simon, was just as sullen. When the therapist asked him how he felt about discussing their therapy outside the session, he said, after a struggle with his own feelings, that it made him feel threatened and inadequate. He resisted his wife's questions and assertions because they challenged his view of himself as competent and confident. For their therapy to advance, Simon needed to recognize that his resistance kept him from the truth about himself, namely, that he often feels the opposite—inadequate and ashamed. To be sure, Nora also has a responsibility not to be so shrill and nasty in her accusations, and this became a major focus in her therapy. I would repeatedly have to ask her to take a deep breath and rephrase her complaint in a more respectful way. Her anger, I told her, stopped Simon in his tracks and scrambled his thinking. In that state, he could not hear his wife *or* his therapist.

I worked one-on-one with this man for a long time before he became ready for the intense interactions of marital therapy. I showed him that resisting the strident messages of others may have kept him sane when he was a child, but now this automatic shutdown was keeping him from encountering the world, especially the world of his children, something he wanted very much to share. With Simon's realization that he was shutting out most people in his world, not just Nora, he became stronger and was able to express his difficulties growing up with bossy, scary parents. He began to move toward life instead of away from it. In the process, he developed a remarkable sense of humor, and with encouragement, began teasing Nora in a loving way. She was initially offended and countered with her usual put-downs. She softened when she saw that her therapist appreciated Simon's wonderful humor and the way he used it to express his need for Nora. Therapy showed this couple how much *love* they actually shared.

Projection

Our amazing ability to disown unwanted parts or aspects of our own motivation is called "projection." We attribute these part-aspects to another person and then experience them as coming *from* that person. It sounds like magic, but it happens—often with little awareness on the part of the person doing the projecting. Consider this example:

A couple is coming into the therapist's office. The husband looks at his wife and says, "Don't be surprised if you hear some things you don't like." The wife gives her husband a sideways glance. *She* had arranged for the therapy. She knew that therapy involved hard questions. It was clearly the *husband* who was apprehensive about what he would hear. He had projected his fear onto his wife. He believed that *she* might be the uncomfortable one. This belief made him feel better. (Does this begin to sound like a sitcom? We can only laugh because we know how it works.)

In therapy, this defense pattern is examined. To the degree that the husband can understand that he is projecting his feelings onto his wife, and how often he does this, the couple will make progress. This is not a simple matter, but people *can* take back their projections and own them. The husband can realize that the emotion he attributes to his wife is really his own fear.

Holly and Gerard had moved here from Canada for her job promotion. Gerard is a graphic artist who had been working for one of Holly's firm's accounts. When they met, Gerard's eyes held Holly in a fateful lock—an undeniable connection both disconcerting and exciting. Although he was only a year younger than her, she began calling him "the Wood Child." He was a quietly attentive person whose mood seemed to dance just below the level of euphoria. Holly is an efficient, no-nonsense executive who worked long hours. They would not have seemed a good match, but they knew they were drawn together by an ineffable bond.

In the therapy session, Holly was in her element. She presented a careful argument why Gerard should change. "He wants to live like an aging teenager," she said, "who, by the way, is adorable." (It was this last phrase that alerted me to Holly's central conflict.) Her complaint continued. Gerard would start home-improvement projects then leave them in various stages of undone. He would work intensively on a computer assignment then sit up late at night—in their home—drinking wine with his friends. He would be asleep the next morning when Holly would kiss him and leave before daylight.

I looked at Gerard and asked how he felt about Holly's complaints. His eyes widened with a combination of alarm and mischief. He always lived in a world of color, light, and art. Now he was here sitting in a chair talking to a therapist. He smiled but was clearly in a mild torment. (One really got the feeling that at any moment he could shrink to the size of a nymph and leap onto the bookcase.) With an embarrassed grin, he answered my question. "When Holly complains" he said, "I just kiss her."

As therapy progressed, I asked about their childhood experiences. Gerard had grown up with two kind parents. His grandfather was an artist who talked about the colors of light and taught him to draw. Holly had been raised by a successful father who told her: never be late; do more than is expected of you; never leave a job undone; don't sleep in. Her father's proscriptions, internalized by Holly, were now part of her conscience. They represented the identical demands she now *projected*, without realizing it, onto Gerard.

It became clear that this intelligent, very-much-in-love couple was being threatened by Holly's harsh conscience—the excessive demands she made of herself and of Gerard. What she had found in Gerard was her own lost childhood—the happy, carefree girl she had been before her well-meaning father clipped her wings. She recalled writing bits of poetry she never finished. She remembered designing clothes with her friends, and plays to go with them. She and her friends had sneaked out of the house and hopped onto a bus to wherever it took them. Holly's father disapproved of all this, and she believed him. She "should" be more responsible. I told Holly that whenever she used the word "should," she could be sure it was coming from *outside* of her, not from her own self. It represented someone else's ideas about her responsibilities. But her father's plan for her worked: Holly became more disciplined and successful. She now earned more than her father at the height of his career.

When I questioned the cost to her health and her marriage, Holly was incredulous. She stared at me and blinked. "But I'm *happier* this way," she said. She didn't yet see that what she loved about Gerard mirrored her complaints. She blamed him for the charming impulsiveness of starting creative projects as they occurred to him and leaving them unfinished when he became tired—something she never allowed herself. She didn't realize she also wished to be free and spontaneous.

Holly wanted therapy to "make" Gerard more responsible, because she could not bear to see that he had all the freedom she had given up and now sorely missed. But (I worried) if therapy were to change Gerard—her stated goal—would he still be "adorable"? I could agree he should not be drinking so much wine, and we could begin with that. But I cautioned her that therapy cannot change a person's inborn temperament—nor is that desirable.

Gerard became interested in what I was saying. He *knew* that Holly was just like him. But Holly was alarmed. She was beginning to see that Gerard was living the life she sorely missed and that although she admired that in him, she also resented his freedom to do so. *Both feelings* were there, causing a painful and recurrent conflict in her. Gerard, the one she thought had to change, had an essentially healthy personality. Holly herself was the conflicted one, and she *projected* that conflict onto Gerard. Holly's projections contained four complex emotions: loving Gerard for his free spirit; resenting him for being free; grief for her lost girlhood; and guilt for wanting it back. These feelings were pushed out of awareness because Holly could not consciously resent her father's over-control without guilt. All this existed in her mind without her conscious awareness. Without therapy, Holly would have clung to her belief that Gerard needed to "grow up," and Gerard would likely have continued to drink too much because Holly was so critical of him.

With continued therapy, Holly's insight grew. She felt a slowly developing amazement that the complaints she now made about Gerard were the actual proscriptions of her father—her father's words, now in her voice. She projected these words out of guilt for wanting to defy her father and guilt for wanting the freedom Gerard enjoyed. She must punish Gerard for being free—and herself for wishing to be—because she *must hold together* the life she had created for herself; she was "happier" that way. Holly cried openly during the discussion of all this. She was beginning to see that her father's formula for success, so valuable to her, was also an onerous burden.

One of my recommendations for this couple was that they take a brief vacation, where they could *both* play and rest. Also, that they discuss what the goals of their therapy might be. Holly could hardly give up her executive position. It was an important part of her identity and the basis for the couple's financial security. But they *could* make her schedule more congenial; at least one morning off per week for love making. She could delegate more of her responsibilities to willing assistants. And Gerard, a computer "geek," would help with some of her reports. My task was to help Holly appreciate her very *normal* childhood wishes without guilt, to complain about and understand her father (and how his motives may have originated), and finally to love Gerard freely without resentment. Projections operate subconsciously. Without therapy, Holly would never have come to these realizations. This wonderful marriage might have ended with both Holly and Gerard wondering why.

Transference

We should mention the mechanism of transference, which refers to a phenomenon occurring in therapy. It describes the patient's projection onto the therapist of unresolved issues from her past. These issues often get in the way of the patient's being able to trust the therapist. Well-trained therapists are aware of this and accept the patient's complaints and accusations, which are a reflection of what she has historically lived with. They show her ongoing struggle and the very areas where she is caught in the effort to outgrow her past. By encouraging the patient to complain about the way she experiences the therapist as a person, much grief and pain are uncovered: "You treat me just the way my older sister did!" The therapist then understands who is represented in the transference. And over time, the patient comes to understand the sources of her life's pain. This is the value of the transference.

THE IMPORTANCE OF PSYCHOLOGICAL DEFENSES IN DEVELOPMENT

One reason children are so charming is that they are so disarmingly naïve. If they have received adequate care, they show none of these defenses. They boldly ask: "Where does the sky end? How do birds swim? Why doesn't God have a wife?" They can seek the answers to these profound questions because they are not anxious. Children entreat *parents* to resolve their anxiety. It is a tenet of healthy parenting to quickly resolve an anxious moment for a child or to teach him with humor, love, and patience how to resolve it for himself.

We may have evolved with the psychological defenses described in this chapter (Varki & Brower 2013). Some researchers (Dinnerstein 1983) have called them normal psychopathology. In *Totem and Taboo*, Freud concluded that our capacity for neurosis separated us from the animals. This capacity was the result of our spectacular cultural advancement. Civilization "makes us crazy," but now we cannot live without it.

Ironically, psychological defenses have been shown to have some *healthy* adaptive functions. John Zinner (1972) has studied projective identification intensively and describes it as the basis for empathy and "attunement" among family members. Projective identification, he says, changes a person's inner turmoil into a shared conflict that a person can observe and deal with. Rochelle Kainer (1999) also observed projective identification leading to empathy. Recall that when Holly projected her anger with herself for wanting a more relaxed life onto Gerard, she began to resent him for enjoying his artistic happy life. Only then did she realize that she was not "happier this way" (as a harried executive). She began to empathize with Gerard's joy and creativity and finally with her own.

Being realistic and insightful means taking responsibility for all our behavior. There are four categories of behavior: words, feelings, thoughts, and actions. We struggle during our normal development to take responsibility for all four categories, which inform one another. If we separate our words and actions (external behaviors) from our thoughts and feelings (internal behaviors), we create a "false self." This means that the way we feel inside is different from the self we show to others. You will read about a number of personalities like this in the chapters that follow.

This brief overview of some of the psychological defenses should give an indication of how they operate, complicating and simplifying our lives. We gain respect for these concepts as we see them expressed reliably and predictably in the lives of real people, hence the need for examples. We have seen how the particular mechanism each individual "chose" suited his or her need at that stage of life. It protected that person from the painful reality he or she was struggling with. And as we saw with repression, the defense pattern can cause secondary problems of its own—for example, phobias. Our growing personality is changed by what we have to adapt to and the way in which we adapt.

We should not be surprised that defense patterns, as well as increased realism and self-responsibility, are functions of brain processes.

The temporoparietal region is . . . important for taking the first-person perspective, perceiving ourselves to be the agent of our actions. This region may also help us appreciate other people's minds, and is important to the pathways that allow us to empathize with others. . . . Many cortical areas are critical to put the self together, like the prefrontal and posterior cingulate [involved in self-reflection]. (Nelson 2011, 143)

Developing self-responsibility, in and out of therapy, retrains the brain, refining our sense of self and increasing self-efficacy. But it takes focus and determination. "[W]e need to be wary of our left hemisphere, the explainer and confabulator in our brains" (Nelson 2011, 259). We are only too quick to make up a story to explain an uncomfortable situation, a story that relieves our discomfort and that feels justified but is not realistic.

There are more defense patterns than have been discussed here. For example, we have not discussed "reaction formation," in which a person changes an emotion to its direct opposite and then experiences only that opposite consciously. For example, one can experience a person as admirable when we actually resent that person. "Magical thinking" is perhaps the most conscious defense (Hutson 2012). This is why couples will not want to keep a bed where one of them had slept with a former partner. Both know there is nothing wrong with the bed, but it represents an intrusion into their new life.

Defense patterns *may* be the evolutionary consequences of the anxiety caused by increased self-awareness. This in turn may have resulted from the enlargement of our neocortex, the newest part of the human brain. Defenses operate largely subconsciously. The actual defense pattern we develop has much to do with the amount and type of stress assessed by our subconscious mind and how much we need to keep it out of awareness:

> Because both enhance survival, conscious and unconscious processes coexist, assessing information in parallel. The human social order is based on the preeminence of conscious circuits. In consequence, the emergence of unconsciously determined behaviors and emotional states may disrupt people's ability to work or maintain important relationships. (Viamontes & Beitman 2012, 54)

Consciousness itself is an automatic process. "Nearly all neuroscientists now believe that the thalamus and cortex are the part of our [brain] anatomy where our consciousness attains its unique human content" (Nelson 2011, 54). But defenses themselves—denial, resistance, repression, etc.—*require conscious effort and energy*. It takes strong motivation, often fear or anger, to keep an idea or meaning *out* of awareness. So even though defenses operate subconsciously, they can exhaust us and constrain our lives. People who use repression and denial have weaker immune systems (Dreher 1995, 60–65). Moreover, internal conflict is not only a brain function. Brain peptides (information-carrying compounds) are found throughout the body, in the immune system, the endocrine system, the hormones, and the blood, as the result of changing emotions (Pert 2003). This is a major reason why our psychological functioning can affect our general health.

Each of us must struggle with the parents, the culture, the language, and the stamina and gene structure we inherit, as well as the amount and quality of nutrition we receive, in our adaptation to reality. This struggle makes each of us unique. The increased self-awareness described above as an effect of brain enlargement forced us to live in three time zones: the past, the present, and the future. We remember our past, we live in the present, and we project ourselves into the future by imagining and planning it. And we need to hold all of this information together, a task that requires the four maturational skills with which we started this chapter—intelligence, patience, courage, and commitment. If we manage this well, we have the big picture: realism. Or—to use a synonym—we have *wisdom.*

REFERENCES

Anderson, M. C., Ochsner, K. N., et al. (2004). "Neural Systems Underlying the Suppression of Unwanted Memories." *Science;* 303, 232–35.

Brown, N. O. (1959). *Life against Death: The Psychoanalytical Meaning of History.* Middletown, CT: Wesleyan University Press.

Dinnerstein, D. (1983). Afterword: "Toward a Mobilization of Eros." In M. Murray (Ed.), *Face to Face.* (294–309). Westport, NJ: Greenwood Publishing Group.

Doidge, N. (2007). *The Brain That Changes Itself.* New York: Penguin Books.

Dreher, H. (1995). *The Immune Power Personality.* New York: Penguin Group.

Ferentz, L. (2012). *Treating Self-Destructive Behaviors in Trauma Survivors. A Clinician's Guide.* New York: Routledge.

Flynn, J. R. (1998). "IQ Gains over Time: Toward Finding the Causes." In U. Neisser (Ed.), *The Rising Curve: Long-Term Gains in IQ and Related Measures,* 25–66. Washington, DC: American Psychological Association.

Freud, A. (1966). *The Ego and the Mechanisms of Defense: Revised Edition.* New York: International Universities Press.

Herman, J. (1992). *Trauma and Recovery.* New York: Basic Books.

Howes, R. (2013). "Wearing Your Heart on Your Face: The Polyvagal Circuit in the Consulting Room." *Psychotherapy Networker* 37(5): 67–69.

Hutson, M. (2012). *The Seven Laws of Magical Thinking: How Irrational Beliefs Keep Us Happy, Healthy and Sane.* New York: Hudson Street Press, the Penguin Group.

Kainer, R. G. K. (1999). *The Collapse of the Self: and Its Restoration in Therapy.* Hillsdale, NJ & London: The Analytic Press.

Kubie L. S. (1969). *Neurotic Distortion of the Creative Process.* New York: Noonday Press.

Lin, F., Zhou, Y., et al. (2012). "Abnormal White Matter Integrity in Adolescents with Internet Addiction Disorder: A Tract-Based Spatial Statistics Study." PloS ONE 7(1); e30253 doi:10.1371/journal.pone.0030253

Nelson, K. (2011). *The Spiritual Doorway in the Brain: A Neurologist's Search for the God Experience.* New York: Dutton.

Pert, C. (2003). *Molecules of Emotion: Why You Feel the Way You Feel.* New York: Scribner.

Shedler, J. (2010). "The Efficacy of Psychodynamic Therapy." *Journal of the American Psychological Association* 65(2): 98–109.

Sifneos, P. E. (1996). "Alexithymia: Past and Present." *American Journal of Psychiatry,* 153(7 suppl), 137–142.

Varki, A. & Brower, D. (2013). *Denial: Self-deception, False Beliefs and the Origins of the Human Mind.* New York: Twelve.

Viamontes, G. I. & Beitman, B. D. (2007). "Mapping the Unconscious in the Brain." *Psychiatric Annals,* 37, 243–256.

Viamontes, G. I. & Beitman, B. D. (2012). "Neural Substrates of Psychotherapy." In R. D. Alarcón and J. B. Frank (Eds.), *The Psychotherapy of Hope: The Legacy of Persuasion and Healing.* Baltimore: The Johns Hopkins University Press.

Zinner, J. & Shapiro, R. (1972). "Projective Identification as a Mode of Perception and Behaviour in Families of Adolescents." *International Journal of Psychoanalysis,* 53, 523–530.

Chapter 2

Self-Esteem and Self-Confidence
The Bedrock of Healthy Personality

Trust thyself: every heart vibrates to that iron string.
—Ralph Waldo Emerson

The deepest principle of human nature is the craving to be appreciated.

—William James

Self-confidence and self-esteem are indeed the foundations of a healthy personality, although they are not the same thing. These two concepts sound the same, but they are actually very different experiences for us, although they work together to reflect much of our satisfaction in life. They both develop quite early in life, although for most of us, they represent an ongoing project. This conceptualization of the dual structure of self-esteem is the work of Nathaniel Brandon (2001):

> Self-esteem has two interrelated aspects; it entails a sense of personal efficacy and a sense of personal worth. It is the integrated sum of self-confidence and self-respect. It is the conviction that one is *competent* to live and *worthy* of living." (110, italics his)

THE BEGINNING OF SELF-ESTEEM

That self-efficacy (a sense of power) and self-worth (a sense of deserving) are separate but interrelated experiences is a valuable concept. Although both can be thought of as convictions and beliefs, the research findings of developmental psychologists—notably Bowlby, Mahler, Ainsworth and, more recently, Brazelton and Greenspan (2000)—show that a child's confidence in himself or herself is an *effect* of the attachment to a caring parent, and thus profoundly emotional. Without that caring, conveyed through touch, smiling, and soothing verbal messages, babies can die of anaclitic depression. This fatal form of depression occurs when babies are fed and kept clean but are not held and spoken to (Spitz 1965).

Confidence in oneself, then, is the *gift* of a loving parent. It is the result of having been valued, indeed cherished, by a parent deeply bonded to his or her child. As such, the experience of self-worth is emotional—deeply felt *before* it is understood. The message to the baby is that she is loveable, and thus safe. Self-worth is the comfortable awareness a baby feels of the love and joy her mother and father experience with her. "Our quest for empathy is a *longing to be known*" (Kainer 1999, 183; emphasis hers). The baby can see his very existence passionately reflected in the eyes of the mother. This conviction of being loveable and worthy emerges in the child as a result of the strong attachment mother and baby feel toward each other. Psychologists call this the attachment phase (Bowlby 1969, 1973). Another line of research by Margaret Mahler (1979), one of the earliest researchers of infancy, identifies the mechanism of attachment as "mutual gaze"— the baby literally holds the mother with his or her eyes. This mutual gaze can be so intense the infant will stop nursing in order to stare at the mother.

Constructing the Self

This phase can hardly be overestimated. Quiet staring, indeed all the interactions between baby and mother,

> may serve as an important mechanism of the transmission of neural organization from parent to child. It is rare to find a child who is able to be still and centered and feel safe in the presence of chaotic adults. We believe that early caretaking builds and shapes the cortex and its relationship with the limbic system, which supports emotional regulation, imagination, and coping skills. To this we must now add the development of the parietal lobes in the construction of internal space. (Cozolino 2010, 146)

An infant's sense of self is *constructed* by the day in, day out interaction with the caregiver. Without this reliable interaction, the child's sense of self will be scattered and disorganized. Many brain areas contribute to this cohesive sense of self. "The temporoparietal junction may . . . be central to the ability to see ourselves as consistent, carried through the past, present and future" (Nelson 2011, 232). And this takes time.

> The development of a sense of self requires periods of freedom from external threat and inner turmoil. It also requires the development of frontal-parietal systems responsible for inner imaginal space. Children constantly buffeted by external chaos can remain trapped in a "selfless" state where they are witness to interior impulses and exterior behaviors with little or no ability to either understand or control what they are doing (Cozolino 2010, 195–196).

This crucial process of constructing a self from the interaction of a vulnerable infant and a parent's responses is complicated by the fact that it must occur during a "critical period"—that is, during the time that the brain *can* be influenced.

> Our brains *lie in wait* for the inputs we need to wire foundational systems like vision, language, *attachment*, and social cognition. This process of experience-expectant plasticity involves sensitive periods during which the brain is . . . acutely responsive to instructions from the world around it. . . . [S]ensitive periods create windows of vulnerability. If the experiences we expect are corrupted or absent, the damage may be hard to undo. *A child who suffers severe neglect early in life may have attachment problems that last a lifetime.* (Smoller 2012, 325–326; emphasis added)

In sum, constructing the self is a synthetic process that occurs very early in life and involves time-sensitive wiring of the brain. Epigenetics is the new science providing evidence of how information from the environment actually turns on some genes and turns off others. It is a process in which a baby needs much assistance. A strong confidence in the early mothering person's reliability will lead to "a well-secured identity, object constancy [the belief that a mother who can be frustrating is the same mother who brings food and love] and the structure of the superego [conscience] which *regulates* self-esteem" (Horner 1979, 305; emphasis added).

The *normal* reaction to babies is universally one of delight. As evolution prepared us, we are powerfully drawn to a baby's babbling, squealing, and cooing. This behavior on our parts has recently been shown to be hard wired in humans. Looking at a baby's face—but not at an adult's—activates facial recognition sites in the brain, as well as a part of the brain involved in both movement and speech. And not just any speech. There is actually a special kind of speech reserved just for infants that all people use around the globe (Winerman 2013). This research was carried out by Marc H. Bornstein as part of his massive contribution to the field of parenting. While all his work is fascinating, some data are truly stunning. For example:

> some research has found that mothers' brains actually grow in size in the early months of parenting. In the first three months after their babies were born, gray matter in mothers' brains increased in certain areas, including the hypothalamus, amygdala, and prefrontal cortex, related to motivation, reward, and emotion processing, and reasoning and judgment (Bornstein quoted in Winerman 2013, 30).

In another study, Bornstein found that women—but not men—were equipped to respond instantly to a baby's cry. This was true even in women who were not mothers.

Winnicott's "False Self"

What happens when a child is *not* overvalued and cherished at the beginning of life? What happens if a child learns during the first weeks and months that support and comfort are not always forthcoming? Psychoanalysts and other therapists believe with good evidence that babies can make these distinctions about their own safety (Mahler et al. 1975; Bowlby 1969, 1973.) Such a child will feel shaky and lack what is called "confident expectation"—the accumulated evidence of ongoing support. The nervous system can register the frequency of feedings and other interactions. Fear and apprehension "may take place in the amygdala below the conscious level" (Nelson 2011, 175). Babies can actually tell from the way they are diapered how safe their bodies are in the hands of the one doing the diapering. And as the baby grows, he will work harder and harder to get the attention and care he needs from the parent. Such a child cannot feel good about himself *internally*, and he will lack confidence and become dependent upon *external* evidence of support.

Psychoanalyst Donald Winnicott called this syndrome the "false self." Anxiety rises, and the child becomes hypervigilant, watching the people around him and accommodating his responses to their behavior. He abandons his "true self" (his own inner needs) to the service of others. He learns to meet *their* needs, and in that arena, gets some of his own needs met. The trade-off is a serious distortion of the child's personality, a loss of self that makes the child unhappy from that point on.

Children who grow up this way put most of their efforts into performance—that is, getting attention for what they *do* rather than for who they *are*. Actually, we need attention for both, and these needs are complementary. But without a strong *internal* conviction of self-worth developed in infancy, a child becomes too dependent on praise from others and comes to value herself *only* for what she can do—like the teenager we discussed in the introduction. And like that girl, she begins to neglect what she herself may want, because what *she* wants is not important to her parent.

In sum, healthy self-esteem cannot develop in a person who has not received the requisite parenting. In contrast, the experience of having been cherished can "inoculate" a child against depression and anxiety for a lifetime (Mahler 1979). Even if trauma and loss do occur later in life—as it will for most of us—a person who has had this steadying early support can more easily withstand the strain and recover her stability.

SELF-ESTEEM IS ACHIEVED THROUGH OUR OWN EFFORTS

Self-esteem develops quite differently from self-worth. We have said that with a strong positive attachment, a child feels safe and secure. This child can relax and begin to explore the world. From this point, she can begin to develop self-esteem, which is based on what some psychologists call *mastery*—reaching out, learning new words, fiddling with toys, successfully putting things together. Early attempts at this are the cute ones, like fitting the right peg in the right hole and first attempts at putting one block on top of another. When these attempts elicit joyful responses from the mother and others, the baby laughs and feels a sense of mastery. Her self-esteem grows. It is a victory, nothing less, and these little victories accumulate.

Later in life, our focused efforts at achievements are called "executive function," the sum of activities in the prefrontal lobes. "Executive function" refers to a clear sense of self, our skills and roles in our own fates. No less a person than Eric R. Kandel (2013), the famous neurophysiologist and Nobel Laureate for the year 2000, has said that "the prefrontal cortex . . . is the seat of executive function and self-esteem" and that this is one of the areas that can be disordered in depression.

A note about narcissism. Self-esteem is not narcissism. Self-esteem leads to *self-expression*, which does not (as it does in narcissism) exclude other people's right to do the same. With healthy self-esteem, we enjoy expressing our skills and talents, at the same time that we know other people have the same right to express their own skills and talents. That is not true of narcissism, which is characterized by intense self-centeredness. A narcissistic person feels that he or she is more deserving than others and thus should have special rights and privileges others don't have. The narcissistic person feels entitled to take advantage of others and is angry if his or her specialness is questioned. Narcissists are intolerant of any competition. Narcissism is only normal at around the age of two, when it is actually helpful for a toddler to believe that he is the center of his parents' world. As they grow, children can be grandiose, enjoying power over other children. But with good guidance, they can be helped to see that such an attitude is unfair to others and can damage relationships.

Self-esteem grows—*must* grow—from a child's own efforts. Every new skill builds on these early efforts. Learning to dress oneself, performing little chores, or learning to ride a bicycle all elicit praise from the parent and contribute to the sense of a child's own efficacy. This is healthy self-esteem, built on the foundation of internalized self-worth. Again, without that internalized self-worth, a child will put too much effort into what he can *do for others*. If he cannot be valued for the person he is, all efforts become centered on overachievement, on being the best. It shifts the center of gravity in that person from an *internal* psychological stability to the *exterior*, to somewhere out there in the world. Appearance, dress, makeup, and accessories become too important. He or she feels that the outside of the body must be perfect because the inside feels insecure. Degrees and titles become overvalued, not just as the achievements they truly are, but for the status they confer.

Self-esteem continues to grow through adolescence and does not show differences between males and females. In a longitudinal study spanning ages 14 to 30, researchers found that high self-esteem correlated with emotional health, outgoing behavior, and conscientiousness. People with strong self-esteem also showed low risk-taking and better physical health (Erol & Orth 2011.)

Experienced and dedicated clinician Madeline Levine writes, "The central task of growing up is to develop a sense of self that is autonomous, confident and generally in accord with reality" (Levine 2012, 8). She cautions that doing things for a child that he can and ought to do for himself deprives a child of his autonomy.

> [I]t is the inability to maintain parental boundaries that most damages child development. When we do things for our children out of our own needs rather than theirs, it forces them to circumvent the most critical task of childhood: to develop a robust sense of self. . . . It is psychological control that carries with it a textbook's worth of damage to a child's developing identity. If pushing, motivation and reward always come from the outside, the child never has the opportunity to craft an inside. (Levine 2012, 8)

Doing your child's homework or writing her letters of application to college damage her self-esteem and are more clearly filling the parents' need for success and affirmation rather than the child's. Rule-making parents, Levine says, help their children by teaching standards and encouraging children to meet them. It teaches children to be self-starters.

Psychologist Angela Duckworth (Duckworth, Peterson, Matthews & Kelly 2007) has identified aspects of academic functioning—separate from IQ—that predicted success. She developed the concept of "grit," perseverance in pursuit of a passion, a combination of patience, persistence, focus, resilience, and stamina. Duckworth, 1 of the 24 recipients of the 2013 MacArthur Award for outstanding research, says that "grit" may be as important as intelligence, because this set of skills allows a child to stay with a task over the long term until he or she masters it. She found that children with the most "grit," not the smartest ones, had the highest grade point averages. Duckworth has also, it would seem, defined the features of self-esteem more precisely than anyone to date.

And high self-esteem correlates with happiness. This book's quest is, in part, to clarify the parallels between emotional health and happiness. Arthur C. Brooks, president of the American Enterprise Institute, offers this:

Work can bring happiness by marrying our passions to our skills, empowering us to create value in our lives and the lives of others. . . . The secret to happiness through work is *earned* success. . . . Americans who feel they are successful at work are twice as likely to say they are very happy overall as people who don't feel that way. And these differences persist after controlling for income and other demographics. (2013, 7; italics added)

SHAME AND GUILT AS NORMAL MOTIVATORS

Children do not always comply with what we ask. About this, Levine takes a curious position. "A loving parent is warm, willing to set limits and unwilling to breach a child's psychological boundaries by invoking shame and guilt." Yet how do we avoid these? Shame and guilt are normal childhood emotions and do much to shape a child's cooperative behavior, as well as a child's self-esteem.

In brief, "shame" refers to our acute discomfort when we fail to meet our own standards (Wurmser 1981). When we feel shame, we have been found inadequate by our own measure. Shame is a painful internal state, but it is a major motivator that steers us forward to eliminate that pain by trying harder or changing course. Children learn quickly how to avoid embarrassment or shame, but guilt is another matter. It is the painful self-hate we feel when *others* accuse us. It is *their* judgment of what we ought to do—and we believe it. We would not feel the pain of guilt if we did not believe the others. Unlike shame, which is often positively motivating and builds self-esteem, guilt is a downward spiral of increasing *self*-hate, immobilizing us and damaging our self-esteem. Having said this, guilt is still important in childhood because it increases a child's sensitivity to his parents' wishes and requirements. Guilt thus protects the child's relationship with his parents and helps to shape a normal conscience—as long as the parents have healthy standards.

PREFERENCE VERSUS COMPULSION

A preference comes directly out of our experience of self-worth. Preference represents a choice, a self-expression. A preference comes from your heart; it is gratifying and connects you to your life. An example might be preferring one type of literature or music to another. More broadly, the choice of a career is a preference. Loving astronomy, fashion, genetics, or playing the cello can be a source of joy and inspiration throughout life. What type of art we love, what kind of garden we want, what type of terrain we want to live in—all are preferences. Just planning this kind of enterprise is edifying, and making it happen enriches one's whole life.

A compulsion, on the other hand, is a driven behavior. It does not feel good for very long, simply providing relief from some tension, but we feel we must do it anyway. Compulsive handwashing, wherein no amount of washing is enough, is a familiar example. A truly compulsive person will not be able to stop himself from counting the tiles on the floor. And then he will do it again. Preferences make us happy and support more good choices; compulsions make us miserable and anxious, but we cannot stop performing them. Thus, our general mood is a good test of any particular behavior. Preferences are emotionally healthy; compulsions are emotionally unhealthy.

BEING COMFORTABLE ALONE: PROOF OF GOOD SELF-WORTH

Another consequence of low self-worth is difficulty with being alone. For some people with low self-worth, this engenders a feeling of abiding loneliness. For others it is worse, a feeling of emptiness. This can be a perceived emptiness in the room, or it can be internal, a perceived central emptiness in one's being, a kind of "spaciness." This disconnectedness can cause a person to rush to other people compulsively, to social settings that are noisy and even risky, or to social media that are constantly stimulating. Others can become workaholics. Persons with low self-worth are *essentially unable to be comfortable when alone.* They seek attention from others to help them feel better.

First described by pediatrician and psychoanalyst Donald Winnicott (1958; 1986), the ability to be comfortable when alone is an achievement of early childhood. It is experienced when an infant is able to be alone—to "tune into" herself—in the presence of her mother or other reliable caretaker. This allows a certain organization to develop in the child's brain. The child's imagination and fantasy life can begin, and the emotions she feels are not overwhelming. The calmness and safety allow a child to develop self-regulation of her emotions, as well as her motives. "In this state of mind, the need to employ defenses to cope with external threat and inner emotions is at a minimum. At the same time, parietal-frontal systems involved in imagination and the creation of an inner sense of self become activated" (Cozolino 2010, 194). It seems strange that the elaborate system of emotional defenses we discussed in chapter one, Realism, would begin this early. But recent research shows human infants capable of a "brain signature of consciousness" similar to that of adults, but weaker, by about five months of age (Koch 2013). Defenses only develop when they are needed—that is, when the child is threatened or uncomfortable both alone and with others.

Difficulty with being alone, the corollary of poor self-worth and self-esteem, can lead to an attraction to alcohol and drugs, which only briefly reduce anxiety. The main effect of alcohol and drugs is to deaden feelings. The person's pain is numbed by drinking and drugging, but this only complicates the whole project of coming to terms with his or her problems. If this goes on long enough, brain damage can occur, making the person even less amenable to intervention. This is the sad experience of many people who have family members with substance abuse problems. A person's discomfort with being alone can be addressed in therapy. In the presence of a supportive therapist, the emptiness and fear the person feels can be tolerated long enough to understand its source and to develop the inner strength to overcome it.

WHERE DID THAT COME FROM?: OWNING OUR MOTIVES IS PART OF SELF-ESTEEM

We often feel that the way people treat us has nothing to do with our own behavior, that we are just living our lives and things happen to us. But studies of subconscious motivation—mostly by psychoanalytic researchers—have shown that other people's behavior toward us is, to a certain extent, *caused* by us. Our needs, our aversions, and our hostilities are expressed verbally *and* through nonverbal behavior. These can structure the responses we receive from others as well as their attitudes toward us.

Consider that you can predict the behavior of each of your friends and associates, what they like and don't like, and especially what will make them angry. This knowledge determines what you will say to each of them and what you will avoid. In the same way, we cue others about our own internal world, attracting the behaviors we want, or can tolerate from others, and warning them away from our deepest sensitivities.

These mechanisms of mutual cues, both conscious and subconscious, operate in healthy as well as unhealthy relationships. One serious, abnormal—and sad—complication that can develop is the condition of masochism. Complex and deep, this is the problem of persons who have grown up with a hostile, engulfing parent who binds them to herself in mutual need and pain. A son or daughter's attachment is thus to a person who will repeatedly hurt him or her, perhaps in a sneaky way not apparent to others, but the victim cannot let go of that person. This bond, along with the suffering that comes with it, secures a person's attachment to her oppressor. But it also guarantees a total loss of healthy autonomy for her (Wurmser & Jarass 2013). When she is grown, she may continually complain and even seek help for her suffering. It is very difficult to resolve, even in therapy, essentially because the suffering is gratifying to her on some deep level she can neither understand nor relinquish.

The lesson for the rest of us is that the way people treat us is not independent of our own behavior. It is linked to cues and signals *from* us that we, wittingly or unwittingly, convey. We are not neutral receivers of the actions of other people, and we must have an awareness and a sense of responsibility for the messages we give to others and ask ourselves if we have elicited the response that now is bothering us. It is another answer to the question: What is really mine? These are the types of issues that are explored and resolved in therapy.

THE PROCESS OF THERAPY

Therapy is a course, and like any course, each session's findings are dependent on the content of each preceding session. At first, people hardly know what to bring up, and some are annoyed that the therapist is interested in their background. A kind of curiosity about one's own psychology would seem the best preparation—being able to say: "I am not happy, and I don't want to go on this way. I think I may be contributing something to this situation, and I would like to find out what." Then therapy can begin.

I have come to think of progress in therapy as a sequence of stages.

In the first stage, the person sitting in front of me is distressed and confused, often not understanding the connections I make.

In the second stage, the person does understand some of those connections, but they offend her and make her uncomfortable or ashamed. Thus the second stage may be the most unstable and is the point at which a person may leave therapy.

In the third stage, the person becomes more comfortable with and confident of the interpretations her therapist is making. Indeed, she can begin to *predict* what her therapist would say. Humor, a good sign, often emerges in this stage, indicating to the therapist the beginning of insight, a broader self-understanding, and some distance from the symptom.

The fourth stage begins when the person can stop herself, at least some of the time, from doing something that would repeat an abusive situation before it happens. *It is only the insight—the ability to predict the sequence of behavior—that gives us the power to stop it before it occurs.*

Consider this sequence of stages as you read Amy's case.

Amy: "I only feel good when I give in."

When Amy first came to therapy, she was a 21-year-old college senior but looked significantly younger. She was an only child who constantly sought her mother's approval and affection. She did this with a compulsive compliance to her mother's expectations and needs. When this pattern was revealed in therapy, I gently asked, "Was this your mother's idea or yours?" At this, Amy would pull up her knees to her chest and start to cry. "I used to think that what my mother wanted *was* what I wanted." At those times, she looked like a very unhappy little girl.

Amy's mother was an outgoing woman who held an important position in a financial institution. She was very demanding, especially of her daughter. Whenever Amy would differ from her mother, the mother would angrily say, "Why can't you just do what I ask?" From this, it is fair to infer that Amy's mother had a difficult time getting adequate caring and approval from the important people in her own early life. Amy's mother grew up to be very like her own parents, repeating the pattern of discounting what her child, Amy, asked or wanted. Because Amy's needs and wishes were ignored by her mother and by her stepfather, she grew up feeling very unimportant, unloved, and powerless.

While still a little girl, Amy developed a pattern of seeking attention by allowing inappropriate touching by older boys. She said she was about 6 years old when this kind of relationship developed with a boy of 11. Both of them were reprimanded for it, but Amy remembers that she *loved the experience of being held and appreciated.* Then, when she was about 14, an older cousin forced himself on her. There was a big fuss in the family, and Amy was taken for a medical exam. She had not become pregnant, but the experience with her cousin frightened her. She became wary of freely giving hugs and kisses. She was beginning to believe she could make this decision for herself, that she should not let the other person make it for her. Her body belonged to her, not to other people.

Amy graduated from college with high honors. She applied to and was accepted by several graduate programs. She chose one and promptly met an interesting man, a classmate, and they began what promised to be a mutually gratifying relationship. And so it was, for several months. Then it became clear that he wanted her to admire him, take care of all his needs, and in general be focused on him. She was not to have any expectations of him, and he was impatient with her complaints, simple and warranted though they may have been. Amy loved this man, and she wept when describing his behavior in therapy. But she finally had had enough of his criticisms and demands. As she put it succinctly, "He was eerily like my mother."

It was interesting and a little nerve-wracking for Amy when her mother actually asked to come to a therapy session. This had to be Amy's decision, not her therapist's, and with some apprehension, she said yes. Her mother did come in, chatting enthusiastically about the therapist's garden and laughing about her own efforts. Amy looked quite miserable, feeling that her safe haven was being invaded. For this reason, many therapists would refuse to allow a parent or other to join an individual's therapy, but the session proved very illuminating.

When I asked Amy's mother the reason for her request to share a session with her daughter, she began to criticize her daughter for being messy and rude at home. At this point, Amy was still living with her parents. The mother said that Amy was unwilling to go out to eat with the family and that she complained about the food served in relatives' homes. No consideration was expressed by her mother that Amy was a vegetarian and often could not eat what was served. The mother's complaints filled the session, while Amy said nothing. It was painful to witness in real time the ongoing criticisms Amy had grown up with. Here was the evidence for the pervasive self-esteem deficit I was treating in this very deserving young woman.

During the next session, I asked Amy how she had felt with her mother present during the session. Looking wounded, she said, "You are *my* therapist," clearly feeling her mother could usurp even this very private part of her life. I then asked Amy if she had noticed that her knees were pulled up and her arms wrapped around them during that session with her mother, and that she had been silently tearful much of the time. Even in the presence of her therapist, Amy didn't feel she could refuse her mother's nonstop criticisms. She was crying at the time I asked this question, but she suddenly stopped, sat up, blinked, and said, "Oh, my God! Do you think I'm doing this to myself?" Yes, Amy was right. She was silently consenting to the ongoing abuse. But she was not powerless. She could refuse it, I said. She could refuse to be put down and humiliated. She could say "Enough!"

Although it may seem painfully obvious to you, this is not a step that can readily be taken by a person with severely damaged self-esteem. *A person cannot separate from a mother who does not permit it*, who blames her for wanting a separate life and the right to make her own decisions. A mother must be healthy enough to allow a child her autonomy. That is, a mother needs to be capable of enduring the pain of watching her child move away from her. This is not easy, but it *is* normal. In therapy, this point must be made again and again. It is strengthened by the therapeutic relationship: a valued and respected therapist/teacher who provides interpretations and validation, almost in a parental way, to a person who is asking—in Emily Dickinson's phrase—"Shall I bloom?" (The way Dickinson phrased that question shows that "blooming" can be difficult to do.)

It was at this point that Amy began to realize, "It's not me. I don't have to feel guilty. I have the right to be alone. I have the right to refuse to go out to dinner with them." These realizations were, of course, intellectual and unstable. She would still give in to her parents, only now with more insight. Finally, Amy felt it was time for her to live alone or perhaps with a friend. A final proof for the family dynamic I had been observing was this: when Amy told her parents she was thinking of moving out, they angrily gave her one month to do so.

Almost as soon as Amy moved out, she began to have more relationships with men characterized by power struggles. If she had the upper hand, she was glad. If the boyfriend tried to control things, she was miserable. It was control or be controlled. Her control issues came directly from her past, unchanged by time, as did the boyfriend's from his own past.

I explained to Amy how quickly she reinstated the early struggles with her mother in each new relationship. While hating the behavior, she irresistibly became tearful and needy within weeks of starting a new relationship. In the early weeks, all had seemed well, with both of them enthusiastic and energized. Indeed, we are all prone to this early exhilaration. "This time it will be different," we say. "This time all our dreams will be fulfilled." When the relationship is healthy, there is nothing in life to compare. But like Amy, some of us can quickly project our early unresolved issues onto a new relationship, and it can rapidly become unhappy. Amy's relationships showed this pattern. One man who was demanding and insecure would angrily blame her. The next man, emotionally healthy, would become disappointed and pull away. Her little-girl neediness was ruining each new opportunity.

The task for her therapy was clear: that Amy try to become more realistic about herself. She was no longer the helpless child her parents needed her to be. She did not need to cling to people to be loved; indeed, that was the turn-off for many of the men she was dating. I continually reflected back to her what was real: she was an intelligent and competent young woman *who could meet all her own needs.* She could support herself financially. She could cook for herself all the favorite foods she loved. She could structure her day around school and friends. Most importantly, she could appreciate her friends as equals, people she enjoyed for their own talents and accomplishments. Co-equal and co-powerful.

She had learned in therapy that she did not have the right to expect people to take care of her, and indeed, she did not need them to do so. If she did not remain conscious of the possibility that she could project the little-girl neediness onto any new relationship, it would happen automatically, since the motivation was subconscious. In time, Amy could observe her own behavior, saying, "Yes, I'm doing it again. I'm expecting this man to baby me." These changes only happened because Amy had been patient with my questions. She did not run away when her therapist held her to a difficult point. And she had let her therapist meet her mother, which clarified the whole picture.

Slowly, Amy's conviction of her own self-worth emerged, her intrinsic value to herself and others, but this time along realistic lines— no little-girl meltdowns. She was able to take responsibility for all her behavior—words, feelings, thoughts, and actions. She could enjoy her wonderful accomplishments. She had the confidence to speak up in class and assert to friends. She limited her mother's intrusions into her life. She found people who enjoyed the same music she loved. Each time we discussed these things, there was a bit more awareness, more growth, and more relief. Amy was seeing herself as a person among people—not taking herself too seriously, respecting herself and others equally and able to give and receive love and appreciation. Amy is still working on all these issues, with notable regressions, but the goal of therapy is being achieved: *maturation of her entire personality.*

You can see that Amy could absorb only a little information from each session. That is because each question I asked and each interpretation I made changed her emotions, sometimes confusing, sometimes frightening her. Her reactions , either of acceptance or resistance, actually structured the therapy. Let's review Amy's improvement in therapy using the system of stages I am proposing.

In the first stage, Amy was, in her word, "clueless." She could make no connections between what was happening to her and her own behavior. During the second, most difficult stage, Amy began to understand these connections, but they offended her and made her uncomfortable or ashamed. At times she was frankly angry with me and would say, "Stop. Stop!" At this point, Amy may well have left therapy, but she had a strong motivation to understand herself. "I want to go to graduate school," she said, "and I don't want to be a mess while I'm there." She was learning that much of her suffering, as we explored it in therapy, was the result of situations to which she had silently consented. As the second stage of her therapy progressed, Amy became more confident in recognizing and "owning" her reactions: she could say "Oh, my God! Do you think I'm doing this to myself?"

During the third stage, Amy could almost predict what her therapist would say. She would come into the therapy session tearful about an interaction with her father then hold out her hand toward me firmly, palm up, saying, "I know what you're going to say!" Amy had been describing her primitive father's penchant for showing anger toward her by leaving his mess in her toilet. Her reaction to these incidents had always been tearful helplessness. She had been apprehensive about telling me this because I would say—again—that she was all grown up now and far from helpless. As an adult, she had power she was not using. "Yes," Amy could say to me, "I can see that I'm doing it again." Amy could see that she was letting her parents humiliate her without making any complaint. She was very afraid to express her anger.

It was during the fourth stage of her therapy that Amy could actually stop herself, some of the time, from submitting to an abusive situation—for example, enduring her mother's tirades of criticism. She would leave the room without too much guilt. She could say with conviction, "I know I'm doing this to myself." She was finally beginning to make her life what she wanted.

In therapy, we often find that deficits in self-worth and self-esteem underlie many of the issues for which people seek treatment, especially depression and anxiety disorders. People do not know what is normal and what behaviors constitute symptoms. They do not notice the connection between the anxiety they feel and the substance they reach for to calm themselves be it alcohol, food, or drugs. As in the case of Amy, a better prognosis can be made for those who have not been involved with substance abuse. This is especially true for the most common substance abuse, alcoholism, which destroys precious brain tissue, making therapy much more difficult. But significant self-esteem issues also underlie another type of substance abuse—the addiction to food.

While you read the story of Ben below, you may notice that, in contrast to Amy, Ben had much difficulty expressing himself verbally. Amy's verbal skills served to discharge much of her anxiety. But among food bingers like Ben, one of the major motives is the need to stuff down angry or anxious feelings. Ben discovered that overeating calmed him (food is a good anesthetic). But that is exactly what inhibited his growth in life and in therapy. Yet Ben and Amy's progress in therapy followed the same path: the ultimate achievement of a dependable, strong self-esteem by taking responsibility for their own decisions and not living according to the proscriptions of others.

Ben: "Nothing to fall back on."

Ben was born someplace in central Europe. Although he is not certain, he believes it was Hungary. His mother, a girl from the countryside, had moved to a big city to work as a maid in a hotel. Tragically, many of these young girls were offered money for sex, and Ben was the result of one of these encounters. Expectant mothers were not welcome at the hotel, but Ben's mother found work with a private family nearby.

When Ben was a toddler, his mother returned to work at the hotel. Each day (he was later told), he would cry to go to work with his mother but had to stay with the kind family who took his mother in. This was a difficult time for his mother as well; she was still nursing

Ben. But at the hotel, one of her clients, an American businessman, befriended her. This man grew to love Ben's mother during the ensuing months, and eventually, after several trips back to the United States, he was able to marry her and adopt Ben. When they finally arrived on American soil, Ben was four years old.

Notably, it was a move that Ben remembers resisting fiercely. The day the family was to leave for the United States, Ben disappeared. He had been told they would not be returning to the village, so he hid in the trees around the only home he had known since birth. He remembers hearing people calling his name for a very long time, and finally, tired and hungry, he emerged from his hiding place. His mother tearfully expressed her relief, and they all left for America.

During the next years, Ben remembers his mother as warm and kind but not protective. Ben's mother remained a frightened person who needed protection herself. Although she had poor self-esteem herself, Ben's mother found ways to comfort herself and her child. She would sing to Ben each night in their own language. Ben loved these songs and learned all of them, singing them to himself when school was difficult. Increasingly, however, Ben was being encouraged to speak English. Ben's adoptive father still traveled for business, and Ben and his mother were often left alone in a community that was not always welcoming. Ben went to a school where some of the children giggled at his accent. He thinks he also may have stuttered a bit. He remembers trying *not* to speak while at school. This was a serious problem, because speech is our major tool for self-assertion.

Ben's self-esteem deficits ran deep. He had only vague images of the country in which he was born. His birth certificate was a copy of a line in a church registry. He still thought and dreamed in a language he and his mother had come to believe was inferior. Perhaps worst, his biological father was a person his mother had barely known. There was no surname for this man which would allow for some search of his whereabouts. This man did not know of Ben's existence. Ben had, in his poignant words, "nothing to fall back on."

Then tragically, when Ben was 10 years old, his mother died, he said, of tuberculosis. People do still die of tuberculosis, but I wondered if her condition had not been compromised by a fragile constitution, poor nutrition during childhood, and little or no medical care during her pregnancy and after Ben's birth. The loss of his mother was devastating to Ben. He then had no blood relatives in this country. But with his mother's death came strong positive changes for Ben.

Suddenly there was more community support, a vital connection with his school counselor, and a grief support group for children who have lost a parent. There Ben made friends with the other group members and listened to the phrases they used. For the first time, he learned to express his feelings verbally in English.

For the six years Ben had been in this country, he had remembered everything in his early life as shapeless and unclear, and his body image reflected that. Growing up, his body image was of someone weak and thin, uncoordinated, uncomfortable, and insignificant. He and his mother had developed a pattern of overeating "junk food," especially on nights when his stepfather was away. After his mother died, Ben's food binging began. He would buy chips, soda, and cookies. Although he was gaining weight, he still felt frail, weak, and uncoordinated. At age 18 and on his way to college, Ben was significantly overweight.

His weight increased over the next decade. After college, Ben worked in sales and had a van at his disposal. He said he would work a few hours in the morning then go to the drive-ins and buy many entrees and drinks. He would binge in the back of the van all afternoon. Ben's increased weight gave him an unexpected "benefit." He had noticed years before, when he was becoming obese, that as he came through a door, he would hit both sides of the door frame. He had felt "big and strong" for the first time in his life—a presence, visible and permanent. (Do women feel more powerful and positive when they gain many pounds? I think not. Overeating has other "benefits" for women, but feeling better about their bodies is not one of them.) Thus the symptom of overeating had at least two major effects. It was, in Freud's term, "overdetermined"—providing more than one advantage to the person. In Ben's case, overeating gave him solace, lulling, the experience of being with his mother again, *and* the added benefit of feeling big and strong. This last was to produce a crisis in therapy. As Ben lost weight, his feelings of being thin and weak, shapeless, and a bit unreal resurfaced. As we have seen before, a symptom is often a defense against anxiety. Being overweight protected Ben from the anxiety of feeling weak and insignificant.

At age 38, Ben came to therapy because he had been fired, in part because he was not working very hard, and also because he was discovered bingeing in the back of his company van. He was angry and embarrassed, but as we went through the history-taking process, he softened and used some expressions in his native language. When

I asked what they meant, he smiled and said, "No translation." He allowed himself to be weighed, a good sign. Then we went through his food history—what he eats throughout the day and what he eats on weekends. Like many obese people, Ben ate no breakfast but took in most of his calories late in the day. He understood how unhealthy this was. We went through the requirements of a healthy eating plan, emphasizing lean protein and lots of fruits and vegetables.

As I do with other overweight people, I asked Ben to eliminate one "junk food" per week, starting with soda, the worst offender, then chips and other bagged horrors during the second week. The third and fourth week's designees were doughnuts, sandwich cookies, and full-fat ice cream. Portion size was his biggest challenge, but he mastered that by taking large portions of green salads, medium portions of meat and fish, and small portions of brown rice or cooked barley. He chose to give up pasta altogether because it was a binge food. He learned to eat something every two to three hours—a cup of yogurt, a piece of fruit, or a handful of raw, unsalted nuts. He kept supper light, eating only a small protein portion, like a chicken leg, a hot vegetable, and a big slice of cantaloupe.

After many months, Ben was doing admirably, losing several pounds a week at the same time that he was looking for a new job. Part of his success came from working out at a gym several times a week and enjoying much encouragement from people there. The crisis came when he had lost about 50 pounds and began feeling all the old inadequacies. He was no longer big and imposing and was not noticed by people on the street. He did not hit both sides of the door frame anymore! He began to feel weak and uncoordinated again. But this time, he was getting strong kinesthetic feedback from his body during his workouts. His muscles were getting stronger. He was feeling strong in a new way.

Finally, with the confidence from working out and the support he was feeling in therapy, Ben began to weep. The tears were about all the early losses—his mother, his country, his language, and his nameless father. The bodily fragility he felt was really *emotional* fragility, "nothing to fall back on." Ben's difficulty with verbal expression made his loneliness complete. He had lost his childhood home, his language, and his mother but could not tell those stories in English. The relief we might feel by pouring our heart out to a friend was not possible for Ben. During each therapy session, Ben would gravitate to that void. He was losing weight steadily, but his depression would not lift. Since he was no longer binging on huge amounts of food, Ben was now encountering his early history in a raw, preverbal form. Ben wept silently too—a gentle implosion of grief.

Ben did speak English adequately, but it was mainly descriptive. He did not have that deep, poetic layer of language wherein our earliest longings are encoded; Ben did not have metaphor. Then I suddenly realized that he did have words for those deepest feelings, but they were *Hungarian* words. If psychologists are correct that personality forms principally between birth and about three years of age, then Ben's early longings and losses were relatable only in his native language. When his mother died, Ben feared their language had died with her. But I realized his mother had actually left him a vital link to their language: her *songs.*

I suggested that, while Ben was at the library researching job opportunities, he spend some time in the music section listening to CDs of folk songs and traditional as well as modern groups. Ben did this, spending hours listening to music with headphones. A librarian helped him find listings in Hungarian. He had never before seen his language in writing.

With this, Ben's search intensified. He was on a quest, listening for a certain dialect, and, one day, there it was! He would close his eyes, and the woman singing on the CD transported him to his childhood home. Triumphant, he came for his therapy session. This quiet man, who had hesitated before saying anything, now sat in front of me smiling. His excitement was palpable. His eyes shone, and he began to sing! From deep within his body came this "little-Ben" song, full-voiced and unafraid.

He sang so beautifully. Could he sing in a group? During the next months, Ben researched and found a singing group who specialized in traditional European folk songs in many languages—Polish, Hungarian, Czech, German, Russian, and others. He liked singing in other languages but was most moved by his "mother tongue." He began singing with this group as they toured around the state and in their Christmas concerts. He made friends. He suggested songs for them to do. As for his therapy, his serious weight problem would not have been resolvable without treating his self-esteem issues, which, as always, were rooted in his early childhood.

Ben is still singing.

MOTHERS AND THERAPY

Hollywood has made a laughing matter of the influence of mothers in their children's lives, blaming Freud for this reductionist view. The answer to any transgression, any problems with teens or marriages, any inability to reach a goal could be reduced to the quality of a person's early mothering or lack thereof. Yet with realism and some courage, we will readily see that our parents' personalities have deeply affected us. The way they raised us sensitizes us to their values on the one hand and to resentment of those values on the other. It comes in with the very air we breathe: their intonations and inflections; what they consider funny, important, sacred, or expendable; how anger is expressed (or repressed); how holidays are celebrated; how relatives are treated; and—most of all—how children are to be raised.

If we were lucky enough to have caring, helpful parents, all those categories are easy and comfortable for us to negotiate. But if we didn't, therapy can teach us what went wrong and how to correct it. We learn how to parent although we were not adequately parented.

> A parent's unconscious [mind] is a child's first reality. Interestingly, negative events in childhood are not necessarily predictive of an insecure . . . future parenting style. Working through, processing, and integrating early experiences, and constructing coherent narratives are more accurate predictors of a parent's ability to be a safe haven for his or her children. This *earned autonomy* through the healing of childhood wounds, appears to interrupt the transmission of negative attachment patterns from one generation to the next. (Cozolino 2010, 204–205. Emphasis his.)

In early childhood, *primary identification* is one of the most important achievements. It refers to the identification with a child's same-sex parent—a girl with her mother, a boy with his father. Primary identification (the resolution of the Oedipal Conflict) prepares a child to incorporate the behavior of the same-sex parent as part of that child's socialization. The passionate identification a girl, for example, feels with her mother also helps secure her mother's identification with, and pride in, her daughter.

How all this operates at the family level—for ill or for good—is illustrated by a young woman who came for therapy explaining that she grew up with a tense mother who was easily upset. Her mother would then become shrill and abusive, blaming the little girl for aggravating her. My patient hated the yelling, saying her mother would "go from zero to sixty" very rapidly. During much of my patient's childhood, and interspersed with "the good times," she would live in dread and apprehension that her mother could start yelling unpredictably for slights not always discernible by a little girl. Thus her stress was compounded by "anticipatory anxiety"—that is, her stress hormones were always high, a very damaging situation.

I asked this young woman if this was one of the issues for which she was seeking therapy. "Oh no," she exclaimed. "I want to work on *my* screaming. I swore I would never be like my mother, but when I get angry, I sound just like her. I look at my own little daughter and I can see the pain, confusion, and hurt in her eyes. It breaks my heart."

This young mother did not yet realize that the only way to overcome this behavior was to understand and respect its derivation. She came by it honestly. Sociologist Edward Shorter (1982) remarked that experience inscribes itself on our bodies. Our nervous system developed such that it can encode our lives. For a thoroughly modern discussion of how this happens, see Doidge (2007).

Learned patterns of behavior descend down (redundancy intended) through the generations unaltered by time. Any unresolved problems a woman has with her own mother, she will likely project onto her first or only daughter. She will do to her daughter what was done to her, without insight, without understanding. Her body will need to discharge stored tension. Her mind will not allow her to know she is doing that. The result is often a familial trap that can bind family members together in need, guilt, ambivalence, and love.

The process of identification requires that a girl identify with her mother not only to be attached to life and nurturance but also to be able to grow up and use the body she was born with. For this woman (who had a screaming mother), there had been a long period of running to her mother for a hug and running away from her mother's frightening outbursts. This builds tension in a little girl who loves, needs, and fears the same person. The careful task for both therapist and patient is to analyze those aspects of the early mother that are beloved and to be cherished, and those parts of the mother's behavior that have caused pain. We try to do this without blaming the mother. It is accomplished within the therapy relationship, allowing all feelings without judgment. The project in life—and in therapy—is to decide what parts of the parental identification to keep and what parts one does not want. How to keep the fun, the joys, all the parent's best gifts, but to become oneself.

CHANGING THE PAST IN THERAPY

People often feel we cannot change the past. But in therapy, we change a person's *understanding* of the past and thus her *experience* of it. And that changes the past. She can never again think of a particular incident in the naïve way she had before therapy.

The mistakes in perception that a person made in childhood were unavoidable (Celani, 2010). In normal early childhood, the experiences of safety and satisfaction (comfort and gratification of physical needs) are *unitary*. Safety and satisfaction are both experienced together in the hands of a loving mother or other caretaker. But if the mother is neurotic (unreliable, or even hostile), the child will do anything to stay safe and attached, even if this means *giving up* satisfaction. This instinctive, subconscious shift in the child causes a fateful split in her experience, *such that safety feels ungratifying and gratification feels unsafe.*

In therapy, this split is uncovered and treated. The person is helped to see that the safety she chose as an infant—that is, remaining desperately attached to an unreliable parent, now serves as a straitjacket. The anxiety that forced her as a child into the safety position, submission, is no longer necessary. As an adult she is no longer at risk, and the old choice now inhibits her growth.

Consider this as you think about your relationships. It is a mistake to believe that all comforting, reassurance, and protection must come from others. While it is very nice to have that reassurance from a parent, friend, or supervisor, we need to feel certain within ourselves that we are deserving and worthy. When it comes to love relationships, it is even more important to be confident of our own worthiness and that we deserve love. If we seriously doubt that, then our whole approach to a love relationship will be one of desperation rather than interest or excitement. It will feel like a life or death situation. *That is too great a burden to put on your loved one, and he or she will resent it.*

Every emotionally healthy person is a good parent to himself or herself. This means you can learn to carry within yourself the capacity for reassurance. Along with this, you are certain you will not allow yourself to be mistreated. You have the ability to remove yourself from a relationship that tears you down or a job that is depleting or unsafe.

For those who are willing to discuss their early histories in therapy and endure the vulnerability we feel when our life events are interpreted, true self-understanding and relief can be achieved. The early derivatives of the problems are examined. It is usually found that the person loved his or her parent, but ambivalently. That ambivalence is examined and expressed with guidance from the therapist; it is all right—indeed normal—to have mixed feelings about your parents. As described above, the therapist reaches back and provides corrective experience for those episodes in which, for whatever their reasons, your parents could not be "there" for you when you needed them or could not protect you when you needed protection. And what emerges is this: You deserved that caring attention. You were a healthy child ready to live and love, but people could not reach down to you when you were reaching up. You have the same basic human worth as any other person. You are good. You are worthy. And you are deserving of love—just for yourself. No achievements required.

REFERENCES

Bowlby, J. (1969). *Attachment and Loss*. Vol. 1: *Attachment*. New York: Basic Books.

Bowlby J. (1973). *Attachment and Loss*. Vol. 2: *Separation, Anxiety, and Anger*. New York: Basic Books.

Brandon, N. (2001). *The Psychology of Self-Esteem*. San Francisco: Jossey-Bass.

Brazelton, T. B. & Greenspan, S. I. (2000). *The Irreducible Needs of Children*. Cambridge, MA: Perseus Publishing Co.

Brooks, A. C. (2013, December 15). "A Formula for Happiness." *The New York Times Sunday Review*, 1, 6–7.

Celani, D. (2010). *Fairbairn's Object Relations Theory in the Clinical Setting*. New York: Columbia University Press.

Cozolino, L. (2010). *The Neuroscience of Psychotherapy*. New York: W. W. Norton & Company, Inc.

Doidge, N. (2007). *The Brain That Changes Itself: Stories of Personal Triumph from the Frontiers of Brain Science*. New York: Penguin Books.

Duckworth, A. L., Peterson, C., et al. (2007). "Grit: Perseverance and Passion for Long-Term Goals." *Journal of Personality and Social Psychology* 92(6): 1087–1101.

Erol, R. V. & Orth, U. (2011). "Self-Esteem Development from Age Fourteen to Thirty: A Longitudinal Study." *Journal of Personality and Social Psychology* 10(3): 607–619.

Horner, A. J. (1979). *Object Relations and the Developing Ego in Therapy.* New York: Jason Aronson.

Kainer, R. G. K. (1999). *The Collapse of the Self: and Its Therapeutic Restoration.* Hillsdale, NJ: The Analytic Press.

Kandel, E. R. (2013, September 9). "The New Science of Mind." *The New York Times Sunday Review,* 12.

Koch, C. (2013, September–October). "The Conscious Infant." *Scientific American Mind,* 24(4), 24–25.

Levine, M. (2012, August 5). "Raising Successful Children." *New York Times Sunday Review,* SR 8.

Mahler, M. (1979). *Selected Papers of M. Mahler, Volume 1. Infantile Psychosis and Early Contributions.* New York: Jason Aronson.

Mahler, M., Pine, F. & Bergman, A. (1975). *The Psychological Birth of the Human Infant.* New York: Basic Books.

Nelson, K. (2011). *The Spiritual Doorway in The Brain: A Neurologist's Search for the God Experience.* New York: Dutton.

Shorter, E. (1982). *A History of Women's Bodies.* New York: Basic Books, Inc.

Smoller, J. (2012). *The Other Side of Normal: How Biology Is Providing the Clues to Unlock the Secrets of Normal and Abnormal Behavior.* New York: William Morrow.

Spitz, R. (1965). *The First Year of Life: A Psychoanalytic Study of Normal and Deviant Development of Object Relations.* New York: International Universities Press.

Winerman, L. (2013, August). "Primed for Parenting." *Monitor on Psychology* 44(8): 28–33.

Winnicott, D. W. (1986). "The Mother's Contribution to Society." In C. Winnicott, R. Shepherd & M. Davis (Eds.), *Home Is Where We Start From. Essays by a Psychoanalyst.* New York: W. W. Norton.

Wurmser, L. (1981). *The Mask of Shame.* Baltimore: The Johns Hopkins University Press.

Wurmser, L. & Jarass, H. (Eds.). (2013). *Nothing Good Is Allowed to Stand. An Integrative View of the Negative Therapeutic Reaction.* New York: Routledge, Taylor and Francis Group.

Chapter 3

Spontaneity
Playing with the Whole Keyboard

Stunning my sensibilities you came,
Swarming the inner caverns that were cold.
How brilliantly you wrest from joy its flame,
From truth its fiber and from grief its soul.
                              —Camay Woodall, "Wakened"

How frustrating it is to try to play an instrument that has a bad key or string. We can't compose on it, because every time we need that key or string, the instrument can't respond. Something like this happens when we are unable to feel all our emotions. Important parts of our reality are not available to us, simply because we cannot connect with a specific feeling. "Spontaneity" refers to exactly that. Being spontaneous means that we have access to all our feelings. This may sound boringly obvious, but it is critical for emotional health. We need access to the *whole panoply of emotions* a person can have, feelings like excitement, happiness, fear, sadness, anger, terror, and joy. And what about curiosity, apprehension, wonder, confusion, contentment, loneliness, anticipation, or apprehension? We can feel baffled, miffed, intrigued, thrilled, pensive, daunted, annoyed, impatient, shamed, appreciative, surprised, aggravated, repelled, exhilarated, flummoxed, exhausted, inspired, curious, and glad. These emotions may sound similar, but they are all somewhat different. They have nuances that refine our experiences.

FEELING IS A LEARNED PROCESS

Feeling our emotions is just the beginning. We also need to hold onto them and then *decide* how we want to react. Think of this process in four consecutive stages: (1) being able to feel the emotion, (2) being able to name the emotion, (3) being able to hold on to the emotion and not push it away, and (4) deciding how to act on the emotion.

Stage 1. Being able to feel the emotion. This requires a conscious relaxation of the body that allows that feeling to flood our senses. The feeling must be welcome to us, meaning that we *allow* ourselves to feel all emotions. We give ourselves permission to experience whatever reaction we may have to the events going on around us. We are good receivers of information, witnesses to our own lives.

Stage 2. Naming the emotion. This has a lot to do with the words available to us. If our parents and the other people with whom we interacted as children taught us many different words for feelings, and if they validated our feelings, then we will be more able to refine the meaning of our own experiences all our lives. For example, we may be feeling annoyed with the person we are talking to and then realize that we are annoyed because the other person is not agreeing with us.

Stage 3. Being able to hold on to the emotion and not push it away. The capacity to hold on to a feeling is a function of our patience and our tolerance for frustration. It's easier to stay with a *happy* feeling than one that annoys us, but that is the only way for us to get the big picture. If we stay with the feeling of annoyance—and not run away from *any* negative emotion—we can expand our perception to see the other person's point of view. Are we strong enough to stay with the discussion until we can agree, or compromise, or agree to disagree?

Stage 4. Deciding how to act on the emotion. This decision to act on an emotion or not depends on impulse control (what psychologists call "affect regulation"). It is the recognition that all feelings are permissible but that behavior may have to be limited, according to social or personal morals and constraints. If the person we are talking to disagrees with us, we may feel the impulse—familiar to us when we were four—to smack him with the nearest object at hand. But *if we truly believe that other people have the same rights and privileges we want for ourselves*, it will be easier to be patient and to limit our response to one that is assertive rather than aggressive.

An important point: spontaneity is not impulsivity. As we have said, "spontaneity" refers to the capacity to *feel* all one's emotions.

"Impulsivity" refers to *acting on feelings* that are not well thought through and are often unfair or destructive.

SPONTANEITY REQUIRES FLEXIBILITY AND TOLERANCE FOR AMBIGUITY

How is spontaneity accomplished? We achieve it by being flexible, allowing all feelings to develop. As we have said, this is an effect of the quality of early care we received as children. Emotional flexibility cannot develop if a person is very anxious. It thrives on a healthy sense of humor, patience, and a caring attitude toward your body. Flexibility embodies a kind of curiosity you may have about how far a feeling can go and what it will develop into. For example, do you long to develop a new skill? Or to try for another degree? Or to move to a different part of the country? It's exciting and scary, but you will be able to make a better decision if you allow yourself to feel all the pros and cons. Spontaneity is the end result of being emotionally flexible.

FEELINGS ARE BODILY PROCESSES

Harvard physiologist Walter B. Cannon (1871–1945) was the first to demonstrate that emotions *are* physiological changes. He described the reaction of frightened animals as a mobilization of the sympathetic nervous system with adrenal hormones that readied the animal for "fight or flight," a term he coined. The return to "homeostasis," also his term, required the action of the parasympathetic nervous system that restored normal gut mobility. Cannon was a major researcher in the emerging field of psychosomatic medicine. He differed with his early teacher, William James, who said that cognition precedes emotion—we know something then we feel it. Cannon alleged it was the opposite; we feel something then we name it.

Neuroscientist Candace Pert (2003) says emotions and cognitions are intertwined and "bi-directional." She writes:

> *The body is the subconscious mind!* . . . [W]e can no longer consider the emotional brain to be confined to the classical locations of the amygdala, hippocampus and hypothalamus. For example, we have discovered other anatomical locations where high concentrations of almost every neuropeptide receptor [the place where a protein or hormone "docks" and becomes biologically active] exist, locations such as the dorsal horn, the back side of the spinal cord, which is the first synapse

within the nervous system where all somatosensory information is processed. . . . In fact, we have found that in virtually all locations where
information from any of the five senses—sight, sound, taste, smell and
touch—enters the nervous system, we will find a high concentration of
neuropeptide receptors. We have termed these regions "nodal points"
. . . to emphasize that they are places where a great deal of information converges. . . . Emotions and bodily sensations are thus intricately
intertwined, in a bi-directional network *in which each can alter the
other.* Usually this process takes place at an unconscious level, but it can
also surface into consciousness under certain conditions, or *be brought
into consciousness by intention.* (141–142; italics added)

A heady notion, that emotions are perceptions *and* cognitions. But
it makes eminent sense. The "information molecules" were created on
the basis of experience. Pert adds: "If we accept the idea that peptides
and other informational substances are the biochemicals of emotion,
their distribution in the body's nerves has all kinds of significance,
which Sigmund Freud, were he alive today, would gleefully point out
as the molecular confirmation of his theories" (141). And Freud did
write, "the ego [self] is first and foremost a body ego."

AMBIVALENCE (MIXED FEELINGS) IS NORMAL, INHIBITIONS ARE PROBLEMATIC

It is normal to feel several conflicting emotions at once—for example, excitement and fear, curiosity and apprehension, nervousness and
humor. And they can act on one another. Curiosity can be modified
by apprehension, fear can limit excitement, and humor can relieve
tension. Ambivalence—having mixed emotions—is the experience
of having a number of emotions at the same time, some of which
frankly oppose one another. Some dramatic examples are being sexually attracted to someone we know is not good for us, or a child's
strong attachment to a parent or other grown-up who continually
frightens her. Or wanting to accept a job that requires us to leave a
house and city we truly love. It builds emotional health to not run
away from dilemmas but to tolerate the ambiguity until a solution is
found. Tolerance for ambiguity simply means that we can put things
on hold, wait for clarification, and seek further information or advice.
It is a form of patience, and it helps us grow stronger. An *in*tolerance
for ambiguity is regularly found in impulsive people—those who are

driven to act on their feelings, whether fearful, sexual, or angry, without adequate reflection and planning.

What happens when we cannot feel a particular emotion? It means that somewhere in the progression of the four stages, a feeling is buried, denied, or worse, not perceived at all. Whatever the mechanism, the emotion is inhibited; it does not become part of that person's conscious life. The emotions that are most frequently banished or avoided are anger and fear. The reason for this is usually that, because of early nonsupport, we cannot feel trust. Basic trust—the outcome of a child's happy encounter early on with loving parents—permits the child to relax and to feel confident and supported. If a child cannot feel trust, he will be afraid and angry, two emotions that are likely to distort the trajectory of his subsequent growth.

To be sure—elaborating on Donald Winnicott's (1986) idea of the "good-enough mother"—children often get a mix of nurturance and neglect, patience and impatience. Parents are not robots; once in a while we run out of energy. In general, children are happier and healthier if they have parents who enjoy their children, understand good nutrition, care about rules and schedules, and tolerate a less than perfect house. (As a guide to parents in their struggle, I unhesitatingly recommend Marc Bornstein's [2012] five-volume contribution to psychology, *The Handbook of Parenting.*)

Children are damaged by parents who say they love them but then abuse or neglect them. Children are also emotionally damaged by parents who want their children to fulfill the parents' needs. Such children are heartbreakingly described by Madeline Levine (2011) as "trauma victims." Levine, a clinical psychologist, cites the familiar yet vital advice that children need time and attention for their own development, their own goals and interests, playing outdoors, and walks together with parents—in a word, unstructured time. Levine faults school systems for emphasizing standardized tests and competition for the "best" schools. These oppressive if not impossible standards can overwhelm children's ability to adapt, leading to inhibition and also acting-out behaviors.

Many types of mental illness and emotional suffering stem from the lack of a nurturing environment, as recently surveyed by Biglan, Flay, Embry, & Sandler (2012). In the following account, one man describes his lifelong struggle with the anxiety and confusion of not having had even minimal support and its ultimate effect on *his own children.*

TIM: A DICKENSIAN CHILDHOOD

Tim was raised by an angry, sarcastic mother who worked compulsively. His father had to travel frequently for work, and although this man was a caring father, his schedule made him unavailable to his children. Tim's older brother reacted to their mother with belligerence. They would get into loud verbal battles that no one would "win." Tim, who had watched these tense interchanges between his mother and brother, consciously or subconsciously, did the opposite. He sympathized with his mother completely, feeling that anything he could do to help her was the right thing to do. He would be "the good boy," making no trouble and being the person his mother wanted him to be. He "decided" that only what his mother needed was important. Thus, he had to push away his normal feelings of anger since his mother did not treat him any better than she treated his older brother. Tim struggled for reasons to justify her behavior: "She was tired. She had a hard day. She doesn't feel well. She does so much." These reasons effectively distracted him from the fear and anger that his own needs—*normal childhood needs*—were not being met. Tim and his brother needed attention, affection, support, encouragement, and protection, all the things that healthy parents give their children most of the time. He could not know, as a little child, that because of his mother's own early experiences, she could not enjoy her own children or be maternal toward them.

When Tim pushed his anger away, he was making a fateful error. When anger is deliberately pushed away, it can form an inhibition. After a while, the person cannot feel anger at all. As Tim explained in therapy, "You weren't supposed to feel anger." Anger was considered wrong, he said, and unwarranted. Compliance was good, at any cost. But when such a strong and normal emotion as anger is constantly pushed down and away from consciousness, it doesn't disappear. There is a backlash. It comes to be expressed in other ways. One such way is through forgetting. The child simply forgets to do what the parent asks. This gives the child some relief from the exhaustion of constantly complying with the parent's requirements. He then develops a *pattern* of overtly remaining the "good" child. He simply forgot. He is not aware that his forgetting represents a sneaky, passive-aggressive way of expressing anger at his frustrating parent. This defense pattern is then used in other relationships without insight.

Forgetting is a good example of a behavior that both hides and reveals—*at the same time*—unacknowledged motives. Forgetting hides his motive from himself and reveals it to a therapist. In this way, not being able to express an emotion affects a child's *cognitive* development as well. Anger is a normal emotion, which infants usually express by crying. They normally modify their crying when they are comforted and reassured. Through multiple interchanges of this kind, their crying becomes less desperate, and they eventually learn to complain verbally. Little children are *normally* very assertive, letting us know in no uncertain terms what they like, what they don't like, and why. Tim never learned to assert as a child. It would not have been welcome to his angry, controlling mother. Put another way, children need their parents' *permission* and assistance in order to say clearly what they want. Without that permission and assistance, children do not learn to assert but remain angry.

By the time Tim came to therapy, he was suffering from depression that was affecting his work. He had been married for 10 years to an angry, alcoholic woman who berated him and their children and neglected everyone, including herself. The first 5 years of their marriage had been tolerable; his wife's drinking had not been so frequent, and he had had more hope. But he sought therapy after two life-changing events. His boss and co-workers were complaining that he was running home too often, neglecting his work duties. Then his nine-year-old daughter ran away from home to an aunt's house and refused to come back.

In therapy, Tim said repeatedly, "How could I be angry with her [his wife]? She's sick." He also gave evidence that he was asking his older daughter—the nine-year-old—to take care of her mother. *This was the same role that Tim had taken on as a child.* When his daughter had pleaded for his help, he had insisted that she "respect" her mother. After many years of this—years of coming home to a frightening, drunk mother—the girl ran away.

The most difficult task for Tim in therapy was to see the connections his therapist was making—putting all these experiences together, logically and realistically. But Tim would often frown and look confused. When we cannot feel all our emotions, our reality is distorted. As long as Tim believed his wife should be supported at all costs (like his mother), he could not see the dangerous neglect his children were suffering. His need to protect his relationship with his wife created blinders, which narrowed his experiential field. Even his daughter's pleas—and they were many—were not understood for what they really were, and Tim could not empathize with her pain, or with his own. He could not allow himself to feel any anger toward his wife, just as he could not feel anger toward his mother. Therapy taught him that these two were experientially linked and protected by the same need. He was still feeling "Don't make waves. Be the 'good,' patient one." Moreover, the whole idea of a possible divorce and the question of placement for his children left him tremulous and nauseated. He had to persist, and he must have his older daughter's assistance. Their whole way of life depended on it.

Slowly, Tim began to understand that what he wanted was just as important as anyone else's needs and that he had the right to make decisions that supported those needs. Most of all, he learned that he was worthy of love without having to "earn" it through self-sacrifice. And with many repetitions of my question, "How do you think your daughter is feeling?" Tim was finally able to see it. "How could I have been so stupid?" he asked in recognition of his compulsive need to justify his wife's behavior. Tim wept as he described his little daughter's anguish as she begged him to let her stay with her aunt.

Realistic living requires courage. During the course of his therapy, Tim moved his children to an apartment near his work so that he could drive them to school. A year later, when he was able to see that it was unfair and unnecessary to allow himself to be abused over and over in the name of loyalty, he filed for divorce. Tim's difficulties did not come primarily from anger. Initially they derived from fear—fear of hurting or alienating the person he had needed most as a child. Fear then damaged his developing spontaneity. That fear is what made him wary of his justified anger, which came from not being listened to and respected. Children need and deserve respect. Then they can welcome all their feelings.

The definition of "childhood" includes the often missed point that it is normal for children to be dependent; they are not taking advantage of their parents. Complicating this, children realize at a very early age that they are powerless to meet their own normal needs. When these needs are not met, they react with anger, as Tim's brother had done, producing a stormy interaction with their mother. Or children can react with fear, as Tim did. A fear of his own anger made him push the anger away, out of conscious awareness, so that it was not available as a reaction to his mother. He did this so as not to be "bad" like his brother and punished for his anger. Moreover, little children fear that their anger can actually damage the mother. And this becomes even more frightening, because now the mother could be harmed or dead, and it is the child's *fault*. Tim would offset all these horrible consequences by being the good, appreciative son, who did what was expected of him, no matter what. As Freud would have predicted, as an adult Tim was attracted to a needy, only superficially caring woman. As her drinking progressed, he struggled over many years to "cure" her. His mistake was to believe that he could change his wife's destructive behavior through his own effort or, failing that, that he had to blindly endure. Depending on the situation, sometimes the best, and the healthiest, thing to do is to give up.

WE THINK WITH A PART OF OUR BODY: THE BRAIN

It takes a lot of energy to keep anger out of awareness. You have to keep your foot on that devil's neck constantly, or the anger may surface, making you feel terrified and vulnerable. You can never learn to be assertive—that is, you can't speak up on your own behalf. Without the skill of assertiveness, you will be uncomfortable having any kind of power, because power can be so destructive. All this is in the service of keeping anger out of awareness. Neurophysiologist Antonio Damasio (2005) has shown in his work with variously brain-impaired patients that the inability to feel emotions compromises our reasoning:

> The organism interacts with the environment as an ensemble: the interaction is neither of the body alone nor of the brain alone. . . . The physiological operations that we call mind are derived from the structural and functional ensemble rather than from the brain alone; mental phenomena can be fully understood only in the context of an organism's interacting in an environment. That the environment is, in part, a product of the organism's activity itself, merely underscores the complexity of interactions we must take into account. . . . [A]nd suffering, whether it starts in the skin or in a mental image, happens in the flesh. (introduction to the second edition, xxi)

Here is evidence for what I stressed earlier. What Damasio means is that when feeling is inhibited, thinking is impaired. *Not being able to express an emotion affects a child's cognitive development.* What finally resolves a person's rigid defensiveness is a slow process of learning. This is what happens in therapy, signaling to the person and his therapist that the therapy is accomplishing its goal. But it *can* happen simply as a result of having good relationships around you. The formerly rigid person realizes he doesn't have to worry so much anymore. The people around him now love him and want him to be happy. He develops a trust in himself, his life, and his future that he never had before. And his symptoms—anger, defensiveness, sarcasm, unresponsiveness—begin to fall away, like crutches he no longer needs. He is among friends. He can relax. A gentle sense of humor develops, allowing him to laugh at himself when he "goofs up," the opposite of the vicious self-hatred he used to feel with any little mistake. He is free to feel all his emotions.

How does therapy work this magic? Contrary to older neurological information, the latest evidence establishes that brain growth, and therefore learning, continues throughout life. A person cannot have full and easy access to all his feelings unless he is relatively free of anxiety. Our bodies will not allow us to feel any emotion that is developmentally linked, subconsciously, to excessive anxiety. But this is no longer seen as a life sentence. As a result of recent findings in brain plasticity, we now understand how growth in therapy, and in life, proceeds.

> It is now known that neurogenesis continues throughout adult life from neural stem cells in just two locations. The first is in the walls of the brain's lateral ventricles—part of the system through which cerebrospinal fluid flows between the brain and spinal cord. New neurons born here migrate to the olfactory bulb, where our sense of smell is processed. The second is located in a part of the hippocampus called the *dentate gyrus.* The hippocampus is well known to be crucial for learning, memory and regulating stress responses, and neurogenesis here is part of the brain's response to new experiences. (Smoller 2012, 127)

When this neurogenesis is blocked, Smoller emphasizes, the stress hormone cortisol remains high. Neurogenesis, the birth of new neurons throughout life, "buffers" the effect of this cortisol. As Smoller puts it, "*resilience* may depend in part on the brain's ability to generate new neurons in the hippocampus" (127–128; italics added). These new findings fit beautifully with those of psychiatrist and psychoanalyst Norman Doidge (2007), who said—building on the work of Eric Kandel—that psychotherapy works by altering the anatomical connections between brain cells and turning on the "right genes" (221).

This is the mechanism by which we can outgrow inhibition. No matter how "stuck" we may be, with enough determination, courage, effort, and perhaps a good therapist, we can see the larger picture and understand the connections that were blocked by fear. In this process, feedback from others is essential. Just as we want to be taken seriously, so do our spouses and other family members, especially our children. In Tim's case, his little daughter's disappearance forced him to listen to what she had been saying for years. The new research tells us that not just his mind, but his brain was changing—at the same time. The birth of new neurons coincides with the emotional realizations that free us from the past because we now understand and no longer fear it.

FEELING EMOTIONS WE DO NOT WANT

The process of emotional growth is not smooth. Allowing ourselves to feel all our emotions can hurt. Jealousy, for instance, is uniquely painful. As an example, someone we work with gets a promotion we had hoped for. We feel sad and angry at the same time, and resentful of the lucky co-worker. These are normal and expectable feelings, generated by the conviction that we also deserved that opportunity. The discomfort stays, making us sadder and unhappier. Slowly, with patience, we begin to appreciate that our co-worker and her family are much better off, and we can begin to be glad for them. And we begin to set our sights on another position, or another company, or even graduate school. There are other opportunities, other chances for us. Thus jealousy can be outgrown.

Grief and loss are emotions that ravage the mind and heart. The pain is so unbearable that people often welcome some pill or drug that will anesthetize them, at least for a time. Alcohol can be abused at these times; it is also a good anesthetic—its health hazards forgotten for the moment. People who have lost a spouse or a son or daughter often report that they could hardly remember the details of the year or more after the loss. They also report feeling quite numb, as if they had thrown a total body switch, thereby canceling all feelings. This does not happen consciously; the body simply "turns off" to avoid debilitating pain and to conserve energy and sanity. This numbing comes at a price, however. Only when they can begin to feel again can grieving begin. Grieving *requires* feeling the pain of loss and expressing it—in words or in works of art: a poem, a painting, a song, or in a profound connection to nature. Finally, at some point it begins—a deep turn back toward life.

Among the unwelcome feelings that definitely upset us are unwanted sexual feelings. Our society is so full of sex symbols that we have to actively tune them out so as to avoid becoming unwittingly aroused. Our bodies simply react, if we have adequate hormone levels, and most healthy people do. These reactions are amoral, rather than immoral, if we find ourselves aroused but uncomfortable with our response. We should not blame our bodies for being healthy. A healthy body will respond to pleasurable or painful stimulation from the environment. At that point, our prefrontal cortex, the decision-making part of the brain, must decide if our reaction is appropriate or not, is fair or not.

A striking example is the distressing testimony of sexual assault victims. They will often lament that, at some point in the assault, they actually found themselves sexually aroused. In therapy, they feel ashamed of this reaction, which can lead to some confusion and guilt. I have explained to more than one such patient that, as stated above, our bodies simply react. To make an analogy with another appetite, if someone put sugar on your tongue, it would taste sweet whether you wanted it or not. Thus it is only *after* the excitation that we have the opportunity to make a judgment: is this a good situation for me or not? It is only then that our moral and social values can be imposed on the situation. Sometimes being spontaneous—being able to feel all our feelings—can make difficulties for us, but it is worth it. Being fully spontaneous is the only way we can truly be in contact with reality, with the big picture, and with all the players in our personal life. Then, as Damasio (2005) has asserted, our decisions are better, richer, more nuanced, more humane.

Vera: The Body Autonomous

The preceding discussion helps us to understand that it is healthier to deal with unwanted sexual feelings than to deny them. The worry that a troubled mother brought to therapy exemplifies this. Vera was a professional woman accustomed to efficient problem solving. Now she was upset on a daily basis by the way she was reacting to her son, who was 19 and living at home while attending college. Vera found herself more and more intrigued by the sight of his body, especially when he came down for breakfast nude to the waist. "What's wrong with me?" she lamented. "This is my own son. I shouldn't have these kinds of feelings about him."

We discussed her feelings in detail during her therapy sessions. The feelings had only begun within the past few months. I explained to her the way the body works. Her body was just reacting. It is like a

5-year-old child who wants every treat she encounters. The body does not make judgments about what is or is not appropriate. That is the brain's job. The brain—especially the prefrontal lobes—is involved in choices about what is and is not appropriate. But before getting that far—that is, to the thinking and judgment phase—this woman's body was simply reacting as it would to any other attractive man. (It was a sign her hormones were working well.) Moreover, I asked, didn't this 19-year-old remind her of how his father had looked at this age? A sight she had surely reacted to in exactly this way? Vera laughed. "Yes, of course," she said, but what was she to do now?

As her therapy progressed, I learned more and more about Vera's methods of problem solving. Usually she was too hard on herself and was accustomed to quick solutions. She could agree that this attitude was not helpful. First of all, it showed that she blamed her body for the problem, when as explained above, it is a normal appetitive reaction, although one she needed to understand and limit.

There were, I stressed, several important considerations. First, it would, of course, be totally inappropriate to tell her son how she was reacting or to communicate her feelings to him in any nonverbal way. Second, she would protect herself from the unwanted stimulation by leaving the house earlier in the mornings before her son was awake and in the kitchen. Then, on weekends, she could request in a friendly way that her son come down to breakfast with a shirt on. At first Vera said she would be embarrassed to request this. I reminded her that this was not different from a considerate parent not walking around half-nude in front of a growing child. Lastly, I told her that we need not feel guilty about our body's reactions as long as we take responsible steps to act morally. Here was the inevitable link between what is normal and what is moral. In a word, all *feelings* are acceptable, at first, as information about how our body is reacting. But our *behavior* must be scrutinized and limited on the basis of what is fair, appropriate, and moral.

Vera's therapy became focused on her son's father, from whom she was now divorced. She had endured the separation and then the divorce proceedings with much hurt but not disorganization. She had found out about her husband's affair through his own verbal fumbling and had confronted the whole thing directly and responsibly. Once we understood her real adult needs, as well as her feelings of grief and abandonment, her regressive longings made sense. Our bodies are amoral, and like children, need redirection.

It is the same when we are dieting. It's crucial to protect our bodies from the arousal we would feel while shopping the aisles that feature cookies, candies, and pies. Our bodies—our little girl or boy self—would immediately start campaigning for them.

MEANING: SYMPTOMS ARE PERSONAL

The only way we can understand behavior is through *meaning*. The same symptom can mean different things in different people. For example, the symptom of compulsive housework in one woman was consistent with the other features of her obsessive-compulsive disorder (OCD). She described her need to wash the kitchen floor after breakfast and again after lunch. She would have to fight the impulse to scrub it again after supper and could only be dissuaded from doing so by her caring family.

Another woman came to therapy describing the same pattern of compulsive housecleaning, but her neediness centered on constant vacuuming. This woman showed no features of OCD, nor any other symptoms. What was happening here? This was a rigid but accomplished woman with strong religious convictions. In therapy, she discussed her compulsion as a much-needed protection. Protection from what? Finally, she was able to say that as long as she was vacuuming, she could resist urges to leave her house on weekends and seek other men. Floor scrubbing for the first woman actually made her more anxious: compulsions reduce anxiety only briefly. But for this woman, it was the opposite. She said the constant hum of the vacuum *calmed* her. "It's almost like praying," she said.

Therapy for the first woman included her psychiatrist's recommendation for medication. For the second woman, treatment involved a careful analysis of her marriage and why she felt so unfulfilled. Therapy helped her understand her personal dilemma and resolve long-standing developmental conflicts. Helping these two very different women depended on understanding the totally different *meanings*—and purposes—of compulsive housecleaning.

Similarly, being overweight can act as a kind of protection against private fears. For one man, losing weight made him feel weak and insignificant. To be fat was to be big and imposing, a person to be reckoned with. Another person, a woman in therapy, revealed that her obesity protected her from being unfaithful. She explained that being very overweight assured her she was unattractive to men and curtailed her impulses to flirt. Two people; two very different meanings for the experience of overweight. Often it takes a serious course of therapy to achieve this level of clarity.

A final example. In therapy we often hear people expressing a fear of "going crazy." It is usually described in the context of high anxiety as a fear of losing control. A person will report desperate tactics to maintain control, such as writing in journals, sometimes writing over his or her own writing when all empty pages have been filled. Or a person will not venture beyond a certain perimeter, perhaps her own front porch. People desperately attempt to manage their anxiety through rituals like these. At the time I was working at the Johns Hopkins Hospital, we were evaluating a woman for possible admission. She gave her history responsibly and seemed sensible and practical. Her husband had brought her to the hospital complaining about her refusal to talk to him and cooperate with his wishes. She explained with an embarrassed smile that she was "afraid of going crazy," yet she exhibited no "crazy" behavior. When the other staff had finished their questions, I asked the woman what she meant by "going crazy." She stared at me, somewhat alarmed. "You know. Go crazy. Go out dancing!" It turned out that her husband was very religious and did not approve of dancing or music in general. His wife felt unbearably constrained, and she feared her own impulses to defy her husband and *go out dancing*. That was what she meant by "going crazy." This woman did not need hospitalization. My recommendation was that she seek group therapy.

Meaning is what makes a symptom personal. Despite the claims of recent books on the "new science of meaning," there is nothing new about it. Psychology was founded on philosophy—a word that means "the love of knowledge." William James, who wrote the *Principles of Psychology* (1890), was essentially a philosopher trying to render demonstrable the observations of earlier thinkers. Meaning, he said, is the *interpretation* we give to an event, which then causes the physical reactions we call emotion.

We have to look behind a person's words for the unspoken motive. It is not just deprivation of our bodily needs that can make us anxious. Ideas and concepts—for example, the notion of "going crazy," can activate the fear center of our brains. William James would have appreciated knowing that the amygdala, our anxiety and stress center, is regulated by *language-processing areas*, which produce the fear-promoting ideas and concepts in the brain (Berkowitz, Coplan, Reddy & Gorman 2007).

When you can feel all your emotions, you bring to every encounter the best instrument for experiencing what is really there in front of you, not what you fear is there or hope is there. This is never a perfect process, of course, but the more open and patient we are with each situation, the more accurate and fair our participation will be. We are always analyzing the events of our lives and how we feel about them. This keeps us open to all possibilities and connects us to the real world. Thinking and feeling are inherently integrated, and they inform each other in our effort to be realistic. Returning to the opening metaphor, to lose even one key prevents you from playing the whole song.

SPONTANEITY HELPS RELATIONSHIPS

Spontaneity is an essential feature of emotional health. It is an easy, joyous, and unconflicted attitude toward the world, opening us to all its emotional riches. In another setting, this could be called a vigorous *curiosity* about the world, or a *mindfulness* (Holzel 2011; Kirk 2011) of its particulars. However we describe spontaneity, it addresses our ability to respond to any situation with a full range of feeling. You can easily see that this also means we will *suffer* more; we will feel more sadness, frustration, loss, anger, fear, and conflict. Why in the world would anyone want to do that? Because it is the only way to be realistic and to stay in touch with the real world. In addition, it is the only way to learn how to regulate our emotions—to figure out what we want and need to do about a particular emotion—and then how to manage those feelings.

Thus, if you are feeling uneasy about an assignment you were given, you may need to ask more questions to better understand what is being asked of you. If you are angry, stay with that feeling long enough to understand where your anger is coming from. The same is true if you should feel neglected or rejected by someone important to you. First ask yourself, "Is this really true, or is it coming from earlier feelings of neglect and abandonment that have nothing to do with the present moment?" If the answer is yes, the feeling is coming from the here and now, then a clear, fair statement—an assertion—to the person causing the feeling would be the next step. Find the moment to meet with that person and to be candid. Listen to his or her version; it may be a statement about *your* behavior. Take the opportunity to complain on your own behalf. Assertion is a skill; people learn it. *And each time you use the skill of assertion, you become stronger.* So that the next time you need to assert, it will be easier.

An Affair: When Emotions Are Overwhelming

We have said that being a fully feeling person is emotionally healthy, but it can also make for problems. When you are open and receptive to all your feelings, you may at some point find yourself in a uniquely human dilemma—sexually attracted to someone and your feelings reciprocated—while one or both of you is married to someone else. An affair can change and sometimes wreck lives. Reactions to this event vary wildly. Some people consider this type of attraction the "spice of life." Others call it sin. Literature, poetry, and opera rely on the love triangle as the quintessential human drama. These feelings are so compelling as to seem irresistible. Some earth-centric force—probably evolution again—impels you toward this person. What do you do? And how is it that these feelings are so often mutual?

Sometimes the new relationship is true and real and represents the next, necessary step in your emotional growth. When this is the case, the two people must clarify their earlier relationships and make their peace, as much as possible, with family members. *Every relationship, especially with our children, must be rebuilt.* Siblings often take sides. Fathers and mothers cry, rant, and then stop answering their phones. Rejected spouses become uncharacteristically greedy and punitive. They storm out of the house and have car accidents. Older children act out, punish, and switch sides. Then they switch back. Everyone in the extended family has an opinion and a prediction. The whole community is abuzz. Jobs are given up, sometimes unnecessarily. Houses change hands. Wills are rewritten and fortunes lost. The state is interested in the tax consequences. At least two lawyers wait for their thousands. Alimony is not dead; it can double child support payments. Are you ready for all this? Is this worth your spontaneity?

You decide it has to be. Life is inconceivable without your new love. That is your answer. The actual breakup, though, can be wrenching. Watching someone you have lived with actually packing and leaving is like being slowly eviscerated. Each of you will leave the life you have known. You and your new love will make a new life, perhaps in a new place, where your children, and as many family members as wish to, may visit or live. The mind-numbing complexity of all this may cause you to give up the new relationship a time or two—or for good, if the loss of so much family history outweighs the gain of even true love.

In the end, it is the undeniable rightness of your new love, his or her uniqueness and irreplaceability, that pushes you, head down and out of the old one. If, instead of landing in hell, you find yourselves in an empty, clean house with boxes to unpack—and you kiss before starting that lesser task—you will feel you made the right decision.

If, on the other hand, you are certain you will end in hell, don't go. Too often, the new relationship is a dalliance for one and a tragedy for the other. If this is true in your case, what a dangerous place you now stand in. Lying is always wrong, but it is criminal to lie in a love relationship, especially when little children are involved. You may feel transfixed, unable to move forward or backward. How can you go on, as if this great attraction had not occurred? My bias is that this, and indeed all the situations we have been discussing, deserve the respectful and careful analysis you will get in therapy. It is perhaps too great a decision to make alone. For your emotional health and your future, you must take this challenge seriously. You are suffering a loss the other person does not share. But it can be outgrown, because so much of our brain is dedicated to inhibiting impulses. "Although the capacity for learning is to some extent present in even the simplest creatures, willpower is the uniquely human 'ghost in the machine'" (Pert 1997, 135). You can stop your pain, in time, by skillfully developing willpower—and insight.

INTENTION IS THE KEY

To elaborate, large, major areas of the brain are devoted to inhibitory circuits, those that limit unwanted behavior (Doidge 2007). These most advanced circuits govern social behavior. They are located in the front part of the head, behind the eyes and between the temples. This area, the prefrontal cortex, contains most of the inhibitory networks that allow a person to wait and consider a choice before acting on it (Viamontes & Beitman 2012, 39). But it does not function automatically. We must focus our attention and consciously state our intention of limiting that impulse. It must be consciously refused. This takes practice and determination, which causes a stress of its own. We are fighting our impulses. We walk around conflicted, but the longer we tolerate that stress, the more clarity we gain. An internal dialogue emerges: "What is going on here? Where am I going with this? Who is it hurting?" Your body is in withdrawal, but your brain is helping.

You have as much power to inhibit feelings as you have to experience them, but you must feel them first in order to know what to limit. To stretch our musical metaphor, it is a kind of symphony. There are brass instruments, wind instruments, strings, and percussion. *You are the conductor.*

REFERENCES

Berkowitz, R. L., Coplan, D., et al. (2007). "The Human Dimension: How the Prefrontal Cortex Modulates the Subcortical Fear Response." *Reviews in the Neurosciences*, 18, 191–207.

Biglan, A., Flay, B. R., et al. (2012). "The Critical Role of Nurturing Environments for Promoting Human Well-Being." *American Psychologist* 67(4): 257–271.

Bornstein, M. H. (Ed.). (2012). *Handbook of Parenting*, Five Volumes. London: Psychology Press.

Damasio, A. (2005). *Descartes' Error* (2nd ed.). New York: Penguin Books.

Doidge, N. (2007). *The Brain That Changes Itself*. New York: Penguin Books.

Holzel, B. K., Carmody, J., et al. (2011). "Mindfulness Practice Leads to Increases in Regional Brain Gray Matter Density." *Psychiatry Research* 191(1): 36–43.

Kirk, U. (2011). "Interoception Drives Increased Rational Decision-Making in Meditators Playing the Ultimatum Game." *Frontiers in Neuroscience*, 5–49. doi:10.3389/FNINS.2011.00049

Levine, M. (2012). *Teach Your Children Well: Parenting for Authentic Success*. New York: Harper/Harper Collins.

Pert, C. B. (1997). *Molecules of Emotion: Why You Feel the Way You Feel*. New York: Scribner.

Smoller, J. (2012). *The Other Side of Normal: How Biology Is Providing the Clues to Unlock the Secrets of Normal and Abnormal Behavior*. New York: William Morrow.

Viamontes, G. I. & Beitman, B. D. (2012). Neural Substrates of Psychotherapy. In R. D. Alarcon & J. B. Frank (Eds.). *The Psychotherapy of Hope: The Legacy of Persuasion and Healing*. Baltimore: The Johns Hopkins University Press.

Winnicott, D. W. (1986). *Home Is Where We Start From: Essays by a Psychoanalyst*. New York: W. W. Norton & Co.

Chapter 4

Work and Play
The Antidote to Depression

It may be that when we no longer know what to do
We have come to our real work,
And that when we no longer know which way to go
We have come to our real journey.

The mind that is not baffled is not employed,
The impeded stream is the one that sings.
—Wendell Berry, "The Real Work"

Work and play can be discussed together because they often exist together, and, ideally, they become one another. That is, fulfilling and creative work can seem like play. And play can often be expressive but hard work. The work and play that we are drawn to, that pull us along with growing intrigue, contain expressive and evolving interests, sustained since childhood. They can be fascinating and endlessly variable, and they can be fun. Imagine having all that together. Finding something you love to do—that you would do for nothing—and getting paid for it! Broadly speaking, "work" can be defined as a focused effort toward a future goal. It gathers many points. The goal is a mental construct. It is complex: building a tree house, writing a report, plotting a journey. And all the steps leading to that goal are present in the mind as a plan. The steps have a particular sequence. Finally, the energy and time that each step requires are also carefully considered. All this takes intelligence, stamina, vision, and focus.

Whether for payment or not, the ability to work reliably is another hallmark of healthy personalities. A sense of responsibility to ourselves and to our employer goes along with that. Supporting ourselves, at least in part, is the important result. Work and play, and their individual interpretations, are our natural habitat, and the required exercise of our imagination is part of what makes us human. It is the source of all art, music, poetry, literature, science, and engineering. We make work and play an individual expression by projecting our own unique skills and talents into each endeavor and making it our own. The more we can make our work and our play into our *art,* the happier and more fulfilled we will be.

Well and good, you say, but is this a world where mail gets delivered, kitchens get cleaned, articles get published, and children get helped with their homework? Some work, while not oppressive, is hardly a religious experience (taking out the trash comes to mind). Yet—I persist—if you love your home, then cleaning it will not be (too much of) a chore. And if we are loved by our families, especially by our significant other, then whatever we do for them will not seem enough. It is just part of that loving. Any work we do that sustains those relationships—even taking out the trash—will be annoying at worst, but worth it.

Psychologically, we are happiest when we have the liberty to choose work that engages us at many levels: intellectually, emotionally, physically, and even spiritually. The work of scientific research, for one, is brain wracking, demanding, exhausting at times, but immensely rewarding. (One colleague called research "the hardest and best game.") Even the failures are interesting and recentering. There is always the promise that some new finding will move the field forward or change it forever. Our minds reach for complexity and innovation. We have to force ourselves to think simply, applying old, established data to the new.

Every child's project is to imagine her life in a future she is not experienced enough to understand. So she dreams. There is not yet a distinction between work and play. Money is not a childhood value. She does not know what is impossible. Thus, childhood is a place of perfect possibilities, endlessly generative. It is a place we cannot stay, but it is the place to which—later, in a quandary—we must return.

There are lists of books about finding the right and best job for you. But I am stressing the *psychological* elements involved, how we react to the work situation, and most of all, what it means to us. We *identify* with our work; it becomes part of our self-definition. This includes not just the work itself, but the setting, the type of people around us, and the rewards, monetary and otherwise. If you love music, then any task involved in the making and recording of your kind of music will be a joy. If you love the sea, then taking whatever skills you have to a coastal area, at least for part of the year, will transform your work experience.

Some people love city planning, history, canoe building, dress-making, or pottery. (Musicians seem to be the pinnacle of this happy crowd. Conductors are said to be among the longest lived people; maybe it's the amount of time spent at the heights.) The point is that we can see our work as both a contribution to community and as a personal expression of our connection to it. It develops our abilities and imagination in a unique way.

That our work can also be frustrating only adds to this complexity. For me, each patient or couple brings a new set of issues. I often come away from the first session or two thinking, "What is this person doing?" But if we continue, eventually the answer puts itself together in my mind. Each person brings a unique dilemma, *peculiar to his or her history*. I am most useful, and I understand the dilemma best, when I honor that uniqueness.

WORK FRUSTRATIONS

Much depression *is* work related and happens normally as a reaction to a *loss*—for example, loss of meaningful work, loss of any job that held body and soul together, loss of the status and respect the job gave us, or loss of a start-up business. Having been passed over for a coveted promotion ranks as a particularly poignant loss. If you are among the currently unemployed, the helplessness you may feel is a realistic reaction to the situation around you. I mention this because some people are feeling ashamed and diminished due to a job loss. The longer one is unemployed, the more it can affect one's life. Unemployment puts a strain on marriages, damages a person's self-esteem, and can lead to poor physical health. The stress, while psychological in origin, can end up causing adrenal fatigue. Ongoing stress can lead to overeating and substance abuse.

It doesn't have to be this way. If you are currently unemployed, try very hard to keep a reasonable schedule. Use your resources for the most important things, like food and shelter. Everything else can wait. Seek help from those you trust, especially your family. Adversity can actually strengthen marriages. Rather than suffering because they can't have the latest gadgets, children can be taught about priorities. It can be an opportunity to learn patience and endurance. For example, the resources of the family must go first to that person—or persons—who have the full responsibility for the support of the family, that is, the parents or single parent. If there is only one car, then it must go to the person whose work sustains the family. In family therapy, this is not always an acceptable point.

In the case of a current work dilemma, plan your steps. What is the worst approach? What is the least bad approach? What is the best outcome? What will be your losses? Do you consider any loss unthinkable? Why? When you know all you need to know about resolving your dilemma and have talked to enough people—including a therapist if necessary—then the next step will be intellectually and emotionally compelling. There will be nothing to do but that. And you will do it.

Not everyone can do this. At times, a person cannot go forward *or* backward. That sense of stuckness—that equal mix of helplessness and hopelessness and the painful self-rejection that ensues—we call depression.

EXPERIENCING DEPRESSION

Some depressed people experience agitation and obsessive thoughts. They have trouble sleeping. Recent brain research has found "excessive communication" between cortical areas and the limbic system (Leuchter, Cook, Hunter, Cai, & Horvath 2012) that may account for depressive symptoms. Other people show the opposite—slowed reactions and sleeping too much. This type of depression is characterized by a slowing down of our energy and a feeling of exhaustion about life in general. As stressed above, it is *usually a response to a loss*. Loss—of a relationship, a job, a scholarship, and perhaps most of all, the loss of our health. We feel depressed when our marriage is threatened or when a son or daughter leaves for college. The more serious the loss is perceived to be, the greater the suffering. Your body and mind will react to the degree of importance you attribute to the loss. This estimate includes the inner resources and the outer supports you believe you have.

Physical symptoms include loss of appetite or eating too much, not being able to sleep or sleeping too much, and a loss of sexual arousal. Psychological symptoms include not being able to enjoy the things you used to enjoy, like music or going out with friends; crying, sad moods, and feelings of hopelessness and helplessness; and feeling disconnected from life and not being able to imagine a future. Depression can also affect our self-esteem, making us feel unworthy and inept. To be diagnosed as clinical depression, these feelings must persist for most of each day and for more than two weeks. Peak ages for experiencing depression are 24 to 44.

A common notion is that it is "normal" for people to become depressed as they grow older. If depression is associated with loss, then it is reasonable to feel that the loss of youth will be depressing. People vary widely in their response to aging. The richer a person's emotional life, with a gentle sense of humor and a loving flexibility, the more acceptable the prospect of aging will be. Good nutrition, a commitment to exercise, avoidance of bad habits—drinking, smoking, and drugging—and a varied social life are our best supports. There is evidence for a gain in hippocampal volume (a correlate of memory) in older adults who exercised versus a group who did only stretching (Erickson et al. 2011). But age we all shall, however gracefully. The most effective mitigators of that process are all the skills and accomplishments we have been discussing—nurturing mutually satisfying relationships; the capacity for gratifying and fulfilling work; all types of creativity, like writing or painting; research; sports of all kinds; or caring for pets—in general improving our lives through our own effort. These are the best compensation for the loss of youth (a normal process) and the best antidepressants.

Normal—and Expectable—Depressive Reactions

If depression is usually a response to a loss, it follows that at some point, every one of us will feel depressed. It is normal to feel depressed after losing or having to give up a relationship, a valued job, or an educational program we had our heart set on. The pain of the depression is often proportional to the *perceived* meaning of the loss. For example, in the teenage years, the loss of a first boyfriend can seem like the end of the world. A 16-year-old cannot appreciate that we all go through, and survive, something like that. The pain she feels is so acute because it is so shockingly new. We learn a lot from that first loss: the sense that it can be integrated and can become part of our life history and that, paradoxically, it really is a treasure—an experience we would not have wanted to miss.

Then there are losses that are shattering. The loss of a child is so traumatic that it can threaten the foundation of the marriage itself. There is the threat to a marriage from an affair. This can throw people off balance and make them feel there is no future. To receive a serious medical diagnosis for yourself or a loved one can make time stand still. You feel stunned and immobilized. The information does not go in. You want to turn it around and make it untrue. All your senses come to a thud against this intrusion. How can this be? Our complex brains search for reasons. You must wait for the shock to subside somewhat before you can think more clearly and decide what to do. It is essential that you have responsible people to talk to, knowledgeable people and trusted others. Talking about it with these people clarifies the problem, takes it down to size.

All of life is in cycles, wave like in nature. On the way up, they are full of tension and feel unbearable. On the way down, they provide relief and vision. The course of every human illness is unique—that is, anyone who has an illness has it in his or her own way. The new sciences of epigenetics and nutrigenomics teach us that we can influence our own genes through the *nutrients* we eat. Even our *intentions* can affect which genes are expressed and how they are expressed (Pert 2003; Smoller 2012). Stay close to your professional advisers and take good care of yourself. Not eating, not drinking enough water, and not sleeping make everything worse.

The loss of a job contains many other losses. One is the work itself, which may have been highly gratifying because it used our skills in a unique way. We also lose every friend and co-worker and a social environment we had valued for its own sake. We lose the momentum of that job's daily requirements and the excitement of the trips and conferences it allowed. We lose the stability and confidence that having a job offers. We perhaps lose the mentors who taught and encouraged us. We lose a certain status with our families, who in a sense define us by what we do. And last but not least, we lose the income we had come to depend on. How can we go on without that? And this may be the most frightening of all: the looming project of the job search.

Stress and Its Effects

Stress alone can lead to depression. The World Health Organization's estimate is that depression will be the second greatest global problem by 2020 and the first by 2030 (Caril 2012, 5). The World Health Organization cites stressors such as abuse and neglect of children, aging, domestic violence, workplace stress, and suicide. This is significant because it finally addresses mental health as a global concern. Depression is twice as prevalent in women as in men. This incidence is found worldwide and begins at puberty, when girls begin to menstruate (Brizendine 2006, 2).

Cumulative stress is built into modern life (Kendler, Thornton, & Gardner 2000.) We can be overwhelmed by too much responsibility, too long and hectic a commute, workdays that stretch into the evenings, and people around us who are mean or unhelpful. In addition, we vary in our ability to withstand stress. Some people can take much more than others without developing symptoms like fatigue, headaches, gastrointestinal symptoms, cardiac complications, or skin conditions. Stress can even make us fat, as discussed below. We feel a loss of control in our lives, and that depresses us. It makes sense, in the light of new research, to do all we can to relieve the pressures on us.

We evolved to take stress in short bursts—the famous fight-or-flight response. Once the threat was dealt with, our stress hormones, mainly adrenaline, would drop to normal levels. Modern life is very different. The pressures on us are often ongoing, persisting throughout the day. This means that the *other* adrenal hormone, cortisol, stays elevated for long periods. It is this condition of elevated cortisol that is so damaging to our bodies. One effect caused by chronically high cortisol is an increase in appetite (Epel, Lapidus, McEwen, & Brownell 2001) and belly fat. It is a factor in the development of all the conditions we are discussing. Chronic stress can lead to heart conditions, high blood pressure, stroke, diabetes, and gastrointestinal illnesses, as well as to generalized exhaustion. For this reason, treatment of depression should always include a physical examination and a nutritional analysis. One's mind and emotions cannot improve if one's body is not well taken care of.

Anxiety can coexist with depression. Recent research finds about 60 percent of depression cases complicated by anxiety, sometimes referred to as "agitated" depression. Whereas depression is felt as a loss, anxiety is experienced as a *threat*. Anxiety is a heightened level of nervous system arousal in response to a real or an imagined threat. If the threat is immediate—for example, if we have to get out of the way of an oncoming car—the threat is fixable by a swift move in the right direction. This kind of anxiety is organizing and adaptive. Mediated by the adrenal hormone adrenaline, it is done and gone. We can calm ourselves down.

Another kind of stress is chronic and *dis*organizing, an unhealthy response to a difficult situation. It is experienced as a lower level of agitation, such as an unhappy job situation or a chronically frustrating relationship. This stress is ongoing and is mediated by the other adrenal hormone, cortisol. It is considered much more damaging to the body, leading to the litany of conditions noted above, in particular, becoming overweight. Chronic anxiety is also associated with alcoholism and substance abuse as an attempt to self-medicate.

Recent research is alleging that depression is not simply a reaction to a loss. It—and other mental disorders as serious as schizophrenia—can be the sequellae of early *infection* (Brown 2011). Pre- and postnatal infections produce an inflammatory response that can predispose people to depression as adults (Williamson, Smith, Sholar, Mistry, & Bilbo 2011). Maltreatment in childhood increases the likelihood of depression and even post-traumatic stress disorder in adulthood (Weir 2012). Ongoing stress and the resulting high levels of stress hormones, acting during long periods of development, are the links with mental illness (Lupien, McEwan, Gunnar, & Helm 2009). What we had not known until recently is that *inflammation* is a major actor in the stress response. Special cells in the brain called microglia are involved in brain growth, but they also produce signaling molecules called cytokines, which are crucial players in the brain's inflammatory response (Weir 2012).

What all this is saying is that pre- and postnatal infections set up an inflammatory response that can alter behavior years later. For example, cytokines produced by inflammation can prevent the synthesis of serotonin in the brain, and serotonin is considered necessary for normal mood. Moreover, depressed people who have suffered early life trauma do not respond to treatment with selective serotonin reuptake inhibitors (SSRI) as well as do people without such histories (Nemeroff et al. 2003). The conclusion is that while inflammation and its effects are present, the drug treatment is not effective. However, psychotherapy alone produces relief and change in depressed people with many types of histories (Doidge 2007; Yalom 2009).

In order to minimize the potential for infection and inflammation, it is worth stressing the importance of good prenatal care for the benefit of both mother and baby. This includes the usual monthly checkups and vaccination. A healthy diet for the mother-to-be, including the important anti-inflammatory omega-3 oils, does much to protect the baby, as does reducing stress at work, getting proper rest, and abstaining from alcohol.

Abnormal or Clinical Depression

You may already be aware of the types of depression that warrant immediate professional intervention. One of these, suicidal statements or actions, should always be taken seriously. Even if the person has threatened self-harm before or tends toward self-dramatization, it is better to err on the side of safety and seek an evaluation. Other important signs of worsening depression: not being able to get out of bed (also associated with bipolar depression), sitting in the dark for long periods, feelings of worthlessness, withdrawing from social interactions, or the person weeping easily and saying she can't enjoy anything anymore. This degree of "painful" depression has been newly designated as "melancholia" by historian of medicine and psychiatry Edward Shorter (2013). (However, the nervous system may not be able to distinguish between psychological and physical pain. A lost love affair or a lost position at work can bring us to tears and drain our energy as effectively as an arthritic hip.)

A person who locks herself in her bedroom or one who leaves the house for days with no communication is deteriorating and in need of medical care. Be alarmed as well if a person's depression leads to drinking or drugging binges or follows a head injury. If the depression alternates with periods of high activity, loud and constant talking, grandiose thinking and risk-taking, as well as hypersexuality—all symptoms of bipolar disorder—it is time to intervene and protect him or her.

The persons who will benefit from a course of psychotherapy often show considerable insight into the ways their lives have dramatically changed, and they realize that their coping skills are exhausted. But they keep going until all meaning and purpose seem drained, and the future looms empty and frightening. They come to therapy because they want to know how to get their lives back and in what way they may have contributed to this impasse.

The Story of Liz: "Depression that stalks you and then sits on your head."

The above quote about her experience of depression demonstrated that Liz was capable of penetrating realism at the same time she was experiencing daily psychological pain. When she described her depression to me as "stalking her," she expressed surprise that she would ever be talking to a clinical psychologist, that she would ever feel so "done with life."

Significantly, this 44-year-old widow had not an inkling of depression until almost five years after her husband had died. His death had been so tragic. At only 39, he had died unexpectedly of a rare, possibly familial blood disorder. It had mobilized the whole community. Everyone rallied to the support of her family. Liz's children were then 10 and 12, and because their dad (a local official) had been so beloved by everyone, they received attention and affection from all. Their pictures were in the paper, and they were asked to officiate at fairs and games.

Liz herself was completely devoted to her children's protection and welfare. She encouraged her younger brother and his wife to spend time with her 12-year-old son. They were all having difficulty with the grieving process. Liz and her daughter were part of the community activities, dressing up for fairs and celebrations. Their feelings of loss were integrated into this community life. No one said much about Dad, except in front of a microphone. Life went on. Liz's energy seemed dependable, and she slept well from sheer exhaustion.

One of the most important questions to ask in therapy is: why is this happening at this moment? Almost five years had passed. Liz's son was now 18 and would leave for college the next August. Her daughter had "500 friends" and no longer confided in Liz with that intensity of little-girl news. It was a natural development. Liz knew it, but she was unprepared for how sad she actually felt. With her children growing up, she was feeling more loss than she had felt after her husband's death, coupled with some agitation and anxiety. Her children's doctor was a family friend; he had prescribed an antidepressant, which she had been taking for more than five months at the time I was scheduled to see her. Significantly, Liz complained that the antidepressant had eliminated "what was left of my sexuality." She was "modern," she said, about the whole issue of masturbation, for herself and her children, but the drug had left her with no sexual feelings. I admired her candor and felt it was a good sign that she wanted to be sexual again.

She said she had a demanding job requiring more than eight-hour days and that this was important for the protection and support of the community. She had two younger male co-workers who reported to her. They called her Elizabeth or "Boss." She had three monitors on constantly, in a windowless office. To me, it sounded like a sensory-deprivation experiment. A total lack of connection. Her isolation was complete.

When I evaluated her mood, she made the striking statement I quoted above about the long-delayed experience: "Depression stalks you and then sits on your head." It was a heaviness she walked around with. I asked, as I must, if she ever felt so bad she would think of hurting herself. Her deadened attitude toward life was summarized in her reply. With dark humor, she said, "Well, someday my computer and I will merge, and that will be that." A ghoulish image of her internal experience, to be sure. Clearly this woman was feeling dehumanized, like a robot, not really alive.

I asked Liz if she felt a benefit from the medication. She replied that it made it easier to get to work. Significantly, she had not missed any days of work, a common finding in serious depression. We worked on her history, but I was more concerned with her current state, which she described dutifully. She was facing age 45, with no relationship prospects. She was feeling increasingly lonely, a good sign. Loneliness is normal and impels us out into the world as a positive move. (However, loneliness, when accompanied by isolation, is damaging to the immune system [Cacioppo & Patrick 2008].) Her children were happily into their own lives, and they consulted her less and less. Her friendships with other mothers had been centered on school activities, now outgrown. She had an exhausting job, although one she could not leave. And she wanted to get off the antidepressant.

I explained to Liz that weaning off an antidepressant must be done under her physician's guidance, since he was legally responsible for prescribing it. I was seeing her twice a week at that point, and I would monitor her mood. She was also in phone contact as needed. (My decision not to hospitalize her was based on this close contact, plus my judgment that, although she had little energy for life, she was not suicidal. She could negotiate her daily duties. She was always on time for appointments.) I sent her to a colleague for a physical, including an assessment of her hormonal status. She was at the age when progesterone especially needed to be supplemented with bio-identical (human) progesterone. After age 40, women are making little or no progesterone (Reiss 2001). She was also prescribed bio-identical estradiol, which is finally recognized as safer than the conjugated "horse urine" estrogens (*Journal of the American Medical Association, Int Med*, Sept. 20, 2013).

I also continued with my careful history. Her relationship with her husband sounded ideal, very close from high school on. But Liz had not been able to say goodbye to him because her husband had been in denial about the seriousness of his illness. They had never talked about it. So Liz had never grieved, and she badly needed to begin that process. Antidepressant drugs often suppress the very brain region—the prefrontal cortex—that we need in order to analyze our feelings and do the necessary thinking to change them (Mayberg et al. 1997).

A few days later, we had the results of her physical examination. Liz was basically healthy, but physically and emotionally exhausted—a condition some clinicians call "adrenal burnout." Whatever the "cause" of depression, it interferes with our neurotransmitters, especially serotonin and epinephrine. Normalizing these neurotransmitters is the aim of the SSRIs, but their effects are often accompanied by unacceptable side effects, like *increased* depression, agitation, and decreased sexual feelings. As an alternative, serotonin and epinephrine can be normalized safely and effectively by giving one's brain the proper *nutrients* to make them. These are the B vitamins, omega-3 fatty acids (as in fish oil, flax seed, and walnuts), l-theanine (an over-the-counter amino acid that is both calming and centering), vitamin D3, and the adrenal hormone DHEA (Emmons 2010). I taught Liz about these nutrients and carefully examined her eating habits, especially on weekends (when people often ignore what they know about healthy food).

"Let's look at your strengths," I told Liz. "You are healthy and trim. You have not succumbed to the usual response to low mood—overeating. Your children are happy with their lives. You are not worrying about them. Although you are quite depressed, you are not attracted to alcohol, which is usually a tragic move. You have a job that supports you and your children very well." Liz agreed with all this, smiling weakly. "What you don't have," I continued, "is light and air. A connection to life that is *both work and play*, that provides you with interest, solace, beauty, and enthusiasm."

Liz looked at me, puzzled but intrigued. "I don't want to use the online dating sites," she said. "I've heard too many stories." I understood that but recommended she do something else: make a list of all her trusted associates—family, friends, and co-workers—and let them know she was looking. "Everyone knows someone who is single or becoming single," I said, "especially if they think a while. That is one of the best ways to meet someone new."

But I was really considering something else for her. I told her that we are happiest as adults when we can reconnect with whatever we loved, or wished for, when we were 8 to 12 years old. It is actually the time of life when children are most idealistic. The dreams we had then came out of our deep, unique longings and our secret image of our-selves. It is the time when you fall in love with an idea. "What did you love as a child?" I asked. Liz sat quietly, staring at the floor. She said nothing. When the session was over, I said, "That is a good homework question. Try to remember the things you loved when you were *little*, Liz. What was your nickname? What did your friends say about you? What were the secrets too precious to tell anyone?"

At the next session, we went over the nutrients I had recommended to boost her mood, as well as the "non-foods" she should eliminate, those that raise insulin levels and increase inflammation. For the record, those are white potatoes, including chips; white sugar; and most baked goods, except the rye bread she liked. She had already given up soda and was drinking filtered—not bottled—water. Sim-ply adding a good-quality fish oil will improve both mood and brain health. (Fifty-five percent of the brain is made up of these oils, but to be utilized, these require saturated fats like those in butter and eggs and meat [Enig, 2000].) Moreover, omega-3 oils are anti-inflamma-tory. "DHA and EPA (the major natural omega-3 FA [fatty acid] con-stituents of fish oil), mediate potent anti-inflammatory effects" (Oh et al. 2010, 692) through an elaborate sequence of cell signaling mechanisms. (These researchers further demonstrated that omega-3 oils *reverse insulin resistance* in obese mice. This is a momentous finding because of the association between insulin resistance and diabetes.) With her diet improved and twice-a-week therapy, Liz's energy was returning. But we still had no information about her pre-pubertal years. And how, she wanted to know, was that supposed to help her now?

We talked about how she would feel if she delegated some of her work to one of her associates, actually promoting him. It would give her more time, she said, but time to do what? I persisted. Happiness in adulthood is often the continuation and actual fulfillment of dreams that began in childhood. Experiences that you loved as a child, including those you had wished for and never had. Experiences that were both comforting and exciting and that helped you develop a strong sense of your own efficacy. It was a time when you could dream "big," when you didn't know what was impossible.

Liz looked at me. There was a new urgency in that look. Once on a vacation when she was 10 years old, she said, she had watched two teenagers riding their horses around the lake. She remembered thinking how happy and free they seemed. A few days later, she saw the teens again, this time walking their horses to the stable. They smiled and asked if she wanted to come along. Yes, it was all right with her parents. Little Liz spent the rest of that day helping the girls "muck out" the horse stalls. The two teenagers explained that this was the way they earned riding time. It was hard, smelly work, but they loved it, talking to their horses and laughing through it all. Liz remembered feeling an ineffable connection to that life. This was hard work that she loved. This work was *play!* She had been connected to those horses in a way she felt but could not describe. There would be one more summer at that lake, riding lessons, and riding alone! Then her family moved away when she was 11.

I asked if she had ever gone back to riding. No, she said. She became absorbed in schoolwork and kept at it until she had a master's degree. Then came marriage, a baby boy, and two years later a baby girl. What about now? Did she know of any riding stables within a reasonable distance of home or work? She said she didn't know. But now she was smiling. "I know," she said. "That's my homework."

By the next session, Liz had found a riding stable about 45 minutes away. She actually took the next day off and drove out there. She parked and walked slowly toward the barn, the ground yielding to her grown-up feet. She remembered her 11-year-old self, excited, half-frightened the first time one of the horses nudged her. It was a message: Let's play!

Now the air was heavy again with that never-to-be-forgotten scent of horse presence. It was the smell of the earth, of *life*. She closed her eyes and breathed in that life.

"Liz?"

Her eyes flew open.

"You're the lady who called me?"

"Yes."

"Let me show you Patrician."

The woman led Liz into the first barn. There was Patrician. He was the tallest horse she had ever seen. Could she ride this giant?

As Liz described all this to me at her next session, she was filled with amazement and pleasure. Lessons were so much more expensive now, she said. She was grateful she could afford them, for herself and for her daughter, who was asking to join her and Patrician on their jaunts. I had only asked that she try to get out to the stable a few times a month. Liz began riding on most weekends, happily looking forward to it all week. Within a few months, she was helping with the management of the stable. Her daughter and her friends were helping too. Then she told me that she was working on a horse rescue project. By the time Liz left therapy, she was the owner of Patrician and another horse she had rescued. She had moved closer to the stable and cut down on her work hours. Her new social group revolved around the horses and the families that support and love them. (Note: Experience with horses is now an accepted intervention for emotional healing. One of these is at www.greatstrides.org. See also the book by Trotter 2011.)

When I had first seen Liz, I felt that if she were not already physically ill, she could become so. Our immune systems are weakened by chronic stress, making us less able to fight off infection. Moreover, research has shown that having the sole responsibility for decision making is a major stressor. Liz was responsible for mobilizing her two subordinates and their staffs. She was good at it, but it eventually became a crushing burden. She reported driving to work each day, even able to smile, but inside she felt nothing, a kind of numbness people experience when they cannot feel grief. Liz was at risk for physical illness; our moods can affect our immune system (Pert 2003, 190).

Over the next few months, Liz and I talked about the loss of her young husband and the mysterious turn his illness had taken. Liz wept openly, almost shouting the outrage she felt watching her dreams shatter along with her marriage. She had received much appreciated support from the community and her extended family, but at night she would climb into an empty bed. We talked about the "loss" of her son, then her daughter, to friends, school, and life. It is the "empty nest," a loss we laugh about for years, until it happens. We are not quite ready, but still they leave because they must. I explained to Liz that our children do come back—as quite different people—when they marry or form partnerships, and especially when they have children. The significance of family traditions then becomes newly relevant.

Until then, Liz was on her own. She was discovering that we are all really alone. Our early experience of ourselves as children, then teens, becomes a wellspring from which we may draw new purpose and meaning. Her depression was now gone: it had been resolved through her own effort to take her therapy seriously, reforming her diet, giving her brain and body the nutrients they needed, and most of all, reconnecting to her history and the innocent, passionate child she had been. Deliberate and right action—both work and play—take effort and planning. But together they counter the torpor of depression.

PLAY AND ITS THERAPEUTIC EFFECTS

Physical activity helps in the treatment of depression (Otto & Smits 2011; Walsh 2011). It lends an exhilaration of its own, whether it is walking, running, dancing, or, as in Liz's case, reconnecting with what she had loved as a child—riding horses, being with horses, and finally rescuing horses. Physical activity not only treats depression but has been shown to *prevent* it long-term. A longitudinal analysis of 26 years of research findings showed that even 30 minutes of activity, like walking and gardening, can prevent depression as people get older (Mammen & Faulkner 2013).

But a recent hypothesis (Dietrich 2006) suggests that the psychological benefits of exercise result from specific brain changes that occur only when the aerobic threshold is reached. At that point, and not before, metabolites are recruited *away from the prefrontal lobes* and toward the motor cortex. This, Dietrich says, provides the relief from emotional symptoms.

> Building on the fundamental principle that processing in the brain is competitive and the fact that the brain has finite metabolic resources, the transient hypofrontality hypothesis suggests that during exercise the extensive neural activation required to run motor patterns, assimilate sensory inputs, and coordinate autonomic regulation results in a concomitant transient decrease of neural activity in brain structures, such as the pre-frontal cortex, that are not pertinent to performing the exercise. An exercise-induced state of frontal hypofunction can provide a coherent account of the influences of exercise on emotion and cognition. (Dietrich 2006, 79)

Thus when exercise is vigorous enough and sustained, energy is shifted *away* from the thinking, worrying part of our brains. Dr. Roland A.

Carlstedt, chairman of the American Board of Sport Psychology and a research associate in psychology with Harvard Medical School and McLean Hospital, has researched the transient hypofrontality hypothesis (THH) and helped me understand its dynamics. Commenting on the proposed effects of the THH, Carlstedt referred to a "nothingness, worry-free state people experience as their frontal lobes go into [Dietrich's] idle-mode" (personal communication, Dec. 22, 2013).

Exercise has been shown to alleviate the symptoms of depression as effectively as sertraline (Zoloft) with none of the unwelcome side effects. This may correlate with the finding that running increases endorphins, our natural opioids. Blumenthal et al. (2007) concluded that exercise, both supervised and "home-based," was generally comparable to antidepressants for patients with major depressive disorder. The researchers stressed that exercise was also effective for preventing relapse. Exercise also reduces the incidence of anxiety in those prone to react with panic, says Jasper Smits, coauthor of a book on exercise in the treatment of anxiety. Smits makes a connection between the physical responses to fight or flight—that is, heavy breathing, heart pounding and sweating, and those that accompany exercise. Whatever the mechanism, exercise manages and reduces anxiety as well as depression (Otto & Smits 2011).

Among the evidence-based treatments for depression (as well as social phobia and substance abuse) is a group of interventions loosely called wilderness therapy (Association for Experiential Education, www.aee.org). Groups are taken out in the wilderness for as long as two months. Usually these groups are small and share painful histories like drug addiction and depression. The groups are staffed by psychologists, and the participants have regular therapy sessions throughout the trip. Among the first of these groups, Second Nature was started in 1998. Each participant is thoroughly assessed before placement in a group. They typically spend several months together, hiking, cooking, and journaling. The idea is that surviving in the wilderness boosts self-esteem and fosters greater physical and emotional health. It also inspires bonding with healthy mentors.

Play of all types is one of the most *original* aspects of our lives. As described by psychiatrist Lawrence Kubie (1969), play is the result of our preconscious capacities with

> their automatic recall, their multiple analogic and overlapping linkages and their direct connections to the autonomic processes which underlie

affective [emotional] states. The rich *play* of preconscious operations occurs freely in states of abstraction, in sleep, in dreams and as we write, paint or allow our thoughts to flow in the non-selective paths of free association. (Kubie 1969, 45; italics added)

For lasting effect and real personal meaning, I have found that the activity that lifts mood reliably is some component of a person's history that draws on this preconscious function and is often a *combination* of work and play. The early sessions of a person's therapy are often a period of painful, tearful repetition. Each time the issues are discussed—as realistically as she can—she discharges more of her tension. It is often during this period that the memory of some type of creativity will emerge.

But before this can happen, what depressed people need most is *to rest,* to stop trying. To breathe in and breathe out, and eventually to talk. Through much grieving and some obsessing, a new vision emerges. We must build the ground in front of us before we can walk on it. But one day it is ready, and our whole being moves to a new alignment. The amount of time this takes varies with each person, but the process must be respected. It works toward a renewal, retaining elements from the past, but engendering a life not yet lived. It leaves behind some experiences for good. (Discussing a failed marriage, which is a grieving process of sorts, is like that.) The future cannot be rushed.

The tension reverberating in that person's nervous system is slowly, and at times dramatically, released as *words.* What brings relief is the very process of transforming bodily experience—what is *felt*—into words, concepts, metaphors, that are *known.* The therapist listens carefully to those words and metaphors. They contain the essence of that person's suffering—the germ of her emerging selfhood. The way forward is often a look backward, to the hapless child who stumbled upon joy during that magical Middle Earth of prepuberty.

This essential period, from age 8 to 12, is currently at risk. It requires stretches of solitude and a dearth of outside stimulation. It entails falling back on one's own resources. That solitude has been infiltrated, perhaps forevermore, by social media (Tifflin & Terashima 2001). It is difficult for young people to be alone anymore, and their creativity suffers for it. An October 2011 article in *Monitor on Psychology* reports that children from elementary school through high school who used the most hours of social media were more unhealthy, more narcissistic, and had worse grades than those who used the least amount. When parents intervened and monitored their time on social media, the children's performance and health improved. Here is another "monster" we must protect our children from, along with fast cars, drinking, and drugs. An addiction to constant, superficial stimulation *steals* the time and opportunity to build a personal space, a place of emerging selfhood, of *psychological "stem cells" that can be reclaimed later*. Like actual embryonic stem cells, once that critical period is past, it is lost forever.

I mourn the loss of peaceful, reflective childhood. It holds the source of creativity we can tap in therapy to help our patients emerge from painful, deadening depression. Liz had those wonderful summers at the lake with her friends and their horses. It took a course of therapy to tap that resource, but it was there for her when she needed it. And then it connected her to her future!

For another woman, it was the rediscovery of her sewing machine (the gift for her 12th birthday) and the alchemy of transforming a bit of fabric into a blouse that actually fit her body. She had worn the blouse to school the very next day, feeling she had taken a giant step into the realm of grown-up life. In therapy, I suggested to this depressed woman that her sewing machine represented a unique source of personal efficacy for her. She took the machine out again, a month after her mother's death, and could feel that magic moving into her hands again. It was a link, a kind of continuity with her mother's life, a connection that could sustain her. (This is not the whole of therapy, but refinding purpose and creativity encourages a person to keep trying.)

Dramatically for one man, it was flying kites. He had loved this at age 10, along with his father and his cousin. Now, as a depressed adult, he tentatively tried his hand at designing a kite. He educated his therapist about the types of materials that were suitable for kite making. Between discussions about his deceased father and his daunting work responsibilities, as well as competitions within the extended family, he talked about the polyester "creature" his kite was becoming. He brought the creature to therapy, and it required a chair. The kite was so successful that he began an online group that designs and builds kites. The site hosts long, obsessive discussions about places for flying these creations. It renewed my patient's connection to his history, and ultimately, with the help of therapy, he resolved the longstanding family issues. For his tension, I had suggested l-theanine, 100mg in the morning, and a homeopathic preparation called *Calms* to help him sleep.

For another man, exercise—and creativity—took the form of "blues dancing." Depressed and apathetic in therapy, angry and embittered by a painful divorce, it seemed at first that this man could enjoy nothing (a major feature of depression called *anhedonia*). This is not unusual during the first months of therapy. He had no energy for dating, and I suggested this was not a bad thing for the time being. But there seemed to be nothing he wanted to do except ruminate about his misery and his resentment about the divorce. He did need to talk about that, but I wanted more for him. What had he enjoyed doing as a child, in the magical period of 8 to 12? He went back even further. He had loved dancing to "Thriller" at age 6. He talked about *Dance Fever*, a dance show, and how *Solid Gold* showed him "break dancing." So now, within four months of moving out on his own, he was willing to try. Could he go to a dance studio by himself? I encouraged him to go and to stay for one hour. Although shy about meeting new people, he made a pact with himself. He would go for an hour. If he did not find people to talk to or to dance with, he would leave. He connected with some people doing East Coast Swing dancing. A few months later, he tried the Lindy Hop. He started taking lessons. The lessons alternated with several weeks of Blues Dance. He then remembered his dad had liked blues music. He could connect with this music. The dancing began to structure his week. Before long, he was building his life—and his new social life—around dancing. It was hard work. And *play*.

Lastly, there is the capacity to use *humor* as an assertion against depression. When we live in an impossible reality, our hearts long for a way to suspend natural law. This last example is from a man who had always loved the Tolkien classic *The Hobbit*. He saw this as a daring projection of the imagination into a new reality. Life and experience could be altered. Now as a depressed adult, this man's wit flew into the room, suddenly there between patient and therapist. It was swift, glistening, a transcendent presence that penetrated his hopelessness and created a pluperfect present, however brief. It was humor as Freud described it: "the [self's] unwillingness to suffer."

In therapy, it became clear that this man had a penetrating wit informed by years of studying history. With a flourish, he announced in one session that he believed all the wars of antiquity had been fought because the participants had not had access to chocolate. All would have been averted if only Switzerland had refined chocolate centuries earlier. Laughing, I protested that the South American natives who *did* have cocoa beans were not exactly peaceful, were they? Undaunted, my patient pressed on. It had only been, he said, the occasional human sacrifice. We were both laughing so much I feared no useful therapeutic work would be done. Then I realized that humor was this man's antidote to depression. If life was going to be absurd, he was going to enjoy it.

A FINAL NOTE

Clearly, play is a place in our sentience where creativity, art, and spirituality intersect. Play described in these terms has all the elements of *flow*, the experience described by the Hungarian researcher Mihaly Csikszentmihalyi. He posited that when we are involved in very absorbing and challenging tasks, we do not notice the passage of time. We are so involved in what we are doing—so *happy* with what we are doing—that we lose track of time, and we do not tire. Csikszentmihalyi (pronounced *cheek-sent-me-high*) says that when we are in a state of flow, our emotions are neutral—that is, we are tension free. He found that the more people were able to achieve a state of flow, the happier they were at work and in their other activities. He stressed that flow must not be confused with the mindless state of watching television. Flow only accompanies those goals that are important to us. Then work and play become deliquescent, melting into one another.

When asked what we must do to have a normal, healthy life, Freud designated work and love as the essential elements. But we must add one more: *play*. Play represents activities we engage in for no further purpose than to enjoy them. Play rejuvenates us, expanding our lives beyond our loss. *And play heals*. It leaves us, in Emily Dickinson's words, "A little newer for the time / Upon enchanted ground."

REFERENCES

Blumenthal, J. A., Babyak, M. A., Doraiswamy, P. M., et al. (2007). "Exercise and Pharmacotherapy in the Treatment of Major Depressive Disorder." *Psychosomatic Medicine*, 69, 587–596.

Brizendine, L. (2006). *The Female Brain*. New York: Three Rivers Press.

Brown, A. S. (2011). "The Environment and Susceptibility to Schizophrenia." *Progress in Neurobiology* 93(1): 23–58.

Cacioppo, J. T. & Patrick, W. (2008). *Loneliness: Human Nature and the Need for Social Connection*. New York: W. W. Norton & Co.

Caril, E. (2012, July–August). "World Health Assembly Passes Action Plan Resolution for Mental Health." *National Psychologist* 21(4): 5.

Dietrich, A. (2006). "Transient Hypofrontality as a Mechanism for the Psychological Effects of Exercise." *Psychiatry Research*, 145, 79–83.

Doidge, N. (2007). *The Brain that Changes Itself*. New York: Penguin Books.

Emmons, H. (2010). *The Chemistry of Calm*. New York: Touchstone.

Enig, M. G. (2000). *Know Your Fats: The Complete Primer for Understanding the Nutrition of Fats, Oils and Cholesterol*. Silver Spring, MD: Bethesda Press.

Epel, E., Lapidus, R., McEwen, B., et al. (2001). "Stress May Add Bite to Appetite in Women: A Laboratory Study of Stress-Induced Cortisol and Eating Behavior." *Psychoneuroendocrinology* 26(1): 37–49.

Erickson, K. I., Voss, M. W., Prakash, R. S., et al. (2011). "Exercise Training Increases Size of Hippocampus and Improves Memory." *Proceedings of the National Academy of Sciences, USA*, 108, 3017–3022. doi:10.1073/pnas.1015950108.

Kendler, K. S., Thornton, L. M., & Gardner, C. O. (2000). "Stressful Life Events and Previous Episodes in the Etiology of Major Depression in Women: An Evaluation of the 'Kindling' Hypothesis." *American Journal of Psychiatry* 157(8): 1243–1251.

Kubie, L. (1969). *Neurotic Distortion of the Creative Process*. New York: Noonday Press.

Leuchter, A. F., Cook, I. A., Hunter, A. M., et al. (2012). "Resting-State Quantitative Electroencephalography Reveals Increased Neurophysiologic Connectivity in Depression." *Plos One* 7(2):E32508.doi:10.1371/journal.pone.0032508

Lupien, S. J., McEwan, B. S., Gunnar, M. R., et al. (2009). "Effects of Stress throughout the Life-Span on the Brain, Behaviour and Cognition." *Nature Reviews Neuroscience*, 10, 434–445.

Mammen, G. & Faulkner, G. (2013). "Physical Activity and the Prevention of Depression: A Systematic Review of Prospective Studies." *American Journal of Preventive Medicine*, 45(5), 649–657. DOI:10.1016/amepre.2013.08.001

Mayberg, H. S., Brannan, S. K., Mahurin, R. K., et al. (1997). "Function in Depression: A Potential Predictor of Treatment Response." *NeuroReport*, 8, 1057–1061.

Mayberg, H. S., Lozano, A. M., Voon, V., et al. (2005). "Deep Brain Stimulation for Treatment–Resistant Depression." *Neuron* 45(5): 651–660.

Nemeroff, C. B., Helm, C. M., Thase, M. E., et al. (2003). "Differential Responses to Psychotherapy versus Pharmacotherapy in Patients with Chronic Forms of Major Depression and Childhood Trauma." *Proceedings of the National Academy of Sciences* 100(24): 14293–14296.

Oh, D. Y., Talukdar, S., Bae, E. J., et al. (2010). "GPR120 Is an Omega-3 Fatty Acid Receptor Mediating Potent Anti-Inflammatory and Insulin Sensitizing Effects." *Cell* 142(5): 687–698. doi:10.1016/i.cell.2010.07.041

Otto, M. & Smits, J. A .J. (2011). *Exercise for Mood and Anxiety: Proven Strategies for Overcoming Depression and Enhancing Well-Being*. New York: Oxford University Press.

Pert, C. B. (2003). *Molecules of Emotion: Why You Feel the Way You Feel*. New York: Scribner.

Reiss, U. (2001). *Natural Hormone Balance for Women*. New York: Pocket Books.

Shorter, E. (2013). *How Everyone Became Depressed: The Rise and Fall of the Nervous Breakdown*. New York: Oxford University Press.

Smoller, J. (2012). *The Other Side of Normal: How Biology Is Providing the Clues to Unlock the Secrets of Normal and Abnormal Behavior*. New York: William Morrow.

Tifflin, J. & Terashima, N. (2001). *HyperReality: Paradigm for the Third Millennium*. New York: Routledge.

Trotter, K. (Ed.) (2012). *Harnessing the Power of Equine Assisted Counselling*. New York, NY: Routledge.

Walsh, R. (2011). "Lifestyle and Mental Health." *American Psychologist* 66(7): 579–592.

Weir, K. (2012, February). "The Beginnings of Mental Illness: Autism, Schizophrenia and Other Disorders May Have Roots in Life's Earliest Stages." *Monitor on Psychology* 43(2): 37–39.

Williamson, L. L., Smith, S. H., Sholar, P. W., et al. (2011). "Microglia and Memory: Modulation by Early-life Infection." *Journal of Neuroscience* 31(43): 15511–15521.

Yalom, I. D. (2009). *The Gift of Therapy: An Open Letter to a New Generation of Therapists and Their Patients*. New York: Harper Perennial.

Chapter 5

Self-Soothing and Comforting
The Legacy of Parental Love

> You will see that a great deal that a mother does with an infant could be called "holding." Not only is actual holding very important . . . but also much of infant nurture is an ever-widening interpretation of the word "holding." Holding comes to include all physical management, in so far as it is done in adaptation to an infant's needs. . . . The family continues this holding, and society holds the family.
>
> —Donald Winnicott, *Home Is Where We Start From*

If realism, the ability to see things as they really are, is the single most important distinction between healthy and emotionally troubled people, then the ability to calm oneself is the second. Or, more accurately, if realism is the right hand of our emotional stability, then self-soothing is the left. If anything helps us to bear the heaviness of reality, it is the ability to steady ourselves that comes from within. And again, as with all aspects of personality, that ability is developed very early and is a precious resource throughout life.

Even for the strongest among us, the ability to calm ourselves is not inborn. It is a learned phenomenon that shows some male–female differences. There is evidence that girls retain larger communication and emotion-processing areas in the brain from the intrauterine period and throughout life, which allows them to respond to their mother's soothing efforts better and more often than do boys (Tannen

1990). The process of "mutual gaze" is the intense staring behavior between mother and infant and is considered to be the mechanism for "attachment" (the term psychologists use to describe the strong bonding of mother and infant). Some research has found that girls are better at this skill (mutual gaze) as well (Leeb & Gillian 2004). *All* small children are easily frightened, and their emotions are constantly shifting. The nervous systems of infants are, in William James's (1890) inimitable phrase, "a blooming, buzzing confusion" (488). It is only the consistent comforting a baby receives from a caring parent that calms and organizes her nervous system. Each instance of comforting is encoded, and the baby learns a basic trust in her parent and the extended environment.

Like other aspects of parenting, soothing and comforting does not have to be perfect. Allowing a baby to cry himself to sleep may help the baby to learn to comfort himself, although this is a challenged view. There is no way to measure the long-term harm to the baby. Infants cannot judge how long it will be until help will arrive, and all it would take is a reassuring touch. The ability to develop self-comforting can be most seriously damaged in this early period if exposure to stress *overwhelms* an infant's adaptive capacity (Celani 2010). This will negatively affect brain development if it occurs during the first 24 months (Fisher & Gunnar 2010).

No one has written more poignantly about the vital mother–infant relationship than D. W. Winnicott, an English pediatrician who practiced in the 1950s and 1960s. Winnicott, who began studying Freud late in life, went on to become one of the most innovative and influential psychoanalysts. Because he was a pediatrician, he was in the perfect position to understand the relevance of Freud's ideas for the very earliest stages of life. Using psychodynamic insights, and following many of the innovations of W. R. D. Fairbairn, Winnicott studied the significant relationship between mothers and infants. He described the mother's preoccupation with the baby before and after the birth and her pulling away from other concerns and relationships as an important sign of the mother's growing bond with her infant. This "holding environment," as Winnicott described it, includes all the nurturing aspects of the baby's world—warmth, feeding, softness, verbal soothing, and "cooing"—as well as actual physical holding.

Winnicott wished to avoid Latin terminology and other psychiatric "jargon." He developed concepts we can all relate to, like "the good-enough mother," recognizing that most mothers were good—but not perfect—providers and protectors of their children. Perfection was not required for a baby to grow strong, healthy, and happy. Winnicott (1953, 1971) and Fairbairn (1952) give us the best evidence that the baby's personality develops *in the interaction* with the mother and is shaped by her behavior. The baby of course has his own genetically decreed abilities and stamina, but the mother's needs and requirements will determine where the baby puts his energy.

This is a crucial point. In the early years of a child's life, safety and gratification—holding, playing, feeding—are combined and continuous. The baby feels both safe and satisfied. But if the child is not reliably held and fed, the link between safety and satisfaction becomes *uncoupled.* The child becomes insecure and frightened; he then wants only safety and connectedness. At this crucial point, safety no longer feels satisfying, and satisfaction feels unsafe. To avoid this uncoupling of safety and satisfaction, consistent comforting and reassurance are vital to babies, day in and day out. There is some protection against this dilemma in the first months of life. Very little babies cannot tell that they are separate from the mother's body. The mother's breast or the bottle is felt as continuous with the baby's body. Slowly, the baby's nervous system matures, and she realizes that the thumb or fist she sucks on is part of her own body; she has full control over them. But the breast or bottle comes only when the mother arrives. That recognition is frightening to babies, and they need regular assurance that they are safe.

WINNICOTT'S ORIGINAL TERMS

If we consider three of Winnicott's (1953) concepts—transitional objects, boundaries, and self-soothing and comforting—we learn how early infant experience supports the person throughout life, providing the essentials skills we need to steady ourselves in all sorts of adult situations. The importance of these skills cannot be overstated. They are essential features of normal personality.

Transitional Objects

Winnicott was the first pediatrician and researcher to recognize that a baby's special toy was not simply a cute favorite. It represented an important stage in development. Quite early, usually in the first year of life, the mother will give the baby a toy—a doll or a teddy or a blanket—often at bedtime. The baby will choose his favorite, and that object becomes more special than any other toy or object in his world. He must have the toy or blanket when he sleeps and in the car. He drags it around, like Linus in the *Peanuts* comic, and no one dares to wash it. This is the baby's "transitional object." Why transitional? Because this blanket or teddy actually stands for the mother, as a kind of surrogate parent. It allows the baby to endure the mother's occasional absence, and it can accompany the baby to sleep or while traveling, as if the mother were actually there. It was the gift of the mother and contains her magic. The transitional object is so beloved that even as the child grows up, he does not want it thrown away. Some people even take a doll or teddy to college.

Boundaries

A crucial point is that the transitional object is chosen *by the baby*. This doll, teddy, or blanket, which Winnicott termed "the first 'not-me' object," provides an intermediary space between herself and the world. The infant actually constructs her relationship with reality out of the interaction between herself and others (transitional space). In every interaction with her parents and other caretakers, the infant is expressing her separateness from them. And with every response from the mother, acknowledging her child's separateness, a boundary forms between the child and the other person. It is the place where she ends and the mother begins. This process creates an inside and an outside for the child. If that boundary is respected by the mother, then the infant has made a psychological achievement. The space between herself and her mother, the space occupied by the transitional object, is the place where she can play and rest. She is blissfully satisfied and safe.

What happens if the mother does not validate the child's separateness? What if her child's independent play makes the mother uncomfortable? It is a problematic situation when a mother wants her baby to be an extension of herself. She wants the child to meet her own needs for connectedness. She fears being alone (Miller, 1981). Then the boundary between herself and her baby will be diffuse and unclear. As he grows, the child will not be comfortable as he attempts to live a separate life with friends and classmates. He may vaguely feel he is taking something away from his mother, something she needs from him. In this situation, it is unlikely that he had a favorite toy or teddy, because his mother would have been jealous of it. Attempting to separate from this needy, dependent mother will be a life long struggle fraught with self-doubt and guilt.

Self-Soothing and Comforting

The ability to comfort ourselves, as we have described, must come from the experience of having been comforted regularly as a child. This recurrent comforting teaches us to be a good parent to ourselves. Most of us have experienced or witnessed a scene like this: If a baby should fall and cry, her mother picks her up and comforts her. She treats the cut or scrape and then, for good measure, kisses the hurt knee or hand. Over time, psychologists have found, children begin to use the same words and tone for themselves when they get hurt. A three-year-old who falls will be observed to get up wailing loudly. Then she will suddenly stop, say, "Oh, boo-boo," and kiss her own cut or scrape. *She could not do this if she had not had a caring parent or grandparent who did that consistently.* Psychologists say such a child has introjected—taken in—the aspect of the mother or grandmother who reliably comforted her. Later in life, the ability to calm ourselves is important on a daily basis. As adults, we can then say to ourselves, "We'll cross that bridge when we come to it," or "That job was one opportunity. There will be others," or "Losing that house is not the end of the world. We'll keep looking and maybe we'll find a better one." All these are examples that show that, when we were little, somebody nice kissed our scraped hand or knee.

COMFORTING: ITS EFFECT ON COGNITIVE AND EMOTIONAL GROWTH

Infant–mother interaction that is intimate and ongoing provides the baby with the opportunity to derive meaning. Tronick and Beeghly (2011) contend that the only way to accumulate clinical data on infant "meaning-making" is to study the mother–infant communication processes they call "matching, mis-matching, and reparation" (116). This ongoing process teaches the infant how hard he will have to work to achieve a supportive relationship with his mother. "Our focus on the dynamic moment-to-moment changes between the infant and caregiver highlights the concept that every infant–caregiver relationship is unique" (116). As an illustration of this concept, these researchers describe a baby and mother happily chatting when the baby suddenly pulls the mother's hair and won't let go. The mother squirms and cries out, tugging back her hair. The mother's reaction frightens the baby, who does not make a connection between pulling hair and pain. The baby begins to wail. The mother quickly tries to reassure him, comforting and holding him. But he does not calm down so easily; the mother must stay with him and repeat her reassurance until eventually he is reassured and smiling again. But, the researchers warn, not all mothers have the time and patience for this whole sequence. If the mother turns away angrily when the baby pulls her hair, he is left with the knowledge that his mother is angry with him for reasons he cannot understand. However, unlike theorists who say that time closes over the personality at an early age (childhood amnesia), Tronick and Beeghly, and others, stress that correcting early mistakes continues throughout life. But for infants who have suffered a fright, rehabilitation must be swift and persistent, since they are in such a dynamic stage of growth. The authors extol the importance of therapy for a troubled mother, together with an alternate caregiver to support both mother and infant.

Some researchers have addressed the same type of intervention for adults in therapy (Weir 2011). Psychologists and other therapists "teach" people "self-compassion." The findings show that this kind of training reduces depression and anxiety and raises feelings of well-being. There are several problems with this intervention. Encouraging people to feel compassion for themselves when they are already depressed will surely reawaken early conflicts, which must then be addressed in therapy if there is to be any lasting relief. Moreover, I feel it is important to credit Winnicott for being the first to describe self-soothing and self-comforting and for placing its development squarely in the interaction between infant and mother. I believe Winnicott's careful descriptions of the importance of early nurturing and the "holding environment" in which an infant develops were groundbreaking and represented the growing edge of research at the experiential level. Although Winnicott, a pediatrician, did not explain it in these terms, self-soothing gives us the tool to quiet down our amygdala, the anxiety center in the brain. We can do it for ourselves. No drugs needed.

Winnicott was not the first psychoanalyst to study early deprivation. W. R. D. Fairbairn (1952) had observed the effects of such deprivation in Scottish orphanages. In addition, during the mid-19th century, several studies were done by Rene Spitz (1965), who studied babies in foundling homes in New York City. Spitz found that, although these babies were kept very clean and well fed, they died at an alarming rate—about 80 percent. He hypothesized that the babies died because they were well fed but not cuddled and played with. These babies died in much less time than it would take for them to starve to death. Spitz called this condition *anaclitic depression*. Then in the 1930s, infants in foundling homes were noted to have lower IQs than infants of similar ages who were not in institutions. Researcher Harold Skeels (Karen 1998) brought in girls from a home for the mentally deficient and gave each of them a baby from the foundling group. The babies continued to be fed and diapered by the professional caretakers, but the girls played with the babies all day. They dressed and undressed them. They chatted with them and sang to them. These babies survived and thrived on the attention and cuddling they received from the girl "mothers," and they developed higher IQs. These studies show unequivocally that attachment, comforting, and caring are essential to life and to normal IQ development. This was also shown by the striking findings from the Bucharest Early Intervention Project (Fox, Almas, Degnan, Nelson & Zeanah 2011).

In order to grow and thrive, a child must have at least one unequivocally good person to depend on and to trust. Psychologist Ruth P. Newton (2007) asserts that, despite the current emphasis on cognitive development in children, the need for attachment is more crucial for a child's general well-being. Newton gives a good overview of attachment theory as well as the evidence that attachment is essential for emotional health. Comparing both organized and disorganized attachments, Newton follows their progression throughout infancy. To the degree that a parent is responsive and attuned to her child's needs at any given moment, the child develops trust and thus can rest and enjoy his feedings. As this continues, he will be more able to integrate and regulate his negative emotions—that is, he will be able to experience anger and not become completely overwhelmed. He can respond to alternatives offered by his parent. He can tolerate the parent's periodic absences without panic.

Attachment and its stabilizing effects can hardly be overstated. All the impulse disorders we can mention—bulimia, gambling, sexual addictions, drug and alcohol abuse, disorganizing rage reactions like partner-battering, and, I would wager, even mass shootings (meaning simply that the shooters have not been found to be stable, comfortable, emotionally healthy persons)—likely stem from a disordered attachment period and the fact that it was not rectified by some effective intervention later in the person's life.

Early attachment is not without its complications. The attachment to a parent can be *ambivalent*—for example, as when a child is bonded to an unreliable parent who is nurturant one day and unavailable (or intoxicated) the next. The normal need for intimacy becomes contaminated by fear. The child (and later the adult) avoids intimacy in order to feel safe but then feels abandoned for lack of intimacy. The splitting defense, described by Melanie Klein, and further developed by Fairbairn, identifies a person's need to keep separate the gratifying and frustrating aspects of the parent so as to stay attached. The gratifying part of the parent remains conscious while the frustrating parts are repressed. Disorders of attachment are so complex, with their significant subconscious motives, that I believe they are most thoroughly treated and best understood in psychoanalysis (Brandell & Ringel 2007) and other psychodynamic therapies.

ANXIETY: GOOD AND BAD

To be clear, anxiety can be and often is a normal part of everyday life. Examples of normal anxiety would be the task of applying for and starting a new job; moving to a new, strange city; the challenge of college on the first day of class; or a first date. Anxiety accompanies us during medical evaluations and stays with us while we await the diagnosis. It grips us when our child is hurt and we don't yet know how seriously. Anxiety freezes our thoughts when we are confronted with a major decision. In each of these instances, we will be able to cope if we feel the early reassurances that calmed us as little children.

Every loving mother the world over has known this intuitively. Self-soothing and self-comforting are learned skills that steady us in all sorts of situations throughout life. Among all the features of emotional health, *this one is unique* in that it is the *gift* of loving parents or other dedicated caregivers. And it is vital for protection against anxiety. Excessive and unrelenting anxiety is the accompaniment if not the cause of many of the psychological symptoms we are considering— low self-esteem, phobias, attachment disorders, and panic reactions. This would not be true for schizophrenia and bipolar disorder or for other conditions considered to be genetic in origin. But panic disorder, as well as overeating, substance abuse, alcoholism, gambling, risky sexuality, and excessive anger all represent conditions in which the suffering person cannot comfort herself, cannot calm herself down without her "fix." When people with these conditions come for therapy and *stay long enough* to learn a few things about their behavior, they often respond with great relief, significant maturation, and the development of a kind sense of humor. Their anxiety becomes less frightening, and eventually they learn to manage it well and then outgrow it.

The compulsions described above have as their main effect an avoidance of reality, and to be fair, sometimes we do need a reprieve. But that reprieve should not include a drug that will "hi-jack" the brain and destroy the liver, a "drug of choice" that then leaves a person with *no* choice. It takes years to die of alcoholism or drug abuse, but years before death, many an alcoholic has already lost home, job, marriage, and children. Healthy ways to wind down do not avoid reality; they embrace it. Talking and laughing with friends, and especially with children, fostering a sense of fun together—games, sports, movies, volunteering, decorating, learning to cook healthy food, do-it-yourself projects, gardening, reading, crafts, taking courses, community improvement, prayer and faith—are all activities that relieve a high level of anxiety and celebrate life. And most effective is a deep and profound conviction that we carry within us the power to calm ourselves with memories and imagery of a comforting relationship early on.

Sexual experience can be comforting and tension-relieving as well as exciting and gratifying. When people are very anxious or depressed, however, they often report that it does not "work" for them anymore. The reason for this may be that it takes pleasant, arousing mental images to release an orgasm. For a person who is feeling very tense, rejected, or who has other self-esteem problems, such pleasant, warm images may not be possible. Potency, arousal, and sexual satisfaction return when emotional problems are resolved in couples therapy.

EPIGENETICS AND RESILIENCE

Anxiety can exert its damaging influences even in the womb. Women have always felt that their experiences while carrying a baby matter to the child's well-being. This is certainly true for nutrition; the fetus takes what it needs from the mother's bloodstream, and if important nutrients are absent, fetal growth will be delayed or damaged. Bailey, Luback, and Coe (2004) found that infant monkeys had fewer lactobacillus and other beneficial microbes in their gut when their mothers had been frightened by loud noises while pregnant. More mysterious by far are the epigenetic changes, which affect the parent's own gene expression and are passed down to the baby, and even to *her* children (Meaney 2001; Smoller 2012). How can this happen? How can environmental influences affect anything as seemingly unreachable as our genes?

Trauma to the mother even before she becomes pregnant can alter the mother's genes in a way that gets passed down to her baby and can influence that child's reaction to stress throughout life (Smoller 2012). Similarly, trauma to the father can affect the quality of his sperm production. Judith Shulevitz (2012), science editor for the *New Republic*, reported the scope of epigenetics as affecting fathers equally. "Our genes can be switched on or off by three environmental factors, among other things: what we ingest (food, drink, air, toxins); what we experience (stress, trauma); and how long we live. Epigenetics means that our physical and mental tendencies were not set in stone during the Pleistocene Age. . . . Rather, they're shaped by the life we lead and the world we live in right now" (6–7). Research shows that epigenetic switches can be thrown by experiences a man has in the present that affect his sperm production later in life.

So it is not only our genome that affects our development and our behavior. Epigenetics refers to a parallel system that operates literally "above" our genes and determines *which* of our genes are turned on or off, or turned down, and even *when* this happens. These epigenetic factors work by being *sensitive to environmental influences*—nutrition, stressors—and they react by locking down certain genes or gene sequences, or allowing their expression, thereby dramatically altering our development:

> A variety of environmental factors are known to alter the epigenetic state . . . of DNA and chromatin, including diet, low-dose radiation, and various drugs and chemicals like cigarette smoke and alcohol. Thus, the epigenome serves as a gateway by which the world around us can change how our genes express themselves. Recent research is showing that early life experiences can also affect the brain's epigenome. . . . During a sensitive period early in life, subtle and not so subtle differences in how parents treat their infants can change the chemistry of the chromosomes in ways that alter how stress response genes are expressed. This sets off a cascade of cellular events that may govern how a child's brain and stress hormone system responds to challenges and threats for the rest of her life. (Smoller 2012, 114, 117)

The old debate about nature versus nurture has finally been resolved. They are not separate. Nurture *becomes* nature. With the new information from epigenetics, we now know that nurture—environmental effects—can alter our genes, which then program our biology, and this in turn is affected by nutrition, by pollutants, and most of all by our relationships.

To complicate matters, there is evidence that stress in utero affects girl infants more than boys, because girls have larger areas of their brains dedicated to relating and communication than boys do. "Stressed mothers naturally become less nurturing, and their baby girls incorporate stressed nervous systems that change the girls' perception of reality. This isn't about what's learned cognitively—it's about what is absorbed by the cellular microcircuitry at the neurological level" (Brizendine 2006, 20). After birth, through a process called epigenetic imprinting, the moods and temperaments expressed around her affect a little girl's developing attitudes and beliefs about the world, beliefs that can persist throughout her life. Her *sensitization* to conflict and discord causes her to be more anxious and hypervigilant than actual events may warrant.

Does this sound like the beginning of an anxiety disorder? It can be. And it is more evidence that infants need to be protected, not just from unsupportive environments and poor nutrition, but also—and mainly—from the complication of an anxious, frightened mother who cannot cope. *Both mother and infant* must be helped, and urgently. Mothers of infants and small children are often emotionally overwhelmed and dangerously isolated. They are struggling with their own issues of early deprivation and even abuse and may not be strong enough to fulfill the day-to-night-to-day needs of a baby. Any program that can offer morning get-togethers with other mothers and children, hearing stories and singing together, will be supportive, like the exemplary Early Head Start. Helping infants begins with helping young mothers. That is the first and best therapy.

Building resilience in children is increasingly understood to be the outcome of psychobiological and sociocultural influences. Researchers Stephen M. Southwick and Dennis S. Charney (2013) write that inner strength or resilience consists of several related skills—for example, being able to face one's fears while planning new ways to solve the problem. It is the ability to hold on to hope and realistic optimism. Reaching out to others is part of this. Persisting in these ways causes measurable brain changes, notably the secretion of neuropeptide Y, which is associated with successful resolutions. In contrast, these researchers say, the brains of depressives show high levels of the stress hormone cortisol. The *effort* of coping itself induces brain changes (Nechvatal & Lyons 2013). Beneficial brain changes will not occur, however, in children who are afraid to "try" or who are overwhelmed by reasonable tasks. The point is that reassurance must come before coaching.

LOVING MOTHERS FOR ALL: RESEARCH ON THE MARCH

Psychologists, psychiatrists, and other researchers are now saying bluntly that we cannot put up with community environments that compromise the health and safety of infants. Neglected and abused babies grow into children who cannot do well in school, cannot relate fairly to peers, and can end up in trouble with the law. This has always been the case: here is the sequence. If parents don't adequately care for their children, the schools have underperformers who are often disruptive. The schools then send the children to psychologists, where these children's problems can be assessed but may take years to resolve. If the children are *not* brought to psychologists or do not do well in treatment, they can become a problem to the police. Unhappy, depressed, and angry, these children often grow up to be inadequate parents themselves. And so the cycle goes. *Enough*. There is a better way.

How do we define a nurturing environment? Researchers have identified the components. What Winnicott and others said earlier— and more quietly—these researchers are now declaring stridently: "If we want to prevent multiple problems and increase the prevalence of young people who develop successfully, we must increase the prevalence of nurturing environments" (Biglan, Flay, Embry & Sandler 2012, 258). Their first criterion for a nurturant environment is to "minimize toxic conditions" (259). These range from physically, emotionally, and sexually abusive relationships to biological toxins such as pollution, smoking and secondhand smoke, dangerous non-foods like trans fats, and lead in the environment. The authors recognize that many of these stressors are associated with poverty. Alcohol consumption during pregnancy is cited as the cause of fetal alcohol syndrome, which is associated with sometimes severe mental and emotional issues. Children's IQs can be adversely affected by even light drinking during pregnancy (Lewis et al. 2012). Significant benefits to poor families can be provided by programs that directly help mothers in the middle of divorce proceedings as well as their unhappy, anxious children.

The second criterion Biglan et al. identify is the practice of teaching and encouraging pro-social behaviors. These include sensitivity to the needs and feelings of other people and sharing and celebrating with others. They stress that conflict resolution and impulse control should be actively taught. People from depressed, dysfunctional families may not realize that this is possible. Recently, many efforts have been focused on eliminating bullying. One-third of schoolchildren have reported being bullied—2.7 million incidents each year (Taffel 2012). These innovative programs have been featured in the media, and school policies are at long last becoming more stringent on this issue. Biglan et al. also discuss the complicated principles guiding the proper and creative use of reinforcements, which are—surprisingly—a controversial issue. They discuss the use of certain games that have been shown to change children's behavior for the better even years after they were played. They restate the finding that after-school programs protect children from taking risks, getting into substance abuse, and ignoring homework and grades.

Biglan et al. are calling for a community-, state-, and countrywide orientation to the requirements of environments that will guarantee infants and children safety, comfort, and good nutrition as their birthright:

> Now that we understand the importance of nurturing environments, we should aspire to a society in which we would be shocked to find that an environment did not nurture its children.... The highest priority environments are families and schools, because they influence child and adolescent development and because most problems develop during childhood. (Biglan et al. 264)

These innovative researchers have thrown down the gauntlet. The challenge is on: to *guarantee* babies and children the nurturant environment vital to their mental and emotional growth. Once grown, a secure child *retains* the capacity for calming, comforting, and clear thinking—all the components of resilience necessary to use the assets he or she was born with. But we need to start these interventions early.

Mental health researchers and practitioners have been saying this for a century, but it is heartening to hear it from eminent persons in other fields. "Current programs don't start early enough," writes

James J. Heckman (2013), professor of economics at the University of Chicago and Nobel Laureate in economics,

> nor do they produce the skills that matter most for personal and societal prosperity. The cognitive skills prized by the American educational establishment and measured by achievement tests are only part of what is required for success in life. *Character skills* are equally important determinants of wages, education, health and many other significant aspects of flourishing lives. *Self-control, openness, the ability to engage with others, to plan and to persist*—these are the attributes that get people in the door and on the job, and lead to productive lives. Cognitive and character skills work together as dynamic complements; they are inseparable. Skills beget skills. (5; emphasis added)

If we examine Heckman's recommendations for character skills more closely, we can see that he has intuited the features of "normal" personality, as I am outlining in this book. *Self-control* is the combination of realism (chapter 1), strong self-esteem (chapter 2), and the ability to comfort oneself (this chapter). "Openness" is another word for vulnerability (discussed in chapter 10). *The ability to engage others* combines openness with assertion (chapter 9) and empathy (also discussed in chapter 10). The *ability to plan* is part of Work and Play (chapter 4). Lastly, the *ability to persist* describes the resilience we are discussing here. Heckman is also implying, in his comment on skills begetting skills, that IQ and character skills develop together. He thus echoes my major premise: "normal" personality can be taught and learned—and is much helped by good nutrition.

What a challenge. It will take more than just identifying the features of nurturing environments (although the reader is encouraged to read the article by Biglan et al., which gives many more details of their entreaty). It will take legal influence and vigorous media campaigns. But one change we can make, I propose, is *to have hospitals take a greater role.* Hospitals are set up to treat patients and have many coordinated departments. They can add a new one: outreach. Every new baby born at the hospital would go home with some clothing, food, toys, and an *advocate.* A trained hospital worker, perhaps a special nurse, would accompany mother and baby home, and the nurse would evaluate the home environment for safety, nutrition, and emotional support. If the mother has the help she needs from family and friends, and the home is clean and stocked with food and staples, all is well. But if she needs help on any of these levels, she will receive it then and there. No waiting or applying for programs. Everything would be in place, as it is for other hospital-based programs. I believe that this is a better use for our taxes than for programs that do not even start until the child is older and possibly already damaged. This would be a way to guarantee that early needs are met at the time and place when each baby cries. Does this sound too ambitious? Let's try it.

In fact, Nicholas Kristof (2012) cites just such a program that has already been implemented: the Nurse-Family Partnership:

> It sends nurses on regular visits to at-risk, first-time moms, from pregnancy until the child turns two. The nurses warn about alcohol or drug abuse and encourage habits of attentive parenting, like reading to the child. The results are stunning: at age fifteen, these children are less than half as likely to have been arrested as kids from similar circumstances who were not enrolled. (SR11)

Interventions that come later are also helpful. Early enrichment programs are beneficial for socially disadvantaged children (Barnett 2011) but, as we have stressed, infancy is the period when the right interventions will do the most good. Joy D. Osofsky and Alicia F. Lieberman (2011) address the ongoing need for the integration of services to at-risk families that now are hampered by frustrating and damaging delays in the court system, lack of coordination of services, and inadequate training for mental health workers. The programs these writers are calling for include five interrelated components: "financing, policy, training, service delivery, and system collaboration" (121). Some of these intervention teams are court teams—for example, Zero to Three (www.zerotothree.org) which focuses on decisions for abused children:

> Children ages birth to five years have disproportionately high rates of maltreatment, with long-term consequences for their mental and physical health. Research on normal development and developmental psychopathology has shown that early development unfolds in an ecology of transactional influences among biological, interpersonal, and environmental domains. (Osofsky & Lieberman 2011, 129)

These researchers cite the enormous contribution of Early Head Start, a learning and play program targeting infants and mothers. (Funding for such programs can wane depending on government priorities.)

Just as heartening is the report by Florence Nelson and Tammy Mann (2011) highlighting the role of psychologists in educating policy makers about the urgency of early childhood programs. The major risk factors are clear: "poverty, pre- and post-natal parental depression, family isolation, parental mental illness, or parental substance abuse" (131). The focused and efficacious Early Head Start program is "required to screen children for developmental/behavioral concerns" (131) and shows measurably good results—for example, children who are less violent and more interactive. Psychologists, the authors say, should be involved in building "a knowledge base for policy decisions. . . . Psychologists are credible experts who can be a voice for babies in public policy discussion and in raising public awareness about infant mental health and social-emotional wellness" (Nelson & Mann 2011, 137).

Increasingly, the *parents* of Early Head Start children are taking advantage of services offered to them, "including treatment for depression, crisis intervention, child abuse and neglect services, substance abuse prevention and treatment, and domestic violence services" (Nelson & Mann 2011, 134). The authors also review the elaborate and changing insurance issues. Many companies are expanding coverage for treating babies and their families, but more and more these issues are requiring government intervention. Hopefully, these programs will no longer be among those that are cut whenever government spending needs to be curtailed. Psychologists and other mental health specialists can bring their expertise to educate representatives and policymakers both as individual clinicians and through our professional groups. The American Psychological Association website dedicated to infant and early childhood policy issues is http://www.apa.org/pi/families/children-mental-health.aspx.

WHAT OUR CHILDREN WANT

What children want does not cost a great deal of money. Jonathan Baylin and Daniel Hughs (2012) offer a description of parenting as a hard-wired, oxytocin-mediated endeavor. "Parenting . . . is an ancient mammalian mind-heart process, which allows a caregiver to stay engaged and regulated enough to sustain the mind-to-mind, heart-to-heart connections that are vital for a child's development. Parenting is rooted in openness and safety, not in survival-mode self-defense" (41).

It's true. Children do not care if the roof is leaking as long as they have a parent who gets on the floor and laughs with them and who is reasonably reliable. Similarly, money is not a childhood value (until children are indoctrinated), nor do they care about our concepts of nutritious food, or clothing styles (until other children start teasing them for the lack of these). Programming children's days with one activity after another, with hardly a chance to exhale in between, is not normal. The so-called "tiger parenting" style has been roundly criticized as unhealthy for children regardless of the milestones achieved (Juang, Qin & Park 2013).

Most of all, children want to be appreciated and respected for each age and stage of their development. They want their small and big victories celebrated. They want to know, as Gordon Allport (1968) taught us, that they can influence us and make a difference in our decisions, at least some of the time. They want to be reassured and comforted when they are disappointed or frightened. If they do not get these, it does not matter what else they are given. It will never compensate for love. (Ironically, their harried parents also need the same things. But it is unfair to expect little children to fill our adult needs for appreciation, comfort, and reassurance. Later in this book, there is an extended discussion of how adults can nurture each other.)

SMALL COMFORT: WHEN THINGS GO WRONG

Given an adequate nurturing environment, normal growth is autonomous. It opens up like a flower, following its genetic decree and responding to environmental cues, including nutritional stimuli. Neurosis, then, can be thought of as *the sustained pressure against normal growth*. It is the consistent and unfair requirement of a parent that "bends a child out of shape," as the saying goes. A child cannot be made neurotic overnight. It takes months or years of those particular parental pressures or negligence. Children will learn to accommodate their parents' neurotic needs because they are dependent and need the support. Children who are not supported grow up tense and anxious. When they are routinely anxious, people cannot then calm themselves, and they may reach for alcohol, food, drugs, or sex. Or they become phobic, trying to manage anxiety through the avoidance of spaces and places they believe will set off a panic attack. Their personalities can also become cynical and sadistic, showing a sinister need for revenge.

FEAR OF INTIMACY/COMMITMENT: THE OBVERSE
OF SELF-SOOTHING

The chronic deficit of soothing and comforting in early childhood often leaves the child fearful. But in many cases, the child's reaction can be intense anger. In adulthood, such children feel a need to "take out" their anger on others. I believe that fear of intimacy/commitment is one such example. A source of much pain for romantic partners, avoidance of commitment is a puzzle of many dimensions. Sometimes it is simply a more-or-less conscious refusal to financially support a partner. Or it can be a fear of being owned and "engulfed" by the partner. At other times, it seems to stem from a poignant psychological wound reaching deep into childhood and buried from awareness.

The cause of fear of commitment can be a massive disappointment or betrayal that the person *cannot transcend*. For reasons historical, genetic, or both, the person lacks the capacity or will to *grieve* his or her great loss. Grieving requires the recognition of the gravity of the loss, as well as the courage and resilience to endure the pain. Grieving is a form of emotional processing that takes into account all the ambivalent feelings we may have toward a person or a situation. It is a *form of self-soothing* that consoles us and lets us rest. But it cannot be experienced if a person does not sympathize with his own suffering and lacks a caring attitude toward his own body. Grieving also shows vulnerability, the recognition that we had no control; we could not stop the loss from occurring. Grief comes in waves, and after each bout of tears and pain, the person processes more of his loss—its history and meaning. In this way, and by accretion, more relief and balance are gained. The process is similar whether the loss is of a parent, sibling, child, or spouse/lover.

When grieving overwhelms or is not permitted us, the person can become numb. Psychological pain too great to be repressed will be dissociated (Celani 2010). While the subconscious features are complex, fear of intimacy on the conscious level often plays out as an opportunity for vengeance. *The person could not stop the loss* but *he can cause it.* And this gives him some power over the helplessness he had felt and relief from his pain. A man who suffers a disorganizing humiliation and loss as a child or young man may develop, without noticing it, a pattern of "love them and leave them." He can enjoy a new relationship for a few months, genuinely feeling desire and love for a partner. Then at a certain point—when the partner's longing for him is obvious and constant—something changes in his feelings. The opportunity for vengeance and gloating become irresistible, and the partner is deliberately rejected. *The sado-masochistic need thus overrides real feelings of love and longing.* This is of immense clinical importance because *the man is also sabotaging himself* and guaranteeing he will never have a gratifying and enduring love relationship. His enjoyment of frustrating his partner eventually trumps his own legitimate need for love.

This sounds incredible. Why would a man do that to himself, and to the sequence of partners unlucky enough to love him? Where could such a cruel motive come from?

Through the Crack in the Door: Drew, a Man Divided against Himself

Rural Norway has idyllic small villages reminiscent of Christmas card scenes. Drew lived his early life in such a setting, the only child of a logger and his wife. His mother was kind but said little. It was Drew's father who read to him each night before bed. They would play cards and games and talk about their day and laugh together. Drew's father was his world. Life was peaceful and happy for this family until the father, a lifelong smoker, became ill with cancer. As his father's condition worsened, five-year-old Drew was pushed out of his life. Finally his father withdrew to his bedroom, and his mother told him *he couldn't see his father anymore.*

As an adult in therapy, Drew tried to describe the torment of his father's final weeks. Forbidden to see his father even at the end, Drew would hide behind the door, which was left slightly ajar, and peer through the opening. I asked Drew what he was feeling in those long hours behind the door. He said he had to be very quiet, but crying, he would mouth the words over and over: "Papa, Papa, I love you. I want to see you. I'll read to you." He wanted to give his father the good experiences he had given to Drew. He could hear his father's voice, but he wept all the more because *his father did not want to see him anymore.* Although they may not have realized it, the cruelty of the parents' decision was tragic for their son. Exhausted, he would fall asleep on the floor behind the door. This went on for months. Drew does not remember his father's death, nor much about the rest of his childhood.

Ironically, when I expressed sympathy for little Drew, grown-up Drew angrily rejected it. He said emphatically that his mother's decision to exclude him was correct. "It was necessary," he said. He had to hold on to his belief that his parents were good and so resented my reminding him of their cruelty. This is a defense called "splitting," the need to keep separate the gratifying and the frustrating aspects of the parent (Fairbairn 1952) that then allows a person to preserve a positive relationship or memory of that parent. (It is emotionally healthy to be able to see both sides of a person's behavior; this mollifies the bad parts, consoles us, and fosters normal ambivalence.)

Drew had come to the United States as a visiting scientist and worked in one of the many laboratories of a prestigious research foundation. He was enthusiastic about his work and wanted to publish several scientific papers here before returning to his academic position in Europe. He came to therapy apologizing for his English, which was quite good. He was also a good observer of his feelings and expressed them well. The problem, he said, was that he could not "stay with" a woman for more than a few months. All would start out well and was mutually enjoyable for two or three months. He could not fault any of his girlfriends, he said. Something changed in *his* feelings.

This is an amazing insight on Drew's part. Many men and women who show fear of intimacy simply become angry when they are questioned. If they are married, they angrily withdraw from the discussion. But Drew struggled to describe his emotional change. After genuinely enjoying intimacy with a woman, he said, his feelings of love for her would one day melt away. In their place arose a dark urge: a frank need to frustrate her—to bring her to his room, undress, and then sit back and refuse sex. The woman would clearly be expecting sex, since that is what had happened for weeks, and with mutual enjoyment. This scenario usually had the expectable result. The woman was at first puzzled, then weeping and pleading, and finally angry and verbally abusive. Throughout these stages in the woman's feelings, Drew said he would be smiling, which sent the woman's frustration through the roof and further revealed his sadomasochistic motive.

Drew's stated reason for coming to therapy was to interrupt this pattern. He said he was amazed that the same cycle he had observed in himself while in Europe was happening here in the United States, exactly in the same sequence and, this last time, with an accomplished scientist who he felt would be a perfect partner for him. He loved her, he said. Why couldn't he keep that love? Why was his need to frustrate her so strong? He had come to therapy one week after this remarkable woman had angrily left him, telling him he was "sick."

I asked him, "Do you think you are sick?" Drew thought for a minute then answered with notable seriousness. "Yes, I must be. Last week I drove away this great person. She was naked and beautiful, but I did not touch her. I told her, 'You have to sit there and want me.' She was throwing on her clothes and screaming at me. I was standing next to the bedroom wall, and I felt myself banging my head against the wall *because I could not stop it. I could not stop myself from frustrating her.*" This tall, well-dressed man with a string of advanced degrees looked puzzled, confused, miserable, and defeated.

We had only a few sessions left, because Drew would be leaving for Europe soon. We analyzed this pattern of exciting seduction, love, and mutual pleasure that—seemingly at its most perfect point—devolved into his *greater* need to frustrate. He could understand that he was also sabotaging his own happiness. I explained to him that this pattern did not come out of the blue. It was a repetition of some traumatic experience from his past (Celani 2010). At this point, I had a suspicion that it may have begun with a teenage attachment—passionate and painful—that had broken up. He did report one such relationship that would qualify as causative, especially since it was the girl's *mother* who had told 16-year-old Drew that *he could not see the girl anymore*, ostensibly because her parents wanted her to be engaged to someone else. But there was something deeper, something that *resonated* with that teenage grief: an earlier pain—that of his own mother telling him he could never see his father again. That searing loss to a helpless grieving 5-year-old had lasted for months. *That* had been the original lesion.

And this is the crux of the issue. In such a situation, the child becomes overwhelmed. His ability to cope is exhausted, and his will to keep trying is broken. That pain had been so overwhelming to Drew at the time that his body, his subconscious mind (Pert 2003) had made a fateful decision: if needing someone is going to hurt me this bad, *I am not going to need anyone.* Thus out of unbearable pain, Drew developed a motive to jettison normal human neediness when it reached a certain point of intensity. This was no longer a conscious choice but a deeply rooted compulsion. The child becomes attached to the most intense part of the parent, the most threatening parental requirement (Celani 2010). And Drew was right. He then could not stop it.

Analytic thinkers like psychologist George Strutt go further. There is a pattern, a motif, Strutt said (personal communication, December

13, 2013), of the "relationship at a distance" as a structure in Drew's life. It was forced on him during his father's ordeal, but then it became his torment and his compulsion. It was a pattern he tried to master by recreating it with every woman he was intimate with; at a certain point he had to push her away as he was pushed away. He could not prevent the imposed distance from his father, but now he could *cause* it in his adult relationships, and that revived his sense of personal power.

Could therapy stop this pattern? Possibly, given enough time as well as Drew's remarkable insight and curiosity about his own behavior. The necessary condition for learning self-soothing is vulnerability, and this can be developed in therapy. Drew found the psychoanalytic interpretation of his lifelong struggle interesting but a "bit of a stretch." He could hardly believe that his poignant loss at age five could affect him now as an accomplished adult. I reminded him that intellectual growth can be a separate continuum from emotional growth, and that our nervous systems are sensitized to pain. The vulnerable child grew up to be a sensitive teenager, and the pain of his early loss of his father had been compounded by the loss of his first girlfriend. Most importantly, no one had helped him to grieve as a child. No one had comforted him. Eventually learning in therapy to soothe and comfort himself would have helped him to outgrow the devastating pattern of needing to frustrate women *as he had been frustrated*—Freud's *repetition compulsion*. But by then Drew was gone.

MAKING THINGS RIGHT: THERAPEUTIC INTERVENTIONS

Can people who were never adequately comforted in childhood learn to steady themselves in adulthood without resorting to some kind of compulsion? Yes, probably, and to the degree that the person is interested in outgrowing her or his problem. My bias is for individual therapy—thoughtful, respectful, and serious interchange between therapist and patient. This is the model for psychoanalysis and psychodynamic therapy. Giving a person time and encouragement to talk, to mention everything that bothers her, especially recurrent issues, and eventually to make some connections that provide growth and relief.

As we have said, children who grow up with a history of neglect, and even abuse, cannot regulate their emotions and often struggle with unbearable anxiety. Phobia, panic attacks, and other anxiety disorders may be the result. The sufferer will then try to "self-medicate" with smoking, alcohol, gambling, or drugs. They may become addicted to food. Excessive sleep and even compulsive sex can be recruited in the attempt to manage disorganizing anxiety.

According to Sally Winston, codirector of the Anxiety and Stress Disorders Institute of Maryland (www.anxietyandstress.com), current treatment for anxiety disorders incorporates mindfulness and acceptance-based interventions. Most significant "in the treatment of panic disorder itself is the identification of the trait of anxiety sensitivity," which is the fear and shame, as well as the misinterpretation of anxiety experience, both the physical and emotional symptoms. "This fear and shame is passed from generation to generation, both directly as an inherited trait and indirectly in the teachings of parents and the experiences of the child. Treatment of the *fear of fear* forms the core of the treatment for panic disorder" (Sally Winston, personal communication, November 5, 2013; emphasis hers). Winston stresses that perfectionism, fear of dependency, and hypervigilence constitute major features of personalities with anxiety disorders. These personality traits are systematically examined in therapy to show the patient's collusion in her own suffering. She feels that if she is not hypervigilant, the sky will fall. Until she has effective therapy, she cannot let go of that fear and begin to trust.

Addiction treatment is a complex, multifaceted enterprise with its own literature and practitioners. The findings of laboratory researchers and those of counselors in the field do not always match up. That is because what "works" in controlled research settings with college-age subjects may not work for diverse, long-time "users" (Winerman 2013). Much of the treatment involves teaching addicted persons to be aware of their impulsivity and how to protect themselves from settings and people that can pull them backward. Through group discussions, they learn to understand their feelings and to take responsibility for them. Most importantly, they learn to comfort—not numb—themselves, and to give themselves what they never had on a reliable basis in their early lives—protection, encouragement, and reassurance.

LEARNING TO CARESS

Lisa Ferentz, president and founder of the Institute for Advanced Psychotherapy Training and Education, Inc., and a private practitioner, has created a treatment model that serves as an alternative to standard safety contracts when victims of trauma, abuse, or neglect feel the urge to engage in a self-destructive behavior. Many of the people she treats exhibit behaviors such as cutting and burning themselves, addictions, and eating disorders, behaviors that clients believe are necessary and relieving in the short term. "CARESS allows clients to experience the positive outcomes they were getting from their self-destructive behaviors by offering alternative behaviors that avoid the injurious and re-victimizing outcomes" (Ferentz 2012, 15). This innovative approach replaces self-destructive acts with creative, expressive, and comforting alternatives. Participants are taught that CA means "communicate alternatively," RE stands for "release endorphins," and SS is for "self-soothe."

Working with each person individually, Ferentz begins by forging a trusting therapeutic relationship and helping clients become curious about a connection between their current struggles and their family-of-origin experiences, which often include trauma, abuse, neglect, or pain narratives. The intervention (the CA, communicate alternatively part) includes the client's own drawings of the body part he or she is driven to cut or burn. Clients are encouraged to write about their self-harming behavior, to draw or even sculpt in clay the body part they wish to hurt. They set a timer and do this intervention for about 15 minutes each time they have an urge to harm themselves. This empowers the person to interrupt self-destructive behaviors at home. The second part of the intervention (RE, release endorphins), also performed for about 15 minutes, is to engage in one of the prescribed activities, usually a full-body workout such as running on a home exercise machine or jumping in place. If preferred, they may also watch a funny movie, read a favorite book, or—just as Winnicott would advise—hug a stuffed toy, or better, a live pet.

For the self-soothe, Ferentz offers "wrap in a quilt and rock in a rocking chair; take a warm shower or bubble bath; light scented candles or oil; read positive affirmations; massage your hands with soothing lotion; listen to a relaxation tape or play soothing music; blow bubbles to slow down breathing" (141–142). Participants are encouraged to create a CARESS box that contains all the objects they need to do the three-part intervention. When the urge to self-harm is experienced, they can quickly go to the box and find the resources they need to begin the protocol.

Part of the beauty of this program is that the CARESS model provides people with a new way to articulate their painful past experiences, safely short-circuit overwhelming affect (emotion), and then self-soothe in healthier ways without the residual by-product of guilt or shame that often accompanies destructive acts. In time, clients will build on these suggestions and come up with new ones that resonate personally for them. The message the person receives is that she does have alternatives. She is in control of her behavior. This radical intervention moves beyond the usual therapy process of using words to describe and explain feelings. Many traumatized people cannot use words in that way, at least not yet. The CARESS model allows them to share their pain narrative and find resolution through self-soothing. This makes them active agents in their own healing process, moving them beyond the victimhood of their earlier environments.

A DELAYED REACTION: PANIC ATTACKS IN AN ADOLESCENT

The absence of the ability to calm ourselves does not *always* mean that one's early environment was harsh or that one's mother was cold, detached, or negligent. Sometimes essentially normal parents are struggling with difficult issues of their own, and are distracted and exhausted. Nonetheless, the result can be an anxiety disorder in their child.

Chrissy came to therapy after she had suffered a full-blown panic attack in her second year of college. This attack had come "out of the blue," as they often do, and she left class in a cold sweat. Her heart was pounding, her breathing labored. A nameless feeling of terror gripped her. She called a girlfriend to sit with her, but the friend soon tired of what she called "drama" and left. Tearful and confused, Chrissy called her dad, who came to the campus and took her home. A careful checkup with their physician established that there was nothing wrong with her heart. Panic disorder patients become terrified that their hearts will not be able to endure the pounding. They often end up in the emergency room, convinced they are having a heart attack.

The major fear in panic disorder is that another panic attack will occur, causing a total loss of control. For some people the fear is specific—fear of vomiting or of becoming incontinent. A fear of heart attack or stroke can follow the experience of a pounding heart and a cold sweat. Other people fear they will start screaming or cursing, or that they will "go crazy." Indeed, these people may avoid psychological treatment because they fear being considered "crazy." Some patients have reported a smothering sensation or difficulty breathing. Feelings of depersonalization—feeling unreal—can be caused by hyperventilating on a daily basis. The abnormal levels of blood gases that result from hyperventilation are the cause of these frightening feelings. Their pounding hearts convince patients that their panic cannot be "psychological." They do not yet know that all psychological experiences are effects of biological changes (Pert 2003; Smoller 2012).

In therapy, Chrissy was impatient, angry, and embarrassed. She wanted her therapist to "fix" her so that she could return to college, but a recurrence of her panic attacks convinced her that she could not do that. She felt her body was betraying her. As we went over her history, it became clear that Chrissy had no sympathy for her body or for her life. When her body was hurting, or hungry and tired, she would get angry with herself. *She had never learned to be self-comforting.*

Chrissy had much difficulty describing her early life, and sad as it was, she did not cry. When she was very little, she was the adored child of her father and her grandmother. Her mother had been there but was somewhat distracted. Her mother had a son from an earlier marriage, and she spent much time with him. When Chrissy was three years old, her mother left with her son to rejoin the boy's father. Although she had a very loving father and grandmother, her mother's leaving must have been a tragedy, but Chrissy said she had no memory of crying for her mother. And there seemed to be nothing in the house to remind Chrissy of her. Her grandmother had disposed of all her mother's possessions.

I asked Chrissy if she had ever seen her mother again. She said yes, a few times, but she had no particular memories of these visits. Earlier, her mother had given her a little blanket, which she had kept in the toy box, but eventually that too disappeared. Chrissy's father was devoted to her, but his sadness for his absent wife was undisguised. He would weep openly at the dinner table. When she was five years old, Chrissy remembered clinging to her grandmother the first time she was taken to school. Eventually school became her favorite place. Teachers and friends became her world. They were always reliable and kind. They did what they said they were going to do, whereas her good and loving dad was usually depressed and unavailable. When her dad was home, they talked about school. No one talked about her mother.

Panic disorder patients may be more easily sensitized—easier to scare—than other people, a trait that may be inherited. Like bipolar disorder, panic disorder has genetic roots (Smoller 2012). The first panic attack is all the more frightening because it comes "out of the blue"—at a meeting, on a plane, or a bridge. For Chrissy, it was much more generalized. She felt that her whole body, indeed her whole life, was threatened. She reported that before the panic attack, she had felt completely normal, and after it completely disorganized. She was particularly unhappy that she had to leave the college she loved. That conflict is what brought Chrissy into therapy. As frightened as she was, she wept about wanting to return to school.

Panic disorder patients are often perfectionists. Also, they have difficulty with confrontation and with strong emotions in general. For example, falling in love can make them fear dependency; they need to feel in control at all times. For some, sexual arousal can cause a panic reaction because sex requires a certain vulnerability and surrender to the experience. They are wary and hypervigilant, worrying that if they are not, the sky will fall. At the same time, they can feel helpless to prevent another panic attack. They often show what psychologists call "a punitive conscience," a feeling that they *should* always be in control. If this sounds like the personality of a high achiever, it is. Fear of failure is another form of anxiety, but if it does not dominate one's whole life, moderate amounts of anxiety can be energizing and motivating.

Chrissy had excelled in high school, winning scholarships, and she had been accepted at a prestigious college. In therapy, I explained that it was the experience of *going away* to college that had likely sensitized her and led to her first panic attack, although not in her freshman year. (Panic is often a delayed reaction.) I believe her leaving for college for the *second* year had activated her memories of her mother's leaving the family. All the feelings of abandonment, unacknowledged since the age of three, would be denied no more.

She saw the connection, but Chrissy seemed as annoyed with her therapist as she was with herself. "Okay," she said. "Now what?" I suggested she tell me a little about her mother, something she had never been allowed to do. She became silent and distant. She could not even begin. I then asked her to talk about the toy box, the box of "gifts" from her mother. What was in it? Chrissy brightened a bit. She could remember some dolls, a fairy dress with wings, and many books. But all this was described dispassionately, as if she were relating the evening news.

Were there any favorites? Chrissy shrugged. Just as she did not sympathize with her body, she had no sympathy for the little girl she had been. She could not comfort that little girl in her loss. She resented the child she used to be because she had been abandoned by her mother. (I eventually learned that Chrissy's mother had pursued her son's father, who had taken their son out of the country illegally. When he refused to return the boy, Chrissy's mother agreed to move to that country because she feared losing contact with her son. And the boy did need her support. Chrissy had known none of this when she was a little girl; no one had answered any of her questions.) When I asked her if she had cried for her mother, she said in the affected tone that some teens use: "I gue-ess."

Through the next few sessions I persisted. We first recounted the previous week's experience with anxiety—when and where these episodes were happening. Then I returned to the early part of Chrissy's life. Was there a "transitional object"—any toy or doll that was very special, that she had taken to bed? What else had been in that toy box that had been summarily emptied by her grandmother? Was there *anything* she kept, at least for a little while, that came to bed with her and felt, and smelled, like her mother? Chrissy's expression softened. She said it slowly, in a voice newly needy, newly aware:

"My . . . blankie."
"Your blankie," I repeated. "Was it a baby blanket? What did it look
    like? Do you remember the color?"
She did not answer. She turned her head. She did not want her therapist
    to see her crying.

Nothing was said. It was enough that Chrissy had gotten this far. Those tears were not of the moment; they belonged to a little three-year-old girl who could not know what was happening to her. In subsequent sessions, she remembered the mother who sat on the rug with her, talking about little-girl things, dolls and fairies. The mother who read to her. And when her mother seemed distracted with her other life, Chrissy had her "blankie." Just as Winnicott (1953) taught, the transitional object—the doll or blanket—substituted for the mother when she was not there. Chrissy's memories slowly emerged in therapy. Her mother would wrap her in the little blanket when they went to the car. Then Chrissy would drag it from the car and bring it to bed. It was fuzzy, she recalled. It had fringe, and it was yellow.

Over the next weeks, we were able to make many connections in therapy. We discussed how her mother may have been conflicted. How much was her mother influenced by her first husband, her son's father? Her mother may not have been a strong person, perhaps very needy herself. She may have been unhappy in her second marriage, dominated by her mother-in-law. She may have been quite torn, not able to see any way to combine these two families and have her son and Chrissy together. We considered the probability that any cards or gifts that had been sent by her mother had been confiscated by her grandmother and how the loss must have been unbearable to Chrissy at age three.

Chrissy considered these things. She loved her grandmother, but knew there was no disagreeing with her. Now that Chrissy was aware of the source of her early helplessness and terror, I could help her learn the skills she had never learned at that crucial time. Therapy teaches patients that panic is a bodily overreaction. It is their *thoughts* that terrify them. They are not actually in any physical danger at the moment. Their most significant need is to *sympathize* with their bodily reaction, not blame themselves for it, and to learn to soothe and comfort themselves like a good parent. At this point, a person can become angry with her therapist for "not getting it," as Chrissy alleged. "I feel terrible! Don't you understand?" A good therapist must sympathize with her pain but stress that her *brain* is reacting with panic to a *past* frightening event which was never processed and integrated. In Chrissy's case, it was her mother's leaving her when she was three. She had been asleep when her mother left. No explanation was offered to her the next day. Chrissy remembered that she often pleaded for her mother, but her grandmother ignored her questions, turning her back to Chrissy, and life went on. Significantly, this teenager did not experience panic until her *second* year at college.

As therapy progressed, Chrissy could speak about her early childhood more easily. She slowly developed a respect for her body's—"little Chrissy's"—fear reaction. Her adult self could say, "Oh, I'm feeling afraid that I'll have another panic attack at my friend's house tonight." I recommended that she take steps to prevent that, like calling the anxiety "it" and experiencing it as separate from her body. She could "float" her anxiety, as Claire Weekes (1990) advised, willfully letting it go, like a balloon or a kite. And most importantly, she could take measures to calm and comfort herself, verbally, as a good mother would, saying: "It's all right. You're fine." Little children need this reassurance because they cannot predict the effect of a fall or a fright; they need much reassurance that it is limited and not fatal.

Chrissy's panic attacks became infrequent and less frightening. She was learning to comfort herself, first by grieving for her early loss but also by connecting with the reassurances of her therapist. Her "fear of fear"—that another panic attack could occur—lessened dramatically. We talked about caring for the little child she used to be. She wept during those sessions and realized that tears can be very comforting.

Tears are a generalized release of tension that is curative. Von Glahn (2012) advises therapists not to stop their patient's crying but give the person the opportunity to cry until the tears are finished. The discussions that follow such episodes can thus be more insightful.

Chrissy talked about school plays when other children had their mothers there. She mentioned the embarrassment of her first period, when her wordless grandmother simply set out the items she needed. Birthday after birthday went by with no card or gifts from her mother. Notably, Chrissy said she hated feeling sad. I asked her why she would hate feeling sad. She replied that it made her feel *weak*. Sadness is normal, I said, and is not weak. Normal human neediness is not weakness. It was not fair to belittle herself or her friends for normal human sadness. *Only by grieving can we begin the deep turn back toward happiness.*

We began talking about her strengths. She loved getting As in school. She loved being "looked up to" by her friends. She loved certain teachers who had encouraged her to do her best. She was able to apply to colleges because of that encouragement. And she loved her dad, who was "the best!" He often felt sad, but Chrissy now could cheer *him* up. She learned to appreciate herself and all her accomplishments realistically. (This reminded me how much self-esteem is built on a foundation of reliable soothing and comforting.) Chrissy had regained the memory of her early mothering experience. She told me she had even tried to find a yellow blanket that resembled the one she lost, laughing about the embarrassment of looking at baby things in the infant department.

By the time she left for college again, her panic had largely resolved. Her relationship with her dad was sympathetic on both sides. Her ability to comfort him and herself was reliable and efficient. She left therapy smiling and saying, "I'm going to be all right. I'll be fine." Chrissy completed her college degree with no other anxiety except what accompanied exams. The absence of panic meant that Chrissy felt *safe*. She had learned in therapy to provide that safety for herself.

SELF-COMFORTING IN ADULTHOOD

Paul Horton (1981), using Winnicott's concepts of Transitional Objects and Transitional Space in therapy, explains that adults need solace as much as children do, and throughout our lives. Relationships are probably the richest source—the steadfast presence and loyalty of our partner, watching our children develop their own interests, and the deepening meanings of family as we grow older. But so are *places* that nurture us, like our gardens, the sea, and places of worship, as well as various forms of art and music. Especially reaffirming is having *time* free of electronic and other interferences.

In addition, I believe that *words* themselves can be transitional objects, whether they are the remembered words of a loving person or a poetic phrase that stays with us year after year and reassures us. For me, an example would be this line by Walt Whitman:

> From imperfection's murkiest cloud / Darts always forth one ray of perfect light.

Words, especially in the form of metaphor, connect our bodies to the outside world. A metaphor contains a known part that illuminates an unknown part—for example, "a curiosity as sharp as hunger." Hunger, the known part, clarifies the quality of the unknown part, a curiosity. Moreover, the known part is a *body* experience, while the unknown part is a concept, the meaning of which we are trying to convey to another person. We will say, "She makes me sick to my stomach," a powerful image of the revulsion one person feels for another. In therapy, metaphor is the way a person conveys her inner experience. A teenager said, "I feel like a guest in my own home," reflecting the distance she feels from her family. A woman reported feeling "light as air" after we had come to a solution to a chronic problem that was "weighing her down." A body experience—"weighed down" and "light as air"—clarified her psychic troubles and their reprieve. Words can be transitional objects, as comforting as a perfect cup of tea.

The things, experiences, and people that were comforting to us as children remain precious all our lives. We may not realize how much they shape our preferences and our longings. Carried into our adult lives, they support us in ways that are hard to describe to others—how our kitchen should smell, the music we come home to, the way we want our bed made. They offer us not just comfort but connection and continuity. Yet many of us lacked such comforting experiences. When this is the case, the need for such solace can leave us with an ongoing longing. How can we fill that empty space?

Learning to be a good parent to yourself is a major theme in therapy, encouraged by a sensitive therapist who cares about your history. Therapy is one of the best ways to learn how to become self-comforting, but certainly not the only way. For example, you *can* have a second chance for fulfillment in a very supportive romantic relationship, and when this is going well, nothing compares. However, it is a mistake to believe that reassurance and protection must always come from *outside* of you—that is, from others. That is too great a burden to put on a romantic partner, and it will be resented. With good self-esteem (and with some of the experiences described below), you can carry within yourself the conviction of "loveable-ness" and worthiness, as well as the ability to reassure yourself when you doubt this. Of special importance is the quality of the relationship. Be certain you will not allow yourself to be mistreated, trading loneliness for submission and abuse, a fair definition of masochism (Wurmser 1993). Healthy people have the courage to leave any relationship that is demeaning. Normal "masochism" is the willingness to endure pain and deprivation for a higher, conscious goal, such as sacrificing for a child's benefit. Loneliness itself *is normal and resolvable*, and enduring it builds resilience.

Adult self-soothing that addresses our physical, emotional, and spiritual needs comes in many forms. Religious faith can be an important source of comfort. Many people feel, as they get older, that faith is their primary source of comfort. Developing a love of art is a superb way to self-soothe, especially if it includes dabbling with paints. Music is another source that can be both calming and exciting. Joining a singing group is a truly transcendent experience. Dance, too, allows for abundant self-expression. And writing as well; just sit down and write a poem about the vacation that fulfilled a life-long dream, the last hike you took, or an account of the family get-together where you saw your now grown-up cousin, who seemed like a different person. Maybe you would like to do a short story or even a novel. For some people, being outdoors in nature—hiking, boating, or camping—is the best way to unwind (if they can separate themselves from their mobile devices). Travel, getting far away from our day-to-day obligations, is a favorite comforting activity. The important point is that creative self-expression is rewarding and comforting in and of itself.

And as we have been saying, family is a major source of comfort. The irreplaceable relationship with a sister, a cousin, or a parent is a place where we can feel completely understood. The experience of feeling understood is quintessentially comforting. A friend who has known us since childhood is a treasure who grows in significance as the years go by. But we can make new friends all our lives, and some can be as comforting as family. We can form a lunchtime group to learn a new language. We can join, or start, a book club on a favorite theme.

We should remember that much comfort comes from treating our body as if it were our own child. Your body depends on you to feed it when it is hungry, put it to bed when it is tired, and take care of it when it is sick. Who else is going to do that? This is *how* we learn to be a good parent to ourselves. *When we do that, the body can relax at long last and rest.*

I would be negligent if I didn't point out that pets are wonderful friends and a rich source of comfort. Most of us have had at least one pet who was so precious to us that we remember him or her with a combination of pain and gratitude. That wonderful dog or cat or horse is all but irreplaceable. Pets are truly members of the family. If this is the way you feel, the rescue foundations need your help—and resources. A few hours a week can make a difference in their lives and yours. You may end up with a new pet—or two.

The most comforting experience is that of touch. Touch is a basic foundation of our existence. The infant feels the mother before he sees her, and throughout our lives, touch is an important source of solace. Caring touch can lower the heart rate all by itself, possibly because touch releases endorphins, our pleasure molecules (Pert 2003). Because touch is so profoundly relaxing, massage should be administered only by someone you trust. I recommend massage therapy and yoga for persons who have experienced early deprivation of nurturing and holding. They help connect people to those needs and are helpful adjuncts to conventional therapy that uses words and concepts. Mindfulness (Hofmann 2010) and meditation relieve anxiety and lift depression as well, but they do not supply touch. Comforting others with hugs and kisses can comfort us as well. A moving report on Alzheimer's patients noted that their agitation could be calmed by cuddling a doll (Abrahms 2012).

Reading and learning are comforting and stimulating at the same time. The pursuit of a topic of interest can engage us intellectually throughout our lives. We can collect the works of a favorite writer or concentrate on books about cooking and serving special types of food. We can follow the development of a certain invention—cars, recreational fishing boats, computers. Taking courses with other people is a perennial treat although online courses do not give us the human connections we need.

Food retains its early capacity to comfort. Food—as separate from the mother's body—becomes a transitional object for all of us. Food is calming and comforting. A major reason for this is that most of the body's serotonin (the gratification neurotransmitter) is in the digestive system (Weil 2012). The danger is that, in this tense world, our need for calming and gratification is extraordinary, and food is regularly recruited as a cheap, effective antidepressant (especially sugary and fatty "foods"). But we should never forget the warm gratification that comes from eating wholesome "slow" food. Gathering, preparing, and cooking food is an artistic—even a sacred—endeavor. In many if not most traditions, a prayer or blessing is said before a meal, reflecting the gratitude we feel for the sustenance provided. The fellowship we share in dining together is part of that comfort. Those we share food with are special; eating together signifies trust and a unique bond. The whole experience of food, fellowship, aromas, and laughter can center us. It is perhaps the earliest and most enduring connection and a life-long comfort.

Gardening is unique in that it provides peace and calming, as well as an opportunity for great exercise of the body and the imagination. Clearing a piece of land and standing back to see where the sun rises and sets and imagining what trees and shrubs would be best for that place is both a challenge and a joy. The English method of continuous bloom requires research and hard work, but with diligence and good planning, flowers can be had from February to November (at least in the mid-Atlantic region). The early bloomers, snowdrops and cro-cuses, are a special treat.

To expand on a topic mentioned earlier, romantic love is perhaps the greatest and the most sought-after comfort in adult life—and may be the hardest to achieve because it derives from and is influenced by our earliest, most vulnerable period. Some psychologists and psychi-atrists see a connection between falling in love in adulthood and the capacity for transitional relatedness (attachment and bonding) in early life (Horton 1981; Winnicott 1986). Psychoanalysis teaches that the experience of comfort, support, and intense joy in early childhood is the foundation for all later healthy relationships and may be the prototype for falling in love. Love then gives us not only comfort and support but also access to our own vitality and talents. The excite-ment, the passionate possessiveness, and the comfort are continuous with the original connection to the treasured early parent with one dramatic difference—the sexual response. And as long as it is not exploitative, sex continues to be a source of comfort and gratification throughout adult life.

Finally, sleep is a major source of comfort. Physical and emotional exhaustion, difficulty with a particular decision, and sometimes disillusionment can be helped by deep and restful sleep. Chronic sleep deprivation is a known physical and psychological stressor that can affect our mood, energy, time perception, metabolism, and even our insulin response (Knutson 2012). An obvious source of sleep-disturbing stress is the overstimulation we get from computers, tablets, and our ever-present cell phones. We may not realize that, with practice, these devices can be banished from our bedrooms. It is supremely worth the effort. Adequate sleep is essential and sanity-saving.

A balanced life needs both activities like work and play that require energy, *and* these experiences that *restore* our energy—art, music, dance, faith, food, travel, gardening, family, friends, reading, writing, sleep, touch, love, and sex. And sometimes just peace and quiet. Breathing deeply and consciously. A walk in the woods. Listening to the rain. A hot cup of tea. Take comfort.

REFERENCES

Abrahms, S. (2012, July–August). "A Comfort and Joy Approach." *AARP. ORG/Bulletin*, 14.

Allport, G. (1968). *The Person in Psychology.* Boston: Beacon Press.

Bailey, M. T., Lubach, G. R., & Coe, C. O. (2004). "Prenatal Stress Alters Bacterial Colonization of the Gut in Infant Monkeys." *Journal of Pediatric Gastroenterology and Nutrition* 38(4): 414–21.

Barnett, W. S. (2011). "Effectiveness of Early Educational Intervention." *Science*, 333(6045), 975–978. doi:10.1126/science.1204534.

Baylin, J. & Hughs, D. (2012). "Brain-Based Parenting: What Neuroscience Is Teaching Us about Connecting with Our Kids." *Psychotherapy Networker* 36(1): 38–43, 56–57.

Biglan, A., Flay, B. R., Embry, D. D., et al. (2012). "The Critical Role of Nurturing Environments for Promoting Human Well-Being." *American Psychologist* 67(4): 257–271.

Brandell, J. & Ringel, S. (2007). *Attachment Theory and Dynamic Practice.* New York: Columbia University Press.

Celani, D. P. (2010). *Fairbairn's Object Relations Theory in the Clinical Setting.* New York: Columbia University Press.

Fairbairn, W. R. D. (1952). *Psychoanalytic Studies of the Personality.* London: Routledge and Kegan Paul.

Ferentz, L. (2012). *Treating Self-Destructive Behaviors in Trauma Survivors: A Clinician's Guide*. New York: Routledge.

Fisher, P. A. & Gunnar, M. R. (2010). "Early Life Stress as a Risk Factor for Disease in Adulthood." In E. Vermetten, R. Lanius & C. Pain (Eds.), *The Impact of Early Life Trauma on Health and Disease*, 133–141. Cambridge: Cambridge University Press.

Fox, N. A., Almas, A. N., Degnan, K. A., et al. (2011). "The Effects of Severe Psychosocial Deprivation and Foster Care Intervention on Cognitive Development at 8 Years of Age: Findings from the Bucharest Early Intervention Project." *Journal of Child Psychology and Psychiatry* 52(9): 919–928.

Heckman, J. J. (2013, September 15). "Lifelines for Poor Children." *New York Times Sunday Review*, SR5.

Hofmann, S. (2010). "The Effect of Mindfulness-Based Therapy on Anxiety and Depression: A Meta-Analytic View." *Journal of Consulting and Clinical Psychology* 78(2): 169–183.

Horton, P. C. (1981). *Solace: The Missing Dimension in Psychiatry*. Chicago: University of Chicago Press.

James, W. (1890). *Principles of Psychology*. New York: Henry Holt.

Juang, L. P., Qin, D. B. & Park, I. J. K. (Eds.). (2013). "Tiger Parenting, Asian-heritage Families and Child/Adolescent Well-Being." *Asian American Journal of Psychology*, 4(1).

Karen, R. (1998). *Becoming Attached: First Relationships and How They Shape Our Capacity to Love*. Oxford: Oxford University Press.

Knutson, K. (2012). "Does Inadequate Sleep Play a Role in Vulnerability to Obesity?" *Americam Journal of Human Biology* 24(3): 361–371.

Kristof, N. (2012, October 21). "Cuddle Your Kid!" *New York Times Sunday Review*, SR 11.

Leeb, R. T. R., & Gillian, F. (2004). "Here's Looking at You, Kid! A Longitudinal Study of Perceived Gender Differences in Mutual Gaze Behavior in Young Infants." *Sex Roles* 50(1–2): 1–5.

Lewis, S. J., Zuccolo, L., Smith, G. D., et al. (2012). "Fetal Alcohol Exposure and IQ at Age 8: Evidence from a Population-Based Birth-Cohort Study." *PLOS One November 14*. doi:10.1371/journal.pone.004907

Meaney, M. J. (2001). "Maternal Care, Gene Expression and the Transmission of Individual Differences in Stress Reactivity across Generations." *Annual Review of Neuroscience*, 24, 1161–1192.

Miller, A. (1981). *Prisoners of Childhood: The Drama of the Gifted Child and the Search for the True Self*. New York: Basic Books.

Nechvatal, J. M. & Lyons, D. M. (2013). "Coping Changes the Brain." *Frontiers in Behavioral Neuroscience*, 7, 13. doi:10.3389/fnbeh.2013.00013

Nelson, F. & Mann, T. (2012). "Opportunities in Public Policy to Support Infant and Early Childhood Mental Health: The Role of Psychologists and Policy Makers." *American Psychologist*, 66(2): 129–139.

Newton, R. P. (2008). *The Attachment Connection: Parenting a Secure and Confident Child Using the Science of Attachment Theory.* Oakland, CA: New Harbinger Publications.

Osofsky, J. D. & Lieberman, A. F. (2011). "A Call for Integrating a Mental Health Perspective into Systems of Care for Abused and Neglected Infants and Young Children." *American Psychologist* 66(2): 120–128.

Pert, C. B. (2003). *Molecules of Emotion.* New York: Scribner.

Shulevitz, J. (2012, September 9). "Why Fathers Really Matter." *New York Times Sunday Review, SR* 1, 6–7.

Smoller, J. (2012). *The Other Side of Normal: How Biology Is Providing the Clues to Unlock the Secrets of Normal and Abnormal Behavior.* New York: William Morrow.

Southwick, S. M. & Charney, D. S. (2013, July–August). "Ready for Anything." *Scientific American Mind* 24(3): 32–41. doi:10.1038/scientificameri canmind0713-32

Spitz, R. (1965). *The First Year of Life: A Psychoanalytic Study of Normal and Deviant Development of Object Relations.* New York: International Universities Press.

Taffel, R. (2012, January–February). "The Decline and Fall of Parental Authority and What Therapists Can Do about It." *Psychotherapy Networker* 36(1): 22–54.

Tannen, D. (1990). *You Just Don't Understand: Women and Men in Conversation.* New York: William Morrow.

Tronick, E. & Beeghly, M. (2011). "Infants' Meaning-Making and the Development of Mental Health Problems." *American Psychologist* 66(2): 107–119.

Von Glahn, J. (2012, May–June). "In Praise of Therapeutic Crying: Therapy's Best Kept Secret." *Psychotherapy Networker* 36(3): 48–49.

Weekes, C. (1990). *Hope and Help for Your Nerves.* New York: Signet.

Weil, A. (2012, January–February). "Psychotherapy at the Crossroads: A New Vision of Integrative Health." *Psychotherapy Networker* 36(1): 45–50.

Weir, K. (2011, July)." Golden Rule Redux." *Monitor on Psychology* 42(7): 42–45.

Weir, K. (2012, February). "The Roots of Mental Illness: How Much of Mental Illness Can the Biology of the Brain Explain." *Monitor on Psychology* 43(2): 31–33.

Winerman, L. (2013, June). "Breaking Free from Addiction." *Monitor on Psychology* 44(6): 30–33.

Winnicott, D. W. (1953). "Transitional Objects and Transitional Phenomena." *International Journal of Psycho-analysis* 34, 89–97.

Winnicott, D. W. (1971a). *Playing and Reality.* London: Tavistock Publications.

Winnicott, D. W. (1971b). *Therapeutic Consultations in Child Psychiatry.* New York: Basic Books.

Winnicott, D. W. (1986). "The Mother's Contribution to Society." In Winnicott, C., Shepherd, R. & Davis, M. (Eds.), *Home Is Where We Start From: Essays by a Psychoanalyst.* New York: W. W. Norton.

Wurmser, L. (1993). *The Riddle of Masochism.* New York: Springer.

Chapter 6

Love and Sex
The Eternal Knot

My hands
open the curtains of your being
clothe you in a further nudity
uncover the bodies of your body
My hands
invent another body for your body

—Octavio Paz, *Touch*

Among the features of healthy functioning, as well as reasons for seeking therapy, love figures prominently. New love, old love, lost love, love you can't live without, love you wish you could get rid of. How can you stop feeling love, how can you find it? Why does it motivate us the way it does? Can it be saved?

When we love someone, we invest that person with many kinds of meaning—a process psychoanalysts call *cathexis*. These meanings come from our own history, and some of them may not be conscious at all. There is just "something" about this new person that intrigues us, something we feel deep in our being—a feeling not always sexual, although it can be enhanced by sex. It can also transcend sex, creating a connection both new and old, at times beyond our wildest dreams.

We feel very vulnerable in love; we are baring our heart and soul to another person. This is tolerable only because the other person is vulnerable, too. In love, we become profoundly influenced by the loved one, often making decisions more in keeping with his or her experience and expectations than our own. There is also a wish to emulate that person, to become like him or her, and to share more and more experiences, such that two lives can merge.

That uniqueness may be the most sustaining part of a loving relationship. We *overvalue* the loved one. There is just no other person like this one, something felt rather than understood. It is something undeniable that we cannot quite specify, but it creates a "centeredness" and a continuity that can last a lifetime. It feels reverential, even a bit unreal. We say, "I feel as if I have known this person all my life." Seemingly out of nowhere, we feel a profound trust, a rightness. Indeed, it is often the betrayal of that trust that brings people into therapy.

It is crucial to point out that a relationship such as I describe above has a good prognosis in therapy. Let me underscore its characteristics:

- Uniqueness of the partner
- Profound trust on both sides
- Feeling deeply loved, even overvalued, by the partner
- A wish to emulate or become like the partner
- Vulnerability or openness (Only those who are willing to be vulnerable can truly love.)

This type of loving relationship has an importance and value to the two people that is greater than any problem they may encounter. When a relationship or marriage is this strong, all problems are *external* to the couple. Conversely, if a relationship lacks most of these essential attributes as outlined above and is, instead, based on neurotic needs—a need to control the other or to take out all one's frustrations on the other—it will not survive serious problems. Or the pair will stay together quite miserably.

COUPLES IN THERAPY

Very often, a couple may be "stuck" in their growth or progress—and happiness—because each needs something from the other that is not forthcoming. Each feels unheard, misunderstood, and most of all, dissatisfied. The longer each feels misunderstood and dissatisfied, the more each feels increasingly disillusioned and even hopeless that the other can change. Feelings about the fate of the marriage become increasingly bleak. Years can go by with both partners expressing more and more cynical views of their relationship to relatives and friends, often in weak hints about the spouse's negative behavior. How can a good marriage get to this point? Like an infected tooth, it gets worse and worse until even the most skilled dentist cannot save it.

Couples therapy is such a huge area that it is better to confine ourselves to the major questions that couples bring to therapy. Chief among these is the reason most people suffer, give up, and even contemplate divorce: disillusionment. "Disillusionment" refers to the realization that our spouse is not the person we thought he or she was when we married and that the dreams we had at the beginning may never be realized. All the enthusiasm, hope, and trust we felt in the beginning are gone; we feel betrayed, or at least abandoned. Trust must be rebuilt, and this requires realism and honesty, with both partners taking responsibility for their own behavior. We then work on developing a keen awareness of each partner's needs and on increasing the motivation to meet them. What does your partner need from you? What needs of yours are being ignored by your partner? The answers are not immediately clear, not all of them. People who have lived together for years often have not learned the important but unspoken wishes and dreams of their partner. They have not observed what makes their partner sad or hurt. Husbands and wives are often surprised by the specificity and poignancy of those needs.

This is equally true for older people. It is notable that older couples, people in their sixties, seventies, and beyond, do not come to therapy for long-standing issues. They did not grow up in an age when sexuality was discussed clinically, and normal sexuality described. They have come to terms with the limitations of their love life or given up entirely, which is sad. Many of them would be relieved to know how health-promoting sex and intimacy can be for them in their later years (Hillman 2012; Lindau et al. 2007). I have heard informal reports that some enlightened retirement communities are encouraging more intimacy among their residents. But it is not the norm. Older people themselves sometimes report that they are ashamed of feeling needy for touch and sex. It is worth restating that these are *normal* human needs, and our needs permeate all of life. This may be an educational issue for families and therapists alike.

Every couple who comes to therapy brings their unique "formula" for the truce they have created and an equally unique conundrum. The resolution of this can evade detection when it is hidden in the unspoken suffering of one partner and, because of shame, kept out of the therapy sessions.

Jamie and Lilli: A Secret inside a Conundrum

This couple came for marital therapy at the suggestion of Lilli's mother. This is a unique situation to begin with, but both husband and wife wanted to be there. Both were talkative and clearly comfortable with each other. They were relaxed while telling me their story. They comforted each other with a gentle touch before telling me any detail each thought the other might feel sensitive about revealing. The light in their eyes was showing me two people in love. What could possibly be wrong with this wonderful couple?

My training had taught me never to suggest what might be wrong. (Unethical therapists have been at least reprimanded for suggesting that a person may have suffered—for example, abuse as a child, and that the abuse is causing their problems in the present. *The data must come from the patient.*) I began with a very general question: What brings you to a clinical psychologist for the first time? Lilli looked a little embarrassed, but she was all right with my question. Jamie smiled at her, and turning to me, he said, "My wife doesn't like sex very much." I noted that and asked if there were any other problems we might also work on. Both answered in unison, no. Sex was the only problem. "Everything else is great!" Jamie added. Then Lilli found her voice, saying how much she appreciated Jamie's help with their little girl. And how he knew how to fix anything. "And we love each other's friends," she added with obvious pride.

I saw husband and wife in separate sessions for their histories, noting many developmental issues that sounded healthy. Both husband and wife had grown up with supportive families, and they were well matched intellectually. (I think couples do better in marriage when they share similar IQs.) They had met in college in a literature course. English literature was Lilli's major; Jamie was in economics. They loved reading a novel and discussing it together. This was notable: *words* were important to both of them. Also notable, their sex histories were normal. (See the Sex History section below.)

In therapy, both were talkative and answered my questions adequately. But something was missing: the frustration I would usually hear when one partner was pushing for an answer. If sex was the problem, why was I not hearing more complaints? Was there enough sex?

Yes. Was sex pleasurable for both? Yes. Was there adequate privacy? Yes. Was there orgasm for both of them? Silence. One of them was hiding something. Judging from her usual behavior, I began to feel that Lilli was *protecting* Jamie. That for her to be truthful would hurt Jamie, or take something away from him. What could that be? I waited and listened.

Then, during one session while Jamie was saying *what he appreciated about Lilli*, she suddenly said, "But you have to stop calling me that name!" Stunned, Jamie stared at her. Lilli started to cry, apologizing for what she had said. But it was out. I began to make the connection. "Jamie calls you a name that offends you?" I asked. A long painful pause, then, "Yes," she said, not looking at us. Jamie looked chastened but now aware. He was putting it together. It was a name, he said, that he had picked up from one of the novels. It was erotic, even crude. "And it makes you feel—" I asked Lilli. She looked at me with alarm and pain. "It makes me feel like a slut!" she said. But she then had a conflict about *telling* Jamie how she felt. Her conflict was this: Lilli knew that calling her that name during sex *increased* her husband's sexual enjoyment by enhancing his self-image. Now she was taking that away from him, and she felt terrible about it. How could she do that? What would it do to their love life? Lilli was inconsolable, dissolving in a flood of tears, and Jamie felt like a loser. They had come to therapy for clarity. Now it all felt like too much.

Over the next sessions, I found that the name Jamie was calling his wife during sex, which enhanced his orgasm, all but eliminated *her* sexual arousal. She would come to bed full of desire for Jamie, each time hoping that he would not call her that horrible name. But invariably, when he became very aroused, he would groan the name again. This almost always had a deadening effect on Lilli; mostly, it left her angry and feeling demeaned. Lilli knew what would happen if she revealed her dilemma. Words were very important to both of them. But Jamie understood. He was amazed that he had never made that connection before. He had thought the name was arousing for *both* of them, just as in that juicy novel. His insensitivity—and Lilli's reticence—were ruining their otherwise good relationship. They had much to learn, and relearn, about their arousal patterns. And some happy experimentation!

It is difficult to convey the essence—and the richness—of months of therapy in just a few pages. The crux of the problem was Lilli's fear of her revelation's effect on Jamie. This may sound romantic and naive on Lilli's part, but her professional areas of study were Jane Austin, the Brontë sisters, and others. In these novels, one person's belief or decision could profoundly alter another person's life forever. Jamie had learned to love literature from Lilli and was delighted that he could vicariously enjoy the escapades of a hero through discussion of these novels with Lilli. This vicarious enjoyment became part of Jamie's sexual fantasy—a whole new world for a man who spent his day with numbers and economic theory.

No, the problem had to be dealt with carefully and respectfully, and therapy gave them that opportunity. Perhaps other women make this kind of decision, to sacrifice their comfort for their partner's comfort—but the stakes are high. A decision like this may seem innocuous, made for convenience or comfort, but it ends up constraining the sexual enjoyment of both partners. Part of the problem was that Lilli did not yet understand herself well enough. Her mother had suggested therapy for them because Lilli had always been a very private child, saying little about her deepest feelings. Her mother understood that and would draw her out, gently suggesting that she felt sad or curious or angry. Lilli had become accustomed to other people "just knowing" how she felt. That presumption left her vulnerable with friends and in marriage. Jamie did not know how to encourage Lilli's honesty. Not being able to speak up on her own, Lilli may not be able to help her own little girl to express her feelings. One of the successes of Lillie's therapy was that she learned to be clearly assertive *without* hurting Jamie's feelings.

A SEX HISTORY SURVEY

In the context of doing research on the sexual development of eating-disordered girls and women, I developed a series of questions that speak to one's early experience. For couples, I refined and limited the questions that I felt were not relevant for most of them. For example, I do not ask about crossdressing if there is no evidence that that was ever an issue for either of them. All the questions may not be needed for any particular person. But I always ask about sexual abuse. These data are not forthcoming in therapy without specific inquiry. Nonetheless, I keep the survey lighthearted and respectful.

General Questions

Is sex easy or hard to talk about? What was your mother or father's attitude toward sex? Was sex a good part of life for them? Did you always agree with their views? How do you perceive your parents' relationship? Did you ever suspect an affair? How would you define abnormal or "kinky" sex? What do you think is normal sexually for men? For women? Have you ever taken a medication that interfered with sexual function? That enhanced it?

Gender Identity

Can you remember your first experience of being a girl? A boy? When and how were you certain you were a girl? A boy? Was it a happy thing to be a girl (boy) in your family, or did your parents want a child of the opposite sex? If yes, how did that affect your early years? If no, did you yourself ever feel it would have been better to be born the opposite sex? How would that affect your relationships? Do you feel that you are gay? Lesbian? If yes, is that a good part of your life or not?

Body Image

How do you feel about your body in general? Is your body a valued part of yourself? Do you resent its care and its needs? Do you feel you are attractive? When did you feel most attractive? Why? Who did you feel was more attractive than you? Why? What body part displeases you? Was that always true? What would you want to change? Any racial concerns? What body part pleases you the most? Was that always true? What aspect of your physical self do others react to? Does that please you? Are you satisfied with your height? Your weight? Have you ever been overweight? What did you do about that? How did you feel about pubertal body changes? Getting your period? Do you exercise? Play sports? What kinds of exercise/outdoor skills do you want to try?

Questions Pertaining to Arousal

How do you feel when you are nude? How do/did your parents react to your being sexual? Is sex a good part of your life? Is there a conflict between being sexual and the teachings of your faith? How do you feel about being touched sexually? Do you need alcohol or another drug in order to be sexual? How did you react to masturbation? Was it okay with you or a sin? Have you ever been aroused by someone of your own sex? How did/do you feel about that? Is orgasm easier to achieve alone or with a partner? What would you consider a good sexual experience? What kind of birth control do you use? What parts of sex do you like and what parts would you avoid? Do both of you have orgasms? Do you think that orgasm is harder for you to achieve than for others? Why would that be? How often do you and your partner have sex? Are both of you satisfied with this frequency? Do you and/or your partner look at pornographic sites? Is this part of your arousal alone or with each other? How about cyber-sex/Skype arrangements?

Describe Your Ideal Partner

Consider the physical, psychological/personality, creative, social, cultural, racial, political, ethical, progressive, ambition-related, marital/relational, and religious/spiritual aspects of your ideal. Describe your "dream partner."

Sexual Relationships

Do you remember the first person you were attracted to? Who was your first boyfriend/girlfriend? What was your parents' reaction? Who was your first "real" boyfriend/girlfriend? Was this also your first experience with sex? How was that experience for you? Have you had an unwanted pregnancy/pregnancies? Have you had any miscarriages? Abortions? How do you feel about this now? Have you had a homosexual experience? How did/do you feel about that? Do you have a "lost love"? How did you react to that loss? Does that experience still bother you? How does that affect your current relationship? Do you feel you are with/married to the "right" person? Why? How much of your "ideal partner" have you achieved? Have you or your partner ever cheated on each other? What have you done about this? How do you feel about this now?

Sexual Abuse

When you were a child, did anyone ever approach you sexually? (I ask about all possibilities—babysitter, neighbor, older child, friend's older brother or sister, sibling, father, uncle, stepbrother, cousin, grandfather, teacher, custodian, priest or minister, guardian, adoptive parents, mother's boyfriend, stranger. Although rarer, I also ask about mother, aunt, sister, grandmother, stepmother, and the parents of friends.) Had there been a long-term incest relationship with a member of your family? How do you feel about this? What could you do about this? Did anyone ever pay you to be sexual, or reward you in other ways? Did anyone ever threaten you or your younger sibling with harm if you did not agree to sex? Did anyone ever beat you and then engage in sex with you? Has anyone asked you to beat him/her and then engage in sex with them? Were you ever date-raped? Were you drinking at the time? Did you ever agree to sleep in a bed with someone because of unavailability of other sleeping arrangements then realize the person had had sex with you without your consent? Have you had experiences with sex that involved drugs? Have you ever been raped by a total stranger? Ever gang-raped? Any experience with group sex? How do you feel about these experiences now?

Questions about Disease/Dysfunction

Have you ever had an STD? Has your partner had an STD? What was/is being done about this? Have you or anyone in your family experienced premature ejaculation, anorgasmia (inability to achieve orgasm), or dyspareunia (painful sex)? Has any doctor talked about developmental or genetic abnormalities of your or your partner's genitals? What has been done about this?

Summing Up

Could we go over some of the findings? How many pregnancies have you had? Miscarriages? Abortions? Experiences with forced sex? How many sex partners have you had? Is there any aspect of your sexuality that we have not discussed? Any questions?

Therapy as a Course

When people finally come to therapy, they want to complain about years of mistreatment. While it is important for the therapist to understand how partners currently relate, the pattern will surely persist if attitudes and goals do not change. The single most important thing to establish is: *Do both partners want the relationship/marriage to succeed?* This is not guaranteed by the fact that they are now sitting in front of a therapist. People are often ambivalent when they start therapy, feeling unsure that anything can help. They often have put off seeking therapy for years, and the marriage has degraded during that time. This is profoundly true if an affair has occurred, but the feeling of abandonment can exist without an affair. People often do not know how to conceptualize their problem and slowly give up on trying. Therapy reverses this. The reestablishment of attention to each partner's needs is a major goal of marital therapy.

After I have heard about the central conflicts, I work with each partner alone to understand his or her history and the history of the relationship from each person's point of view. This is not the practice of all couples therapists. Some training programs insist that seeing the partners separately can, for example, set up an alliance with the one seen first and engender a bias on the therapist's part toward the other. Even if that is not true, the person seen second or, perhaps, less frequently, may start to believe such an alliance exists and feel disadvantaged in the treatment. This requirement can result in one partner being sent home if the other cannot make every session. I feel this is too high a price for troubled couples to pay. I see them separately at the beginning of therapy during history taking, and I ask about any "favoritism" they may feel. I work to eliminate any biases or disadvantages they express. While stressing that a therapist cannot work on half a marriage and that both partners need to attend each session, I will still see them separately if one is ill or away.

I often find that each partner is "living" a different marriage. That is, one partner's assumptions and beliefs about the marriage are quite different from the other's. Some psychologists refer to our set of beliefs about ourselves and our relationships as our "assumptive world"—all the beliefs we carry into our marriages. *Of course* weekends are spent like this, and *of course* this is the way children are raised. Taking separate histories reveals just how different the two individual's assumptive worlds can be.

The central diagnostic questions I ask couples are these:

1. Do you feel you are with the right person? The immediate response to this question orients the couple. If one feels he is with the right person, and the other is not sure, it changes the vectors in the therapy.
2. At what point did you feel out of touch with each other, not able to talk about problems in a respectful interchange? Most

couples identify such a point. Often it coincides with a move to a new place that one partner feels was a huge mistake. Or it happens after the birth of a child, when parents' energies are taxed to the limit. Much disillusionment is born of sheer fatigue.

Again, a deficit of caring and attention is found; attention, affection, and respect for each other—the way it was in the beginning. It must first be established that both partners want the therapy and the marriage. If one wants out of the marriage then therapy will only clarify their impasse.

However, sometimes the one who has given up is amazed to understand that change can indeed occur. Schedules are examined for the opportunity for partners to actually talk together. Therapy becomes the first instance of this new attention, an hour spent with a therapist committed to their progress. But a weekly date is agreed upon, preferably outside the home, when both are able to relax and make decisions about how to take the pressure off. This can be as simple as shutting off our mobile devices. It works! Or it can be as difficult as switching jobs or agreeing to spend less time with one's parents. If the relationship is worth it, the choice will be worth it.

3. What is the solution that each person sees to their problem? If a wife wants her husband to work less and spend more time with their children, that is a healthy and reasonable goal we can work on. If instead she wants him to work a second job so that she can buy more expensive clothes and shoes, that is unfair and must be confronted in therapy. If a man wants his partner to appreciate his interests—for example, woodworking, cars, playing guitar, or skiing, all those can be reasonable requests. If he wants his wife to *do nothing else but help him with his interests*, that is unfair. In both these cases, the unfair spouse is seeking to be treated in a special way and to dominate the family's time and resources.

   Marriages, like other partnerships, must be based on fairness. A husband and wife or live-in partners are coequal and co-powerful. She is not more important than he; he does not have more power than she. Understanding and accepting these principles is the basis of therapy.

4. What are the things or experiences both partners enjoyed in the beginning of their relationship? These could be the very

reason they met in the first place. Was it playing music with a group or listening to the same band? Were they in a language class together? Did they both ski or hike or go kayaking? Are they both interested in politics or have actually worked on a campaign? Did they both have Peace Corps experience or wish that they had? What do they love to do that they now feel there is no time for? There needs to be special time for each partner to talk about his or her goals, wishes, and frustrations, a time that does not necessarily include the children.

Having fun together engenders respect and trust in each other again. It is time well spent; it is mutually stimulating and is essential to keeping a healthy, vigorous sexual relationship. The link between happy shared experiences and sexual attraction was clear to both of them in the beginning. Therapy asks them to think about this again, to take the course.

Communication: The Problem or Not?

When couples become disillusioned, they often feel their problem is communication. But is it? They are probably using the same words they always used, but the partner is not responding in the same way. When they ask for attention or help, the partner ignores them or angrily protests. When they ask for sex—something that happened easily in the beginning—the partner refuses or starts a fight. It isn't a lack of communication but a change in attitudes, feelings, and behavior. Instead of seeing the other as a source of happiness and satisfaction, they have begun to see each other as a source of frustration. So they avoid each other more and more. And the frustration grows.

This situation becomes complicated when an unusual problem or a crisis occurs. Both partners become frightened and mobilize to work together. They pool their efforts and get through it. In the relief and joy they feel, they find themselves again in each other's arms, and for a time they feel they have their old relationship back. And they do! It happened because they were reliably there for each other: (1) they paid attention to what was needed; (2) they discussed it as equals, respectfully; (3) and they each did their part toward the same goal, which benefited them both. They can keep that feeling of closeness *if they keep the attention to one another*, trusting that the other is deserving of it.

In therapy, couples are asked to discuss their own and their partner's emotional needs. Each need—and wish—is discussed independently.

We must be specific and honest. What are the crunches for you when you need help? What can your spouse do to make you feel safe and loved? What does your spouse need from you? Is this need new or long-standing? What are the difficult times for him or her? How can you help? Do you want to help? Why not? Therapy requires that we discuss these issues again and again. Every little thing you might now think is unimportant is not. *We all interpret attention to our needs as evidence that we are loved.* A woman will protest, "My husband leaves dirty clothes all over the house. He doesn't care." A man will tell the therapist, "My wife never has supper ready on the nights she knows I have classes. She doesn't care." Again, if the relationship is worth it, the effort will be worth it. Is this relationship worth every effort you can put into it? If the answer is no, then Sigmund Freud could not help you. If the answer is yes, you can probably do it with the therapist you have.

Power Struggles: The Need to Win

When both members of a couple are competitive, each seeking the upper hand, the prognosis is not good. Power seeking is included here only because, although it is a pathological behavior, there are times—if the marriage is very important to them—that power seekers can express exhaustion and a wish for change. They are unaware of the secondary gains their marital pattern affords. When such a couple comes to therapy, the first four or five sessions are filled with mutual accusations. Having the therapist there seems to stimulate their memory to dredge up every insult on the part of their spouse over the span of their entire marriage. Their style is competitive bickering, and the reason they do not change is that *they absolutely love it.* They love presenting themselves as a victim of the other's abuse. They love dramatizing their spouse's failings. They love being able to yell at, interrupt, berate, and blame *someone who will not go away.* Yes, it is sadistic. The perverse satisfaction derived from this abuse is more important than the couple's stated wish to overcome it.

Their good moments are notable. They often report they enjoy sex, but it is fitful and brief, when both are exhausted. They report they very much want to sleep together in the same bed. And they feel close holding hands in church, as if the congregation seeing them holding hands wipes away all the bitterness in their relationship. And once in a while, when one of them has a serious problem—a parent is suddenly ill, or a son or daughter has an accident—this couple will pull together in a sincere, sensitive way. They will both report this in therapy as a "good week." We will celebrate it briefly, and then, often in the same session, they are "at it" again. We can see the compulsive nature of this behavior—the need is to dominate and to win. The need is also to humiliate the other, perhaps as they were humiliated in their childhood. Each partner refuses to learn or to change, all the while protesting that they long for relief. Each wants the therapist to side with him or her. There is no insight on either side, and each has a motive to resist developing it.

Any intervention the therapist offers is considered intellectually interesting or amusing. Neither is interested in taking any responsibility for his or her behavior, because each believes he or she is just reacting to the partner's insults. It is "one-upmanship" all the way. Often, each has such a fierce need to win that he or she can hardly hear what the therapist is saying. The therapist persists, saying that their anger and mistrust for each other is historical and likely displaced from some event or person in their respective pasts.

For example, if a woman's father or mother clearly favored a sibling all through her childhood, she would feel resentment, jealousy, and mistrust toward her parents that could not be expressed or resolved with them. Those feelings would remain with her, covered over with other interests and experiences. But when she marries, her husband inherits all the unresolved issues the woman had with her parents. He now is the person she can finally vent on; all the pain, anger, and feelings of abandonment she has been storing come out with a vengeance. She accuses her husband of not doing what she had asked that day and for deliberately frustrating her. He is made to pay for what her parents did to her, and since he can't compensate her for any of her assumed deprivations, her accusations are endless. The husband in this pair also has unresolved issues from his past that he brings into the marriage unchanged by time. He also does not realize that he uses his wife as the repository for all his historical anger. They rail at each other, actually relieved to have someone to scream at, and their marriage becomes an endless merry-go-round of mutual accusations.

Some people realize this on their own, and others learn it in therapy. But if neither of these happens, the marriage becomes the power struggle described above. Why is the prognosis so poor? *Because of the unwillingness to give up blaming*. Because one or both partners are unwilling to work with the therapist on the roots of the problem, experience their vulnerability, and begin to grieve for their losses. Each must be willing to stop blaming the other and honestly discuss his and her individual histories. Each one needs individual treatment as well, and sometimes they accept this. What really happened in their family of origin? How did they really feel? To explore all of that for two such people who are this defensive would take another book. The central problem is this: *Living in the past interferes with living in the present.* To the degree that a person believes this, therapy can begin. There is no substitute for doing the necessary thinking, discussing, and connecting. Each spouse must quiet down, accept individual responsibility, and look inside.

In an investigation of "perceived threat" and "perceived neglect," Keith Sanford and Kristin Wolfe (2013) report that the single most desired outcome of a marital conflict is for one's partner to accept a more equitable sharing of power and to admit culpability. No surprises here. We are born with a sense of fairness and justice that our well-being requires to be satisfied from babyhood on. The longing for fairness pervades song, poetry, literature, and drama and is the engine for social unrest worldwide. Being treated with fairness (one of the features of normal behavior we are considering) gives people hope in their marriages and relationships. It also makes us happier, supporting the notion that happiness is a correlate/outcome of emotional health.

This points to perhaps the most glaring limitation of the new "positive psychology": namely, that positive behaviors, like trust and forgiveness, function differently in healthy marriages than they do in disturbed ones. An attentive therapist will observe that forgiving a person who repeatedly hurts you simply gives him or her license to hurt you again. Conversely, forgiving someone who is usually good to you is largely unnecessary. Similarly, trusting someone who has shown himself to be trustworthy makes for ongoing happiness. But trusting someone who continually abuses you communicates your consent for continued abuse.

As psychological researchers James K. McNulty and Frank D. Fincham (2012) have shown, any "positive" interventions we make must consider the *context* in which they are employed:

> Four ostensibly positive processes—forgiveness, optimistic expectations, positive thoughts, and kindness—can either benefit or harm well-being depending on the context in which they operate. Although all

four processes predicted better relationship well-being among spouses in healthy marriages, they predicted worse relationship well-being in more troubled marriages. . . . Any movement to promote well-being may be most successful to the extent that it (a) examines the conditions under which the same traits and processes may promote versus threaten well-being, (b) examines both healthy and unhealthy people, (c) examines well-being over substantial periods of time, and (d) avoids labeling psychological traits and processes as positive or negative. (101)

Books about couples therapy often propose "rules" and recommendations. My worry is that people cannot simply *read* a rule and put it into practice. For example, the frequent recommendations to do nice things for one another or to celebrate each other's achievements often stop at the reading stage. The reason: they are so angry with one another. Years of hurt cannot be erased by one kind deed, however well intentioned. As stated before, the early sessions of therapy are filled with complaints of historical hurts and omissions; a shy man had to pace around the room in order to say how he felt. (One of my graduate school professors used to say, "The good feelings can't come in until the bad feelings are out.") A therapist's role is to support people while they say their truth, cautioning them to do this without shouting, profanity, or put-downs. When that is accomplished, the two know each other much better, and the books will then be interesting and useful. But it is cruel, if not impossible, to ask a very hurt man or woman to be kind to the person who hurt them.

Money: A Mask for Power Issues

One of the more traditional areas of contention, money, figures prominently in the complaints heard in marital therapy. Not the amounts of money (that is hardly a therapist's business), but categories of money—the way money is used and valued by the couple; the way it is talked about, spent, and saved. Money is indeed power, and in marriages especially, it can be used as a control or a support by both partners. Money is important for all of us, of course. One crucial indication of emotional health is that we be self-supporting as adults. If an adult is not self-supporting, and he or she is not disabled, retired, or elderly, there is usually a problem with maturation or mental health. But individual attitudes toward money are still complex and personal. It is a challenge to devise and commit to a spending and saving plan with even one other person. This is often the first area where candor and secrecy clash. It is discussed here because conflicts over money can result in one or both persons refusing sex or being so angry it prevents sexual arousal. (Anger is one of the enemies of sex, as discussed later.)

One of these clashes comes early in a relationship: gift giving. Therapists hear accusations like these: "I gave you this; you only gave me that," "You gave your sister a this, but I only got a that," "I'm not giving your parents this, because we only gave my parents that." It may be impossible to prevent gifts from being manipulative, and the manipulation often comes from the amount of money a gift represents.

A successful if imperfect plan that works well for couples in therapy features three categories of money: hers, his, and theirs. This plan stimulates vigorous discussion from the beginning and even humor—a good sign. The "our money" category carries the couple's budget for food, housing, transportation, utilities, phones, electronics, and some clothing. This category is contributed to by each partner in proportion to the amount each person earns. The same ratio also helps determine the amount each of them contributes to savings. This discussion, as we might expect, brings out their comparative reactions to risk and even their notions about aging. It definitely brings out their issues about control.

If a couple's financial picture is so complex that they need a financial planner, that decision is made at this point. But if both feel empowered by the "our money" discussion, we go on to the even more complex "her" and "his" money. Ideally, these are categories for which there need be no accounting. We all need a stash of money we can use as we wish for personal needs and wishes that are often creative, like a yoga class or a pair of boots. I say "creative" because such purchases often give us a boost in mood. Sometimes, instead, the "his" and "her" money discussion releases a burst of contention, new to the couple's therapy. Allegations of selfishness emerge; a spouse who feels cheated in another area of the marriage may find it easier to complain about his or her spouse's use of money, which can move their therapy to a new level. New feelings of victimization are expressed in answer to the therapist's validations that money can be the arena where other power struggles are staged. Again, money is power and power must be used judiciously.

SPECIFIC SEXUAL ISSUES IN THERAPY

Complaints about sex can dominate the therapy hour; it is possibly the single most important reason for a couple to seek therapy. Limiting our discussion to their most frequent concerns, here are five:

1. Affairs
2. Disparity in sexual appetite
3. Lack of sexual arousal
4. Jealousy
5. Cybersex

Before we begin discussing these five issues, I must mention another important one, that of sexual abuse. The inability to form and sustain an intimate relationship is often rooted in one of the partner's prolonged sexual abuse. This is a major area of research and treatment, and I mention it here only to refer the reader to specific texts on the subject. Many of these books have actually been written by victims of sexual abuse. They vary widely in tone and quality, but I feel confident referring the reader to two valuable sources: Christine Courtois (1988) and Lisa Ferentz (2012).

In addition, it may not be widely known that forced sex in marriage is legally considered rape in the United States (Russell 1990). This may be disputed by some ethnic groups who believe that a wife is property and/or that she has a duty to provide sex on demand. But the world is slowly changing. In the 1980s, American women who alleged rape were not taken seriously (Brownmiller 1993; Russell 1990). Now the evening news often has stories about women in third-world countries demonstrating about the unacceptability of rape, even when they have few other powers in their lives. The social changes that have occurred (Collins 2009) and those which still need to happen (Kristof & WuDunn 2010; Takei 2012) constitute an encouraging and expanding literature.

Affairs

Although this may be changing, the finding is that men have more affairs than women do (Glass & Staeheli 2003). Even so, all couples have a unique history, and some affairs seem barely intended, as in the couple described here.

Ginny and Dan: Flirting with Danger.

Ginny came to therapy alone, saying her husband wanted her to be comfortable with the therapist first. He said he was willing to come to therapy at a later point. This is not an unusual situation, but they both need to hear what is said and to take responsibility for their behavior. By Ginny's account, she and Dan had all the hallmarks of a good relationship: trust, overvaluation of the partner, and many other attributes I outlined previously. They were both 43 at the time they sought therapy. They had fallen in love in college and had lived together ever since. Ginny had worked in the same company Dan worked for, but she left to be a full-time mother to their three children. They had made this decision together, accepting the loss of her income as a worthwhile trade-off. At the time, Ginny had teased Dan that she would someday write a wicked novel, make lots of money, and make it all up to him.

Two years ago, at one of the many outings the company provided for their employees, a 28-year-old woman walked up to Dan and said—just as she had learned on TV—"I'm attracted to you." Dan laughed and started talking to her about her job with their company. The young woman persisted. Others had pointed out to her that Dan was married, but she said she didn't care. She self-centeredly pursued him. She discovered where Dan had lunch and with whom. She would join them although she had not been invited. The situation progressed to lunch alone, just the two of them, with the woman professing her strong attraction to him. Dan was very flattered and went along with the lunches but nothing more. Then one night, he found her waiting by his car, crying. He allowed her into his car, and they kissed. It progressed until there was orgasm for both of them, but not intercourse. At this point, Dan became sickened by his own behavior. He went home and told the whole story to Ginny. They sat up for hours, stunned, not certain what to do.

Ginny felt angry, betrayed, and frightened. Dan was ashamed and apologetic. But he felt a strong need to remind Ginny that, when they were first talking about becoming engaged, she had had an admirer that she did not discourage. It caused many arguments, with Ginny then claiming there was no harm in their relationship. This was exactly the feeling Dan was having about his new situation. A part of him wanted to keep the attention and affection of the younger woman and somehow have Ginny accept that. Ginny insisted tearfully that things were different now; he was a father. Did he want his children to find out? And what if their parents knew? At this point, both of them felt their love was mortally wounded.

The next day, Ginny got the children off to school and then went to a friend's house. Together they researched and found my name as a marital therapist. In therapy, Ginny said her greatest pain was the sense of betrayal. She told me they had had a similar crisis early on, when Ginny's boss was asking her out. Dan had been so jealous. They had just moved in together, and Dan was worried he could lose her. Ginny easily reassured him that nothing could touch their love. She talked about the "wonderful certainty" she always felt about Dan. They were so sure they were right for each other. What had happened to them?

When Dan joined his wife in therapy, he was understandably subdued. He admitted everything. He was baffled by his reaction to the young woman. Dan was a person who considered himself a very ordinary guy. His questions to me concerned how he could be so "swept away" by this younger woman who was "not gorgeous" but seriously affected his self-image. She had made him feel "fabulous—almost like a different person," he said. I explained that we can be vulnerable to this exaggerated sense of our own importance, this overvaluation. It is normal in love. It is a delicious expansion of our self-image, just the way we feel in return about the person we love. This was Dan's current predicament.

Here it was, offered to him by this new enticing woman. He admitted that his feelings for the younger woman were pushing away his other relationships with his wife and children. I outlined for him the vulnerability he had at this stage of his life. It was so tempting, although he had not gone looking for it. But it was narcissistic and had to be recognized as such—a weakness for that inflated sense of self that others' attention gives us. When it comes from someone who threatens our valued marriage or relationship, it has to be refused—just as he had done in the beginning when the young woman first approached him. The world is full of attractive people, I told him. We will always be attracted to others, and they to us. It is only the realization and appreciation of what we have, and what we could lose, that steadies us and supports our resolve to refuse the new attraction. I put to him the question I ask all couples in a similar quandary: "What do you really, really want?"

Dan understood that. Unlike many people who cannot admit an affair until they are caught, Dan had felt shame, a very helpful emotion and came home to confess. His remorse was growing for Ginny, who was painfully disillusioned. She had cried for hours. How could she ever believe him again? Did she still live in his world? She was feeling more and more out of step with the stylish crowd she used to spend her time with, the world that Dan still lived in. Her family and Dan had been her world, but now that was threatened. They both admitted that for the past few years, sex had not been as frequent. Both were tired and just needed sleep. With a teenager and two preteens, they were rarely alone. *No attention to one another. No care and feeding of this otherwise good relationship.*

In therapy, we discussed a plan. Ginny and Dan would focus on rebuilding trust by redefining their relationship. The affair was to be discussed openly, thoroughly, with Ginny voicing her hurt and pain as much as she needed. Dan would tell and retell his role in it, until both understood how this had happened. He began to understand the younger woman's behavior toward him as narcissistic and frankly abnormal, defined here as a behavior that hurts oneself and/or someone else. She had *disregarded* his first refusal and the fact that she knew Dan was married. Only what she wanted mattered to her. His acceptance of her attention had been unwise and then immoral. He clearly liked the attention, and we talked about how that could happen to women—to Ginny—too. *Flirting is not innocuous.*

Their relationship now became their priority as it had been in college. They decided on a night out, once a week. Ginny was trim and pretty but needed some new clothes. Both joined the local Y and attended classes together. Their teenager would take more responsibility for his life. The two younger children would do more around the house. Just because Mom did not have an outside job did not mean she should do everything for everyone. Most significantly, Dan left his position and took another within the same company that had a shorter commute. He was able to get home for lunch several days a week, and he and Ginny could have something they used to enjoy immensely—love in the afternoon.

This couple's issues show us that one of the most important roles for therapists is saving marriages and preserving families. Although much of our training concerns the identification of pathological patterns in individuals, it is just as crucial to help couples whose marriages are being systematically damaged by another person, as in Ginny and Dan's case—or just overwork and/or overstimulation by electronic devices. Whatever psychologists can do to help families emerge from oppressive conditions, it is laudable and a boon to society (Pipher 1996). Happy, healthy couples grow happy, healthy children.

Rebuilding Trust

People often ask, "How do you rebuild trust?" They may have suffered a painful crisis or breakup because of an affair or even a threatened affair. They begin couples therapy only to find that their problems are more complicated than they ever knew. If they treat therapy as a course wherein each week they learn more about their interactions and their effects on each other—and neither one runs out the door—they will grow together. If their therapist is a caring and wise teacher, the answer becomes clear: *You rebuild trust by being trustworthy.* Each of you takes on the responsibility and the commitment to *reform your own behavior*, not waiting for your partner to do it first. It begins with you. The commitment sounds like this: "I will be trustworthy, not playing Tit for Tat with my partner. I will be unequivocally trustworthy because that is the way I want to be anyway. And now that we have had this crisis, it is all the more important that, no matter what, *I shall be trustworthy.*"

When each partner can make this personal commitment, independently, the couple has a good prognosis. When only one partner can make this commitment, they are no longer a couple.

WHAT "CAUSES" CHEATING?

Dan was able to stop himself—after the affair had gone too far—and remorsefully went home to tell Ginny. Many affairs come to light this way. These are the couples who realize they are in trouble and call a therapist. But people who want to cheat and get away with it—or who believe the rules don't apply to them as they do to others (one of the diagnostic criteria for narcissistic personality disorder)—don't come in for therapy. If they do, it is under duress. A spouse has given the ultimatum: "We go to therapy, or I'm leaving."

The motive to cheat has many derivations—impulsivity or the result of an attachment disorder. Cheating can be part of a generalized immaturity in a person's personality. It starts early. People who cheat in high school have been shown to be more likely to cheat on a spouse and to lie to employers. Moreover, cheaters did not get better grades on exams (Davis, Drinan & Gallant 2009). If the cheating was considered by students a reaction to unfair teachers, there was more cheating (Anderman & Murdock 2006). At least for students, cheating seems curable. When they had to read and sign an honor code *before* taking an exam, it eliminated cheating (Shu, Francesca & Bazerman 2011). Holding people accountable builds character and "normal" personality.

Cheating by Decree: A Couple Caught in Grief

Too often, people who cheat do not interpret their behavior as a betrayal of their marriage or committed relationship. A middle-aged husband blithely said of his sneaky romantic involvement, "You [the therapist] are making such a big deal out of this. It's not as if we had intercourse. All we had was a little oral sex." His wife, who was present in the session, sat on a chair as far from him as my office arrangement would permit. Her husband's bombast routinely upset her. For reasons of his own, however, this husband did not want to lose their marriage. When I asked him why he agreed to come for therapy, he softened and said, "Oh, she [his wife] gets so teary. She'll cry for hours. I hate to see her like this." When asked what he himself wanted, he said that he didn't think they needed therapy because they always made up.

This couple had a tragic history. Their older child, a son, had been killed in a car accident at age 17. He had been driving with several of his friends, all of whom had survived. This is a grief that couples often cannot transcend. The sadness pervading the whole house had driven their daughter to a relative's house and then to a distant college.

Still grieving, this couple seemed to flounder in the session, answering my questions with monosyllables. Neither seemed to have the will to improve their relationship, but both agreed they were suffering. Her husband's affairs had drained this woman of the strength to continue working. She had had a fairly interesting job as an administrator, but she had no close friends. I recommended group therapy for her, a paradigm that helps people develop inner resources and self-expression. Her husband was far less amenable. He saw his pattern of seeking out willing women and engaging in "a little oral sex" as almost harmless and something he needed—a behavior that had started after their son's death. His dilemma was that he and his wife were deeply bonded, affectionate and sexual together—a sanctuary he claimed to value.

But they left therapy, essentially because they could not bear an analysis of their relational pattern. They were both suffering and needy of one another, but their solution was to do nothing. They were not going to separate, and the husband would continue to seek other women, using sex as a diversion. Periodically, his wife would find out, confront him and cry for hours, doubtless for her lost son as well as her lost self-respect. Then they would make up and both would feel reassured.

There are many marriages like this, each accepting the philandering of the partner, and sometimes of both, as the condition of their "truce." Neither is happy nor particularly unhappy. But it is not normal, because it is a deliberate agreement to go on hurting or being hurt. It is a numbed resignation, a giving in to the fear of being alone. It is an abandonment of hope and of responsibility—and ultimately an abandonment of self.

Aiden and Cece: Cheating with Flair

Aiden came to therapy alone, saying that his girlfriend was shy. "She'll be here, practically hiding behind me," he said. He explained that they were in love and that her effusive, "bubbly" personality lifted him out of his isolation. He was an IT professional, spending days at a time unraveling computer glitches that lesser people would sensibly avoid. He was good at it, repeatedly offered other positions. I asked where his girlfriend worked. He explained that Cece was eight years younger than he and that she had worked at several jobs, none of them for very long. She would spend days visiting her parents or friends, but most of the time she and Aiden were together, giving him, he said, "a much-needed reprieve from numbers." They had been together for almost a year.

A month ago, he said—(he became upset and checked himself)—he was told by a friend, someone he trusted, that Cece had been seen with another man, kissing and dancing at a club. She loved to dance, and Aiden didn't do much of that. He tried to dismiss the report. I asked if he and Cece were actually living together. "Sort of. Most of her things are at her parents' house, but they are two hours away. When we're together, it's just awesome. We laugh ... We stay in bed all day ..." His voice caught. He stopped himself again. A long pause.

Aiden looked up, newly confident. "I can't lose her. I know I love her more than any other girl. I know we are good together. We never fight. Her smile pulls me out of my wooden head. She's always happy—like a nymph, an angel." He laughed. "You see, I never talk like this about anyone. I'm determined not to lose her." I asked how Cece felt. He took a deep breath and sighed audibly. "That's just it. I know she loves me. She's so attentive to me and passionate. She adores sex. She would tell everyone how happy we are."

"But now you have doubts," I said. "You called for an appointment. What were you feeling when you called?"

"I was worrying. I was scared. I know I need therapy to understand what is happening."

And there at the next session was Cece. Just as Aiden had described, this tiny girl, looking younger than 25, slid tightly by his side, bringing his arm around her face so that I saw only her eyes. Charming and impish, she had a little-girl voice to go with the picture, protesting with a smile that she was embarrassed to be here. I asked her why she thought Aiden had asked her to come. Suddenly animated, she said she had no idea. Aiden nudged her. "You know—what Hilary [their mutual friend] said."

Cece's face darkened, but still smiling, she said, "Aiden doesn't like it when I go dancing with my friends." She squirmed away from him. "I'm a very good dancer, everybody says. I even took lessons. My dad paid for my lessons. I'm really good." Clearly Cece was not connecting to Aiden's concern. Worried that she may not come back to treatment, I moved beyond my cautious training and asked the hard questions. Their friend Hilary had said that Cece had gone home with the man she was dancing with, I said. Did that happen? How does she think Aiden feels about that? "No, Baby, no!" she said to Aiden. "No, I didn't go home with him." She stroked his face and moved onto his lap. With an embarrassed grin, Aiden put her back on the couch next to him.

"What do you think, Aiden?" I asked. "Of course that is what I want to believe. No. I do believe it," he said. Turning to Cece, he was emphatic. "I believe you. We'll talk about it. I don't want you to think I don't trust you." Cece was crying, apparently feeling cornered and uncomfortable with the questioning of her behavior—any questioning. She looked at me wanly: "People usually like me."

To relieve the pressure both of them were feeling, I asked how they had met. The mood in the room lightened. Aiden laughed and said he had been dragged to a bar by some friends after a particularly grueling day installing new programs. He had been exhausted and quiet, but at one point he looked up and saw some girls who had approached their table. Cece was chatting animatedly with one of his friends, but then she noticed Aiden and turned her attention to him. They had talked all night and made a date for the next evening. She and Aiden had been together since then. He could not imagine life without her.

But by the next week, Cece was gone. Aiden had called everyone but received no real help. Her parents said she was probably visiting friends. "She does that, you know," Aiden was told. "She'll be back." Aiden sat in the therapy session looking desolate. He was certain that his insistence on therapy had scared her away.

"When you question her behavior, does she do this?" I asked. "Or does she stay with you and talk it over?" "I never thought of it before," he said.

"I never questioned her behavior, never had to. I *have* watched her dance with other guys. It never bothered me."

Aiden was thoughtful, struggling with the evidence. But there was a part of him that would not accept the import of that evidence (the psychological defense called *resistance*). And this was his assessment: "She'll be back. You'll see, Doctor. She'll be back."

At the time, Aiden was 33. His father had been killed in a military accident when Aiden was an infant. His mother had remarried, and he talked about his two younger sisters as the ones who brought happiness into their lives again. He laughed, calling his little sisters "my mother's anti-depressant." I pointed out that little girls had been his and his mother's reprieve from emptiness and grief. And now this little girl—Cece—similarly lifted him out of the narrow robotic world he lived in. This was an important link.

At this, Aiden was intrigued but quiet. After a long pause, he said, "It's a poetic notion . . . I guess I like it . . . I do feel that Cece lifts me up. But she does that for everybody. That's just her. But it fits— because the way I feel about her is unreasonable. It's illogical." He seemed mildly conflicted. I asked him to think about what he is calling "irrational feelings" between now and the next session. It was a good "homework question." But at the next session, Aiden came in visibly distraught. "She's with the new guy," he said. Some friends had seen them in the supermarket, buying food, giggling, and kissing. Aiden's skill at resisting the evidence was fraying. "I was so wrong . . . and . . . I guess you were right to question her intentions."

Therapy is full of poignant moments. "Human problems are largely relational," writes Irvin Yalom (2009), psychiatrist and eminent teacher of psychotherapy. "An individual's interpersonal problems will ultimately be manifested in the here-and-now of the therapy encounter" (48). Aiden's "here-and-now" was painful but demonstrated the skills that separate those who will put up with the stress of therapy and those who run away. He had all the essential attributes that can result in significant personality growth. He was bright, probably a superior IQ, and he was sophisticated about therapy. He considered psychotherapy one of many available professions that one sought out for particular problems, on the same par with dentistry and financial planning. It was easy and natural for him to call a therapist. And lastly, he was willing, even eager, to hear what a professional would say about his own thinking. Aiden came in wanting to know *his* contribution to the problem. He just did not know that this knowledge would be heartbreaking.

Nonetheless, we were both surprised when, in a few weeks, Cece was back. They came into the session beaming like happy teenagers, arms wrapped around each other. Aiden was clearly euphoric. "I just knew she would come back, and here she is!" All the doubts that had tormented him in the past weeks evaporated. There was just now, this moment, and Cece. Sitting in her usual place behind his arm, she peered out, smiling. "I wanted *Aiden*," she said simply. "Aiden is 'it' for me. And you are," she said, turning to face him. Aiden could smile again, looking exhausted but happy. The whole episode had taken a toll on him, while Cece looked as bright as ever. Suffering was not for her.

At this point, I was quietly worrying that this pernicious pattern of hers was all too clear but that Aiden was recovering all his fancy rationalizations, resistances, and denial. It would take an arsenal of defenses to keep this out of his awareness, I thought. He looked so relieved. She was saying all the "right" words. For a month of sessions, Aiden brought news of meals happily cooked together, trips to the beach, and bliss in bed. And then she was gone again—this time with a man they both knew at the famous bar where they had met. The news, of course, did not come from Cece. Her new boyfriend was advertising the fact that he was leaving his position at the bar because Cece and he were moving south.

Again Aiden sat before me, conflicted and struggling. He dutifully reported what he had heard. Cece had disappeared from his apartment a few days before. At this point, her pattern—whatever her diagnosis—was painfully obvious. It would be tempting to talk about bipolar disorder; Cece certainly seemed at least hypomanic. She was also hypersexual. But Aiden knew of no frank depressive episodes, and it did not really matter. Whatever was wrong was not going to be treated. A person's capacity for insight was the crucial determinant for growth and change, but this varies with the degree of pathology and defensiveness. We never get the "sickest" people in therapy. We get their spouses, their children, and their employees.

Aiden could not be faulted for believing Cece. After all, every time she came back, she was ebullient, protesting her love for him. She would cling to him and caress his body. A man in love could hardly push that away. It was the single reason he could not give up on her. Nor could he be angry. One of Aiden's great strengths is that he could be sad instead of angry, understanding and patient instead of impulsive (the kind of man who should be cloned). His sad but loving mother had taught him that frustration could be tolerated without acting out.

The word "sadomasochism" can sound quite grim, the kind of thing that Hollywood exploits in film noir. It is in the news lately with stories about revenge porn. But sadomasochism can have normal expressions. Consider the definition: causing harm and enjoying the harm and accepting suffering while benefiting from it. The first healthy example of this has to be willingly giving birth. It is self-imposed pain (usually) and worth it. Simply being in love is an acceptance of the suffering that comes along with it. The sadism part is that this suffering is *self-inflicted*. Another example of healthy sadomasochism (one cannot resist adding) is graduate school. The important distinction is that *normal* sadomasochism is a time-limited and conscious choice. The goal—a degree, a baby—is worth the suffering. Cece's behavior, however, was *pathological* sadomasochism, enjoying the "game" of flirting, sexual exploitation, and "dangling" Aiden and other men. She had a need to deliberately frustrate, and could not allow herself any vulnerability or sadness. Her behavior likely had significant subconscious roots peculiar to her history, which I was never to learn about.

Pathological sadomasochism shuts down the personality and stifles growth, insight, or change (Basseches, Ellman & Goodman 2013). Examples include torturing animals and the revenge porn mentioned before. Sexual sadism is the most dramatic example, with orgasm being dependent on experienced pain. The most familiar example of pathological sadomasochism is battered wives. They might cry about their abuse, but they are compulsively bound to their torturer. Often, a woman in this situation will tell a clinician that after she is beaten, the two can have passionate sex. It was Sigmund Freud who defined masochism as sadism (cruelty) turned against the self.

The dance that Aiden and Cece were in kept them together, but it also kept them apart. Cece was, by her pattern of behavior, guaranteeing that she herself would never have a lasting love relationship. One could argue that she did not want a long-term, meaningful relationship. That would be too normal. But what was she left with? She would enjoy her trysts until she could no longer depend on her beauty to entice more men. Then she would be in a crisis.

During the next few sessions, we spoke of Aiden's need to hold on to Cece despite the fact that she could not share his dream of a life together. He agonized over the wish that, if Cece would just take therapy seriously, everything could change for them. At the same time, Aiden was a man who lived by "data" and its dogged insistence. If something wasn't working, there was a reason, and that reason was susceptible of demonstration. He had always seen his feelings for Cece as "alogical," and that was part of their beauty. Now all he could feel was the oppressive truth. I asked him how he would feel if she came back yet again; after all, *she* had not changed. At this he looked visibly pained. As he was leaving the session, I said to Aiden, "Think about this. The whip that is over your head—*is in your own hand.*"

Over the span of the next few weeks, Aiden investigated several job offers that had been circulating around his office. A colleague had decided on the only one that interested Aiden—in Denver, Colorado. But the following day, the colleague came in saying he had changed his mind and asked if Aiden was interested. Aiden could then make a decision for his own life and sanity. At his final session, Aiden brought me a throw pillow with the words "Sowing seeds in the gardens of our hearts" on it. "This is what you do," he said. I told him I would keep the pillow forever.

Disparity in Sexual Appetite

It is legendary that men want more sex than do women, but is it true? Often it is, especially after women have babies or after menopause, if the woman does not address her physical changes and the related psychological issues. If this is the major complaint, and they are comfortable in each other's arms, a therapist would encourage the two to stop assigning blame for what may be a hormonal issue. Hormones have profound effects on sexual arousal and mood (Brizendine

2006; Reiss 2001). Given that both enjoy sex, but in differing doses, their therapist might seek to balance things by actually suggesting masturbation for the partner who wants more sex. Many men still resent this suggestion, complaining that they are "not kids anymore," and they now have a wife. And many wives still—even after the Second Women's Movement and all that it accomplished (Eagly, Eaton, Rose, Riger & McHugh 2012)—feel guilty at this suggestion, saying they "should" be willing to have sex more often.

These sentiments might vary with the level of education and sophistication in some couples. But the important thing is that we still hear complaints like this in therapy, and they must be addressed. If both partners are encouraged to accept the man's or woman's masturbation as normal, with or without the assistance of the partner, both are freed from unnecessary anger and pressure. An important sex difference is that men need two to three times more touch in order to maintain the same level of oxytocin—the bonding hormone—than do women (Uvnas-Moberg 2003). In both men and women, oxytocin produces contentment and trust. But in order to maintain that level of closeness, our brains need repeated daily doses of oxytocin (Brizendine 2006). We make that happen through touching, hugging, kissing, stroking, and caressing. Think of pleasure as a *nutrient*; the more you give each other, the better nourished your relationship will be. To be clear, a relationship is more than just pleasure. But pleasure, reassurance, and encouragement—apart from anything erotic—is what sustains it. It is a cycle of caring and gratitude.

This discussion would be incomplete without mentioning the other male hormone, vasopressin. This works together with oxytocin in the male brain to establish strong physical attachment and pleasure. (Actually, both men and women form bonds mediated by the *two* neurohormones, oxytocin and vasopressin. Both hormones are made in the pituitary and hypothalamus, but the male brain has more receptors—docking sites—for vasopressin while women have more receptors for oxytocin.) Both hormones are stimulated by *touch*. I stress this because too many people wait for their partner to reach out. But this is a recipe for frustration. The longer they wait, the angrier and more hurt they become. It can create a damaging pattern in the relationship. The more caring you give, the more gratitude you receive. And along with it, more love. Bonding is all about trust—and oxytocin is the trust hormone.

In the therapy session, the sexual needs of each partner are *accepted* as being different because it is normal and expectable that they would be. It comes under normal variability and is not a symptom. The relief both feel with this recognition can lead to a happier shared sexual experience, which can then increase or decrease in frequency without resentment. Of course, this depends on each accepting that they are equal partners in the adventure. Each has an equal responsibility and right to ask for—or to gently decline—the sexual embrace.

Difficulty with Sexual Arousal

Erectile dysfunction can be the result of an angry impasse between two people resulting in a serious drop in a man's self-esteem. *Or* it can be a harbinger of coronary artery disease (Jackson 2008). Sexual dysfunction can be associated with a variety of health issues, among them neurological issues, diabetes, obesity and metabolic disease, or multiple sclerosis. It can also be caused by medications. Sexual dysfunction should first be evaluated by one's internist to rule out any of the above or other physiological condition.

Alternative treatments reported to have good effect in men include pycnogenol, a pine bark extract, and l-arginine aspartate, an amino acid. For women with problems of arousal, maca, an edible root extract, and cordiceps, an edible mushroom product, have shown good results. These should *not* be taken, however, until an assessment has been made of the woman's hormonal status by a physician trained in bio-identical (human) hormone replacement (www.acam.org). Under the guidance of such a physician, the new botanical combination EstroG-100 (brand name) can be tried. A combination of three plant extracts, EstroG-100 has been shown to be effective in pre- and postmenopausal women in a double-blind, placebo-controlled study (Chang et al. 2012). A fair trial with one of these natural food-derived compounds may be all a woman needs.

Or she may need a careful consideration of her *psychological* needs. Sexual arousal, especially in women, is a complex of her feelings about her partner and about herself. This probably has evolutionary wellsprings, as well as antecedents in the woman's personal history. Seymour Fisher (1973), who wrote a classic book on female orgasm, identifies several of these antecedents to experiencing adequate arousal that are still a useful guide:

Feelings of tenderness and love toward the sex partner
Feelings of unique intimacy

Satisfaction from body nudity and display
Enjoyment in being an object of admiration
Satisfaction from being sexually competent
Sensations of a unique kind of self "release"
Emphatic definition of one's sex identity (394)

Thus, it is not just how a woman feels about her partner, as important as that is. It is also, and perhaps mainly, how she feels about her *own* body. Being uncomfortable with being nude, even with one's intimate partner, is a sign of disturbance in a woman's body image. Much of what we enjoy in sex is our own feeling of attractiveness.

Depending how comfortable the woman is with the discussion, I begin to ask clarifying questions.

Does she "feel fat"?—a subjective judgment if ever there was one.
Does she enjoy being nude, or does she need to hide parts of her
    body?
Did she feel vigorously sexual earlier in the relationship and then
    lose those feelings?
Does she feel that becoming sexually aroused is a good thing, or
    are sexy feelings just for "bad girls"?
Does her religion sanction what she is doing?
If she is amenable, I carefully take a Sex History.

It is sometimes a new idea to people that much of what a woman feels about her body begins with her family's—especially her father's—reaction to her emerging womanhood. A father (cousin, uncle) who teases a girl about her breasts, or worse, makes disparaging remarks about her body, will make that girl ashamed of her developing body and hypersensitive to the criticisms of others—even the presumed criticisms. Conversely, a father who appreciates both his daughter's budding femininity as well as her need for privacy instills in her a pride and satisfaction with her body that will sustain her lifelong. Moreover, this fortunate little girl will comfortably expect similar appreciation from other men when she is grown.

The Vagaries of Orgasm

The notion that a woman needed to have an orgasm in order to conceive dates at least from the second century (Shorter 1982) and was finally dispelled by sex researchers William Masters and Virginia

Johnson in the 1970s. Recent research on a woman's capacity for orgasm has concentrated on the amount and type of stimulation she receives (Brizendine 2006.) It was perhaps Freud's biggest mistake to write that women, as they matured, would progress from the adolescent clitoral orgasm to the more mature vaginal orgasm. The innervation of the clitoris is continuous with that of the outer third of the vagina. Women report orgasms involving this whole area. Yet women's sexual arousal, unlike men's, can be disturbed or eliminated by unpleasant experiences—like a partner's bad breath, too rough handling of her body, and, especially, her crying baby. Historically, many babies would have died if their mothers did not consider the baby's need to be more important than her sexual pleasure.

Sex research also considers "releasers" for orgasm. Again, unlike men, who can become aroused even in noisy settings, women's orgasms usually require more relaxation. Her fear and anxiety center, the amygdala of her brain, must be shut down before that relaxation can occur. Thus, the traditional advice about soothing music and calming scents are still a good idea. Candace Pert, the discoverer of the opiate receptor (pleasure center) in the brain, went on to demonstrate the pleasure-inducing molecules we all make in our bodies during intensely pleasurable experiences like sex and running—the natural endorphins. Pert found that "blood endorphin levels increased by about 200 percent from the beginning to the end of the sex act" (2003, 104).

As of this writing, a new "drug" formulated by Adriaan Tuiten, a Dutch chemist, is being tested by the FDA. It is aimed at the commonly reported drop in female libido in committed relationships. Chemically, this drug is alleged to manipulate the balance among the three hormones testosterone, dopamine, and serotonin (Bergner 2013 a, b). This may be one of few studies that does not assume that female libido is like men's, and similarly requires a hydraulic solution. The framers of this study chose women who stated clearly that they want to be sexual but lack desire. These women—all in committed relationships—said they lost a capacity for passion that was precious to them. All the women reported that they initially felt strong attraction to their partners and were selected on the basis of deep longing for its return. All recognized the importance of a strong sexual bond for their relationships. (It was not clear in the Bergner article whether women taking antidepressants, which notoriously suppress sexual desire, were excluded.) While not openly stating that monogamy itself was the problem, Tuiten was careful to exclude single people from the study.

From talking to couples over the years, my own assessment is that the drop in libido may have more to do with having children. It isn't only the exhaustion and lack of sleep. Evolution may have taken into account that if a women was driven to be continually sexual, she would likely get pregnant again and—at that point in our evolution—not be able to take care of the child already born. Thus libido may have been deliberately turned down. There is evidence that men also experience a drop in testosterone after the birth of their babies.

In the Tuiten study, however, women grieved openly about the loss of their libido. Evolution be damned; they wanted it back. And the drug seemed to work—actually, a pair of drugs, Librido and Libridos—for a portion of the subjects. Sometimes it worked too well, with one woman complaining that she still wanted more after she and her husband had had sex. On that point, the writer cited the ancient male fear: "More than one advisor to the industry told me that the companies worried about the prospect that their study results would be too strong, that the FDA would reject an application out of concern that a chemical would lead to female excesses, crazed binges of infidelity, societal splintering" (Bergner 2013, 49). This incredible quote throws into glaring juxtaposition that *no one is similarly worried about male excesses.*

Anorgasmia has been successfully treated using oxytocin (the bonding hormone) and Dostinex, an anti-prolactin agent (IsHak, Bokarius, Jeffrey, et al. 2010). However, psychiatrist Waguin W. IsHak cautions that the psychological aspects of the condition should be given adequate consideration.

A thorough discussion of the varieties, complexities, and vagaries of orgasm in men and women has been compiled by Komisaruk, Whipple, Nasserzadeh, and Beyer-Flores (2009). Research biologist and psychologist Barry R. Komisaruk found, for example, that orgasm can inhibit pain perception, sometimes by 50 percent. One of his more recent research projects examines the almost mythical phenomenon of spontaneous orgasm (Sukel 2013). Allegedly more common in women, spontaneous orgasm is reportedly possible just with strong imagery. (I would think that this is very much helped if the woman is also ovulating.) Using brain scans, Komisaruk and his group showed that women could simply think about their breasts and genitals being stimulated, and the brain's corresponding sensory areas would light up. It would seem that Komisaruk's Rutgers team is the one to watch for the latest in this fascinating field.

Other Questions Worth Asking

Notably a resurge in sexual feeling is part of the expectable result from good marital therapy. Couples are taught that sex, after little children come on the scene, must be planned for. The enemies of intimacy are exhaustion, anger, no privacy, and no time. *The relationship must be made a priority.* Many draining and unnecessary activities can be given up. Couples are surprised and relieved that when they stop being all things to all people, they have some time and energy for each other. Also a good strategy: for serious issues, seek therapy sooner rather than later.

In therapy, we often find that people will come in complaining they have a sexual problem, but no such problem is uncovered during extensive questioning. What I find instead is that the two people are furious with each other. Unexpressed anger, anger they keep to themselves, is one of the most powerful and most common reasons that two people are not enjoying sex. The resolution of that anger, often of long standing, reveals a complexity and character that surprises both partners. The couple described earlier, whose lovemaking was ruined by the man's idea of a sexy name for his wife, is a good example. The point is that there was nothing wrong with anyone's sexual functioning. It was instead what sex had come to *mean.* The only way to understand behavior is through meaning. The same behavior can have two different meanings to two different people.

Some final questions about major sexual inhibitors of arousal in a woman would include the following (these are questions I would ask when she and I were alone in the session):

Is she afraid of pregnancy? If so, why?

Did her mother have a frightening sexual experience that she relayed to her daughter, and did this also traumatize her daughter?

Has she ever had an abortion? Did she ever seek one and then give up the idea?

Has she ever experienced an STD?

How does she experience masturbation? Was it an accepted phase of growing up or was it a "sin"?

How does she feel about being touched and about touching a man's body?

Does she desire a woman and is daunted by the prospect of a lesbian life?

Was she ever approached sexually by someone who frightened her? Has there been frank abuse? How much of this and what type?

Does she depend on alcohol to allow her to be sexual?

Is she taking a medication that interferes with sexual arousal?

Does she welcome becoming more sexual, or is she angry with her partner for simply wanting sex?

Does she withhold sex as a power play in order to get things she wants? Does she have a need to humiliate her partner?

These issues must be addressed by both partners eventually. A therapist cannot do marital therapy with half of a couple, and a man or a woman cannot make a marriage alone. If, however, each partner is willing, but the capacity for arousal is lacking, it is time for an evaluation of her hormonal status.

Bio-Identical (Human) Hormone Replacement

Sexual response is one area in which reactions and feelings can be a *quantitative effect* of the amount of a hormone present in the body. The capacity to become aroused and to achieve orgasm can be direct effects of the amount of testosterone, and probably dopamine, a person's body makes. This is true for women as well as men. While women, even in youth, make much less testosterone than men do, women's sexual response is still largely a function of this powerful hormone. A woman's individual level of testosterone should always be considered when evaluating all the psychological issues cited above—despite the finding that psychological issues can inhibit the sexual response of a woman whose testosterone level is in the normal range. The consideration of hormone replacement is for those women who are actively seeking an increase in their sexual enjoyment, as well as in their general health and energy.

A drop in essential hormone levels can occur in women well before menopause. Women often come to therapy complaining about diminished sexual feelings in their late thirties and forties. While I always want to discuss their lifestyle and the contribution of fatigue, marital satisfaction, and diet, I always recommend a full physical and some blood tests for hormone levels.

Women's youthful testosterone high is at age nineteen, and by the age of forty-five or fifty, women's levels have dropped by up to seventy percent—leaving many with very low testosterone levels. In these cases ... the sex center in the hypothalamus doesn't have the chemical fuel it needs to ignite sexual desire and genital sensitivity. (Brizendine 2006, 176–177)

So, although we may feel that sexual gratification *alone* does not make for a fulfilling marriage, if sex is important to both partners, it is time to seek a physician skilled in bio-identical (human) hormone replacement. This will include a consideration of the three forms of estrogen: estriol (the safest estrogen), estradiol, and estrone, as well as progesterone and testosterone. Each of us is different, in that our bodies make varying amounts of these hormones. A blood test is necessary to assess the endogenous (internal) level each of us already has in our bloodstream before adding any to our system. An *individualized balance* of these hormones is accomplished, a fine-tuning of the woman's hormonal picture. One need not be apprehensive about this procedure; it is just an extension of a good physical exam. Bio-identical hormone replacement uses creams, capsules, and troches; with the creams, simply rub tiny amounts onto the skin of the inner thighs and the breasts once or twice a day. You may also be prescribed testosterone cream or gel, which you apply yourself as instructed by your physician. An adequate, usually small amount of testosterone in cream form will restore the enjoyment of sex. In addition, taking 10–15 mg by mouth of the adrenal hormone DHEA should be considered for women if their blood DHEA-S levels are indeed low. Women over 40 may make a small amount of DHEA and need replacement (Reiss 2001). When appropriate, DHEA is available over the counter but should only be taken orally when blood levels are low, since DHEA is a "mother" hormone that can turn into other hormones, especially estrogen and testosterone.

Jealousy: Fear of Loss of Love

Jealousy is a very specific fear resulting from the awareness that we could lose a valued love relationship. It is the painful recognition of our vulnerability and of the other person's right to make his or her own separate decisions. If jealousy makes us feel sad, it is healthy. Sadness, like jealousy itself, is normal. Relationships do not come with lifetime guarantees or even a limited warranty that protects us. We are all vulnerable in this way. We have no control, nor should we wish to have control over a loved one. Love is offered as a relationship between equals. We recognize that our loved one is free to leave, as are we. Marriage in some cultures promises forevermore, but in the modern world, even marriage is less and less binding.

Jealousy threatens our conviction of our own lovability. If we are not worthy of love, then we could be abandoned. Because jealousy awakens old developmental fears, it is good to let our loved one know we are feeling threatened. His or her reassurance can make the jealousy go away, and all can be well again. We all need and appreciate reassurance that we are still loved. It is immensely helpful if two people can talk about jealousy openly and regularly, preferably with a bit of humor.

Consider this example: A man asked his therapist if it is normal for him to be jealous of his wife's former lover. The former lover had actually been intrusive in their lives for a time at the beginning of their relationship. His therapist recognized that the man had not felt too secure in the relationship at that point, so some fear of loss was understandable. But then he started to compare himself unfavorably to the former boyfriend, saying that man had been taller than he. (Since both men were quite tall, the therapist struggled to appreciate the point. It may be that tallness is a metaphor for other body parts.) It took not only reassurance from his wife but also therapy to persuade him that it was his own self-doubt that made him uneasy. He needed to be reassured of his basic self-worth and his lovability. His jealousy had more to do with his own history than with anyone in his wife's past.

Why would we doubt our own lovability? For that, we have to go back to the beginning. One of the most painful and determining experiences we can have growing up, especially for the first child, is the birth of the second baby. For many but not all first children, this presents an unimaginable rejection, a refutation of the value and uniqueness of being the only child—seen of course from the point of view of a two-year-old. For many first children, the birth of a new baby is exciting, fun, and a marvelous learning experience. The whole thing is attended with parties, company staying over, and new kinds of attention for the first child. It can seem a natural transition.

For some first children, however, the arrival of a newborn is an intolerable fact. One little boy, while struggling to adapt to his baby sister, asked his mother if she was going to have another child. The mother replied, "No, I think our family is just perfect with the four of us." This precocious four-year-old boy emphatically remarked, "It was perfect when it was just the three of us!" This child was expressing exactly what Freud meant by his concept of "dethronement," the dilemma of the first born.

Consider this scenario. It is as if you yourself had the perfect position at work, a dream come true for you. You had great support, lots of appreciation and cooperation, and a very attractive salary. Then one day your supervisors bring in a new person, and they tell you he is going to share your position. He will also share your office and your salary. You are told that you are expected to help him because, after all, he's new. Oh, and they want you to like him. And if you have any problem with this, you are expected to keep it to yourself. This is what we expect of a toddler the day his sibling is born. Most of us navigate this transition more or less skillfully, although for some families it can be a challenge.

Envy

It is essential to differentiate jealousy from envy. When jealousy makes us angry, envy is born. Envy differs from jealousy in that, instead of feeling sad, we become angry and want to destroy the thing or person who makes us angry. We want control over the thing or the person. We find ourselves resenting the intruder, whether it is a new brother or sister, another child who is competing with us for our place on the team, or someone who has just caught the eye of the person we love. The distinction between jealousy and envy is in the motive: jealousy makes us sad and is normal; envy makes us feel destructive and is abnormal.

If the envy can be contained, if you can laugh at yourself and be reassured, all is well. The experience of a first child has elements of both jealousy and envy. A first child can be helped to accept a new baby because his parents are wise and careful to give him lots of attention and affection. This is an ongoing process of including him in the baby's care and giving him the same cuddling at bedtime. It is normal for children to feel ambivalent about a new baby. Taking the older child to events and lunches without the new baby is reassuring.

If the first child's jealousy of a new baby is not resolved and integrated, it can affect that child's relationships with friends and later, his experiences with dating. He may develop a need to take it out on a friend or a girlfriend. But if it is openly discussed within the family, helping the older child to express his loss and, without too much drama, making him feel special through stories and outings, he will likely outgrow his resentment. Similarly, boys and girls learn that competing on teams is good practice for tolerating the ambiguity that life hands us on a regular basis. And lovers learn that we all live in a world of attractive people, and opportunities are everywhere. It is the deep appreciation of the relationship we have and do not want to lose that keeps us faithful, as well as the appreciation that fidelity itself is a worthwhile goal.

In therapy, envy is often found to be the source of much interpersonal pain. At its worst, envy seeks to destroy what is envied and is complained about in passionate terms. A man envies the influence his wife's family exerts on her and seeks to control it. Or a woman envies certain of the women her husband works with because he comes home and speaks about them enthusiastically. In each case, much of the pain a person feels can be shown to be connected with the *meanings* the particular details have for that person and his or her history. Understanding those often historical meanings can have the effect of *disconnecting* the pain. But the success of this outcome depends on how thoroughly and intimately the therapist understands each person's complaint.

Couples and Cybersex

Crises over cybersex are increasing, even among some committed couples (Smith 2011). With the increasing availability of sex sites, more women are reporting that they use them for sexual arousal and release. Women are also reporting having sex with strangers on Skype. They will argue that it does not constitute infidelity because they have not touched the other person. They also argue that, if they have no other sexual partner, Skype offers them an exciting experience with no hygiene issues and no risk of sexually transmitted diseases. The problem is that their bodies get very used to the ease and convenience of cybersex, as opposed to sex with a person who is physically present and may have some needs of his or her own.

Therapy with such couples involves the same issues of betrayal and rebuilding trust outlined above. We must first discuss their relationship history and their reasons for wanting to maintain the relationship. The same questions are asked about their motives for therapy and the hoped-for outcome. With a convincing recommitment to each other, we then focus on the excitement and self-expression they are seeking when they log onto the sex sites. What aspects of their own sexuality do they feel are stifled, inhibited, or unexpressed in their relationship? The most important sex organ is the brain, with important differences between men and women throughout the life span (Brizendine 2006). Arousal is greatly enhanced by sexual fantasies; would each partner be willing to share his or her sexual fantasies with the other? This one decision can focus their eroticism again on each other instead of "out there in cyberspace." Therapy endorses the exploration of sexual wishes and fantasies as long as they are not cruel and exploitative. In fact, if we want a single criterion to distinguish an unhealthy from a healthy sexual relationship, it would be exploitation.

In the end, it is only a couple's strong resolve to free their relationship from the overstimulation and compulsive lure of the sex sites that saves these couples. Internet sex is very addicting, and people become "hooked" on the easy, accessible gratification. Just as with weight loss and other difficult human endeavors, self-discipline is the answer to successfully outgrowing cybersex. Each temptation is actively refused, with the larger picture of one's own valued relationship in mind. The question is—as always—what do you really want? Then, work for that.

SEXUAL HOOKUPS: THE FUTURE OF AN ILLUSION (WITH APOLOGIES TO FREUD)

An excellent examination of the pleasures and pitfalls of "sexual hook-ups" (Garcia, Reiber, Massey, & Merriwether 2013) concludes that casual sex can become more complex very quickly. Even when agreed upon, the expected cool detachment and breezy enjoyment of the moment barely lasts through the first encounter. We come to any "new" relationship with our whole histories and with our fancy emotional wiring. Although such sexual experiences can be wholesome and happy, regret for sexual hookups can occur at as high as a 75 percent rate for both men and women.

Free love is reinvented by every generation that comes of age, each with its own decade's pressures and anxieties. "It is by now pretty well understood that traditional dating in college has mostly gone the way of the landline, replaced by 'hooking-up'—an ambiguous term that can signify anything from making out to oral sex to intercourse— without the emotional entanglement of a relationship" (Taylor 2013). Out of the pressures for women to "lean in" and put career first, college women push themselves to get excellent grades, and they actively avoid romance because of its potential emotional price. With the energy they have left after their studies, they reportedly are seeking out men they may not particularly like but whose bodies are appealing for sexual diversions. The traditional complaint about men and their exploitative ways seems also to be ancient history; women can beat them at their own game. This could be progress or a questionable move. Marital therapists have to worry what happens to these women if at some point they do wish to consider a baby. Their nervous systems are primed for multiple partners and easy sexual pleasures. The question arises: Could they be "faithful" to one person? Is that even desirable? Do babies do as well with only one parent if that parent is fine with "hook-ups"? It would seem that longing and gratitude, the two healthiest (normal) human emotions, are in danger of going out of fashion. Will humans outgrow our longing for love?

Psychiatrist and teacher of psychotherapy Irvin Yalom asked hundreds of people, over and over, "What do you want?" His group exercise, with the group breaking into pairs and asking each other this question, evoked powerful and immediate feelings:

> successful, well-functioning, well-dressed people . . . are stirred to their depths. They call out to those who are forever lost—dead or absent parents, spouses, children . . . "I want to see you again." "I want your love." "I want you to know I love you and how sorry I am . . ." "I want you back—I am so lonely." "I want the childhood I never had" . . . "I want to matter . . . to be remembered." . . . So much wanting. So much longing. And so much pain, so close to the surface, only minutes deep. (Yalom 2012, xi)

Yalom used this group exercise time after time with the same results. The wrenching feelings harken back to our deep human roots—what we really want—which must be suppressed and silenced if people are to respond to the current requirements for success and meaningless sex.

EVOLUTIONARY BIOLOGY AND US

Evolutionary biology has provided us with much new data about our functioning—for example, findings about our exquisite prefrontal cortex as the main arbiter between impulse and action. This means that pausing to examine an option before we act on it can protect us from doing something really stupid. But evolutionary biologists also stress that hormonal influences are the major regulators controlling our behavior. I worry that this is too narrow a view. For instance, sexual attraction is not the only or even the main motivator for humans. Among the reasons for choosing a partner are higher-level *social* categories. For example, you may be attracted to a person because you both share a fascination for a particular field of work, or you share a passion for snow sports or literature. Many people feel particularly drawn to someone of their own faith.

We do share a long biological evolution with our closest primate relatives. But what else are we? Other animals cannot deviate one iota from their biological mandate. We are different. We will stay up all night to write a paper, defying every biological urge for sleep and comfort. Some of us leave our privileged lives at home to teach less fortunate people, or to provide medical help, or to advocate for equality. One man left a lucrative career with a big American company to help build schools and libraries for girls in Asia. With these learned and sophisticated choices, we may indeed have borrowed the effects of the bonding hormone oxytocin. We now feel trust and comfort not just with our families but with that wider social group we have come to appreciate.

No, not all of our choices are primarily the effects of hormones. Evolution pushes us to choose a mate with good genes. A person with a symmetrical face and body would be a good indicator of that. But consider that evolution has been largely *amoral*. Some of our most advanced principles—for example, humanism—represent a deliberate refusal of the evolutionary impulse to dominate others. As powerful as hormones can be, our marvelous prefrontal cortex allows us to override them. Our brain is organized by *experience*, which alters blood flow to certain neurons and not to others. In this way, the impulses receiving more blood flow are strengthened and others die off (Gabbard 2000). That is how, era by era, humans can progress.

Most of the couples described in this text are heterosexual, because that has been my professional experience. But gay and lesbian couples share the same problems, worries, and jealousies, although their issues are complicated by secrecy. When gays and lesbians can marry each other and/or live openly, much suffering is averted. For example, the need to distract attention from one's homosexuality in the past resulted in the unstable situation of gay men marrying straight women. More than one wife of an ultimately found-to-be homosexual man has complained to her therapist, "I don't believe him. I think he could be straight if he wanted to be." This statement is insensitive and naïve at best. It ignores the struggle her husband had to hide his sexual orientation. It also ignores the clear evidence that gay people discover their sexuality the same way heterosexuals do: during development. Progress must be made socially and politically so that homosexuality can be appreciated, understood, and studied just as freely as heterosexuality.

The more society becomes sophisticated and fair about the traditional gender roles, eliminating gender bias and unfair expectations, the more our gender choices will be accepted and respected (Bieschke, Perez, and DeBord 2007). *In the end, what is healthy is to be quietly comfortable with your body and the concept with which you identify.* Not needing to be confrontational or defiant.

> The American Psychological Association has been instrumental in advancing knowledge and acceptance for lesbian, gay, bisexual and tran-gender persons since 2001. The last few years have also seen statements questioning the effectiveness of conversion therapy for homosexuality, including from the U.S. attorney general's office, APA, the American Psychiatric Association and others. Unfortunately, progress has not been as swift in many other parts of the world. In the same month as the U.S. Supreme Court rulings, Russia's president signed a law imposing jail terms on people who promote homosexual "propaganda" to minors and who "offend religious believers," ... In a more extreme case, Uganda has been considering a bill since 2009, that would, among other things "prohibit and penalize homosexual behavior and related practices" and punish offenders with life in prison or death. (DeAngelis 2013, 33)

Psychologists, psychiatrists, and other mental health professionals are in a unique position to influence public attitudes about LGBT experience. Several states have enacted laws banning conversion therapy (which was always suspect, considering what we know about the nature of sexual identity). The media have also taken a thoughtful and supportive role.

AN EMOTIONALLY NORMAL COUPLE

I wanted to interview a healthy couple, but one I did not know personally and who had no experience with therapy. This couple, married two and a half years, were introduced as friends of my neighbors. I had heard that their extended family was happy and healthy, exactly what the research findings would predict: that people with better home lives growing up tend to have happier marriages (Ackerman et al. 2013). Normal couples, I theorized, would be characterized by a single idea: they put their relationship first. Is that what I would hear from this pair?

Alan and Annie—whose fluffy red hair made me think she was named after the musical—smiled when I introduced myself. They had agreed to talk to me briefly when they visited my neighbor. I asked my first question: Who gets his or her way most of the time? Again, smiles and easy laughter. "We take turns!" they both answered. (Yes, the relationship comes first. If what you want is your partner's happiness and well-being, discussions don't become power plays.) I asked: Who is more dependable? More laughter. They had never had this problem either. What *was* their most serious problem? With this, they finally looked pensive. Annie looked at Alan, who quietly explained that his father, an alcoholic, had come to visit and had vomited in their bathroom. Annie did not want him as a house guest anymore. They did argue about this and both ended in tears. Their solution was to visit Alan's father and take him out to dinner.

I also noted an easy, friendly sense of humor, a confident expectation that they were there for each other, and an appreciation of each other's friends and interests. Their favorite activity was traveling. Annie's work took her to other parts of the country, and Alan could often come along. There was no talk of babies yet, but I could not leave them without asking. They were undecided, they said. Would they decide not to? (They are currently pregnant.) My last question was: How did they account for their happiness? Annie gave me her usual smile. "Just lucky, I guess."

"What about you," I asked Alan. "Are you lucky too?"

He looked a bit embarrassed. "Yes . . . I'm lucky . . . but I know I'll never get over loving Annie."

WHAT WE ALL NEED

Researcher Sonja Lyubomirsky tells us how ephemeral happiness can be and where we might better look for it (Lyubomirsky 2013). But one thing is certain: relationships grow or they die. The way to transcend this is to relinquish the notion that happiness "happens" to people. Resolve to *cause* it. *Make your relationship a priority.* Let your partner know that he or she is the most important person in your life. Find out what makes him or her happy and make that happen (as long as it is fair). As I said in the introduction, I have found that people are happy when they feel "lucky." You have the ability to make your loved one feel enormously fortunate that he or she met you!

Beyond this, I contend that happiness and health are linked. We all need to have a caring, protective attitude toward our body so that we will not want to hurt it with bad food choices, with poor hygiene, or with risk-taking—for example, having many sexual partners or experimenting with drugs. At this point, the *unhealthy* needs bounce out at us. Unhealthy sexual wishes would include:

Wanting our spouse or lover to read our mind
Expecting or demanding that our partner make us happy
Wanting him or her to do everything we ask
Expecting him or her to be faithful when we are not
Wanting to give or receive painful or humiliating sex
Wanting to get away with lies or deception
Wanting to use any kind of exploitation

As for healthy sexual needs, give what you need. If you need touch, give touch. If you need encouragement—to speak, to share, to be sexual—then encourage your lover.

We all need:

Cooperation (we're in this together)
Enjoyable shared experiences
To be taken seriously
To be treated fairly
To be trusted
Time alone
Gratitude and appreciation

Touch and holding
To feel attracted to our spouse
To feel attractive, sexually appealing
Fidelity

THE LANGUAGE OF LOVE

A man stopped kissing his lover, just as they were beginning to make love. "Tell me," he asked, looking at her intently, "How do we keep this . . . so special each time?"

She smiled and pushed him down on the pillow. "Because," she said, "you are wonderful."

REFERENCES

Ackerman, R. A., Kashy, D. A., Donnelan, M. B., et al. (2013). "The Interpersonal Legacy of a Positive Family Climate in Adolescence." *Psychological Science,* Jan. 10, 2013.

Anderman, E. & Murdock, T. (Eds.). (2006). *The Psychology of Academic Cheating.* London: Elsevier.

Basseches, H. I., Ellman, P. L., & Goodman, N. R. (Eds.). (2013). *Battling the Life and Death Forces of Sadomasochism. Clinical Perspectives.* London: Karnac Books Ltd.

Bergner, D. (2013a, May). "There May Be a Pill for That." *New York Times Magazine,* March 26, 2013, 22–27, 47, 49.

Bergner, D. (2013b). *What Do Women Want? Adventures in the Science of Female Desire.* New York: Ecco/HarperCollins Publishers.

Bieschke, K. J., Perez, R. P., & DeBord, K. A. (Eds.). (2007). *Handbook of Counseling and Psychotherapy with Lesbian, Gay, Bisexual and Trans-Gender Clients.* 2nd ed. Washington, DC: American Psychological Association Books.

Brizendine, L. (2006). *The Female Brain.* New York: Three Rivers Press.

Brownmiller, S. (1993). *Against Our Will.* New York: Ballantine Books.

Chang, A., Kwak, B. Y., Yi., K., et al. (2012). "The Effect of Herbal Extract (EstroG-100) on Pre-, Peri- and Post-Menopausal Women: A Randomized, Double-Blind, Placebo-Controlled Study." *Phytotherapy Research* 26(4): 510–516.

Collins, G. (2009). *When Everything Changed: The Amazing Journey of American Women from 1960 to the Present.* New York: Little, Brown and Company.

Courtois, C. A. (1988). *Healing the Incest Wound: Adult Survivors in Therapy.* New York: W. W. Norton & Co., Inc.

Davis, S. F., Drinan, P. F., & Gallant, T. B. (2009). *Cheating in School: What We Know and What We Can Do about It.* West Sussex, UK: Wiley-Blackwell.

DeAngelis, T. (2013). "Fighting Discrimination Worldwide: APA's Commitment to Applying Social Science to Protect and Expand the Rights of LGBT People Worldwide Is Paying Off." *Monitor on Psychology* 44(9): 33–35.

Eagly, A. H., Eaton, A., Rose, S. M., et al. (2012). "Feminism and Psychology." *American Psychologist* 67(3): 211–230.

Fisher, S. (1973). *The Female Orgasm. Psychology, Physiology, Fantasy.* New York: Basic Books.

Gabbard, G.O. (2000). "A Neurobiologically Informed Perspective on Psychotherapy." *British Journal of Psychiatry*, 177, 117–122.

Garcia, J. R., Reiber, C., Massey, S. G., et al. (2013, February). "Sexual Hook-Up Culture." *Monitor on Psychology* 44(2): 60–67.

Glass, S. P. & Staeheli, J. C. (2003). *Not "Just Friends": Protect Your Relationship from Infidelity and Heal the Trauma of Betrayal.* New York: Free Press.

Gottman, J. & Silver, N. (1999). *Seven Principles for Making Marriage Work.* New York: Three Rivers Press.

Hillman, J. L. (2012). *Sexuality and Aging: Clinical Perspectives.* New York: Springer.

IsHak, W. W., Bokarius, A., Jeffrey, J. K., et al. (2010). "Disorders of Orgasm in Women: A Literature Review." *Journal of Sexual Medicine* 7(10): 3254–3268.

Jackson, G. (2008). "Prevention of Cardiovascular Disease by the Early Identification of Erectile Dysfunction." *International Journal of Impotence Research,* December 20, 2008. Suppl. 2: S9–14.

Komisaruk, B. R., Whipple, B., Nasseszadeh, S., et al. (2009). *The Orgasm Answer Guide.* Baltimore: The Johns Hopkins University Press.

Kristof, N. D. & WuDunn, S. (2010). *Half the Sky: Turning Oppression into Opportunity for Women Worldwide.* New York: Vintage.

Lindau, S. T., Schumm, L. P., Laumann, E. O., et al. (2007). "A Study of Sexuality and Health Among Older Adults in the United States." *New England Journal of Medicine* 357(8): 762–774.

Lyubomirsky, S. (2013). *The Myths of Happiness: What Should Make You Happy and Doesn't, What Shouldn't Make You Happy, but Does.* New York: Penguin Press.

McNulty, J. K. & Fincham, F. D. (2012). "Beyond Positive Psychology? Toward a Contextual View of Psychological Processes and Well-Being." *American Psychologist* 67(2): 101–110.

Pert, C. (2003). *Molecules of Emotion: Why You Feel the Way You Feel.* New York: Scribner.

Pipher, M. (1996). *The Shelter of Each Other: Rebuilding Our Families.* New York: Grosset/Putnam Books.

Reiss, U. (2001). *Natural Hormone Balance for Women.* New York: Pocket Books.

Russell, D. E. H. (1990). *Rape in Marriage.* Indianapolis: Indiana University Press.

Sanford, K. & Wolfe, K. L. (2013). "What Married Couples Want from Each Other During Conflicts: An Investigation of Underlying Concerns." *Journal of Social and Clinical Psychology* 32(6): 674–699.

Shorter, E. (1982). *A History of Women's Bodies.* New York: Basic Books.

Shu, L., Francesca, G. & Bazerman, M. H. (2011). "Dishonest Deed, Clear Conscience: When Cheating Leads to Moral Disengagement and Motivated Forgetting." *Personality and Social Psychology Bulletin* 37(3): 330–349.

Smith, B. L. (2011, March). "Are Internet Affairs Different?" *Monitor on Psychology* 42(3): 48.

Sukel, K. (2013). "Lust's Reward: For Many Women, Orgasm Remains Elusive." *Scientific American Mind* 24(5): 60–63.

Takei, M. (2012). *She-Q: Why Women Should Mentor Men and Change the World.* Santa Barbara, CA: Praeger Publishers.

Taylor, K. (2013, July 14). "She Can Play That Game, Too." *New York Times Sunday Review,* 1, 6–7.

Uvnas-Moberg, K. (2003). *The Oxytocin Factor.* New York: Perseus Books.

Yalom, I. (2009). *The Gift of Therapy: An Open Letter to a New Generation of Therapists and Their Patients.* New York: HarperPerennial.

Yalom, I. (2012). *Love's Executioner: And Other Tales of Psychotherapy.* New York: Basic Books.

Chapter 7

Food
The "Frustrating Goddess"

For me, food isn't just food. Food is a person, a frustrating goddess.

—Patient suffering from bulimia

For so many of us, especially for women, achieving a comfortable relationship with food is a lifelong struggle. Part of the problem is that food is the easiest and cheapest form of self-indulgence there is and a natural mood regulator. In addition, food was the "natural resource" almost completely controlled by women historically. The roots, fruits, grains, little birds, and eggs gathered by women kept families alive and nourished at times when hunting was successful. Learning how to combine and cook different foods made them tastier and likely more digestible. As women shared these cooking methods, whole cultures developed around indigenous foods (Tannahill 1973). Today we call these "ethnic" dishes, some of the most treasured recipes.

EATING DISORDERS: NOT ABOUT THE ENJOYMENT OF FOOD

The quote in the title of this chapter is from a bulimic woman who perceived food as an intimidating presence, at once enticing and frustrating. It lured her to food, promising pleasure that it gave—and then withdrew—when she invariably felt the impulse to vomit. Food only felt good when it was outside of her body; once eaten, it felt like an onerous presence. She became trapped in a binge/purge syndrome that drove her from college then isolated her at home. She became bloated and depressed, avoiding all social interactions. Her dentist saw her eroded teeth and referred her for psychological treatment. She is not alone. Although it is arguable whether women have more problems with food than men do in today's obesity epidemic, women more often complain about it and seek help managing it.

Why is food such a problem for women? Generations of writers have sought to explain this. Popular sociocultural explanations stress that women are exhorted to be thin and scorned for being overweight. Yet the extreme thinness held out to us as exemplary ignores female metabolism and hormonal shifts. Too often it must be maintained with unhealthy practices like starving and purging. But perhaps the biggest offender is the *type* of food—or non-foods—ubiquitous in our modern culture, discussed in detail below. We should also remember that this is hardly a current problem. It was in the early 1900s that insurance companies began compiling weight and height statistics in order to assess longevity. Their actuarial tables showed excess body weight to be a survival risk. And the motive for thinness for its own sake has been with us for some time. American women were first exhorted to be thin by *Vogue* magazine in 1908.

The Hand That Rocks the Cradle: Food as Power

As mentioned earlier, women have had much power over the supply and distribution of food in the family. This is especially significant for children. Mothers and other female caretakers decide what, when, and how much a small child will eat. Still the principal cooks within families, women have primary access to the comfort of food within reach. Notably, part of that gratification is that food is a good *anesthetic*. It lulls us. It eases our discomfort. Food is so soporific that it puts babies to sleep.

All this is learned early. In the beginning of life, food is not experienced as separate from the mother's body, especially when the baby is breast-fed. An infant experiences food, holding, warmth, comfort, and safety all together in the mother's arms. Only slowly, and with continued growth of the body and brain, does the baby come to realize that food, holding, comfort, and mother are *separate entities*. But that early connection of food and comfort can be reevoked throughout life just by eating. The experience of mother and safety remains linked. And if mother did *not* feel safe and comforting, that stays too. Food will then also be *ambivalently* loved. It will be sought again and again to give us comfort and safety, and when it fails, we will blame the food. And then we will blame our body. This is because food is only briefly satisfying. For anorectics and bulimics, food is only satisfying in anticipation—that is, when it is *outside* the body. But first, let's consider overeating.

Motives for Overeating

Working with overweight people supplies much evidence of their need—or demand—that food be there for them as a major support. Some obese people weep as they describe their favorite foods. Especially at the beginning of therapy, they will resist any analysis of their eating pattern and may even refuse to be weighed. They resist mostly the explanation by their therapist that a major motive for their overeating may be a *possessive anger*, anger that is only secondarily about food. It is the task of the therapist to carefully and respectfully examine the person's life story. A thorough history is taken, including current and ongoing concerns. Eating habits and weight history are noted. There is a better prognosis for people who were at a normal weight as children and in teenage years and then gained weight as adults. Those who were overweight as children likely have more fat cells. They may have a history of eating when they are bored or afraid. Many people overeat if they feel guilty. But very often, it is anger.

Why would overeating be an expression of anger and of tension in general? When we look at our evolution, we can see that the mouth and jaw evolved not only for eating but also for *killing*. All the carnivores kill with their mouth and teeth. If you ask children to show you what anger looks like, they will clench their jaws and teeth, and they will make fists. They may even growl! People will often report their favorite foods are crunchy or chewy, offering a satisfying resistance.

This may sound far-fetched or even a somewhat romantic explanation. We can gain respect for these concepts by carefully recording the *metaphors* patients use. One woman had hidden her problem with bulimia for years. She was referred to me by her employer. I was impressed by her skill with words. She described her mother as a "carnivorous conniver." I said I understood "conniver" but was puzzled by the word "carnivorous." The woman paused and then explained,

"She eats me up." Another woman, overweight since her teenage years, told me that every time she had an argument with her boyfriend, she would secretly eat bags of candy. The link between anger and overeating is clear. In the psychoanalytic literature, this is called "oral aggression."

> By eating a lot very fast the patient symbolically tries to *push down* anger—swallowing and burying the anger in food. . . . The intensity of aggression as competing oral motivation depends on the levels of anger and frustration. . . . [T]he emotional associations of eating, love and aggression are felt to derive from these oral stage experiences. (Rand 1982, 187, 190; emphasis added)

We can discharge a great deal of tension by chewing and grinding food. If normal amounts of food calm us when we are relatively free of tension, then it will take large amounts of food to calm us when we are angry, especially if we are unaware of our anger. An overweight woman will complain that she does not *feel* angry, but it is because she is still binging. The symptom—binging—numbs her anger. But this greatest saboteur of a good eating plan emerges when the woman restricts her favorite "junk food." She begins to feel very uncomfortable. This is a crucial moment in therapy: to carefully examine the feelings that bubble up unbidden, unwelcome, and *unnamed*. People are often surprised to learn that they have motives for overeating of which they are unaware. Each person's history is unique, and it is the task of therapy to find the connections between his or her current binge behavior and developmental antecedents. One of the most important questions in therapy is "Why is *this* happening at *this* time?"

There is often a tearful period when a person recognizes a long-standing anger that is acutely uncomfortable. If she persists after the first period of weight loss and continues to take responsibility for her feelings—that is, keeping them in awareness—we make continued progress. *This does not mean she goes home and screams at her parent or husband or boss.* I explain that she may express those feelings to her therapist, describing the actual experiences in as much detail as she can. She is feeling emotions that often began in childhood, and they are compromised by the limited judgment of a child. But the feelings are real and painful nonetheless. With a careful consideration of the milieu and what the others around her were likely feeling, we often come to understand her pain as real but one-sided. Thus therapy changes our *understanding* of the past, and that changes the past. It also changes *us*. A fair definition of "therapy" is *maturation of the entire personality*.

One of the most pernicious problems with eating disorders is sneaking and hiding food so that a person may not seem to be over-eating at all. In therapy we try to establish the time line: When did the weight gain begin? What was going on in the marriage? What are the emotions the person is reporting? Was it anger or helplessness? Or was it shame?

The Wheel of Misfortune: Naiveté and Longing in an Eleven-Year-Old Girl

Beth was 32 when she came to therapy to cope with a dramatic weight gain. She allowed me to weigh her at the first session, which is unusual. She weighed 288 pounds at 5 feet 9 inches. She was cordial but a bit quiet; shy rather than reticent. She explained she had gained over 100 pounds in one and a half years. Happily married with two children, she wept when describing how kind and helpful her husband was. They had a comfortable home, and Beth supplemented the family income by taking care of several small children.

Her beloved father had died when Beth was 8 years old and her sister was 13. Both her parents were "wonderful," and her sister, 5 years older than Beth, was loving and protective. Beth's sister took care of her when they both came home from school, especially important since, after their father died, their mother had to find work in a local mall. But four years later, Beth's sister was off to college. Since her mother had to work on Saturdays, she arranged to leave Beth with an aunt and uncle.

A 100-plus-pound weight gain in one and a half years is highly significant. We had to do a careful food history, and this identified Beth's particular binge food—doughnuts. She described her favorite kinds with a great deal of feeling. She had developed a pattern of eating *boxes* of doughnuts while the children were in school. We discussed her efforts to stop this on her own, but she said the smell and taste of the doughnuts was "so comforting."

What had happened a year and a half ago that had begun this massive binge? During one session, I asked how her husband was reacting to her weight gain. Beth smiled and said he had mentioned it. There seemed to be no tension in her remark, although she said she had come to therapy for weight loss. Several sessions later, she said that she did not feel she was responding sexually to her husband as she had in the past. When I asked how she felt about this, she shrugged and said that maybe she just didn't like sex anymore.

Gaining a significant amount of weight can diminish sexual feelings in several ways. First, a woman feels less desirable, and feeling sexy is a big part of our sexual enjoyment. But—what is worse—fat cells secrete estrogen, and this inhibits testosterone, the hormone responsible for sexual arousal (Zumoff 1988). This affects overweight men as well, with the hormonal changes worsening as weight increases (Cohen 2008; Zumoff 1988). But when we discussed how her husband felt about the weight gain having this effect on *her*, Beth began to cry. From that point, she cried at each session, finally lamenting, "I don't deserve this good husband." She remarked again how kind and loving he was and how patient. Finally, at the end of one session, she said with some hesitation, "My husband wants to talk to you." I asked if that were all right with her. She said yes, and her husband came to the next session.

I was prepared for a hard-working man who might be uncomfortable with a female psychologist and who would find some way to tell me that his sex life was not what it had been. The man who came in was tall and polite with a late afternoon beard, directly from work but neat. In one graceful move, he bent down to kiss Beth then slid into the place beside her that was always his. With his arm around her, Beth softly weeping on his chest, he looked straight at me and said, "Has she told you about her uncle?" I looked at Beth for clarification. She looked frightened but ready to divulge something important. Together and haltingly, they gave me the following account, augmenting each other's details, her husband supporting Beth throughout.

When Beth was 11 years old, her sister left for college. Because her mother had to work on Saturdays, she brought Beth to an uncle and aunt's house in a nearby town. The idea was that Beth would help her uncle with yard work and her aunt with anything in the house. But since her aunt did errands on Saturdays, Beth spent most of the day with her uncle. She liked her uncle; he was talkative and funny. After they did the lawn and the sweeping, her uncle would bring Beth into the basement, where he would get himself a beer and a cold drink for her. Then he taught Beth a new game. He had a game wheel mounted on the wall. He would spin the wheel, and if Beth's number didn't come up, she would forfeit a piece of clothing. Her uncle would spin the wheel again, and if his number didn't come up, he would do the same.

In telling this, Beth shuddered and said she had been "a fat, homely kid, with thick glasses." Her uncle had been the only person who told her she was pretty, so she let him kiss her. They played this game every week, and then the little girl noticed her uncle rubbing himself. This graduated to rubbing against her. And eventually he would simply hold his penis out to her. Beth wept while relating this. Almost with disbelief about the details of what had happened, she said, "Dr. Woodall, I went right into that basement, week after week, knowing what would happen." But she kept it all to herself as her uncle had asked, feeling more and more "like a very bad girl."

Beth couldn't remember exactly how long this had gone on. At some point, her mother stopped taking her to the uncle's house. "I guess I grew up and went to high school," Beth said. She started dating and soon met the boy who would become her husband. He was the only one with whom she shared what had happened with her uncle. She said she didn't feel especially bad about telling her boyfriend. In teenage years, it can be exciting to be a bad girl. Because Beth wanted to preserve family relationships, her boyfriend, then her husband, never confronted the uncle. That had seemed the right thing to do. Beth felt that her naïve mother would not believe it. And upon learning something so weighty, the whole family would have been upset. Still, Beth could not help thinking that her older sister knew something about this and had never mentioned it.

What had happened a year and a half ago that coincided with Beth's doughnut binges? What had altered her ability to keep this whole story well buried? It was because *this uncle had died.* Her aunt was still living at that house. Beth and her husband dutifully went to the funeral. But then the unthinkable happened. After the funeral, a family meal was served in that same basement. *The game wheel was still on the wall.* During and after the meal, Beth could not look around. She had not been in that basement for years, but it had not lost its oppressive presence. She was painfully reminded of her collusion with her uncle. All the shameful feelings flooded back. She went home after the funeral *and began to eat.* Like many women and men, she found that bad feelings could be anesthetized with food.

In subsequent therapy sessions, Beth still avoided discussing her uncle and his behavior. She began talking about a new eating plan and the good things she was already cooking that were compatible with it. But her emotional issues stood squarely in her way. Yes, it was abuse, but Beth felt she had cooperated with it for years. With her father dead, her sister at college, and her mother always working, Beth had felt a constant loneliness. She enjoyed being her uncle's special girl and the attention he gave her. She *was* a bad girl. So she felt she did not deserve to be thin and pretty anymore. If her little daughter were ever to discover what she had done, Beth said she would die of shame.

I explained that she was taking all the responsibility for what had been her uncle's transgression. She was a good mom. Would she allow her children to take responsibility for *her* mistakes? No. In all adult–child interactions, it is always the adult who has all the responsibility for what happens. She had been a vulnerable 11-year-old, naïve and ambivalent, craving attention and affection. The sexual "game" was the uncle's unequivocal responsibility. We agreed that children need to be empowered to protect themselves by coming forward and letting parents and others know what happened. But Beth said she had been such a "bad kid" herself that she didn't even tell her sister, who called Beth from college regularly.

I pursued this last point. Had she *ever* told her sister? Did she know that an incestuous parent or relative will often seek out another family member when the one they had been abusing is no longer available? The holidays were approaching, and Beth would be at her sister's home. Could Beth find the moment to tell her sister? Yes, and the outcome was stunning. Beth and her sister were sitting at the kitchen table talking to her sister's daughter, then 14. Beth's sister was counselling her daughter to be wary of being alone with strangers and said that people were not always trustworthy. Turning to Beth, her sister said, "Like our uncle." *So it was true.* Their uncle had abused Beth's sister in essentially the same way, and neither girl had told the other. Beth was immobilized by this news. How much pain would have been averted if mother, sister, and Beth herself had been able to communicate easily.

Understanding all this and taking it to heart steadied Beth. Eventually, therapy helped her reform her self-concept. She began to feel less self-rejection and learned to encourage her own children to talk about their feelings. All this had a profound effect on her willingness and ability to diet. Without all the shame, she did not need all the food to anesthetize herself. She began to feel revulsion for all the sweets she had eaten. Her children's piggy bank would now be heir to the money she would have spent on boxes of doughnuts. She began to lose weight regularly, each week at least two pounds. And she began walking daily with her very wise husband who had encouraged her to seek therapy in the first place.

Beth's story is a very good example of the layering we see in therapy. She had originally come in for weight issues. Sessions later, she said she was not feeling as interested in sex as she had been. Later still she made the statement that changed her therapy and her life. She said she did not deserve this wonderful husband. That had been the essential clue that she was "stuck" at some painful juncture. She then asked her husband to come to her next session. With her husband's help, she revealed the overwhelming shame she experienced when her uncle died and all those memories came flooding back. This coincidence in time with her massive overeating was crucial to understanding her symptoms and resolving her impasse.

Food and Sex: A Strange and Complex Relationship

A perusal of the many books on dieting and being overweight yields a number of titles by writers who describe their weight gain as the result of sexual abuse. One poignant story after another—as we saw with Beth—is about the horror and betrayal of having been molested and the difficulty of living with the shameful truth. These women—principally it is women who write about this—feel they are bad, damaged, and undesirable. Some women report in therapy that they feel others can know the truth about them just by looking at them. Overeating numbs that pain. In addition, it reduces their body to a shapeless mass. Some women describe that mass as a barrier between them and the world—even between them and their molester. But they are still subject to much self-loathing. A poem written by one such woman in therapy describes herself as "a blob/ Who lives by the light of the refrigerator."

Besides food's numbing characteristics, it is immediately and reliably gratifying. This can substitute for and even override other equally gratifying impulses, mainly sex.

> The psychodynamic connection between eating and sex was reported for significantly more obese (47 percent) than non-obese (7 percent) patients. . . . [S]ome patients ate specifically to avoid intimate involvements, others ate as a *substitute* for sex when no partner was available, and still others ate as a means to maintain their obesity and sexual unattractiveness. (Rand 1982, 186–187; emphasis in the original)

Overeating and weight gain have a stultifying effect on a person's sexual response. Food can be used as a general tension reliever for any number of problems, but it is still surprising when very overweight people tell me that "food is better than sex." This must be one of the reasons that overeating is so difficult to overcome. Following the analytic thinking we discussed earlier, food represents the early union of mother and self. It gratifies at an earlier and less differentiated level than that of sex, which is maturationally later and inspires us toward a relationship. What will life be like once a person attains normal weight? At the end of his or her struggle, a formerly overweight man or woman is confronted with the prospect of romantic involvement and its vicissitudes. Now the person will be attractive to others or newly attractive to his or her mate.

That is not without its own set of problems. People will use food to manage sexual feelings for a variety of reasons. Some overweight women have been thwarted in their attempts at weight loss because of a fear—barely conscious—that, as they become thinner and more attractive, they may be tempted to stray from an unfulfilling marriage or relationship. The extra weight is actually experienced by the woman as *protecting her* from being attractive to another partner. This sentiment may be more common than we think. It is frequently seen in therapy that, as significant amounts of weight are lost, sexual feelings reemerge.

Women differ in their tolerance for newly emergent sexual feelings. Some women are delighted with their now attractive bodies, trying on new outfits and feeling almost like a different person. But for others, these feelings are unwelcome and even frightening. A new relationship, especially a sexual one, will be complicated by new responsibilities to another person and possibly to the children involved. Such relationships can have uncertain outcomes and may not seem worth the trouble. The lure of overeating can return, displacing sexual feelings and calming the anxiety. On the other hand, to be working in therapy during these life changes can strengthen one's understanding and clarify the new relationship and its possibilities. Those embarking on second marriages often seek to understand themselves better and to maximize their chances for a happy, mutually responsible marriage.

The interplay between attitudes toward sex and motives for overeating is a rich area for research. Despite the convincing genetics findings that many of us inherit brains sensitized to seek out and overconsume high-calorie foods as a survival tactic (King 2013), humans are complex in our motivations. Both eating behavior and sexual behavior can reduce tension and can *cause* tensions of their own.

Motives for Restricting Food: Are There People Like That?

As we have said, sexual abuse can lead to overeating. But in a smaller proportion of victims, it can result in the opposite—food restriction, sometimes so drastic it results in anorexia nervosa. Some anorectics have a history of having been raped. These girls (90–95 percent of anorectics are female [Garner & Garfinkel 1985; Andersen 1985]) not only begin to refuse food, they also begin to restrict their activities, often not leaving the house. Or they increase their activities, becoming compulsive exercisers. Many are not able to stay at school. Why starvation? How does that help? Some patients report that food refusal helps them regain their self-respect and power over their lives. Traditionally, starvation has been used as a form of protest—for example, hunger strikes for political gain. Isak Dinesen, author of *Out of Africa,* wrote that restricting food was an ultimate female expression of protest.

Fasting has been considered a purifying ritual. Although women constituted only 17 percent of saints canonized during the late Middle Ages, women were 53 percent of those saints for whom food restriction was the central part of their holiness (Bell 1987). The sleeplessness, hyperactivity, and euphoria reported by saints who rigorously fasted is observable in anorectic patients today. Whereas saints of the Middle Ages were seeking closeness to God, modern anorectics seek thinness for its own sake. Extreme thinness is held out to modern women as a *new kind of holiness,* a unique form of superiority.

Food restriction is not only associated with a history of sexual abuse. In my experience it is more frequently due to a fear of growing up and ambivalence about one's body. The treatment of anorexia nervosa or of less serious conditions of weight loss often reveals that food restriction followed upon having been shamed by friends, teachers, or a dance instructor. Shame is a powerful motivator and should always be considered as such in therapy.

The syndrome of anorexia nervosa uses the drama of food and eating to obscure pubertal difficulties pertaining to maturation. *It causes a stable conflict in a girl who, before developing the syndrome, could not resist her parents' censure without guilt. She could not refuse her parents' requirements of her, but she learned that she could refuse their food.* This gave her a kind of power in the family that she never had before. My work with anorectics was successful when I respected this dilemma. In therapy, they spoke and wrote about their good

childhoods and the shock of pubertal changes. I worked specifically
on their difficulties identifying with, and separating from, parents
who were successful, ambitious, and often controlling. As a teenager,
their daughter then became resistant and controlling. In therapy she
would often become angry with the therapist, who she experienced as
one more adult with an agenda for her. Her anger must be expressed,
tolerated, and understood. Even with this, anorectics are perhaps the
most resistant and reticent of psychiatric populations. Their symptoms are "ego-syntonic"—that is, they identify with their symptoms.

Treating Anorexia: "Leave Me Alone. Whatever I Have, I Like It."

In my work with anorectics at the Johns Hopkins Hospital, I discovered that most anorectics—around 80 percent—were first or only
daughters. Most of these who were ill enough to be hospitalized fulfilled the criterion of 20 percent loss of body weight. It seemed a total
disconnect from the normal reaction to starvation, which is one of
great distress. The body does not lose significant amounts of weight
willingly, especially if the person is close to normal weight to begin
with. These girls showed instead a clear pride in severe food restriction. They ferociously resisted any intervention. A family's frustration is compounded by a girl's reticence. She seems unreachable.

I had written my doctoral dissertation on the treatment of anorexia.
Working with hospitalized anorectics was my first experience with
how resistant they can be. I was convinced I would never graduate if
I didn't find some way to communicate with them. Midway through
my research and desperate to understand my patients' symptoms,
I suddenly realized that *these girls were all A-students!* They loved
English. They were refusing to talk to any therapist. So I devised a
new therapy that encouraged them to talk, not to me, but *about* a
beloved author. I found that most of them loved poetry, and we spoke
at length about favorite poets. The second part of my plan was this: I
had read every poem by Emily Dickinson and concluded that many
of her poems were about feeling insignificant and powerless. Some
poems even referred to starving in the metaphorical sense: "who of
little love know how to starve."

I chose 10 Dickinson poems, copied them, and used 1 at each therapy session with each patient. I read the poem, offered some interpretation, and asked my patient to read it. The first poem began, "I'm

nobody. Who are you? Are you nobody too?" More than one of the patients spontaneously said, "That sounds like me." I gently encouraged each of them to write a poem of her own on that theme. At first many declined, but with encouragement, they produced their own individual statements of insignificance and powerlessness. Within a few sessions with the other Dickinson poems, we were deep into their feelings, strongly articulated, poignantly expressed. They were *writers!* The struggle to put their feelings of inefficacy into words was liberating them from their compulsion. Although many of them had worried what would be left of them if they outgrew the anorexia, their own writing had revealed to them a connection to their bodies and to their lives that was inspiring and empowering (Woodall 1983; Woodall & Andersen 1989).

The term "anorexia nervosa" is a misnomer. The condition is characterized by *food refusal,* not loss of appetite. These two conditions are very different in their motivation. The term used in the 17th century is more accurate: "inedia" (food refusal). We might more accurately call the modern cases "inedia nervosa." True loss of appetite does occur in situations like depression, illness, or trauma. Examples include a car accident, a tragic loss of a child, a prolonged crisis, or a loss of an important relationship. Even a bad case of the flu can leave a person with no appetite. This is experienced as an involuntary reaction, not something enforced every day through a sheer act of will. Anorectics use a number of tactics to control hunger. One of these is compulsive exercise. Another is chewing ice. Ironically, they often enjoy cooking for others.

"Professional Anorexia"

A considerable number of anorectics report bulimic episodes, although by definition they mostly restrict food. Moreover, anorectics only feel in control when they are restricting food; binge eating and vomiting are considered being out of control. It is the ability to severely restrict food that anorectics claim as their pride. Indeed, anorexia nervosa may be the one psychiatric diagnosis that boosts self-esteem. Alcoholics, drug abusers, and persons who suffer from anxiety or depression are not proud of their symptoms, but anorectics uniformly assert they are proud. In a concept that I developed while at the Johns Hopkins Hospital, I proposed that anorectics who *identified* with anorexia the way the rest of us identify with our professions would have a poorer prognosis—they were "professional" anorectics. They insisted, "This is *who* I am." In a questionnaire I used with my own patients, this concept of "professional anorexia" did predict the outcome of their treatment. They were more resistant to treatment and became very chronic in their symptoms. The patients who did *not* identify with their symptoms, who instead said, "I have a disease. This is not me," were more able to outgrow the pathology and connect with the ambitions and goals normal to their age group.

Bulimia Nervosa

In contrast to the superiority and pride reported by anorectics, girls and women who binge and vomit (again, the incidence is overwhelmingly female) report the symptoms as shameful. Most bulimics are normal weight to slightly overweight. They hide their symptoms even from their families. In general, bulimics are older than anorectics and some report a period when they mostly starved. Bulimics also show impulse problems, especially stealing or shop lifting food and other items. They are frequently thrown out of college for stealing their roommate's food. Another important difference with anorectics is that bulimics are more often sexually active and are more often married.

The most striking feature of bulimics is their perception of food; recall the title about food as a "frustrating goddess." In general, they can experience food as a good thing only when it is *outside* of their bodies. Food is enticing and wonderful until it is eaten, whereupon it soon begins to feel horribly uncomfortable and must be vomited. With a number of patients, I felt the vomiting was *aggressive*. Vomiting was sometimes reported as being more important than the binge. I said to one such patient that I thought her vomiting was an angry act. She replied, "Yes! It's like saying, 'Fuck you!'" I pursued this question with other bulimics. Was their vomiting an angry act too? One woman looked at me and said ominously, "Vomiting is a force. It's like killing someone who has been bothering you a long time." I see this as a fairly clear example of the principle that women organize their anger inwardly—that is, internalizing their aggression—whereas men tend to act out their aggression.

One can understand that a person would be relieved to be getting rid of a lot of calories. But why would vomiting be a vehicle for anger?

I see the symptom as a metaphor for the act of striking out in a person who has not come to terms with her anger. Psychologists use the term "acting out" to describe behaviors like hitting that discharge tension outside the body. "Acting-in" refers to behaviors in which tension is discharged within the body and against the self. A kind of relief is felt in both cases. The act of vomiting may be enacting within the bulimic's body tension and anger actually felt toward someone else—a violator or a parent, someone who chronically angered her. Or it could be self-hate for not being brave enough or good enough. For sexually active bulimics, vomiting can be a fear and/or refusal of pregnancy.

My own suspicion is that bulimics may be trying to make food as gratifying *after* it is eaten as it seemed before (Woodall 1987). Food is a "transitional" object for all of us (Winnicott's term for things that reliably comfort us). This means that for healthy people, food feels gratifying both outside and inside the body. But for bulimics, that seems not to be the case. They cannot experience food as comfortable on the inside as it is outside the body. Chronic vomiting may be the evidence they cannot achieve that. But they keep trying. That may be the source of their compulsion and why they feel so trapped and oppressed by food. In therapy they report much secrecy and shame. And the anger symbolized by their vomiting is transformed to vehemence in verse:

In the screaming, silent dark
I drown in seas of red and black
Singing sobs of who is there
(if anyone at all) and
grabbing fistfulls of air
To package my raging thoughts
And seal them (for the moment)
Deep inside.
(Woodall & Andersen 1989, 200)

FOOD AS A DRUG

Humans have substances in our brains and other tissues that can raise mood and regulate pain the way opiate drugs can. We can release these inner opiates—endorphins—through exercising, meditating, and acupuncture. Endorphins are neuropeptides, proteins that carry information in our bodies. Part of that information concerns our emotions, which are affected by eating and weight gain:

Eating, because of its survival value, has been widely designed by evo-lution to be a highly emotional event. (All processes that impact on survival—sex, eating, breathing, etc.—are highly regulated by neuro-peptides, and thus are emotionally directed. The simple emotions of pain and pleasure, signaling us to move either toward or away from it, have been key determinants in whether an animal or human sur-vives and evolves.) Our large and small intestines are densely lined with neuropeptides and receptors, all busily exchanging information laden with emotional content. . . . There are at least twenty emotion-laden peptides released by the pancreas to regulate the assimilation and stor-age of nutrients, all carrying information about satiety and hunger. Too often, however, we ignore that information, eating when we're not really hungry, using food to bury unpleasant emotions. Nervous eating, depression eating—these are the resultant behaviors. . . . Remember, it's the peptides that mediate satiety and hunger, and we can't hear what our peptides are telling us when we are disconnected from, or in denial about, our emotions. (Pert 2003, 297)

Obese people are metabolically and probably genetically differ-ent from nonobese people (King 2013). Some evidence for epigen-etic determination of obesity was reviewed by Sanzone (2011). For example, epigenetic deregulation of the genes for several hormones has been implicated in the development of both anorexia and binge eating. Disturbances in the hypothalamus and in gut-related peptides have been found in persons suffering from eating disorders. Inten-sive treatment of their emotional problems still seems to be the most practical and effective intervention. Sutin, Ferrucci, Zonderman, and Terracciano (2011) found that impulsivity is the strongest predictor of obesity, while people who show personality traits like patience and planning were thin lifelong. Night-eating syndrome is an example of the impulsivity associated with obesity (Colles, Dixon, & O'Brian 2007). Even more ominous, obesity in mothers may be contributing to the rising numbers of children in this country who are diagnosed with autism. Mothers who were obese before pregnancy were 60 per-cent more likely to have a child with autism and twice as likely to have a child with another type of cognitive and behavioral delay than mothers who were not obese (Krakowiak et al. 2012).

In neurobiological terms, binge eating and drug addiction have sim-ilar effects. Both trigger the brain's reward system, releasing dopamine (Grimm 2007). Similarly, the brain reacts to sugar in the same way it reacts to drugs, with a release of dopamine (Macht 2007). One of the most important findings for obesity research was published by Nora Volkov and her colleagues (Wang et al. 2001). They found that very obese persons had *lower* levels of dopamine in their brains' reward centers. These people thus needed *more* food than did non-obese people to provide the same amount of satiation. This fits with the statement of many obese people—that they do not "get full."

These findings are crucial for the project of trying to lose weight. There is some evidence that overweight people are born with unresponsive or poorly responsive dopamine systems. There is also evidence that the process of overeating itself *deregulates* their reward systems (Liebman 2012). It may also deregulate their metabolism. Very obese people who chart their weight loss and their energy expenditure during various activities like gardening and cycling report that they burn significantly fewer calories during those activities than do normal-weight people (Parker-Pope 2012). For most people, food cues themselves—popcorn at theaters, cookie vendors at the mall—release dopamine. That is why they are so enticing and hard to resist.

Another line of research stresses the importance of the type and number of bacterial flora in our digestive systems. Everything we eat affects the ecosystem in our gut—the huge number of bacteria, called the microbiome—which in turn can affect the *mind.* There is now evidence that "the gut microbiome can influence neural development, brain chemistry, and a wide range of behavioral phenomena, including emotional behavior, pain perception, and how the stress system responds" (Carpenter 2012, 51). We know that overeating, especially of acid-producing foods like meat and sweets, changes the normal gut flora and disrupts digestion. Acid-producing foods can also lead to kidney damage, and there is evidence that our ancestors, who depended on game, sought fat and the fatty parts of their game to offset the physical consequences of a high-protein diet—liver and kidney damage (King 2013). Extra acidity also contributes to bone loss. The body has to buffer the extra acidity and pulls calcium from our bones to do this. The point is that our microbiome, the diverse bacteria in our gut that affect so much of our general health, can be altered by the food we choose to eat. If we keep our bacterial flora in good balance, they will in turn support our organs, our metabolism, and our mood.

Overeating may be a weakness we come by honestly. According to new findings by Bruce M. King of Clemson University, we are programmed by evolution to seek high-calorie sweet and fatty foods and to eat them beyond the point of satiation (King 2013), becoming obese in the process. It is the dopamine reward system that is the emotional trigger. People who ate this way during our ancient history survived periodic famines that were a common occurrence in our hunter-gatherer days. But King provides evidence that perhaps a third of us do not inherit that genetic trigger and do not become obese, even when surrounded by excesses of sweet, salty, and fatty foods. The obesity rate is roughly 67 percent, with 32 percent nonobese. Are we at our evolutionary peak?

The evidence is accumulating around us that the problem is the ubiquity of fast food and the relentless advertising of it. In a study of 120,000 people over a period of 20 years, weight gain was shown to be principally due to three foods: potato chips; potatoes, especially French fries; and sugar-sweetened beverages. The same study identified the foods associated with weight loss to be low-fat yogurt, unsalted nuts, fruits, vegetables, and whole grains (Mozaffarian, Hao, Rimm, Willett, & Hu 2011). The *type* of food we eat matters greatly (Lustig 2012), not just reduction of overall calories. Sugar and processed food are the main offenders. And while we think we exercise less than our ancestors, we burn a similar number of calories as our hunter-gatherer ancestors (Pontzer 2012). We simply eat a much worse diet.

Thus the research is telling us that we cannot combat obesity soon enough and effectively enough to preserve our health by depending on individual interest in losing weight. I have spent most of my professional life helping people lose weight. If it were easy, no one would be obese. The path we are on will take us over the cliff like a hoard of lemmings. And weight complications, especially heart disease, hypertension, and diabetes will bankrupt the health-care system in the process. Even Alzheimer's disease is now considered to be an inflammatory disease whose effects are confined to the brain (Clay 2013). The research is arguing for environmental changes. Just as we would not dangle candy in front of a five-year-old and then withdraw it, we must seek food advertisement reform from the fast-food industry. The Center for Science in the Public Interest has lobbied for years to get the soda machines out of schools, and there has been some interest in reducing the number of food ads that children are exposed to. These are good beginnings, but the food industry will not give up billions in profits voluntarily. Parents and legislators must work to limit the onslaught of food advertising and junk food availability that surrounds us. A 70 percent overweight/obesity rate is not acceptable.

OVER 70 PERCENT: HEALTH AND SANITY AT RISK

In 2012, the Organization for Economic Cooperation and Development, along with the American Center for Disease Control and Prevention, released the finding that, worldwide, 1 in 10 people are obese. But in the United States, over 70 percent of men and women are overweight, and over half of these are obese (Flegal, Carroll, Kit, & Ogden 2012). The projection is that by 2020, 8 out of 10 people are expected to be overweight. For children, the numbers are more ominous. More than one third of American children aged 2 to 19 are now overweight, and over half of these are obese (although there has been a glimmer that childhood obesity has peaked, as a result of recent government programs [Rosenberg, 2013]).

Since 1980, the incidence of obesity in children and adolescents has tripled. What is worse, all that junk food, especially the bad trans fats, change children's brains. In contrast, mothers' supplementing with omega-3s was so beneficial during pregnancy and lactation that it measurably increased their children's performance in mental processing at age four (Helland, Smith, Saarem, Saugstad, & Drevon 2003).

Obese children can have serious emotional problems, especially as a result of bullying. They are at increased risk of depression. Their lifestyles are characterized by inactivity with constant cues from the media to want and to eat supersized meals. These problems were incisively addressed by Suzanne Bennett Johnson, former president of the American Psychological Association. We should be careful not to blame the children, she said. It's the "obesogenic environment. . . . The fast food industry, a central player in our obesogenic environment, carefully targets the minority populations who suffer most from high obesity rates" (2012, 5). School cafeterias are improving their lunches, but the biggest problem is still in the families. Too often, obese children have obese parents. When programs can reach the entire family, there is more success. But this can involve a total restructuring of the family's lifestyle—no television in bedrooms, limiting computer time, and teaching the whole family how to cook real food.

Schools do not help this effort when they keep vending machines and packaged snacks around. Children truly live in a toxic environment when it comes to food and eating, an environment they can do nothing about. But we adults can. Fortunately, there is more awareness now about where food comes from and how it is produced. But we need to do more. While mayor of New York, Michael Bloomberg tried unsuccessfully to ban supersized drinks in theaters and restaurants. The truth is that soda needs to be eliminated completely. It is the single-most concentrated source of sugar children take in (Mozaffarian et al. 2011). It is not benign. Children do not know that soda will wreck their pancreas and lead them to develop diabetes, but we adults do.

The only way we can stop this is to become totally fed up—I am, absolutely—with the junk food industry and boycott them. If no one buys bags of artificial snacks, french fries (the number-one fattening "food"), donuts, and soda, the companies will fold. We will no longer have to put up with their relentless advertising. Cold Turkey! Zero Tolerance! Just Say No. Nothing else will work. We can no longer put up with filthy rich companies that routinely profit from ruining our children's health.

INSIST ON GOOD, CLEAN FOOD

A healthy relationship with food recognizes it for the wonderful part of our lives it is. We then want food to be clean and responsibly produced. We don't want it contaminated with pesticides or carried to us from half a world away. We want to cook it ourselves, using all the knowledge we now have about nutrition.

If all this sounds like Michael Pollan, you are right. He is the food journalist who wrote *The Omnivore's Dilemma* about the ways our food is produced and transported. And Wendell Berry, the author, social commentator, and traditional farmer, teaches us not to use any pesticides or chemical fertilizers (Berry 2009). And Joel Salatin (2011) raises livestock holistically, saying grazing is the most efficacious mechanism for planet restoration. And Marion Nestle—www .foodpolitics.com—who writes about the food industry's tactics to hook us on processed "foods." *Salt Sugar Fat* by Michael Moss (2013) will become a classic treatise on these three troublemakers in our diet. These authors, and many others, are reasserting our need for clean food that is raised humanely. Their publications are so wide-ranging that I cannot do better than to refer you to their works, especially to Michael Pollan's book, *Food Rules* (2009), a very readable distillation of his findings.

"HOW DID YOU DO IT?": WHAT REALLY WORKS
IN WEIGHT LOSS

Eating good, wholesome, well-prepared food changes our bodies dramatically for the better, often ending cravings for large amounts of sweet "foods." At this point, it is stunningly clear that sugar is an addictive substance (Moss 2013). Binges are not reported to be of good nutritious food but of candies, cookies, ice cream, and the like. Or of salty, fatty foods like french fries and cheese snacks. When people are eating a good, well-balanced diet full of wholesome food, they report that urges to binge are much less.

But there is no magic here. The bad-for-you nonfoods must be actively refused, and on a daily basis. If people can do this for several weeks, weight loss patients report that it becomes easier; they feel stronger and more disciplined. And they consistently lose weight. We should not wait to be inspired; there is no substitute for the necessary self-discipline. As with everything worthwhile in life, vision, focus, and self-discipline are the ways to make it happen. The experts agree that following a sensible eating plan for 21 days is key to retraining our brains, and we actually feel better within a few days of starting it. No gimmicks, slogans, or amulets, just solid education about nutrition and the will to change your diet for the better. Kate speaks for herself:

> For me, the most important part of my weight loss and a healthy relationship with food all started with an education. I could not have created an eating plan or changed the way that I thought about food without knowing a lot more about what I was putting into my body. . . . *I cannot believe that this is not a strong fundamental part of our education system* [Italics added]. I often wonder how I could have gotten to 30 years of . . . age not have any idea how much fat and calories and sugar were in the foods I was eating. Nor did I really know what all that was doing to my body. . . . In addition, I had to take a look at why and when I overeat and/or make poor food choices. My reasons were not—uncommon. They included feeling tired, overworked, frustrated, or *cheated*. Food has always been a comfort to me. It still is, but now I can apply my considerable knowledge and come up with choices that . . . help my body stay healthy. I have failed many times, but even then I learn. . . . Losing weight made me feel good. . . . I felt clear headed and had more energy for my life . . . [B]ut I didn't know that until I got started.

Kate is addressing the appalling lack of basic nutrition education in this country. It is only recently that nutrition education, especially the value of fresh vegetables and fruit, has been taught at grade-school levels. Moreover, up to the present, *medical school students do not learn about human nutrition* in class, the single subject that would save their patients from the big four major degenerative illnesses: heart disease, high blood pressure, obesity, and diabetes.

It is incomprehensible to me that even some obesity researchers are still saying that all foods are permissible and that people simply need to learn moderation. While it is certainly true that persons needing to lose weight must learn about portion size and train their bodies to be comfortable with less volume of food, the *type* of food is critical (Lustig 2012). Refined sugar is the worst offender, with no redeeming features. The aisles and aisles of snack foods also have no measurable nutritive value, and as we have said before, they hijack our reward systems in an addictive manner. After just a few weeks of not eating these nonfoods, people routinely report how much better they feel—more energy, more ambition, and mentally clear.

It is worth repeating, in this section on weight loss, the findings of the 20-year study of over 120,000 people (Mozaffarian et al. 2011) in which it was shown that weight gain was due to principally three "foods": potato chips, potatoes (especially fried), and sugar-sweetened beverages. This is a stunning finding and good reason never to eat those nonfoods again. Just as impressive, the foods associated with weight *loss* and maintaining healthy weight were four. First, *yogurt, unsweetened,* or *sweetened with stevia.* Then *raw nuts, unsalted.* Third, *fresh fruits,* and lastly, *vegetables* and *whole grains.* The type of food matters greatly, and here is the proof.

The major changes that finally bring a person to that moment of truth about his or her weight are emotional. They are *learned.* If you need to lose fat, then that is the most important thing for you to do this year. Remember: you are the only one who can give that to you. Memorize the principles that successful people have used for years. One or more of these principles will connect with where you are at this moment and put you in the mindset you need. Here are the time-tested rules:

1. Eat the same types of good food each day and on the same schedule. Beginning with breakfast, eat about every three hours.
2. Avoid obese "friends." They will pull you backward.
3. Don't binge on weekends. Follow the same healthy eating plan every day.

4. Aim for a one-to-two pound loss every week. You may lose more in the first few weeks, but after that, one to two pounds is reasonable.

5. Eat slowly, appreciating flavor, aroma, texture, and how your stomach feels.

6. Keep a food journal. Write down everything you eat and the time you ate it. This is much more effective than you may think.

7. Protect yourself from overstimulation, especially at the supermarket. Don't go down the cookie and candy aisles at all. Don't go near vending machines or the cookie kiosk at the mall.

8. Treat your body as if it were a five-year-old child. It is. Like a child, she does not know what is good for her, and she wants the sweets she was given before. Protect her from tempting situations.

9. Avoid the trigger foods. Each person knows what they are. Clean out your cupboards.

10. Always measure your food; be sure you master what normal portions are.

11. Drink the recommended eight glasses of water per day. It flushes out the breakdown products of fat metabolism.

12. Do whatever you can to reduce stress. Don't let yourself get too tired, too hungry, or too lonely.

13. If you slip and eat too much, get right back on your program.

14. Always have good snacks on hand like sliced apples, unsalted nuts, and popcorn.

15. Use stevia to sweeten tea and yogurt. It is the only sweetener that is safe and that doesn't raise insulin levels.

16. Develop patience in planning your food. Impulsivity is the strongest predictor of obesity.

17. Michael J. Mosley has published new findings on intermittent fasting (*The FastDiet*, Simon & Schuster 2013). Some people do well on this.

18. Stop eating about two hours before you go to bed. Digestion slows dramatically during sleep.

19. Find an exercise you love to do, like gardening or dancing. Exercise releases endorphins in addition to burning calories.

20. Give yourself nonfood rewards—clothing, theater tickets, or a new hairdo.

21. Don't eat out if you can avoid it. It can sabotage your resolve, especially at the beginning of your program.
22. Don't leave food out all day on counters. It's part of protecting yourself.
23. Use small plates. Research shows we eat more from large plates and bowls.

Lastly—Get angry at the saboteurs. Get angry at the fast food companies who deliberately make profits selling Americans artery-clogging junk and advertise it as food. They are wrecking our country's health. Let's put them out of business.

FOOD AS HOLY

In many cultures, people "say grace" over home-cooked food, recognizing it for the blessing it is. Historically, the knowledge about how and when to plant crops was available only to the religious leaders or priests. It was sacred information upon which the very life of the people rested. Food was life itself, and it was lovingly planted and harvested and carefully preserved. Harvest festivals have religious roots and emphasize, with music and dance, gratitude for a successful growing season. The reverence we feel for good, wholesome food, beautifully prepared and served, is an extension of this gratitude.

The ubiquity and amounts of "fast food" surrounding us, and worse, the eating of great volumes of this food under conditions of noise and tension (for example, Chucky Cheese's), is the worst situation for children. It is *the making of eating disorders*, priming their nervous systems for preferring large amounts of food in noisy, tense settings. Let's not do this to our children anymore. Let's remember what family meals were meant to be. Eating should be a comfortable, happy affair, free of tension, full of fun and appreciation, in the company of cherished people.

REFERENCES

Andersen, A. E. (1985). *Practical Comprehensive Treatment of Anorexia Nervosa and Bulimia.* Baltimore, MD: The Johns Hopkins University Press.
Bell, R. (1987). *Holy Anorexia.* Chicago: University of Chicago Press.
Berry, W. (2009). *Bringing It to the Table: On Farming and Food.* Berkeley, CA: Counterpoint Press.

Carpenter, S. (2012, August). "That Gut Feeling: With a Sophisticated Neural Networks Transmitting Messages from Millions of Bacteria, Your Stomach May Have a Mind of Its Own." *Monitor on Psychology* 43(8): 50–55.

Clay, R. A. (2013, February). "Could Alzheimer's Disease Be a Kind of Diet-Induced Diabetes?" *Monitor on Psychology* 44(2): 11.

Cohen, P. G. (2008). "Obesity in Men: The Hypo-Gonadal Estrogen-Receptor Relationship and Its Effect on Glucose Homeostasis." *Med Hypotheses* 70(2): 358–60.

Colles, S. L., Dixon, J. B. & O'Brian, P. E. (2007). "Night-eating Syndrome and Nocturnal Snacking: Association with Obesity, Binge-Eating and Psychological Stress." *International Journal of Obesity*, 31, 1722–1730.

Flegal, K. M., Carroll, M. D., Kit, B. K, et al. (2012). "Prevalence of Obesity and Trends in the Distribution of Body Mass Index among U.S. Adults, 1999–2010." *Journal of the American Medical Association*, 307, 491–497. doi:10.1001/jama.2012.39

Garner, D. M. & Garfinkel, P. E. (Eds.). (1985). *Handbook of Psychotherapy for Anorexia Nervosa and Bulimia.* New York: Guilford Press.

Grimm, O. (2007, April–May). "Addicted to Food: What Drives People, against Their Better Judgement, to Eat More Food Than They Need?" *Scientific American Mind* 18(2): 36–39.

Helland, I. B., Smith, L., Saarem, K., et al. (2003). "Maternal Supplementation with Very-Long-Chain n-3 Fatty Acids During Pregnancy and Lactation Augments Children's IQ at Four Years of Age." *Pediatrics*, 111, e39–e44. doi:10.1542/peds.111.1, e39

Johnson, S. B. (2012, October). "Addressing the Obesity Epidemic: Don't Blame the Victim." *Monitor on Psychology* 43(9): 5.

King, B. (2013). "The Modern Obesity Epidemic: Ancestral Hunter-Gatherers and the Sensory/Reward Control of Food Intake." *American Psychologist* 68(2): 88–96.

Krakowiak, P., Walker, C. K., Bremer, A. A., et al. (2012). "Maternal Metabolic Conditions and Risk for Autism and Other Neurodevelopmental Disorders." *Pediatrics online*, April 9, 2012, doi:10.1542/peds.2011–2583

Liebman, B. (2012). "Food and Addiction: Can Some Foods Hijack the Brain?" *Nutrition Action Healthletter* 39(4): 1–7.

Lustig, R. H. (2012). *Fat Chance: Beating the Odds against Sugar, Processed Food, Obesity and Disease.* New York: Hudson Street Press.

Macht, M. (2007, October–November). "Feeding the Psyche." *Scientific American Mind* 18(5): 64–69.

Moss, M. (2013). *Salt Sugar Fat: How the Food Giants Hooked Us.* New York: Random House.

Mozaffarian, D., Hao, T., Rimm, E. B., et al. (2011). "Changes in Diet and Lifestyle and Long-Term Weight Gain in Women and Men." *New England Journal of Medicine* 364(25): 2392–2404.

Nestle, M. (2007). *Food Politics: How the Food Industry Influences Nutrition and Health.* Expanded edition. Berkeley: University of California Press.

Parker-Pope, T. (2012, January 1). "The Fat Trap." *The New York Times Magazine*, MM22.

Pert, C. B. (2003). *Molecules of Emotion: Why You Feel the Way You Feel.* New York: Scribner.

Pollan, M. (2009). *Food Rules: An Eater's Manual.* New York: Penguin Books.

Pollan, M. (2006). *The Omnivore's Dilemma.* New York: Penguin Books.

Pontzer, H. (2012, August 26). "Debunking the Hunter-Gatherer Workout." *New York Times Sunday Review*, SR 5.

Rand, C. S. W. (1982). "Psychoanalytic Treatment of Obesity." In B.B. Wolman (Ed.), *Psychological Aspects of Obesity: A Handbook.* New York: Van Nostrand Reinhold Company.

Rosenberg, T. (2013, November 17). "To Fight Obesity, a Carrot and a Stick." *The New York Times Sunday Review*, SR7.

Salatin, J. (2011). *Folks, This Ain't Normal: A Farmer's Advice for Happier Hens, Healthier People and a Better World.* New York: Center Street.

Sanzone, M. (2011). "Eating Disorders: Genetic and Biological Harbingers." *The Maryland Psychologist* 56(4): 17–20.

Sutin, A. R., Ferrucci, L., Zonderman, A. B., et al. (2011). "Personality and Obesity across the Adult Life-Span." *Journal of Personality and Social Psychology* 101(3): 579–592.

Tannahill, R. (1973). *Food in History.* Briarcliff Manor, NY: Stein and Day Publishers/Scarborough House.

Wang, G-J., Volkow, N. D., Logan, J., et al. (2001). "Brain Dopamine and Obesity." *Lancet*, 357, 354–357.

Weir, K. (2012, November). "Big Kids." *Monitor on Psychology* 43(11): 59–63.

Woodall, C. (1983). "Eating Disorders, Body Image and Self-Hate." Unpublished doctoral dissertation, Rutgers, the State University, Newark, NJ

Woodall, C. (1987). "The Body as a Transitional Object in Bulimia: A Critique of the Concept." In F. C. Feinstein (Ed.), *Adolescent Psychiatry*, 14, 179–184. Chicago: University of Chicago Press.

Woodall, C. & Andersen, A. (1989). "The Use of Metaphor and Poetry Therapy in the Treatment of the Reticent Subgroup of Anorectic Patients." In L. M. Hornyak & E. K. Baker (Eds.), *Experiential Therapies for Eating Disorders*, 191–206. New York: Guilford Press.

Zumoff, B. (1988). "Hormonal Abnormalities in Obesity." *Acta Medica Scandinavica Supplementum*, 723, 153–160.

Chapter 8

Shame and Guilt
What Is Really Mine?

Absolve you to yourself, and you shall have the suffrage of the world.

—Ralph Waldo Emerson

Often discussed together, and often occurring together, shame and guilt are related but distinct human capacities. It is tempting to simplify that distinction by saying that shame is an *internal experience*, concerned with the relationship a person has with himself, and that guilt is *external*, a result of the relationship we have with others, especially their expectations of us. Still, it is helpful to discuss them separately. We will see that shame is a helpful, constructive emotion, whereas guilt—after early childhood—is immobilizing and corrosive.

SHAME: A DEVELOPMENTAL PHENOMENON

A painful and unwelcome feeling from childhood on, shame is actually a very normal emotion. It has been defined by psychoanalyst Leon Wurmser (1981) as the perception of our own failure in not having lived up to our own standards. For psychologist John Bradshaw (2005), the origin of shame "directly touches the age-old theological and metaphysical discussion generally referred to as the problem of evil." We first felt shame because we lost our innocence and ostensibly our "perfection" and are now found wanting.

While we are feeling shame, we feel exposed as inadequate or incompetent. Being laughed at by the whole class is one of the most painful memories of childhood. And how it persists! We wanted to hide, to disappear into the very floor. To compound the indignity, evolutionary biologists have now discovered that humans retain the memory of bad experiences much more readily than happy memories, presumably from the need to prevent bad things from being repeated. Precisely because of this pain, shame powerfully shapes our behavior. Children will learn quickly how to avoid humiliation—another word for shame. Children with a good or adequate sense of self-worth can often laugh at their own mistakes, learn from them, and move on to more acceptable behaviors. Each time this happens, a child's behavior is shaped toward societal norms, and this increases the child's self-esteem.

But children and adults who do not possess a strong sense of self-worth will experience shame as a continuation of their uncertain status in their family of origin (and the life sentence that this can confer). Painful feelings of shame are more often the motive behind puzzling behaviors than we might suspect. Much gruffness, many tearful outbursts, and simple avoidance can be understood as a person's reaction to shame (Morrison 1998; Potter-Efron & Potter-Efron 1989). Being reminded of our shame is unbearable. W. R. D. Fairbairn's psychoanalytic view of shame is that it stems from not having been loved, with the result than the person then feels unlovable (Celani 2010). The observed distress even a tiny child expresses upon failure at a task has been of special interest to developmental psychologists (Kagan & Lamb 1987).

Developmentally, shame can be a *stimulant*, helping us focus on what we need to do to feel better. But shame can also stymie development, catching a child in the quicksand of parental disdain. She does not understand that disdain, because her parent communicates it only with an amorphous discomfort with the child's efforts or the direction of her interests. A child may rush home with her latest creation or a good grade, only to be met by a distracted, impatient parent. The child's achievement becomes tainted; it does not please her parent. The notion that then smoothly clicks into place is this: *I* do not please my parent. Shame then becomes one of the most secretive and hidden emotions (Scheff 1988).

It is encouragement and reassurance that reset a child's confidence and her resolve to try again, and this time to get it right. Each incidence of shame is not just uncomfortable in the moment—for example, completely forgetting to do an assignment; it is compounded by the worry that she was not valued in her own family, perhaps by an older sibling or even her parent or grandparent. Every subsequent experience of shame or failure reinforces her worry that she is not good enough, not worthy of appreciation and attention. This is one more line of evidence showing the importance of sustained positive experience and attachment in early childhood.

On a more serious note, shame is the painful outcome of many cases of incest and other forms of sexual abuse. The person feels not only assaulted but *tainted* and forever defective. This requires a complicated and specialized form of therapeutic intervention (Courtois 1988; Ferentz 2012) that is too broad to cover here, although the case of Terry in chapter one of this book serves as a telling example. The phobia that brought Terry to therapy served to both *hide* and *express* her anxiety about having been raped.

One could argue that the experience of childhood itself has changed. The social media alone usurp much of children's energy. In a world where everyone can have stylish clothes, what is most urgently desired is to have hundreds of "friends" with whom to share the happenings of the day and to chat, share photos, and snoop on others. Now children feel shame about *different things* than in the past. My traditionalist worry is that the more time spent online, the less in actual relationships and in reading and studying. We all get the same 24 hours, and if most of it is spent in front of a screen, most of our reality consists of *internal* mental constructs.

This is another reason for early childhood education. The findings from programs like Early Head Start have actually shown increases in IQ, assertiveness, and achievement in those children lucky enough to have been included, which also offer opportunities for their mothers. Teachers do marvelous work in encouraging shy and defeated children, especially in the lower grades, to have small successes, one after another, that overcome feelings of shame and inadequacy and to start believing in themselves as bright and competent.

To repeat, shame is a normal emotion that helps shape our behavior in order to comply with what is expected by our family and later by our social group. Subjectively, shame is a feeling of having failed. Leon Wurmser (1981; 2007) identified three aspects of shame. First is the experience of shame as the "guardian" of our personal values. Shame alerts us when we stray from our own standards. Second is shame as a depressive reaction that can remain with us throughout life, as in the case of Gustav to follow. The third expression of shame is an anticipatory anxiety; it can make us worry in advance and keep us from making mistakes.

The healthy functions of shame may be stated:

1. Shame helps us to form internal standards in accord with those valued by our parents and peers.
2. Shame keeps us working toward those standards and "cues" us when we fail.
3. It also helps us avoid painful experiences by "cueing" us *before* we do something questionable.
4. It helps build and preserve relationships with those important to us.
5. It is a major motivator toward achievements of all kinds by steering us toward shame's opposite: pride.

The censure, the *pain* of shame may be one of the outcomes of human self-awareness, produced by the enlargement of the brain's neocortex, which allows us to live in three time zones: the past, the present, and the future. We are always making comparisons between and among these, as well as our "place" in them. Our peculiar need for human relatedness and validation motivates us to want to "belong," and this is the setting for shame (and guilt, as we shall see).

A Nameless Grief: The Story of Gustav

The lifelong effects of shame can weave themselves year by year through family life. Tina came to therapy with her husband, Gustav, their 11-year-old son, and 9-year-old daughter. Her husband would not enforce any rules, she said, or reprimand their son at all. The children bickered while the mother complained about having to be the sole disciplinarian. In this first session, her husband said nothing and stared at the books on my tall bookshelves. The children responded to my questions with giggles and sideways glances toward each other. Many, perhaps most, children react with disdain when they hear their parents speak of their own early lives. They consider anything that happened before they were born incomprehensible and irrelevant. This is understandable; we felt the same way about our parents' early lives. Like so many attitudes that relent with maturation, this one yields with a growing appreciation of family history. But for now, these two children were bored and annoyed. Their mother answered the questions I put to them then continued with her complaints. Her husband remained silent.

During one of the subsequent sessions, I commended Gustav for coming to every session, but I worried that his daily silence in the family (his wife's chronic complaint) was being repeated in the therapy session. Knowing the statement could be provocative, I said it might be difficult for him to remember what it was like to be an 11-year-old boy. With that, Gustav seemed stricken. A look of intense pain and anger flashed from his eyes. He seemed impelled to speak. In a low but clear voice and in a soft Belgian accent, he told me his own mother had left the family when he had been about 11 years old. It had thrown him, his father, and his younger sister into a chasm of grief and shock. He remembers feeling as if he were in a daze. He could hear his father sobbing in the middle of the night.

Early one Saturday morning, Gustav sat in the kitchen staring at the place where his mother always stood while cooking. Without waking his father, he dressed and left the house. He started walking, wondering desperately how he could find his mother. He saw a bus stopped at a corner and boarded it. He rode through town after town, scanning the streets, watching people going in and out of stores. He does not remember how long he did this or how he paid for the bus. The driver noticed him and questioned where he was going. Gustav told the bus driver he was looking for someone. The driver smiled and drove him home. After that, he said, he barely could get up and go to school. He felt he had proven to himself that he could not find his mother. He couldn't do anything. Nor could his father. The situation was hopeless.

It was this man's next statement that told me how it had been possible for him to finally tell me his heartbreaking story. "I . . . have been looking at your books," Gustav said. "You read all these hundreds of books. Maybe you can tell me. Where did my mother go?"

Suddenly everything shifted. This silent man with the steady gaze was crumbling in grief. His children were staring at him in amazement and disbelief. Tina had both her arms around her husband tightly, as if holding him together. "I knew the mother had left them," she said. "I didn't know it would bother him this long." I myself was filled with amazement and awe at this man's impressive faith—and naiveté—about what "book people" could possibly know.

Never before had he asked this question, not even of his aggrieved father. But the message left with this boy and his heart-broken little sister—the unavoidable truth—was that their mother didn't love them enough to stay with them. And the fateful mistake that children make when they are not loved is that they themselves are to blame. Researchers, especially those psychoanalytically trained, have repeatedly shown that when children are not loved enough, they tend to blame themselves (Benedek 1973; Celani 2010). They reason, "If my mother does not love me, there must be something wrong with *me. I must not be lovable.*" And this engenders an enduring sense of *shame*, culminating in lifelong depression.

Children cannot, at a very young age, understand that a woman who leaves two young children is showing severe psychological problems of her own. Usually for reasons in her own history, she is not bonded to these children. Or her own sexual attraction to someone else was enough to pull her away from them, or both. Gustav, as an 11-year-old boy, could not see his mother as immature, flighty, or perhaps even as suffering from bipolar disorder, and thus very impulsive. All he could feel was the tragic abandonment and his own abiding shame.

The importance of all this for this family's therapy was now in front of us. This father could not reprimand his son, guide or encourage him; indeed, he could not fully *love* his son, because it was so painful for him to feel anything for his child. Gustav's deserving and innocent 11-year-old son painfully reminded this father of his own 11-year-old self—abandoned, confused, frightened, and full of shame. In therapy Gustav learned that it was not he himself, but his mother's psychological problems that had caused her to abandon the whole family. It was his mother's pathology, or simply immaturity, that caused this tragedy. But as always, this knowledge did not touch the early wound. Only comforting does that; in this case, a combination of the therapist's explanations and reassurance and his wife's dependable touch and holding. Learning *self*-comforting is the best way out of painful feelings of shame. Only when this man could know and *believe* the truth about his mother could he appreciate that he was indeed worthy and lovable—and as innocent as his own son. He could then say *aloud* how much he treasured his wife's loyalty and love—a beautiful thing to hear in therapy. And with many sessions of spirited discussion, Gustav learned the words and phrases to express his deepest feelings. He could then reach out and place his hand supportively on his son's shoulder.

It may be that when a person is very susceptible to shame, he is more susceptible to guilt. Guilt weighs more heavily when a person's self-confidence is shaken by a conviction of failure. These feelings coexisted in Gustav. Although the presenting clinical problem was lifelong depression, gentle questioning soon revealed feelings of unacknowledged shame. He did not have the words to express his feelings and had to learn these words and concepts in therapy. Later, he was able to say that he *knew* his wife deserved more time and support with raising their children, but he could not face that responsibility. I reminded him that he was competent and confident at work; as a supervisor, he was completely responsible to his team. It was on the *emotional* level that he had no energy for his relationships. Depression robs us of energy.

That same confidence would develop side by side with Gustav's realization that his feelings of shame were undeserved. It was not *his* inadequacy that had caused his pain. It was his mother's behavior—pathologically impulsive or immature—that had caused it. The shame was hers.

DIFFERENTIATING SHAME FROM GUILT

"There is a seeming paradox in the *therapeutic responsiveness of shame and guilt.* Whereas it seems evident that shame has definite 'progressive' and 'self-curative' elements in it, it does not follow at all that a pathological condition with the nuclear problem of shame will yield to therapy easier than one of guilt" (Piers & Singer 1971, 51; italics added). Therapy initially *increases* feelings of shame, the therapist's questions and statements actually making a person feel worse about herself. During this crucial phase, it is the patient's growing ability to endure focused feelings of shame that predicts her staying in therapy or not. And the therapist must patiently attend to the person's accusations that therapy is generating not relief but more pain.

In psychotherapy, we speak about psychological boundaries—the sense of what is inside of you and what is outside, the experience of where you end and the other person begins. A strong boundary means that a person feels a certainty about what is his or hers. For example, a strong personality boundary makes me certain of what is my responsibility and what is someone else's, what is my right and what is the other person's right. I must make a careful intervention so that both are preserved. In fact, shame is so ubiquitous in human life that training may be needed to help with *therapist* shame that can be evoked in the therapy hour (Dearing & Tangney 2011).

Similarly, strong boundaries are crucial for understanding the distinction between shame and guilt. We have said that shame is a feeling of unworthiness, incompetence, and deficiency leading to a feeling of failure. Shame is the painful realization that we have failed our own standards. It is an inner conviction that spurs us to correct the problem. Guilt, on the other hand, comes from *outside of us.* It represents someone else's idea about what we should be *doing* (while shame is about *being*). Guilt concerns a thing done or not done that someone else says is our responsibility to do. "Take that job." "Don't marry that person." *If we* believe that the other person is correct—often a parent, grandparent, brother, sister, spouse, or supervisor—then we *will* feel guilt.

When the accusation is deliberate, it is a process known as "guilt-induction" (giving the other person a "guilt trip"). It is crucial to understand that inducing guilt in another person is *a form of* aggression. When someone is trying to make you feel guilty, he or she is attacking you. That attack will cause you to feel ambivalent if you cannot decide who is right. Conversely, if you are certain you are right, then you will react to the guilt-induction as you would to any attack. "Hold on!" would be a fair retort. "Don't put that on me. That's not mine."

The admission of guilt represents a painful rejection of our personhood, a spiral downward that drains our energy and damages our self-esteem. It poses a persistent conflict between what we want to do and what the other person says—verbally or non-verbally—we *should* do. We may know, intellectually, that we have the *right* to do what we want. But the nagging guilt, the *belief* that the other person may be right, interferes with our decision making, as well as with our contentment. How can we be happy if we are not living up to our responsibility? Do we have the *right* to live our own life? A separate life? Guilt begins a process of self-derogation, immobilizing us with the conviction of culpability. Once formed, guilt holds us—in Emily Dickinson's chilling image—"in its claw."

The feeling of guilt is fundamentally one of *anxiety.* Guilt is experienced as a threat. And part of that threat is the fear of retaliation, that we may be punished for our transgression and even for our wishes to transgress. While shame may require an audience—others to whom we unfavorably compare ourselves—guilt is a fateful, *internal* verdict, private suffering, an unsharable hell. Evolutionary biologists tell us, as if it were some harbinger of advanced life forms, that we are born worriers, that we remember bad experiences more easily than happy ones. Misfortune is efficiently recalled, while counting our blessings takes effort (and occurs in a different part of the brain, the prefrontal cortex).

Even the most loving and tolerant of mothers has standards for her child that are mysterious and unacceptable to him. From age two or so, with the competence of walking, running, and climbing, the child is scanning the horizon for exciting opportunities to act on. This is not a "bad" child who deliberately defies his parent's rules. No, he is simply "stimulus-bound" (Piaget 1965); he is "grabbed" by the encounter with a shiny or colorful new object and cannot limit his impulse to reach for it. There is not yet a distinction in his nervous system between impulse and action, one that will permit reflection. That will come later with continued maturation of his nervous system in the form of myelination—damping down the speed of neuronal impulses. For the moment, the child is "quick on the draw," and we must protect him and our possessions by "child-proofing" our home. What does all this have to do with guilt? There *is none* at this stage.

Guilt is the "painful internal tension" (Piers & Singer 1971, 16) resulting from the formation of conscience at age seven or eight, perhaps earlier. Psychologically and morally, a child begins to distinguish right from wrong *as interpreted by his parent*. Guilt feelings are evidence that a strong bond has formed with his parents, such that a threat to this bond is experienced as a threat to his well-being. At age two or three, this threat is experienced as a fear of abandonment. But as he approaches six or seven, any threat to that bond will now be understood by the child as his responsibility. It was caused by his willfulness and is now his to undo.

Whenever we hear ourselves saying, "I should ... ," we may be certain that it is coming from *outside* of us. It is someone else's idea of what is or is not our responsibility. The linguistic and philosophical root for guilt—"schuld" in German—is from "schulden," to owe. Thus, when we feel guilt, we are feeling that we "owe" the other person. This is why we feel guilt in those relationships in which we are most passionately vulnerable. These would be with parents first, and perhaps primarily, but also with spouses and lovers, who inherit the unresolved problems we have with those parents. And finally, we feel guilt toward our children, who embody both our own early experience and the opportunity to blame the past for its inexorable hold on us. Our children also afford us the enticing chance to do things differently.

Raising children often empowers us to verbally refuse the pressures we grew up with. But even if not verbalized, our children intuit the private devils we are fighting. Through the many things said or not said, our children learn what topics we avoid and the things we angrily deride. Out of love, they unwittingly join us in this, although never actively recruited. And those are the issues they will struggle with later.

Our feelings of guilt begin in the relationship with our parents for a very good reason. During childhood, guilt *protects and preserves* our relationship with our parents. This is the *normal* role of guilt. To the degree that we accept their authority over us, we feel safe. These experiences accumulate and lead to the formation of conscience at six or seven, defined as the "introjection" of the parents' rules and proscriptions. It now becomes the child's own voice that he "hears" when he feels guilt.

That conscience develops as a reaction to parental sanctions may be disputed.

> The Comanche, who do not punish children for disobedience and who bestow love and praise for achievement, are said to be free of a sense of guilt, although shame remains a sanction. Where there is neither love given for obedience nor consistent punishment for disobedience, as among the Marquesans and the Alorese, there is no western form of conscience, but there is a sense of shame. (Piers & Singer 1971, 88–89)

We may conclude that an attachment to early parents influences not just our survival, but our self-esteem.

In my own research, this extended to the conviction that a person could feel "owned" by her parent. My early research was with anorectic and bulimic patients (Woodall 1987; Woodall & Andersen 1989). When I pursued their actual subjective feelings, I found that the *outside* of a person's body—"my skin," "my hair," " my face"—was perceived as being owned by her parent, whereas the *inside* of the body—"my thoughts," "my secret," "my heart"—were experienced as belonging to the self, albeit an impotent self. Guilt and submission were properties of the outside, observable body, which was then split off from her true self-experience hidden inside. Therapy with these girls explored this dual existence and developed their creativity and writing skills, which reached their deepest frustrations. Moving their private feelings, often unacknowledged and unpermitted in the parental home, to a celebrated level *shared* with the therapist healed the split between inner and outer body. Food became just food, not the passive-aggressive weapon used ineffectively against the world.

Responses like "My self is non-existent" became, for one 16-year-old, "My self is just emerging."

Our ability to distinguish right from wrong proceeds through several stages, classically described by Jean Piaget (1965) and Lawrence Kohlberg (1973). Initially, children simply try to avoid punishment and will even lie (which I define as the ability to hold two competing versions of an event in mind at the same time—what the parent believes and what the child knows to be true). This can occur sometime between two and three years of age with varying degrees of finesse. The second stage of moral development shows the child avoiding bad behavior because of the strong attachment he feels for his parent and how delighted he is to be called a good boy. In the final stage in Piaget's system, a child is mature enough to appreciate an action's inherent "rightness" or "wrongness," and this guides his behavior. At this stage of development—self-responsibility—no policing is necessary. No one is perfect, however. Kohlberg expanded on Piaget's system, increasing the stages to six and alleging that moral development proceeds throughout the lifespan.

However, Kohlberg's data were gathered from a male cohort. Dinnerstein (1976) and Gilligan (2003) showed how different morality becomes when viewed from girls' and women's perspectives. Dinnerstein, for example, wrote about the problem of differential socialization of girl babies and boy babies. Her argument is impossible to summarize in a few sentences but begins with the early resentment of the mother's control by both girls and boys. Girls integrate their resentment more efficiently because they grow up to become mothers, Dinnerstein said. But boys suffer more from female domination and from being pushed away from mothers earlier in general than girls are. They grow up retaining their need to control women lifelong, an important source of misogyny. This complicates women's wish to compete with men in adult life. "Women's original power over each life . . . not only makes man want to keep her down later. It also makes her want to be kept down by him. But the wish to be kept down is never wholehearted" (Dinnerstein 1976, 192). The ambivalence that women feel in competing with men is in part *guilt* for moving into the mother role and sharing the resentment that all women inherit. Men feel this ambivalence as well, expressed as fear of closeness with women—a "relational dread" (Takei 2012). In a stunning compilation of evidence, Michele Takei turns this argument into an exhortation: women need to "mentor men" because women, Takei says, are the more rational, moral, and creative sex. "They [women] define themselves in the context of human relationships, but also judge *themselves* in terms of their ability to care. . . . This sense of defining oneself as a separate or relational self appears to be a primary difference between men and women" (100–101; italics hers.). Clearly, gender complicates the issues of guilt and shame, as it complicates all of human life.

Moreover, guilt, once formed, is represented as actual changes in brain physiology. According to neuroscientists, guilt feelings are produced by the interaction of several cortical areas:

> Orbitofrontal circuitry embodies many of the functions of the superego [the psychoanalytic term for conscience]. The medial orbitofrontal cortex [OFC] and amygdala detect the presence of both potential reward and danger. In addition, the lateral OFC normally tempers the pursuit of pleasure with considerations of context and risk. (Viamontes & Beitman 2012, 47)

Thus, we may be "hard-wired" to feel guilt. If once we have formed an attachment to a parent, that bond is engraved on our nervous system and protected by its own dragon: guilt.

"Getting Rid" of Guilt: Joanne and Her Sometimes Father

Because our passionate bond with our parents develops so early during the life-or-death whirl of infancy, it is the most complex in our lives. It gathers momentum as we grow, becoming weighted with episodes from early adolescence, fueling our adult decisions and defiance, and is still looming as we watch our parent die.

"Why can't I get rid of this?" Joanne lamented. "Why doesn't therapy help me with this?" I replied that therapy must first examine her ambivalence—lifelong and life-changing—about a father who flitted in and out of her life with maddening irregularity. She had come to therapy confused and angry. She did not want to visit her ailing father who, she said, had left her seven-year-old self, changing the trajectory of her life. But "she felt she should"—*schuld* again. Intuiting the clinical definition of guilt, Joanne felt she owed it to him. "He's my father. I *should* want to see him," she repeated. I told her that at least part of her ambivalence persisted because this man did not know her; he did not know the suffering woman who came to therapy unable to understand her feelings, a flurry of shame, guilt, anger, and longing. At age seven, she had watched him drive away and then ran to her mother's bedroom, only to find the door locked. This scene was bound to engender grief and fear in any child, and Joanne had felt both while "frozen to the floor." She had effectually lost both parents in that moment. Now she was faced with her father's decline. This was the same father who had sent birthday cards, a graduation card, and with the same casual grace, his wedding announcement to "wife number two." Years later, her father had accepted the invitation to attend Joanne's wedding and then disappeared from her life. What now did he want from her? What indeed did she have to give?

Children comply with what their parents want because they feel love and gratitude. Joanne felt neither but still could not quell this feeling of guilt imposed on her by a dying man for whatever his reasons. "Therapy should get rid of this," she insisted. "What about hypnosis?" I sympathized with her plea. She simply wanted to be free of the pain of guilt and, perhaps, to "leave" her father with a flourish of defiance. But, I reminded Joanne, we all need to recognize our feelings and accept them in all their complexity. We do this by *naming* each feeling and describing our reaction to it. What was stopping her from *comfortably* visiting her father was a lifetime of resentment toward him—a *child's* lifetime of milestones. Birthday: no father. Graduation: no father, when all her friends had their dads helping out, driving people around, always available for hugs. The worst was at Joanne's own wedding reception; this now overweight father had to introduce himself to his daughter because she did not recognize him.

There was a part of Joanne that just wanted to scream at him. Her anger was exaggerated precisely because it came from such an early layer of her experience. I encouraged her to tell *me* everything she would say if she did not feel so guilty. This would uncover her feelings of loss and longing. She wrote a letter to her father that she did not mail—a Gestalt Therapy technique that is very relieving and clarifying for many people. She described her earliest happy feelings during her childhood when her dad was still at home. She talked about her mother's depression that had also deprived Joanne of a mother's comfort. She was an only child who described her childhood home as "hollow." She described her embarrassment—*shame*—at school and her loneliness for a dad she could talk about. Later, she said, she had had trouble trusting boyfriends. We talked about a girl's sense of self and body image as being very much influenced by her dad's praise and encouragement. Finally, Joanne's therapy progressed to her present dilemma over feelings of guilt—what she felt she owed her father.

When she was able to fully grieve her historical losses and complain about his self-centeredness, her big-girl decision was that she owed him nothing.

Joanne was relating all this tearfully, all the jumbled feelings, and describing these over and over *in her own words.* There is no substitute for this process in therapy; we have to do the necessary thinking and feeling. Freud had described how moving experiences from the "felt" level to the "known" level by putting them into words was in itself relieving. To *avoid* this process—Joanne's ardent wish—would preserve the conflict indefinitely. The guilt she was feeling is considered a normal progression and must be worked out on an individual basis.

Is Guilt Curable?

Imagine then how complicated things become when a person feels that he or she *did* receive many good things from a parent who—as we might expect—was by turns also frustrating and presumptuous. As children grow, competition for limited resources like money, time, or a parent's graduate work make for spirited family debates. In therapy we hear very specific complaints about even "good" parents.

> "My dad was a good provider, but he never developed any creative interests. I feel guilty for resenting that he's so boring."
> "My mother was a super housekeeper, but we really had to do things her way because she was always rushing. And I always felt guilty for not helping enough."
> "My mother was a very intelligent woman, but she was jealous of me. I got into law school, and that had been her dream. I'll always feel guilty that I got to go and she didn't."

Treatment of guilt will almost always reveal not just a patient's private pain but his private assessment of the issues. It is built up over the years and compounded by the unrelenting and increasing neediness of his aging parent, whose own developmental predicament worsened with the death of *his* parent. We need then to see the problem historically—*that we are victims of victims.* Guilt is a spiral downward that takes with it a person's confidence. "Is this really mine?" we hear in therapy. "What is really mine? Am I carrying the burden of my parent? Of my parent's parent? Is this true? And if it is, how can I learn to put down this burden? Do I deserve to finally put it down? And most of all, what am I without it?"

Is this guilt normal? Yes. As observed above, clinicians, especially those with psychodynamic training, believe that guilt has a normal role in early childhood, when its painful cue informs the child that he or she has displeased the parent. Conforming to the parents' wishes then reinforces the bond between the child and the parents and makes the child feel safe again. But as we grow, especially into teenagers, we must slowly examine parental requirements and try to develop our own values. Instance by instance, decision by decision, we need to develop our own preferences and find ways to *respectfully differ* from what our parents want us to do. It is certainly true that thoughtful, fair-minded parents maintain an open discussion with their growing sons and daughters. But even when parents are adamant and auto-cratic, growing up means being able to increasingly endure parental censure without guilt. This enterprise often continues into adulthood. And when it does, then guilt can be thought of as abnormal—that is, as a symptom.

Guilt and Identity: The "Horns" of Trevor's Dilemma

This question, guilt as normal or not, plagued a man who came to therapy with classic panic attacks. Trevor was 28 and had just started work in the profession he loved: music. His father had another agenda for his son and angrily rejected Trevor for not accepting this. They had been estranged for years at the point that Trevor came for therapy. It had been a year or more into their estrangement when Trevor's father had become ill. Trevor's mother had kept a secret arrangement with Trevor, having early lunches with him that she did not tell her hus-band about. Now, with her husband's condition worsening, she came to his apartment and, in a shrill and blaming manner, said she would not leave until he came with her to see his father. Trevor argued that he would not be welcome, but his mother—lying—said his father had asked to see him.

Trevor was hesitant to do this, he said. He had had guilty feelings for about a year after the falling out with his father. Sometime later, he experienced anxiety that felt like a heavy weight on his chest. At times when he would be playing his instrument, he would feel as if he could not inhale or exhale. Certain it was a heart problem, he sought evaluations from several specialists. In each case, these doctors assured him that his heart was strong. One cardiologist suggested that Trevor seek psychological help, but he declined.

Despite his apprehension, Trevor did go to see his father, whose condition by that point was improving. His mother had told his father that Trevor had begged to see him. (Like many parents caught in this type of intergenerational problem, Trevor's mother was adept at lying and coercion.) His father was not convinced. It took only a few minutes for the father to begin berating his son again. Trevor, never one to argue, left more frustrated, angry, and aggrieved than ever. He could not shake the feeling that he *was* a bad son. Deliberately defiant, ungrateful, and *bad*.

Finally accepting psychotherapy, Trevor described a constriction in his chest. At times he thought he might smother in his sleep, he said. He often felt he wanted to cry but could not. All these are classic symptoms of an anxiety disorder. As a perfect illustration of the requisite for experiencing guilt, he believed he *must* be doing something wrong for this to be happening. Compounding the problem, some people will *seek* suffering as punishment, because it helps alleviate their guilt feelings. Trevor lamented, with clear annoyance, that if only the doctors had found something wrong with his heart, he would not have had to consult a clinical psychologist.

Trevor had a particular symptom that both protected and exposed his inner conflict: a phobia of mirrors. He avoided mirrors and would not have them in his apartment. He would shave quickly, he said, concentrating on the stubble. "Can you look at your face, your eyes?" I asked. "No," he said firmly. He would scan a restaurant before he sat down, so as not to catch his reflection by chance. He was very anxious telling me about this (phobia is accompanied by hyperactivity in the amygdala, the brain's worry center [LeDoux1996]). But Trevor's strong commitment to honesty and his motivation to finally be free of all these painful feelings pushed him to be admirably candid. I gently explained that his phobia was likely protecting him from facing a conflict between the man he is today—the accomplished musician—and the part of himself that accuses him of not doing what he *should* do. As we have seen, with guilt, we have the feeling of "owe." We feel we owe the other, usually the parent, our very lives. I suggested to Trevor that the painful guilt he would feel whenever his central conflict emerged could be avoided, at least in part, by avoiding mirrors.

This explanation intrigued him, that his body would express what he had never said in words! The mirror phobia was to resolve later in his therapy, to his great relief. But its analysis enriched Trevor's therapy, showing how complex a person he is.

"You are twenty eight," I said. "When did this avoidance of mirrors begin?"

Trevor paused. "My mother pointed it out to me. I guess it was a few years ago."

"After the blow-up with your dad?"

Another painful pause. "Yes. My mother was annoyed that I always wanted a table at the back of the restaurant, away from the front counter."

"What about when you were in college?"

"I don't remember feeling uncomfortable around mirrors in college." We were making progress.

"Was your dad unhappy with you when you were still in college?"

Trevor smirked. "He was always a bear."

"We can mean different things by 'a bear.' What does 'a bear' mean to you?"

Never one to waste words, Trevor said simply: "He growls."

I refocussed our discussion on Trevor's panic attacks. In my experience, people who have panic attacks fear bodily harm. Their fears are personal and specific. A man's heart is pounding, and he fears a heart attack. Another person fears loss of control, screaming, vomiting, cursing. In agoraphobia, the fear of open spaces carries a threat of *physical* harm. Another panic disorder patient is convinced she has a terminal illness. The illness can change from week to week. Trevor's fear of mirrors contained a physical threat. It was his own eyes he was avoiding. What was so threatening in his own eyes?

"Are you worrying what people will see when they look at you? Do you notice people looking at you?" I asked. Trevor did not answer and looked pained.

During the next weeks, something happened that changed his therapy and his life. A man who had been in college with Trevor had revealed to his community that he was gay. This man, uncomfortable with the response, had quickly moved out of state. Trevor was discussing this event with his mother at lunch. Later, in the car, his mother confronted him. "Well," she said harshly, "are you gay too?" He nodded yes. His mother said nothing; she quickly started the car and drove him home. He related all this in his subsequent therapy session. All the evidence now seemed to fit together. The eyes in the mirror—the accusing eyes—were not Trevor's but his parents' and the world's eyes.

As his therapy progressed, Trevor's anxiety attacks diminished and were replaced by crying. He was ashamed of crying, too. He was, after all, a grown man. His therapist assured him that crying is normal and very relieving and that men as well as women need to accept crying as evidence of a connection to their true feelings. He could cry in private, but yes, it represented progress. There was progress too in his new openness. Although still understandably cautious, he no longer avoided the eyes of the men who were looking at him. In his profession, there were people who were openly gay. At the rehearsals, he heard them laughing and teasing one another. He would like to talk to them, he said.

We continued to analyze his anxious feelings, the breathlessness, and chest-tightening. Trevor was able to see them as the *physical* expression of his psychological conflict. It was not just Trevor's work that displeased his father; it was *who* Trevor was, his very personhood. His father may never accept him, we agreed. But Trevor was learning how to form a strong boundary between what was inside of him—his own identity—and what was outside of him—his father's disdain. Trevor was taking responsibility only for what was inside of him, those parts of his behavior which represented his emerging selfhood. As we progressed, he could no longer believe that his father had the right to disapprove of him. And with that momentous growth, Trevor no longer felt guilt. But he continued to feel a loss, a *normal* sadness that his relationship with his father may never progress.

Some parents' notion that their son or daughter can and should give up being gay is wrong-minded. "Half a century of scientific research on a variety of SOCE [sexual orientation change efforts] has not demonstrated their effectiveness" (Hancock, Gock & Haldeman 2012, 499). Instead, these efforts have caused "distress, depression, sexual dysfunction, and suicidality" (499–500). Always suspect as an intervention, "conversion therapy" has been outlawed by California, New Jersey, and New York, with ongoing progress in other states. "Bills to ban conversion therapy have been introduced in Massachusetts, Ohio, New York, Pennsylvania and Washington State, but none has been voted out of committee" (*The National Psychologist*, January–February, 2014, 8). Sexuality must be seen as a complex developmental phenomenon. Gay people discover their sexuality, as do all people, during development.

We were left with Trevor's ambivalence about his father and his mother, who also disapproved of his gay self. A turning point in Trevor's therapy came when I told him that his disagreement with his parents did not mean he did not *love them*. Trevor had learned the equation "I don't want to hurt you, but I can't let you hurt me." This was enormously relieving. His father might see him as a disappointment, but Trevor now did not accept that. Therapy had taught him that he was good, worthy, and could rightfully make his own choices.

Although it was not available while I was working with Trevor, I refer all those with similar concerns to the "Lead with Love" documentary at www.leadwithlovefilm.com. There is now a groundswell of interest in relieving the tensions of children who have questions about their sexual identity. And ongoing research is establishing that children at grade and high school levels who attend schools where these issues are addressed openly have fewer depressive and anxiety symptoms (Glicksman 2012). Bullying of all types is finally unacceptable, and it is to be hoped that, if schools strengthen children's understanding of LGBTQ issues, it will find its way back to their parents.

Trevor came to see his oppressive guilt as the confused and primitive construct he himself had made out of the infrequent and hostile contacts he had with his father. Trevor had been a frightened child whose mother did not protect and comfort him. Trevor, the man, externalized his fear of his father, as well as the disapproval he anticipated because of his sexuality, onto *mirrors*, which he could then avoid. This made the fear more controllable—until it became a trap. The more ambivalent Trevor felt about being gay, the more panic he felt, finally depriving him of the very breath he needed to play his instrument. He understood none of this until his work in therapy. We have to *create* the ground in front of us before we can walk on it.

SOME THOUGHTS AND CONCLUSIONS

At this point you may be saying, "I don't care if they are normal. What good are shame and guilt? They make us suffer." Yes, you are right. But many normal emotions make us suffer. *Love* makes us suffer, yet we understand the meaning of that suffering. We see its "place" and its function, and that mitigates our suffering. The same is true for shame and guilt. As stated by the anthropologist Milton Singer and psychoanalyst Gerhart Piers (1971), the function of shame and guilt is to secure that most human of attributes, socialization. Living in families and in groups necessitated the development of psycholog-ical—*internal*—constraints on our selfish and domineering impulses. "Social conformity achieved through shame will be essentially one of identification. . . . Social conformity achieved through guilt will be essentially one of submission (Piers & Singer 1971, 53; italics in the original). Sigmund Freud (1962) also described shame and guilt as *advanced internal regulators* supporting progress in human groups.

Shame is the frequent experience of persons identified as members of racial and ethnic minority groups. The situation becomes more complex when people identify with more than one minority popula-tion (Nettles & Balter 2011). Thus persons may feel stigmatized from outside their ethnic group *and* stigmatized from within their group if they are also, for example, disabled or gay. Their issues with shame can be unique and complex.

Could human societies function without shame and guilt? *Adults* can be shame- and guilt-free through the kinds of maturation we have been discussing—accountability, realism, and self-responsibility. Both shame and guilt make us *think*. They force us to analyze our behavior and to question its rightness. They give us a brake for our impulsivity. Children need shame in order to shape a sense of self that reflects the values of the social group they are part of and to earn them the valida-tion and approval they need. Shame and guilt also provide us with the opportunity to *differ.* While the focus of guilt (in childhood) is on the parents, shame's focus is on one's peers and the larger culture of school and media. As major shapers of our emerging personalities, guilt and shame are allies and guides.

In therapy, much effort and attention is focused on these allies and guides. Shame represents our *inner* conviction of our own failure or unworthiness (Gustav's problem). Guilt causes painful self-rejection when we *believe* we did not fulfill *others'* expectations (Trevor's dilemma). It is our *reactions* to shame and guilt that determine our behavior and our suffering. Joanne's experience of both shame and guilt were well hidden under her readily expressed *anger.* When anger is the obvious and conscious expression of shame, the anger must be addressed first. This reaction is often called "shame-based rage" (Potter-Efron & Potter-Efron 1989). The therapist must patiently and respectfully pursue its roots, which are painful self-rejection and even self-hate, both angrily refused by the patient. Joanne had had her fill of being an unhappy, embarrassed, and *cheated* child. As she grew, she covered her shame at not being loved enough by becoming a strident and intolerant taskmaster who brooked no slackers. This adult Joanne could be a daunting encounter for a therapist, even one convinced by Norman O. Brown (1959) that we "compensate with competence." In the end, Joanne decided that both her shame and guilt were outdated; she "owed" her father nothing.

In his sensitive and accessible book about shame, psychoanalyst and researcher Andrew P. Morrison (1998) provides more evidence that an angry stance is often a defense against, and a coverup for, feelings of shame. He explains that certain people can show a "commitment to shame as a way of life" (154). They hold onto their self-denigration, their dramatic impasse in life, as a living *rebuke* toward those they believe caused it. Psychoanalytically, this constitutes a form of masochism. Their suffering lends to their life a certain importance and purpose, but it is a trap. Morrison further suggested that "shame over convictions about one's imperfections is as powerful an inducer of self-punishment as guilt over wrongdoing" (155). We have seen this in the three people we have been discussing: Gustav's hopelessness and conviction of being unworthy of love kept him from interacting with his own children. Trevor punished himself for disappointing his parents by denying himself the love he wanted. Joanne finally *stopped* punishing herself for resenting the lack of emotional support she had needed and deserved. She did not visit her father before he died.

It is tempting to ask: Is shame more about experiences with mothers? And guilt more about fathers? Are people characterized by shame more mature, allowing for alternatives, nuance, even disagreement? Are feelings of guilt more "primitive"? Intolerant and rigid? To be even more speculative, if shame is about feelings of inadequacy, isn't that more "feminine"? And if guilt is concerned with power issues (Wurmser 1981), isn't that a more "masculine" concern? Researchers have recently proposed that the classic pattern of "fight-or-flight" is essentially a male pattern. When women are threatened, they tend to bond with other women in caring for their collective young. This "female" pattern is termed "tend-and-befriend" (Taylor et al. 2000). Girls do retain larger communication and emotion-processing areas in the brain from the intrauterine period throughout life (Tannen 1990). And men's deficits in these areas have been called men's "relational dread" (Takei 2012).

We feel the pain of guilt more toward those we are bonded to, those who also elicit our empathy (Baumeister, Stillwell & Heatherton 1994). And this of course hearkens back to Sigmund Freud, who wrote that the birthplace of guilt is the family crucible. As Stephen Pinker (2011) irreverently puts it, we tend to "guilt-trip" our friends and family, not strangers or acquaintances. We may more readily admit to shame than to guilt. Shame often garners the sympathies of others, while guilt brings us frowns, shunning, and even punishment. The elements of our shame, at least in childhood, are there for all to see. The elements of our guilt are guarded with a fierce secrecy.

Can shame and guilt be separated in human experience? Yes, in adulthood, when guilt has been largely *outgrown,* and shame becomes a developmental stimulant, encouraging our ever-refined efforts at self-fulfillment. Hopefully the present discussion will help to clarify their separate derivations and help us unravel their separate effects in our lives. Among the most painful emotions we can feel, it is supremely worthwhile to explore shame and guilt—in or out of therapy—to understand their functions in our life stories and finally to come to terms with both.

REFERENCES

Baumeister, R. F., Stillwell, A. M., & Heatherton, T. F. (1994). "Guilt: An Interpersonal Approach." *Psychological Bulletin*, 115, 243–267.

Benedek, T. (1973). *Psychoanalytic Investigations: Selected Papers.* New York: Quadrangle Books.

Bradshaw, J. (2005). *Healing the Shame That Binds You.* Deerfield Beach, FL: Health Communications Inc.

Brown, N. O. (1959). *Life against Death: The Psychoanalytic Meaning of History.* Middletown, CT: Wesleyan University Press.

Celani, D. P. (2010). *Fairbairn's Object Relations Theory in the Clinical Setting.* New York: Columbia University Press.

Courtois, C. A. (1988). *Healing the Incest Wound: Adult Survivors in Therapy.* New York: W. W. Norton & Co., Inc.

Dearing, R., & Tangney, J. P. (Eds.) (2011). *Shame in the Therapy Hour.* Washington, DC: American Psychological Association.

Dinnerstein, D. (1976). *The Mermaid and the Minotaur: Sexual Arrangements and Human Malaise.* New York: Harper & Row.

Ferentz, L. (2012). *Treating Self-Destructive Behaviors in Trauma Survivors: A Clinician's Guide.* New York: Routledge.

Freud, S. (1962). *Civilization and Its Discontents* (translated and edited by James Strachey). New York: W. W. Norton & Co., Inc.

Gilligan, C. (2003). *In a Different Voice: Psychological Theory and Women's Development*. Cambridge, MA: Harvard University Press.

Glicksman, E. (2012). "Psychologists Are Working to Make Schools More Welcoming for LGBTQ Youth." *Monitor on Psychology* 43(11): 32–35.

Hancock, K. A., Gock, T. S., & Haldeman, D. C. (2012). "Science Meets Practice in Determining Effectiveness of Sexual Orientation Change Efforts." *American Psychologist* 67(6): 499–500.

Kagan, J., & Lamb, S. (Eds.) (1987). *The Emergence of Morality in Young Children*. Chicago: University of Chicago Press.

Kohlberg, L. (1975). "The Cognitive-Behavioral Approach to Moral Education." *The Phi Delta Kappan* 56(10): 670–677.

LeDoux, J. (1996). *The Emotional Brain*. New York: Touchstone.

Morrison, A. P. (1998). *The Culture of Shame*. Northvale, NJ: Jason Aronson.

Nettles, R., & Balter, R. (2011). *Multiple Minority Identities*. New York: Springer Publishing Company.

Piaget, J. (1965). *The Moral Judgment of the Child* (translated by Marjorie Gabain). New York: Free Press.

Piers, G., & Singer, M. B. (1971). *Shame and Guilt: A Psychoanalytic and a Cultural Study*. New York: W. W. Norton & Co., Inc.

Pinker, S. (2011). *The Better Angels of Our Nature: Why Violence Has Declined*. New York: Viking.

Potter-Efron, R., & Potter-Efron, P. (1989). *Letting Go of Shame: Understanding How Shame Affects Your Life*. Center City, MN: Hazelden.

Scheff, T. J. (1988) "Shame and Conformity: The Deference-Emotion System." *American Sociological Review* 53(3): 395–406.

Takei, M. (2012). *She-Q: Why Women Should Mentor Men and Change the World*. Westport, CT: Praeger.

Tannen, D. (1990). *You Just Don't Understand: Women and Men in Conversation*. New York: William Morrow.

Taylor, S. E., Klein, L. C., Lewis, B. P., et al. (2000). "Behavioral Responses to Stress in Females: Tend-and-Befriend, Not Fight-or-Flight." *Psychological Review* 107(3): 411–429.

Viamontes, G. I., & Beitman, B. D. (2012). "Neural Substrates of Psychotherapy." In R. D. Alarcon and J. B. Frank (Eds.), *The Psychotherapy of Hope. The Legacy of Persuasion and Healing*. Baltimore: The Johns Hopkins University Press.

Woodall, C. (1987). "The Body as a Transitional Object in Bulimia: A Critique of the Concept." In *Adolescent Psychiatry, Developmental and Clinical Studies* 14: 179–184. Sherman C. Feinstein, Editor in Chief. Chicago: University of Chicago Press.

Woodall, C., & Andersen, A. (1989). "The Use of Metaphor and Poetry Therapy in the Treatment of the Reticent Subgroup of Anorectic Patients." In L. M. Hornyak & E. K. Baker, (Eds.), *Experiential Therapies for Eating Disorders.* New York: Guilford Press.

Wurmser, L. (1981). *The Mask of Shame.* Baltimore: The Johns Hopkins University Press.

Wurmser, L. (2007). *Torment Me but Don't Abandon Me.* Northvale, NJ: Jason Aronson Inc.

Chapter 9

Assertion versus Aggression
The Fair Way to Stand Up for Yourself

[H]umor, more than anything else in the human make-up, can afford an aloofness and an ability to rise above any situation, even if only for a few seconds.
——Viktor Frankl, *Man's Search for Meaning*

"Whatever you call it, it's going to be a fight." I smiled at Marie's comment, but she was not amused. She had been sullen during her weekly therapy sessions with her partner, Carlos. Their once lighthearted relationship was mired in a silent truce. I had been teaching them the essential differences between aggression——fighting——and assertion—— *teaching the other person how you feel*——because he cannot read your mind. Marie was skeptical. Her partner, she said, was not ready to be taught anything.

Carlos had come into my office about 20 minutes later than Marie. (This is a definite "no-no" for many couples therapists who feel that, in these few minutes, a collusion or even favoritism can develop with the therapist. I don't think so. Isn't it important for people to say in private whatever is difficult to bring up when their partner is present? And isn't this exactly where a therapist can be most helpful, encouraging more candor?) Carlos arrived, explaining that he had to take an important call.

Returning to Marie's opening comment, I asked, "Do you argue a lot?" Both Marie and Carlos nodded yes then were uncomfortably quiet.

"What do you usually argue *about*?" I asked.

Marie was still silent, but Carlos sounded resentful. "Her father was a banker."

"Yes," I said, struggling for the connection. "Does that affect your relationship?"

"Of course," Carlos snapped. "Marie runs the show! She's the chairman of the board in our house."

Marie said nothing, looking patient but annoyed. They had met in a library discussion group and were strongly attracted to one another from the start. Although they now lived together, Marie would not agree to marriage. This clearly offended Carlos, who believed that Marie was biding her time until a better man came along.

Marie felt that this was ridiculous. The problem, she said, was "closer to home. I think Carlos is delightful and funny—until you ask him to do something. If he doesn't agree, it's a fight." "Well," I said, turning to Carlos, "what do you say?" He simply looked at me, mildly hurt and a bit sad. These two were from similar socioeconomic backgrounds, but for Carlos, this discussion was affecting his self-esteem. Something about their interchanges made him feel defensive. What was it?

During the next few therapy sessions, I asked Marie and Carlos to sit at opposite ends of the couch and speak directly to one another, ignoring me. At first they seemed self-conscious, and then Carlos remembered an argument they had had earlier in the week and said angrily, "You don't *ask* me to do anything. You *tell* me." What slowly emerged is that it was not the content of Marie's requests that Carlos do this or that task, it was her *tone*. What she was asking of Carlos was usually acceptable to him, but her tone was autocratic and bossy. Further, she prefaced many of her statements to Carlos with "I'd like to see this done" or "I expect to see that done"—statements befitting a chairman of the board.

This was at least one of their problems. Marie's statements, especially her delivery, were demeaning to Carlos, and he reacted angrily. Each thought the other was completely wrong. And both were right. Marie was being aggressive, not assertive. Assertion is always characterized by respect for the other person and/or the wish to be fair. Before therapy, Carlos had not known there was a distinction between assertion and aggression. And when Carlos complained about her behavior, Marie felt his response was aggressive toward her.

For the next few sessions, I stressed this important point, encouraging Marie to listen to her messages and the tone she used. I asked both of them to write out five requests each had of the other. Then I asked them to reformulate each statement, their own and their partner's, this time more carefully and respectfully. Virginia Satir, one of the pioneers of therapeutic communication and group therapy, had said in one of her workshops that we should be able to say anything to anyone and have them receive it as a gift. That statement is an inspiration.

FIGHTING FAIR: ARGUING BY THE RULES

Being able to argue fairly is based on the belief that others deserve the same rights and privileges we want for ourselves. Thus we lead with respect. This is particularly important for our intimate relationships. Marie and Carlos learned to preface their requests with "I wish . . ." "I'd love to see . . ." and "How about . . ." Or, the most powerful way to engage people, especially children—"Let's." They ensured their tone and delivery were respectful. And they observed the following rules:

1. Your request is first and foremost a fair one.
2. Your request conveys respect for the other person.
3. No shouting, name-calling, or profanity.
4. No dredging up issues from the past. (These can be addressed later, by appointment.)
5. Include all the points you wish to make about the current issue, in their order of importance.

As adults, our task is to distinguish assertion and aggression by their intention. Again, the goal of aggression is simply to hurt the other person. It damages or destroys the relationship between the two. The goal of assertion is to *teach* the other person how you feel because he or she does not know. Assertion enhances the relationship with the other person and can make it stronger. Learning to fight fairly is one of the most significant skills for ensuring marital happiness (Parker-Pope 2010).

When a person has been raised by autocratic parents, he or she often does not realize this difference. The person may only have had the experience of protesting to the parent—something the parent took as an aggression—or of submitting, giving in. Developmentally, this person had not had the experience of complaining on his own behalf (a good definition of "assertion") and having the parents accept that. Even if the parent did not react angrily, the assertion may not have been too effective, and these children often grow up to be submissive and/or chronically angry.

It happens so elegantly in a movie. One person says, "When you do that, it hurts my feelings," and the other person answers, "Oh, I see. Well, I won't do that again." Problem solved. But in our own lives, people may not be so accommodating. Thus the art of assertion must be actively developed. If the person you are asserting to is reasonable—that is, emotionally healthy—your assertion will be respected and taken seriously. On the other hand, there are people who will hear your self-expression and react with anger or hurt. That is, of course, *their issue*; it does not negate your responsibility to *yourself* to say how you feel. But sometimes the other person's answer shuts us up. Then what do we do?

DISTINGUISHING ASSERTION FROM AGGRESSION: THE EQUATION

Time-honored in all types of relational negotiations, the equation is this: I don't want to hurt you, but I can't let you hurt me. This equation describes assertion as a skill that people can learn. The statement does not have to be said directly to the other person, just held in mind to allow us to assess the situation. We really do not wish to hurt others but to understand in what way they are hurting us. Thus, the goal of assertion is honest self-expression. Moreover, the assertion contains information, teaching, that, if taken seriously by the other person, can transform the relationship.

Even a confrontation, if given in a concerned and respectful tone, has as its goal *limiting* the other person, not hurting him. But sometimes we can experience our own assertion as a confrontation, especially if we know that it will be heard as one by our partner, friend, or co-worker. Think of a person who has been offensive to you or has been limiting your rights for perhaps months, and you feel certain you must say something. The assertion will be easier with a friend, sibling, or parent when there has been a history of mutual respect. In the spirit of a word to the wise, you say to her, "Well, that wasn't very nice of you!" If both of you can laugh, the point has been made and the relationship can improve. Even if the other person is annoyed, this too can be discussed, and the relationship will grow. Even if the other person still refuses to see your point, be assured you have done the right thing. Remember: assertion is for *your* benefit, for your own growth. When the relationship is worth it, the effort will be worth it. And brain chemistry is on our side. Research has shown that just looking at someone you really like or love inactivates those parts of the brain usually available for making negative judgments about others—for example, the anterior cingulate cortex (Brizendine 2006).

But suppose the situation now seems stalled. You cannot move forward, and you certainly do not wish to retreat. Here's the problem. Most people can do the first part of the equation: "I don't want to hurt you." It is more difficult and significantly more complicated to do the second part: limit another person's aggression against you, be it rudeness, manipulation, or outright hostility. But before we get into part two, let's look at *why* it is easier to say or act out, "I don't wish to hurt you." First, it suits many peoples' tendencies to be passive, to hold back, and to push an uncomfortable issue under the rug. Passive women and men seem "allergic" to any form of confrontation. They say they have "no stomach" for conflict, nor indeed any energy to invest in resolving issues with others.

Sometimes it is more sensible to leave the situation at Part One. If you are working with an aging parent who is not always reasonable, or you decide that pursuing an argument with a certain co-worker is just not worth the stress, it makes sense to leave the project at "I have no wish to hurt you." The concern here is for persons struggling with their own self-growth who *do* wish to distinguish the situations above from issues they ardently want to resolve, but they feel stopped by some inner switch. Those who hold back from confrontation are, in general, fearful of the consequences. And this attitude often has historical roots.

Consider a child who, timid by nature, is daunted by his loud and angry parent and becomes overcompliant out of fear. The nature of the attachment between this child and his parent is thus based on the child's ongoing passivity. Psychologists note that many such children are described as "good" by the parent. But the truth is that something in that child has stopped growing: his ability to say how he feels and his whole relationship with himself. His need to differ, his willingness to plead, and his emergent self-esteem are compromised.

The further tragedy is that this inhibition can become so automatic that it is barely conscious. When this person grows to adulthood, any "whiff" of a confrontation will be swept under the rug in one smooth move, unnoticed by him or the person with whom he is interacting. It has become a pattern, a "personality variable," so predictable that the person is routinely described as "nice," "easy-going," or "shy." The net effect is that this person will come to value himself *only* for being "good" and believe that giving up what *he* wants is the "right" way to be. This is actually the *unhealthy* reason for saying "I don't want to hurt you," because it is motivated by fear of other people's anger (Kainer 1999).

Viewed in this light, our need for assertion is developmental—a part of our emotional growth. The normal—and *healthy*—reason we would say, "I don't want to hurt you," is because we *care*. We want the situation to improve. We respect others and their right to say what they want, as we respect our own right to do the same. We see others as like ourselves, persons of equal intrinsic value. Because we care, we are always trying for consensus, so that our goals and the other's goals can blend. This is the psychological and democratic ideal.

Making it happen takes work. It is every person's individual responsibility, not just our right. We are always making a choice, at any given moment, about what we owe to the other person and what we may owe to ourselves. The goal is to be fair to both. It takes patience and scrutiny, but consider this: Aggression is an "instinctual" act, an "old brain" given. Assertion is instead a *learned* skill. Another way of saying this is that aggression uses primitive parts of our brain, including the amygdala. But being assertive requires thinking and planning—functions of the prefrontal cortex—our source of impulse control!

Speaking Up Is Hard to Do

Why is assertion so difficult? If it is supposed to be so normal, why isn't it "second nature"?

It is. Listen carefully to any two- or three-year-old, and you will hear a passionate argument about why he should have his way. And it gets better. By the age of eight or nine, a child can present a detailed and sophisticated argument for her point of view and why yours is woefully inferior. Often they carry the day. Whole families are swayed by her eloquence and zeal and decide in the eight-year-old's favor.

What happens between 8 and, say, 18, that erodes a person's confidence? Years ago we believed that it was the disparity in power between men and women, in the classroom as well as the workplace, that muffled a woman's voice (Eagly, Eaton, Rose, Riger & McHugh 2012). Indeed, increases in equity in the workplace have enhanced women's opportunities to be heard. I would say at least part of it is maturation. (The hubris of a three-year-old would be out of place in a college classroom.) Difficulty with speaking up on our own behalf is usually developmental, but that difficulty can and should be outgrown. Saying how we feel relieves tension and reestablishes our place in our social world, especially with close relationships. We simply come to recognize that our opinion is one among several. Those around us also have important and hard-won opinions.

The Second Part of the Equation: "I Can't Let You Hurt Me"

One of the most serious drawbacks to this part of the project is that bossy people assert very well! They articulate all the reasons why you should do as they say. While you are struggling to decide if that person is being fair, she doesn't desist. If she would just stop, you might have a discussion. You could even practice your assertion. You have learned that unfair demands must be resisted. (Or, at least, are worth complaining about.)

We all have had experiences like this with co-workers, neighbors, friends, even siblings. With them, there is a relationship of some duration and some trust. You are convinced that in the interest of your own growth, an assertion should be attempted. It takes planning, timing, focus, organization, and considerable courage. In therapy, I have heard people say, "Yes, I know. I ought to assert. But I can't do that yet." The operational word here is "yet."

"What Is Wrong with Me?": Micky and Her Mother

A bright, successful 37-year-old executive with a staff of eight people, Micky came to therapy with an unlikely complaint. She was cordial and effective at work. Her staff loved her. She was realistic, motivating, and kind. They all appreciated her candor and were effective partners in running the department. But with her autocratic mother, Micky recoiled. She would open her mouth, but no sound emerged.

Although Micky had an apartment, her mother would arrive weekly to oversee Micky's life as she had always done. Micky resented this deeply but never complained. She feared she would never have any private space, despite working hard to get this wonderful apartment. Micky reported to her therapist, "I cannot even throw out a bra without my mother going into the wastebasket and pulling it out, saying, 'Why did you throw this out? It's still good.'" How could she allow this kind of intrusiveness? "What's wrong with me?" she would lament in her therapy session. No one else in her life would treat her this way. We agreed that it wasn't good for her to put up with this, but the question was, what stopped her from complaining?

Micky related many past family holidays when her mother described her to others as a "very good girl." She remembered these as happy times. Her mother had been a young widow, and the extended family doted on both of them. All was well until sometime in high school. Micky was editor of the school paper, but if her mother wanted her home, Micky would leave early. Her classmates criticized her for this. She was leaving them with all the work. It only became worse in college when Micky's mother called constantly. Her roommates complained and would tease her. Micky could manage all her responsibilities and was an energetic and reliable friend and classmate. But the strength to confront her mother eluded her. She had developed the pattern described earlier as the "good" child. She had not noticed it happening. Her mother's wishes always came first. Now it was untenable. How do you learn to say no at 37?

The focus and determination—and the humor—that guided her interactions with her employees could not be directed at her mother. Not *yet*. The issue of her mother's intrusiveness continued to be an important part of Mickey's ongoing treatment. I encouraged her to practice in her therapy session. "What do you want to say to her?" I asked. But Micky could not engage my question.

"I just can't hurt her," Micky said over and over. "She still needs me to be her good girl."

I acknowledged that feeling of "should" that still daunted Micky. But my responsibility to her prompted me to ask, "What do *you* need?" This question brought tears, and not a little anger.

"I want to be able to throw out a bra and have it stay in the trash!"

The energy in that response cleared the air. Here was a woman who wanted her life. Micky became quiet, surprised by the vehemence of her first response, despite my encouragement. "Well," she began. "What I would love most is to feel the same way I feel at work—confident, free, intelligent—when I am with my mother. I *lose myself,* that person I am at work, when I'm with my mother." There it was. The evidence that a child's self-esteem can be compromised by a controlling parent.

And here was the crux of the matter. Micky's mother had not set out to do this to her daughter. She was not a mean person. As I had told Micky again and again, the problem was that her mother was very *needy.* But it was not Micky's responsibility, nor was it in her power, to meet those needs. They were mainly *adult* needs, and Micky's mother could have more appropriately sought their fulfillment with other adults, rather than from her little girl. Now the problem was magnified. Micky was no longer just an extension of her mother but a person in her own right. Slowly, with encouragement, Micky was understanding this. She was learning "I am not trying to hurt you. But I have to stop you from hurting me."

Finally, during one session, Micky reported that on the previous Friday night, "The right words fell out of my mouth." Micky and her mother were accustomed to shopping on Saturdays then stopping for lunch to catch up on the events of the week. Both mother and daughter loved these outings, and Micky did not want to do anything to jeopardize them. But the previous Friday evening, Micky's mother had called to verify the time to be picked up. "And," her mother had added, "we'll pick up that navy blazer for you." Micky suddenly and clearly said, "No, Mother, I'd like to get a red blazer." Her mother was silent then angrily said, "We'll see," and hung up the phone.

During the shopping trip, Mickey was nervous and almost gave in. But she was able to pick up the red blazer she wanted and go to the check-out clerk. When I asked how she had felt doing that, Micky replied, "My knees were shaking!" Asked again how she had really felt, she said, "Great!" Micky reported that at lunch that day, her mother had been sullen and angry. But heartened by her healthy assertion, Mickey was cordial and did not reverse her decision as she would have in the past. She had learned how to limit another person's intrusion into her life and decision making but in a fair way. Again, Micky did not have to say that directly to her mother; she simply repeated it to herself during the painful silences.

It was many weeks later, after several more gentle but firm assertions, that Micky and her mother were again having lunch. Something happened that changed their lives and their relationship forever. Her mother took Micky's hand and said with some embarrassment, "I must have been obnoxious to you." Micky almost fell into her soup.

Was her mother really acknowledging years of browbeating that pressured Micky into giving in? Did she really now see that Micky was not an extension of herself? Most important, was her mother no longer threatened by Micky's growing up into an equally competent adult?

"Yes," Micky said, "You *were* obnoxious." Micky laughed and squeezed her mother's hand. They both laughed. They cried. They were finally equals. Competent, mutually respectful adults who loved each other deeply.

This was a victory, nothing less. An accomplishment that would not have been possible without learning and practicing the skill of assertion based on fairness. It is another example of how neurosis—in this case her mother's neediness—freezes people in time and does not permit healthy growth. It is a further example of how hard-won such healthy growth can be. Her mother had never changed because no one—especially Micky—had required it. Her mother really believed that Micky's first assertions had been aggressive, threatening to the mother's self-confidence. Her mother further learned that assertion was *teaching* and that it could enhance both lives. Micky's own growth required it. She could not be a healthy, happy person—the same at work and with her mom—without that skill. Best of all, her mother proved that she could change because fairness to her daughter required it.

That is perhaps the most daunting part. How can we be confident that the other person will listen to us? Assertion is based on a relationship between equals, two persons different in authority and perhaps age but not in basic self-worth. Micky could not progress in therapy until she believed this. Only then was she confident enough to persist.

Assertions from a parent to a child are not usually considered a relationship between equals, but they are. Hardly, you say. Children can be so demanding. Yes, but the "equal" here refers to self-worth. We must take into account the child's level of understanding and not take advantage of the disparity in power between us. Assertion is never a power play, wherein one person tries to coerce, control, and manipulate the other. And with children, this disclaimer is all the more salient.

The differences are huge, to be sure. We always have the greater share of responsibility in the relationship, and our child is hampered by two problems he cannot see—inexperience and impulsivity. His balking and whining are infuriating. The distinction between assertion and aggression begins to crumble.

BECAUSE I SAID SO: ASSERTING WITH CHILDREN

Shelves of books on parenting chide us to watch our language when speaking to our children. Perhaps their most important message is "Lead with respect." Respect, you say. What about me? I'm the one who gets up at 5:30 to do the wash and make breakfast for everyone. I make the lunches and get everyone dressed so that no one is late for school and work. Don't I deserve respect? Yes, unequivocally.

What we don't understand when we complain about our busy life is that our children don't value "busy-ness." Rushing to be on time is not an early childhood value, and little children especially will resist it. As we discussed before, small children do not care if they have clean clothes or if the roof is leaking. What they want and need is a smiling, caring parent who holds them, plays with them, and feeds them regularly. Our busy schedules and frantic communicating styles make children acutely uncomfortable. Then their resistance makes us more frantic and the shouting begins. Sooner or later, we may make the fateful error of assuming that our children are deliberately thwarting our best efforts to be efficient, and we begin to resent them. Our youngest children will feel vaguely threatened, frightened by our shouting and cajoling and resist our efforts all the more.

Family therapist Mary Pipher (1996) has written a sobering description of this modern dilemma. "With more entertainment we are more bored. With more sexual information and stimulation, we experience less sexual pleasure. In a culture focused on feelings, people grow emotionally numb. With more time-saving devices we have less time." (81). Now the chronic overstimulation of cell phones and each family member's insistence on the preeminence of his or her own social demands make it worse. In families harassed by tight schedules and perhaps an excess of ambition, there is no time or energy for respect. What people miss is that there is no "happiness" without it.

What can you do? Think about your schedule. What parts of it can be adjusted or reformed? While your child is little, perhaps your book club can be put aside. Any volunteering might be reconsidered if your family needs more of your time. Responsibilities to clubs, groups, and the like can be put on hold. Streamline your housecleaning. Conserve as much time and energy as you can. Raising little children is exhausting. Try to arrange working from home, at least part of the time. Alternate Saturdays with a friend, sister, or neighbor to share child care and give each of you time to shop alone, catch up on housework, or make love.

In therapy we hear what was precious and what was onerous while growing up. Children's positive memories are uniformly about parental warmth, support, and family fun. And their suffering comes from any prolonged lack of support, as well as fear of abandonment. (This is provoked, for example, by being left at school long after the other children have been picked up.) A generalized lack of support sounds drastic, but it equates with your being too busy every day to talk to your child about her day or to read a bedtime story or stay with little ones until they fall asleep. Too many people—women especially—are seduced by the notion of "having it all." What does this really mean? If we truly want our children to grow up emotionally healthy, they deserve more of our time and energy. But not *all* our energy.

You will agree that much of your stress would be alleviated if you could just get your children to cooperate. Talking to your children *can* be made easier. A number of skills can be learned to help you to communicate with your children briefly and effectively. That's what they want as well. Is this difficult to believe? Consider these:

> *"Let's."* To inspire your children to appreciate that you are both in this together, "Let's" is the preface to use. For example: "Let's get our rooms picked up and vacuumed, and I'll get the kitchen cleaned. Then we can go to the skating rink or zoo" (or wherever they want to go). This teaches children the value of getting responsibilities done before they get to play. It helps to start this early. (It works for us professionals as well.)
>
> *Recruit the fun of competing.* "The first one to be in the car with lunch and school stuff gets a special time with Mommy or Daddy tonight." If you make this fun—no meanness or threats—children are inspired to cooperate. Why? Because, of all the possessions your children have, nothing is more valuable to them than you and your love. Believe that.
>
> *"How about . . ."* When your child is headed toward a decision that worries you or is at cross-purposes with your family's values, present your alternative with "How about . . . doing it this way?" With this, you encourage your child to consider *your alternative.* This is much better than saying, "No. You're not doing that. You can just forget about that." The dramatic truth is this: if you stimulate your child's competition with your authority, your child will win, because he has more stamina and never forgets your put-down. Alternatively,

if you inspire your child's cooperation with a sense of fun and continued support, your child will more likely laugh, see your point, and take on the task. He will feel that you respect him and his growth. A son or daughter is often more ambivalent about their proposed adventures than he or she can say. They still need to be steadied by our support and experience. However, if you threaten them, they may do what they really don't want to do simply to defy your control. Children's self-esteem follows from our support and belief in them.

Recruit the power of absurdity. When your child campaigns for yet another version of his favorite game or tablet, resist the urge to angrily refuse, saying, "What? That costs more than a week's groceries!" Instead, smile and say that if you were to buy him that device, the whole family would have to eat bread and water for a year. The house could not be heated, and the water would freeze in the pipes. Then the bread would get moldy and gross, and you would have to slather it with jam to make it tolerable. Then there would be an invasion of giant ants that would eat the moldy bread and jam, and because they were infuriated that that was all you had, the ants would attack the furniture, but finding that unpalatable would turn to the children, because everyone knows that children are tastier than furniture. By this time, your child will be pleading for you to stop and will get your point. And you will have avoided an angry meltdown.

If your child does not relent and insists that life is not worthwhile if he has to go to school without the latest version of the latest device, he is saying that he is already trapped in the current materialism. But gently reassert your position. Childhood happiness does not correlate with indulgence.

Try moving your children's bedtimes to a half hour earlier. It's amazing how just doing this gives you a chance to exhale at the end of the day. Also, the research evidence is overwhelming that eliminating television, phones, tablets, and games at bedtime helps everyone to quiet down and get the rest they need. This is the time for baths, pajamas, and reading together. It can be done. Memories are made of this. And children who are read to have better verbal skills.

Think carefully about buying your child anything you then have to police. This applies to most games and even computer time on social media. This tactic will not work if you start too late, when your child is already "hooked." But it is worth complaining about at any age, so that Facebook does not become a stronger influence than anything else in their lives. The addictive qualities of games and social media are well documented. Studies are now linking certain video games to reckless driving in teens (Bowen 2012). Learning to control impulsivity helps children at every age. Children who can be patient and put off gratification are able to avoid obesity as adults (impulsivity is the major risk factor), and they have higher SAT scores (Wickelgren 2012).

Privileges Yoked to Responsibilities: An Effective Model for Parents and Children

Raising children well is the hardest work in the world. This is the time parents need one another most. Here is a method for organizing your decisions and helping your children develop realism and self-responsibility. As early as age three or four, give your child more privileges tied to more responsibilities. So an eight-year-old can stay up a half hour longer than her five-year-old sibling, but the eight-year-old empties all the wastepaper baskets and perhaps takes out the trash. A nine-year-old can fold clothes and put them away properly. And for that, he or she gets a ride to a friend's house.

Children need to feel that what they do helps the family in real and measurable ways. This teaches a child the kind of effort and persistence it takes to manage a family so that each member's needs are met. They learn to appreciate all you do day in and day out, because they have daily tasks as well. If you dutifully give your child more privileges year by year, always coupled with responsibilities, by 15 or 16, he or she will understand that there are no free lunches. That adult life is full of responsibilities as well as gratifications, and that self-satisfaction is as important as praise from others.

In a family session recently, an annoyed 11-year-old boy complained, "Why does everything have to be earned?" His father and mother both looked pained. I said to him, "Your father doesn't get paid at work because they like him. They do like him, but they pay him because he works diligently and reliably." The boy looked at me somewhat angrily. Then his face softened, and he seemed a bit embarrassed. He understood my point. I was reminded: Shame (embarrassment) is good. It helps us learn.

Respect and respectful communication—*assertion*—is a central requirement for happy children and families. Lack of respect is strongly correlated with dysfunctional families and with domestic abuse. The American Psychological Association has devised a powerful intervention that is currently being taught in this country and many others, including Puerto Rico, Greece, Italy, Romania, and Bulgaria. The program is ACT: Adults and Children Together Against Violence Parents Raising Safe Kids. It is essentially a training program implemented by psychologists and other trained persons to improve parenting skills and to reduce damaging verbal and physical practices. ACT is available to parents around the globe at http://actagainstviolence.apa.org.

DAVID FLOHR'S PARENTCIRCLE: A UNIQUE THERAPY FOR PARENTS

Psychologist David Flohr has developed the self-as-parent: Pathways Model as self-development for parents in his groups. Each parent—by turns—is invited to the center of the group to be its single focus. The ParentCircle is Flohr's central concept, beginning with therapist-led training sessions that then progress to the group's meeting bimonthly on their own, sometimes for years. It is a brilliant concept that gives parents their own forum, and for long enough to see their children and themselves through significant crises.

Flohr's program is not one in which parents are told what to do. They can express their confusion and ambivalence. They can talk about their failures and state openly that they don't know *what* to do. And that dilemma is "mirrored" by other parents in the circle, who also do not know what should be done. What emerges is that *waiting* is often the best thing and that it is a relief not to retaliate. It builds impulse control. And that parent's son or daughter, often under pressure and overstimulated, benefits from the parent's "backing off."

In this process, the parent in the middle is surely being treated for his or her own developmental issues—unresolved problems from childhood—as they are being expressed *now* in the impasse with that parent's child. The therapist is there watching, guiding the process with clarifying questions and encouraging the other members to reflect (mirror) the struggle unfolding before them. The parent in the center of the circle moves from anger to frustration and then to grief and loss. From the here and now to the lonely child he had been. He cannot initially transcend that child's pain when interacting with his own child in the present. But with the support of the other parents around him, the one in the middle is "being filled up by that mysterious elixir of others' interest and concern for him" (Flohr 2012, 34).

The "container" formed by that validation, back and forth, between the parent in the middle and the group, seems similar to Donald Winnicott's (1971) concept of "transitional space." This space is created between a deeply involved mother and father and their infant, and it holds and supports the infant's psychological growth. In this pluripotent space, the child's very existence is passionately reflected in the eyes of his parent. In this way, Flohr's model is a kind of psychoanalysis for the group. The parent in the middle struggles to put his feelings and thoughts into words. But *each person in the circle around him is feeling his or her own ambivalence with no pressure to reveal it at that moment.* It is a "holding environment" that supports everyone there. Again, as in psychoanalysis, long, potentially rich silences are tolerated. There is progress in eventually finding the words for one's feelings and being able to tolerate the insight that they supply. Achieving that insight in the presence of sympathetic others makes it more real.

All this is possible in Flohr's model because, unlike in group therapy, the focus for each session is on just one person who can take the time he or she needs to finally feel understood. After a period of working with the therapist present, the group moves to working together twice a month to continue the process on their own. They have learned that each of them has the same power and the same need to do so. Flohr cautions that the type of parents who are ready for the ParentCircle are "seeking support and guidance, and are open to slow, steady self-development" (35).

GIVING IN VERSUS DEFERRING: WHAT'S THE DIFFERENCE?

One of the important principles for therapy—important in all relationships—is never to "give in." Why? Because giving in is experienced as a loss of self. One feels one is *giving up* a part of oneself, our wishes and preferences, in order to comply with the expectations of the other person. We feel diminished, even cheated. Giving in makes us decidedly unhappy.

This is different in kind from the necessary compliance we rightfully give to our employer or to the law. "Deferring" means giving *over* the right to decision making in a given instance to rightful authority because we understand it as fair. And this is not resented the way giving in is. (Stopping at a red light is deferring.) Rightful authority includes one's supervisor, who has the right to expect us to do the work we agreed to do when we accepted the job, and for which we are financially compensated. As long as our supervisor is fair to us, that expectation requires our compliance. (If our supervisor is not fair, the need for assertion is clear, using the same skills we discussed earlier.)

The danger of giving in is important in relationships involving family members, relatives, friends, co-workers, even neighbors. What is the effect of giving in to, say, a husband, wife, or other intimate partner? It is often the result of a power struggle, wherein one member of a pair pushes for control, and the other accepts it. This is usually a pattern that causes resentment—the "loss of self" discussed earlier. Or the partner's overbearing behavior is accepted with resignation, which is worse. Assertion in these situations does take energy and some courage. But relationships only improve to the degree that they are challenged. Fairness must come *to* us as well as *from* us.

People laugh when I say that giving in is not good for our mental health. But they are relieved to know that deferring is a healthy alternative. This may appear at the outset to be the same as giving in, but deferring is different *in motive and outcome*. Like all forms of assertion, it describes a relationship between equals, equal power and equal importance. Deferring does not cause "loss of self"—that is, feeling diminished or unheard.

The key to success in this endeavor is mutual respect between the two persons, whether they are spouses, siblings, friends, or co-workers. They agree that neither is more important than the other and that each has equal power in the relationship. That being agreed upon, then what each of them wants—which vacation, car, movie, living room set, or dog—is equally important. Each campaigns for his or her point of view. If they differ, and there can be only one vacation, movie, etc., then they begin their negotiation. And here is the essential premise. If both of them see their *relationship* as the most important element in the discussion, then any one "thing" that each of them wants will be less important than the relationship. Their negotiation will be tempered by caring, patience, and humor. What often emerges is that the issue in question is more important to one of them than it is to the other. The one less affected then defers the decision making to the one more invested. This is done with caring and with the understanding that each gets his or her way enough of the time so that no one feels cheated. At some later point, the one who deferred will be deferred *to*. This stimulates the healthiest emotion humans can feel: gratitude.

To summarize, giving in is a giving *up* of self and a loss of self-esteem, from a position of little or no power. Deferring, instead, is a giving *over* of the decision-making power in a given instance. It is done out of respect and caring for the other person with the understanding that their relationship is more important than any one preference.

DRAWING THE LINE: WHEN THE OTHER PERSON WON'T BE FAIR

The issue of establishing fairness on both sides becomes a central issue for the future of any relationship. How do you accomplish this? One way is to use this important tactic. The next time you feel browbeaten or unfairly criticized, say firmly to the other person, "I don't deserve to be spoken to that way." Then walk away. You will feel uncomfortable the first time, but persist. If you do this repeatedly, and you are certain that you yourself have been fair, it changes the vectors in the relationship. You disengage the other person's abuse. Your walking away is an essential part of this tactic. It is important that he or she *loses your presence* when they are abusive—for example, saying something demeaning or name-calling. And he or she does not want to lose you! Their interest in keeping the relationship encourages them to reconsider their actions. This tactic perhaps works best with the help of a couples therapist, but you can try it on your own.

In other situations, you may not need the other person to change. If you are in an oppressive work situation and you want to stay at that job, assess what it is you are trying to do. If your work is important to you, partial out the offensive person or people. Tell yourself that *you refuse to suffer any more on that account.* Focus on your goal and the nicer people around you. (With this decision, sometimes the oppression stops because it is no longer gratifying to them if you don't react to it.)

SARCASM? REALLY? SOME SURPRISING FORMS OF AGGRESSION

The "aggressive" motive is said to actually begin in infancy when an uncomfortable baby cries, flails, and otherwise lets us know she is seriously unhappy. But can we really call this aggression? Yes, in psychoanalytic terminology, it is "non-destructive aggression" (Parens

1979). This is the energy of life, energy by which the child reaches out and apprehends the world. It powers all our decisions. Learning, inventing, building, traveling, sports, and scientific achievement are all examples of neutralized aggression—aggression without a victim. Of course, this is the energy I am calling *assertion*.

But we all know that some children's behavior can become destructive and no longer victimless. Without protection and guidance, the anger of children in neglectful and abusive households can escalate and, at times, require intervention. Even in healthy families, the societal pressures on children are difficult to manage (Seifert 2006). If aggressive behavior is assessed early on, and the young people affected are in continuous treatment, we are in a better position to protect society from their anger.

Aggression in day-to-day life can take strange and subtle forms. Until it is pointed out, people do not consider sarcasm to be aggressive, although it can be. We all use it, and when it is leavened by caring, we can all laugh at it and it causes no harm. But sarcasm with the intent to hurt is an essential element in bullying and other forms of humiliation. Sarcasm is particularly damaging to children. They often cannot answer it the way an adult can, and they experience it as an attack. Children's self-esteem can be severely damaged by sarcastic put-downs (Morrison 1998). Goading is a form of harassment that can be very subtle but its hostility is unmistakable to the victim. Gloating is a form of shaming with the same effect.

"Passive aggression" refers to the angry but sneaky aggression by which a person, for example, outwardly agrees to do something but then "forgets." He may or may not be consciously aware he is doing this. Some people push things out of awareness better than others. The distinguishing feature about this form of aggression is that it is an abnormal *pattern*. A birthday card to a resented person doesn't get mailed. A task that a person agreed to do just doesn't happen. And the person is full of apologies—more or less sincere. The passively aggressive person has a reservoir of resentment and is searching for opportunities to frustrate the other person. It is a way of keeping an onerous relationship and getting even at the same time.

Any form of racism, bias, or prejudice is aggressive. At base these are sadistic—that is, the prejudiced person feels superior and enjoys belittling those he denounces. Envy can be a fairly hidden, internal form of aggression. Unlike jealousy, envy seeks to destroy the thing envied. A famous example is the murder of John Lennon, which seems to have been motivated by unbearable envy. The murderer was reported in the press to have said to Lennon before shooting him, "There is not room in the world for both of us."

The last example of aggression is more surprising yet: *guilt induction*. When someone tries to make us feel guilty—a "guilt trip"—that person is being aggressive. He is forcing on us painful feelings of self-rejection and labeling us as responsible for things we did not do. The imposed guilt represents an opinion on the part of our accuser, and it is our task to unravel what is real from what is alleged. Another perfect opportunity for assertion!

To summarize, "aggression," by definition, seeks to hurt the other person and damages or destroys the relationship between two people. Hitting the other person, of course, is direct aggression. But in general, we have been considering the more hidden, sneaky forms of aggression. These are shaming and humiliation (bullying), browbeating and overcontrol, bias and prejudice, envy (but not jealousy), passive aggression, nasty sarcasm, goading, gloating, and guilt induction. Assertion, by contrast, is a *self*-expression that seeks to *teach* the other person how you feel with the intention of preserving and enhancing the relationship. It is governed by the equation: I have no wish to hurt you, but I can't let you hurt me. Almost everyone can do the first part; it takes a focused and brave person to do the second.

REFERENCES

Bowen, L. (2012, October). "Certain Video Games May Lead Teens to Drive Recklessly." *Monitor on Psychology* 43(10): 15.

Brizendine, L. (2006). *The Female Brain*. New York: Three Rivers Press.

Eagly, A. H., Eaton, A., Rose, S. M., et al. (2012). "Feminism and Psychology: Analysis of a Half-Century of Research on Women and Gender." *American Psychologist* 67(3): 211–230.

Flohr, D. (2012, January–February). "The ParentCircle: Tapping the Wisdom of the True Experts." *Psychotherapy Networker* 36(1): 30–35, 54–55.

Kainer, R. G. K. (1997). *The Collapse of the Self and Its Therapeutic Restoration*. Hillsdale, NJ: The Analytic Press.

Morrison, A. (1998). *The Culture of Shame*. Northvale, NJ: Jason Aronson.

Parens, H. (1979). *The Development of Aggression in Early Childhood*. New York: Jason Aronson.

Parker-Pope, T. (2010). *For Better: The Science of a Good Marriage*. Boston: Dutton Adult.

Pipher, M. (1996). *The Shelter of Each Other: Rebuilding Our Families.* New York: Grosset/Putnam Books.

Satir, V., Banmen, J., Gerber, J., et al. (1991). *The Satir Model: Family Therapy and Beyond.* Palo Alto: Science and Behavior Books.

Sax, L. (2010). *Boys Adrift: The Five Factors Driving the Growing Epidemic of Unmotivated Boys and Under-Achieving Young Men.* New York: Basic Books.

Seifert, K. (2006). *How Children Become Violent: Keeping Your Kids Out of Gangs, Terrorist Organizations and Cults.* Boston: Acanthus Publishing.

Wickelgren, I. (2012, August). "The Education of Character." *Scientific American Mind* 23(4): 48–58.

Winnicott, D. W. (1971). *Playing and Reality.* London: Tavistock Publications.

Chapter 10

Mutual Respect, Vulnerability, and the Price of Narcissism

If we have become a people incapable
of thought, then the brute-thought
of mere power and mere greed
will think for us.
When we cease from human thought,
a low and effective cunning
stirs in the most inhuman minds.

–Wendell Berry XII, "Leavings"

Why fuss over anything that sounds as dull as Mutual Respect? Why devote a whole chapter to the importance of openness and vulnerability? Because so much of human happiness, especially a happy marriage, is based on these. And because people who are not helped, in their early years, to learn about mutual respect and fairness can become *stuck* at varying levels of self-absorption—narcissism.

Mutual respect—the *equal* regard for self and other—is founded in several simple and crucial premises:

1. That other people deserve the same rights and privileges you want for yourself
2. That you are not more important than the other person, and she is not more important than you

3. That you do not have more power than the other person, and he does not have more power than you
4. That others deserve the same right to privacy that you want for yourself and family
5. That you do not have to be submissive to others, and they do not have to be submissive to you
6. That we should all be protective of each other; this is especially true of children—ours and others' children.

Isn't this just "the golden rule"?, you may be thinking. Yes. It is "live and let live," the basis for ethics. But *it is very difficult to do.* Conflicts over land, power, and wealth are spread across human history. Competition for sexual partners is the stuff of song, poetry, and drama. Just keeping our family relationships relatively harmonious takes ongoing diligence, patience, and humor.

THE DEVELOPMENTAL ROUTE TO MUTUAL RESPECT

Again and again, we see that the early relationship with our primary caretaker—the person who has all or most of the responsibility for the care and feeding of an infant's body—is the prototype for all later relationships. This may sound simplistic, but it is not. Human infants are born both helpless and intelligent; the child can tell by the way he is diapered and fed just how safe and cherished he is. The *quality* of that early attachment determines our ability to form deep, trusting relationships all our lives. A secure, loving attachment can *immunize* a child against much anxiety and depression. It makes us strong, and it teaches us to be fair. Our need for fairness is the root and rationale of "mutual respect" as I am defining it—wanting equal rights for ourselves and others; the willingness to listen to the complaints of others and to work to resolve them are born here. What begins there on the rug with our dad and mom will be just as important in our marriage and to our community and country.

Research by neurobiologist Michael Gazzaniga stresses that a sense of responsibility is not a function of a single brain; it comes from an individual's *concept* of her social group and what they expect from her. Gazzaniga (2011) cites psychological research that shows an awareness of group formation in babies as young as 13 months of age. That this can happen so early is stunning. According to Gazzaniga, a 13-month-old recognizes an "us" and a "them." He knows who he belongs with and why. Much of development is relational. This is also the birthplace of "trust," which I define as the presumed expectation of ongoing support. Trust is what allows the baby to *rest*, so that the whole of his biology can develop.

Can it be that a healthy developing personality is also a moral one? Yes. Psychologists who study babies report that, as young as six months of age, babies showed preferences for individuals who help others and avoided individuals who "hinder" others (Bloom 2011; Tucker 2013). Babies also prefer individuals who *reward* good behavior and punish bad. These researchers stress that, although dutiful parents actively *teach* children to be fair, this learning happens to a brain that is ready for it. From the beginning, we are wired to be receptive to, and to process, input *at this conceptual level.* We should also mention the important finding of "mirror neurons." These neurons fire in the infant's brain when he imitates a behavior, like sticking his tongue out at a person who has done this first. The surprise is that the same neurons fire if the infant simply *observes* that same behavior. Mirror neurons may indeed subserve all empathic behavior, like crying at a movie when nothing comparable is happening in one's own life.

These behavioral trends are heartening. From the beginning, we want fairness for ourselves and others. But morality is still hard work; we are always bucking our other tendency to take all the goodies for ourselves. We have a normal, natural selfishness that gets in the way of fairness in the family as well as in the wider community, a tendency that is only normal in infancy: narcissism.

NARCISSISM'S NATURAL HISTORY

Among history's most colorful characters, narcissists are the people we laugh at, admire, envy, and hate. They take what they want with no regard for others. They are often strikingly attractive or believe they are, and they dress flamboyantly or provocatively. They are masters at getting attention. They have an exaggerated idea of their own importance and boast of their extraordinary ideas and influence. And they are uncomfortable, even enraged, by any competition.

These traits—self-dramatization, grandiosity, and self-absorption—are actually normal at a very important period of late infancy, approximately between two and four years of age. This is the period that Freud called the "normal narcissistic phase." During this phase, the two- or three-year-old child, having reasonably good support and nurturance from his parents, has attained significant physical competence: walking, running, jumping, operating doors and toys. He can essentially do anything he chooses, and it is a heady experience. He feels that the world is his and that he is the center of it. And at the same time that he is taxing our stamina and patience, he is so adorable that we watch his antics and laugh. We are mesmerized by his skills and the new ways he demonstrates them. Two- and three-year-old children are so attractive that we stare at them and smile. All emotionally healthy children have been *over*valued in this way. And they thrive on our attention almost as a form of sustenance.

This, I believe, is the same draw we feel toward celebrities. They too exhibit great physical attractiveness, much grandiosity, and self-dramatization, and they seem to crave attention as a kind of nutrient. They love their attractiveness, and they flaunt it. And we want them to do exactly that. If they are funny as well, we cherish them all the more. The way we are drawn to them, the way they annoy us if they do not behave the way we want them to, and their haughty disregard for what others think of them highlight major narcissistic traits. We see in celebrities the enviable permanence of their narcissistic phase and lament the loss of our own (at the same time that we actually prefer growing up, for a whole new set of reasons). Do you doubt it? Think of your favorite celebrity, his or her striking attractiveness, the prancing about, the dramatic clothes, the exaggerated laughter, the exaggerated embarrassment. With notable exceptions, do you hear any *adult* concerns for what others think? Concerns about the environment, the economy, world peace? (And perhaps they give us the same reprieve from such worries.)

Narcissists are so attractive and successful that we might speculate an evolutionary role for narcissism. Suppose a person happily discovers that he is so breathtakingly good-looking that potential sexual partners are collecting around him. This could be so compelling (if procreation be evolution's primary goal) that the narcissist would see no reason to develop any other aspect of his personality. The need for attention and the need to influence others are so great in narcissism that it usurps all the person's time and resources. Narcissism can thus become a trap that limits development. (This does not apply to certain fine actors, of course, who react to aging as an opportunity to play more interesting and demanding roles. They do want attention, even adulation, but they give back so much. And they do admire other talented actors. They have artistic goals and mature appreciation missing in pathological narcissism.)

The liabilities of pathological narcissism are clear; narcissists cannot exist in a vacuum. They must have an audience. Those who are not strikingly attractive gain attention through wittiness, monopoly of social events, or wearing dramatic fashions. Since they are always seeking new attention from new people, their relationships tend to be short-lived (Horowitz 2013, 83). They often do not want constancy and fidelity. They want variety, excitement, and adulation. (These attitudes are the opposite of mutual respect and openness.) Narcissists become angry if anything is expected of them. They view vulnerability as weakness. This shallowness in their personalities often makes healthier people move away from them. They are very likely to be knocked off balance. There are always younger, more attractive, and funnier people waiting in the wings.

NORMAL NARCISSISM

As previously discussed, narcissism is considered normal in childhood from about the age of two to four. During this phase, the child feels he is the center of the parent's world and can do anything he tries. He can be grandiose and fantasizes about exceptional powers. He does not perceive danger and will do unsafe things unless protected. At about the age of four or five, the child begins to give up his narcissism for a very important reason: *he wants a friend.* One cannot act like the center of the world when one wants a friend. This is the age when children will spontaneously share favorite possessions. Their need to be social is so great that it shapes the child's behavior *away* from self-centeredness. (Not perfectly of course. He can still be demanding, especially with his parents.) But you will see him holding out a favorite toy to another child, and he receives much praise for this. He begins to value togetherness, sharing, taking turns, and "us" instead of "me, me, me." Behavioral scientists speak of these changes as socialization, the emergence of the self-centered child into a shared world where life is better—more interesting, more fair, and safer. This is the beginning of mutual respect. And what eventually emerges from mutual respect plus vulnerability is *the capacity for intimacy,* the capacity to share one's life so completely that one is vulnerable to being hurt. Closeness requires that vulnerability.

That introduces another phase of life when narcissism is normal: falling in love. During the early, magical period when two people find themselves intensely attracted to one another, they feel both humbled and euphoric. They feel overvalued, more attractive, more powerful, and energized. And we find we have extraordinary influence over the one who loves us. It is exhilarating, a kind of "high." All the features of the normal, overvalued child's experience are ours. In love, we feel lighter than air, generous and expansive, happier perhaps than we have ever been. And we wish that time itself would stand still, that we could keep this rarefied experience of ourselves, poised on the edge of time. And not exhale.

Yet even when it does fade, that experience and the person we had it with remains; it shifted our orientation permanently toward one another. Having been loved this way changes us forever. What started out as a normal narcissistic experience (enjoying the feeling of being overvalued) evolves to a focus on one another, shared by no one else. No one else cherishes you this way, just this one person. To the rest, you are just another human being, hard-working, reliable, somewhat interesting, but not otherwise special. Except to this one person. This experience of narcissism (intense self-valuation) is normal *because* you can understand this distinction. You do not expect to be this special to everyone.

The desire for attention is itself a normal need, and beyond childhood. According to the early "needs-press" inventory (Murray 1938), we have some 20 normal needs. Among these is the need to be admired for something we have achieved through our own effort—for example, writing, painting, or building something. We also have a need to "re-try"—that is, not to be discouraged by failure but to redouble our efforts, and this time to achieve what we had been trying to do. (These normal needs persist in the literature as "ego skills.") Both of these normal needs—wanting praise for something we have achieved and the need to retry when we have at first failed—produce a kind of "high" and gain us fame and influence, at least for a time. No one would call these examples of narcissism pathological. Similarly, we want our children to do their best, to develop their skills, and make the best grades they can. The motive is not to humiliate others but to be personally successful. That is the basis of self-esteem, and unlike pathological narcissism, it is not *compulsive* attention seeking.

Adolescent "Narcissism"

Many people consider adolescents narcissistic by definition. And they can be. Yet, from my side of the desk, adolescent grandiosity can have several sources we can consider normal for their age:

1. Compensation for a shaky self-esteem. They are in a new situation with a changing body and do not know how to behave. They do not want to appear afraid or uncomfortable. So they "act arrogant." But it is often simply shyness and worries about inadequacy.
2. Embarrassment in front of the person they are attracted to. This will produce the same dilemma so they act tough, "cool," or loud and silly.
3. An attempt to imitate an admired peer. If you don't know how to act "cool," you find someone who you think is, and you model his or her behavior. Teens are famous for trying out different personalities, accents, styles of dress, etc. We parents can become very worried about one of these, and then they switch to another.
4. Discomfort with their new, insistent sexual feelings. It is uncomfortable to experience almost constant sexual arousal, and boys especially are at great pains to hide it. Loudness, grand gestures, much laughing, can be signs of embarrassment—not grandiosity and arrogance.

The above four situations would constitute normal and expectable issues for adolescents. You can understand, and sometimes relate to, their plight. These types of adolescent narcissism are redeemed by maturation. Each generation fiercely desires something or things that are only theirs. They identify with that feature, perhaps a technology or a type of music, to provide a springboard out of their environment and their family of origin. The more pressured and ambivalent their need for separation, the more intense will be their identification with that feature.

A dramatic example of this phenomenon was the 1960s "flower children" and their exodus to California. It broke many parents' hearts and was distinctly unwise in many aspects. But it boiled down to an angry reaction to the "rat race," the experience of having a corporation run your life, with consumerism as its philosophy. The movement was dangerous to some and not very sanitary. But out of that movement came concepts we now take for granted: stronger laws against sexual harassment, flex-time, increased and more flexible maternity leave. Telecommuting, which many now depend on, came out of the premise that corporations need to be more family friendly and that the environment mattered.

It became reasonable to want a line of work that was congenial. (Of course, from the point of view of, say, the Great Depression, this wish would constitute a presumption. Any work at that time was cherished and a source of pride. Human progress rocks back and forth.) A greater interest in community developed, with the admonition "Think globally, act locally." Over the next decades, organic farming and local agriculture developed, with families buying a share in the fresh produce. A strong stance was taken against pesticides. There was a greater interest in "green" jobs. All these endeavors are ongoing and increasingly effective. To come full circle, all these are social values that stress equality attainable through our own efforts and are based on mutual respect and fairness. They show us that narcissism does not serve families and communities and should remain a feature of late infancy. Adult life requires realism, hard work, and respect for the rights of others. "'Tis a consummation devoutly to be wished" (Shakespeare's *Hamlet*).

Narcissism on the Rise?

A world where narcissism is the norm? Everyone obsessed with power, beauty, status? Manipulating others? It would be a world with very high crime rates, both white-collar crime and violent crime, says Christopher Barry, lead editor of *Narcissism and Machiavellianism in Youth* (APA 2010). Features of narcissistic personality disorder have been increasing among college youth since the 1970s (Stinson et al. 2008). Other psychologists question these findings, saying that today's young people are more environment oriented and seek meaningful rather than just financially rewarding work (Smith & Aaker 2013).

For decades, college students have been filling out the Narcissism Personality Inventory (NPI, updated in Pincus 2013), answering statements about, for example, their comfort or discomfort with manipulating others. W. Keith Campbell and Jean Twenge analyzed NPI data from 85 studies and found that between 1982 and 2006, college students' narcissism scores significantly increased by about two narcissistic answers (Twenge, Konrath, Foster, Campbell & Bushman 2008). A follow-up study published in 2010 added 22 new studies to the meta-analysis and found further increases in narcissism among college students through 2008, although the increase in recent years wasn't quite as steep as it was in the 1990s (Dingfelder 2011). These researchers go on to say they would expect a drop in the incidence of narcissism in young people as a result of the financial crisis of 2008. However, there are other influences, especially the social networks, which can foster self-absorption and self-dramatization.

THE ROOTS OF PATHOLOGICAL NARCISSISM

A consideration of the psychoanalytic roots of narcissism will help us to understand the pathology. The Diagnostic and Statistical Manual states that narcissism begins in "early adulthood." But the word "narcissism" was coined by Sigmund Freud, who drew from his considerable knowledge of classical literature to describe certain traits and syndromes that he was observing in psychiatric patients. Narcissus was the young man in Greek mythology who, upon seeing his reflection in the water, fell in love with his own beauty. Yet Freud places the development of narcissism, not in adolescence, but in toddlerhood, around the age of two to three, naming this the "normal narcissistic phase":

> In this intermediary stage, the importance of which increases the more we investigate it, the sexual impulses which formerly were separate, have already formed into a unit and have also found an object; but this object is not external and foreign to the individual, but is his own ego, which is formed at this period. This new stage is called *narcism* [italics and spelling are Freud's], in view of the pathological fixation of this condition which may be observed later on. (1938, 876)

The narcissistic phase is one of the four "psycho-sexual stages," the progression that children go through in order to emerge as fully functioning, expressive, and sexual adults. "The early infantile ego ... is characterized by omnipotence, a condition to which the later ego will regress under particular stress" (Piers & Singer 1971, 21). But without undue psychological stress, the normal narcissistic phase in late infancy evolves through later stages and becomes the basis for normal interactions with others.

In *pathological* narcissism, the personality does not progress. The narcissistic traits do not mature; they form a "lacuna" (my word; Latin: a blank space; a missing part; a discontinuity in an anatomical structure). The rest of the personality grows up and around this lacuna, and from the outside the person does not appear different. The difference is in his subconscious motives and his reactions, which are narrow, childish, and self-absorbed. Thus we can have perhaps a very bright adult, but one who is psychologically a defiant child—petulant, manipulative, unempathic—who approaches all interactions with a sense of entitlement. The notion that pathological narcissism represents this kind of developmental arrest, or a regression to the early narcissistic phase, is the formulation of Hans Kohut (1971).

Another more ominous formulation of pathological narcissistic development (Kernberg1975) does not simply represent a wish to remain in the normal narcissistic phase or to regress to it when stressed. It is found in those individuals who *never had* a normal narcissistic phase surrounded by a fairly supportive family, and it represents their fixation on that early anger. To avoid overwhelming fear and disorganization, the early frustration becomes generalized. The person compensates with grandiosity; now the whole world shall be his stage and shall reflect back to him his glorious existence.

Through the examination of narcissistic patients, Otto Kernberg states, "one finds from the age of two or three years a lack of normal warmth and engagement with others, and an easily activated, abnormal destructiveness and ruthlessness" (1975, 273). These are people whose early treatment was less than supportive and comforting. As a result, they do not develop a normal deep sense of trust with its consequent opportunity to rest. They become angry and envious. As adults, they *demand* the indulgence and overvaluation they missed. They are described in the psychiatric literature as "schizoid" or "alienated," although the general consensus is that they are not psychotic (Kernberg 1975; Nelson 1977). They are distinguished from borderline personalities in that the latter show considerable self-hate, the opposite of narcissism (Waldinger & Gunderson 1987). Borderline personalities remain estranged from self and society. They cannot form a stable sense of self, and they blame others, beginning with their families but extending to those around them. A child like this ends up with no coherent sense of a supportive parent, *only bits and pieces* of interactions, some of which may have been supportive, while many were frustrating and even scary.

Narcissistic personalities, by contrast, remain passionately connected to others in their bid for attention and their need for control. Winnicott (1986) allows that this type of childhood may be implicated in the development of tyrants. "Indeed, were the psychology of the dictator studied, one would expect to find that, among other things, he in his own personal struggle is trying to control the woman whose domination he unconsciously fears, trying to control her by encompassing her, acting for her, and in turn demanding total subjection and 'love'" (1986, 125).

How can this happen? Babies do vary in their capacity to respond to their caretakers, but it is also true that not all mothers are ready for or comfortable with motherhood. In this situation, she will be ambivalently attached to her infant. Perhaps a child herself, she will not be prepared for the all-day, all-night responsibilities. The sleep deprivation might have her regretting the choice of becoming a parent at all. Thus she may be prickly and fitfully available to her infant. Over time, day after day, month after month, her child has an unpredictable and unreliable experience of his mother. Babies can sense their own dependency. The infant may increase his demands through crying, but much of the time, he will be frightened and angry. This child might develop patterns of manipulation and grabbing what he needs. He might be jealous and even aggressive toward siblings.

From the point of view of this child as an adult, all is justified. One narcissistic patient, angry that he had been caught stealing, protested that the person he had stolen from had a "huge house full of stuff." His reasoning was, "Therefore, I had the right to take what I took." Another narcissistic person was caught looking through the handbags of her co-workers. She insisted she was simply trying to see if they had something she didn't have. That is the narcissistic rationale and sense of entitlement.

Much grandiosity, arrogance, and self-dramatization is not narcissistic personality disorder but the behavior of some bipolar persons in the manic phase. (Handel was possibly in such a phase when he wrote the Messiah in the span of two weeks, hardly sleeping, and convinced that God was dictating it to him. If Handel were alive today, he would surely have been medicated, and we may not have had this incomparable oratorio.) It is essential to distinguish bipolar disorder from narcissistic personality disorder. Bipolar is a *mood* disorder, likely of genetic origin.

PATHOLOGICAL NARCISSISM DEFINED

The first evidence of narcissism is the person's conviction that the rules are different for him than for the rest of us. Pathological narcissists do not have insight into their behavior and usually do not seek therapy (Ogrodniczuk, Piper, Joyce, Steinberg & Duggal 2009). They do not see anything wrong with their behavior and will counter any complaint with an attack on the person making it. It is always someone else's fault. This grandiosity in narcissists has been the focus of the DSM diagnosis of narcissistic personality disorder.

But the current emphasis is on the dual features of grandiosity and *vulnerability*:

> I believe the fundamental dysfunction associated with pathological narcissism is related to intense needs for validation and admiration that energize the person to seek out self-enhancement experiences. Such needs and motives are normal aspects of personality, but they become pathological when they are extreme and coupled with impaired regulatory capacities. . . . Pathological narcissism involves impairments in the ability to manage and satisfy needs for validation and admiration, such that self-enhancement becomes an overriding goal in nearly all situations and may be sought in maladaptive ways and in inappropriate contexts. . . . This definition of pathological narcissism . . . encompasses narcissistic grandiosity and narcissistic vulnerability. (Pincus 2013, 95)

That said, the narcissistic people who do agree to therapy are, in my experience, the grandiose type. Those who are hypersensitive to shame and criticism are intolerant of any analysis of their behavior.

Narcissists in therapy are usually there because of a relationship gone awry. One man, whose wife had come for therapy a few months before, joined one of her sessions to complain. His wife, he said, had become a different person since she had therapy. She was no longer compliant, submissive, or afraid of him. This wife had not wanted to divorce, but she found, as she became stronger, that she could no longer live with this man. Narcissists do not learn from experience; they neither understand nor value mutual respect. Their formula, true especially of narcissists with paranoid tendencies, is "control or be controlled."

Another example: A woman who had been arrested for shoplifting was ordered to come for therapy. During the consult, she boasted about how easy it was for her to steal handbags and CDs, although jewelry was her specialty. She wanted me to write a letter to the authorities excusing her behavior because, after all, she was "a mental patient." Of course, I was not going to do that. She left the session angry and letter-less. Narcissistic persons do not want therapy. They want the world to accommodate to them.

The Narcissistic Parent

Immeasurably more difficult than struggling with a narcissistic lover is the trap of having to grow up with a demanding, arrogant, self-absorbed, and envious parent. I would argue that a person's later attraction to narcissistic partners is rooted in unresolved conflicts with a parent who demanded center stage. Or a parent who so seriously constrained a child's self-esteem that she was an easy mark for the seductions and ingratiations of a narcissistic partner.

Narcissistic women can sometimes enjoy being pregnant because they receive much attention. They even enjoy a new baby, whom they view as an extension of themselves. The attention the baby draws is experienced as her own, and the adulation and clinging of an infant reinforces a narcissistic parent's sense of specialness and power. As they grow, however, healthy children let it be known that they are quite separate people and want to be recognized as such. A narcissistic parent will react with anger to a child's normal assertions. She will punish the child or angrily withdraw. Then the child becomes afraid and aggrieved; he learns quickly to comply with the parent's demand. *And a pattern is born: compliance, compulsive compliance, then resignation. Something in that child stops growing.*

When the compliant child of such a parent starts school, he is quite successful. He has all the behaviors the school wants. He is obedient, attentive to the teacher, quiet, and not too distractible. His longing to please makes him shy and pleasant. He conveys this longing nonverbally, attracting the kindness of every adult around him and some of the children. Since his intellect grows unhampered, he excels in schoolwork. (Intellectual growth and emotional growth can be surprisingly separate continua.) By adolescence, the great push of pubertal hormones will complicate this person's difficulty with low self-esteem and his general lack of self-expressiveness. His normal anger will be well hidden. He is still wonderfully cordial, with an easy-going temperament. But he is beginning to experience conflicts around assertion versus compliance.

A girl with this deficit is even more appealing. She will be perceived as shy, kind, and a hard worker, *until* she develops into a pretty teenager. It is at this point that the conflict with her narcissistic mother will erupt full force. She is now an attractive, bright girl who triggers her mother's undisguised envy. There was nothing maternal in the cold statement of one such mother: "It must be very hard for you to be going to the same school where your mother did so well!" This daughter crumbled in tears. She would never be a separate, valued person to this mother. This gives a chilling sense of the intractability of narcissistic personalities. They are not amenable to therapy precisely because they lack insight; they feel they have nothing to learn, and they angrily reject other people's rights, including their children's. They are happy when accommodated and angry when thwarted; that is the sum total of their stance.

Narcissistic parents can engender other types of neurotic conflict. While working at the Johns Hopkins Hospital Eating Disorders unit with hospitalized patients, I recognized an important subgroup of anorectic girls who were very afraid of competing with a narcissistic mother. The mother's envy of a pretty, emerging daughter was thinly disguised as concern for her health. These girls responded to the scary dilemma of competing with their mothers by cancelling puberty through starvation, stopping time in its tracks. I remember observing one such mother, coiffed and groomed like a Hollywood diva. She was complaining about her daughter, who sat grimly before us, eyes down, an oversized garment covering her frail form. Going through my mind was, "Mirror, mirror on the wall. Who is the fairest one of all?" This was a mother who needed her daughter to be "sick," not a threat in any way. And her daughter complied, all the while showing me the conflict that subserved her entire clinical picture. A symptom *both* hides and reveals a developmental conflict.

Not all the families showed this structure, of course. Many were cordial and concerned. Anorexia nervosa is more often a conflict in the girl herself, a peculiar discomfort with the project of growing up. If a girl *can* grow and leave the family, she does. If she *cannot* leave, she must find a way of leaving while remaining within it. Anorexia nervosa is a brilliant solution to this dilemma.

Narcissism may sometimes be cultivated by targeted merchandising. Parents are as aware as therapists are of the earlier and earlier pressures on girls to be trim and attractive and to be obsessed with all aspects of appearance. As a result, little girls can believe—largely through media pressure—that there is something wrong with their bodies that can and should be corrected by the purchase of specific products. It is not that these products are bad in themselves, just that *little girls can be made unhappy if they do not have these products. And their body image can be damaged by such chronic worries.* All this has been historically addressed by psychologists, educators, and most recently by Peggy Orenstein in her well-researched book *Cinderella Ate My Daughter: Dispatches from the Front Lines of the New Girlie-Girl Culture* (Harper/Collins 2010).

A word about normal parental jealousy, which is different from envy. Many parents understandably feel jealous at times of their young adult children. We see the many opportunities before them. And we cannot help remembering the mistakes we made at that age. We may have made a choice early on that then ossified around us. It may have been a fairly good choice at the time, we just didn't know it would cancel out all others. Young people do not help when they blithely say, "That was your time. This is mine." We mourn the loss of our time. It's normal and necessary. To be clear, *mourning the loss* of an opportunity (jealousy) is healthy and understandable. *Blaming a child* for having a better opportunity (envy) is not. (Jealousy is distinguished from envy in that envy seeks to destroy the thing envied.) And we should not waste our time feeling guilty. Guilt is not warranted; only more caring and "self-soothing" for ourselves and a renewed interest in our own life projects.

A last example of a narcissistic parent: a mother and her two daughters came in for therapy, following a police referral for 12-year-old Sandy. This girl had been caught shoplifting several times. In therapy Sandy was silent, but a vigorous interchange was going on between the mother and her 17-year-old sister, Jillian. The older girl was complaining that the mother always opened her packages and cards (snail mail). The mother haughtily replied, "Oh, isn't it awful that I open your packages and mail!" This clearly narcissistic mother felt that whatever came to the door was hers. This sense of entitlement cancelled her daughter's rights to her own property.

Older daughter Jillian could protest loudly that her privacy was being invaded. Sandy could not protest *in words.* I saw a connection here between the mother's sense of entitlement and the 12-year-old's stealing. Just as the mother constantly made the assumption that everything that came to the house was hers—no matter whose name was on it—the younger daughter aggressively (stealing is aggressive) took things *outside* the house that were not hers. She did not mind being caught. She wanted her defiance to be known. Her anger was not at the store from which she stole but at the mother who consistently stole from her.

This was not an explanation that a therapist could make to this mother. I could not increase the danger to the 12-year-old daughter by angering her mother. My focus was on helping both daughters. Jillian was sufficiently clear about her mother's unfairness and would likely leave as soon as possible. In a private session, Sandy said—rightly—that at that point she would be "it," the focus for her mother's vengeance. She came to understand that her stealing behavior both mimicked the mother's stealing and had the effect of embarrassing her mother.

The key to the resolution of Sandy's stealing behavior was to see her one-on-one. Her relationship with her mother, her whole developmental period, and her feelings about her missing father were examined. She was not the first preadolescent girl whose encounter with the police compensated briefly for a lost father–daughter relationship. Her older sister occasionally shared her sister's session and answered many questions about this family. The shoplifting stopped as the condition for continuing therapy, and Sandy had no problem doing this. Therapy helped her to express herself *verbally.* Now she wanted to be heard and understood. With that, the motive for shoplifting was gone. The sad outcome, however, was that the narcissistic mother remained haughty and unreachable, unaware that both daughters were quickly moving away from her and toward their own lives.

The Narcissistic Spouse

As we have seen, narcissistic persons demand special status, especially within the family. But some, with even less insight, function in a dreamy, contented *assumption* of specialness. They are not flamboyant, except perhaps in one area—for example, their jewelry. They are not particularly aggressive but will crumble in tears if their "feelings" are hurt. They are gloriously themselves and are happy as long as you support their illusions.

Such a woman was the wife of a man who came to therapy with one complaint. She would not move with him to another city to take advantage of an important business opportunity. He seemed helpless to influence her except with gifts, but even these, he was now saying, had become ineffectual. In therapy this lady was cordial but adamant. She told me that her home was here in the city they now lived in; they should never leave. Her children would always support her, she said. Only her husband was complaining. The degree of her morbid self-absorption was brought home to me by one quote in particular. Her husband told me he had recently bought his wife a pair of cameo earrings, the Italian shell carvings usually depicting a classical woman's profile. His wife looked approvingly at the face on the earrings and said, "Oh. Is that me?"

"I Did It All for Her": Robert's Great Risk

The spouse of a narcissist is always working to please and to accommodate. It is striking that they enter these unions unaware. By the time they come to therapy, they describe their plight with grief, confusion, and ambivalence. Such a spouse was Robert.

A man in his early 40s, Robert was referred for therapy by his long-time employer. His problem with alcohol had culminated in a series of drinking binges, and my first thought was to refer him to Alcoholics Anonymous. But his employer was asking for more, a psychological assessment. Robert dutifully told me the whole story. He said that several years ago, he had been caught embezzling funds from his firm. He had been doing this for years. There was a lawsuit, then a trial, in which Robert was found guilty. But before he could be sentenced, his employer suddenly withdrew the charges. Robert was released with the stipulation that he seek therapy at Johns Hopkins and "get his life together." Robert went home and drank for days. His co-workers pulled him together and convinced him to make the appointment.

Sitting in front of me was a well-dressed man with a weak smile and tired eyes. After reading the report, I said simply, "Your friends are quite concerned about you. And your employer . . ." Robert put his head down, crying into his hand. "They know I did it all for her," he said. Haltingly, Robert reported that he was married to a woman 10 years older than he who told him she was related to European royalty. Robert never knew if that were true; it was not important to him. She had been born in Europe and spoke with a charming accent. She was petite and attractive, and this shy man loved her dramatic speech and flourishes. Her striking clothes and jewelry added to the effect. She was not a person to be ignored. It was the upkeep of her expensive life that had Robert in debt, then in trouble with the law. Now his employer, also clearly a good friend, was giving him a second chance. What would he do?

My question to him—the essential existential question—was, "What do you really want?" He could not answer. Finally I said (reflecting my notion of what he was thinking—my countertransference), "I think you want your wife's love."

> "Yes!" His answer was emphatic.
> I continued, "And the only time you get a smile and a kiss is . . ."
> "When I give her a good chunk of money!"
> "And your employer knew that?"
> "Yes."

What often shifts the vectors in a relationship like this is the presence and the opinions of a third party, often a therapist, who is simply trying to understand. I asked if this man's wife would be willing to come in for a session or two, to help with that understanding. I learned that his wife had fled to Europe upon his arrest and had been there for the months he was awaiting trial. There had been little communication during those months, but she had since returned to the United States. After four or five sessions of therapy, Robert felt strong enough to ask her to join him, stressing it was entirely for him.

When his wife was introduced to me, she remarked that I had pronounced her name correctly and began chattering in her native language. I smiled and redirected her, but the connection had been made; she approved of me, at least for the moment. She sat down, and Robert began his usual homage, expressing gratitude that she would come to meet his therapist. She giggled and waved him away. I asked how she felt about Robert's having been released. She replied that she had had a dream that Robert's luck would run out. I said I thought he had been *quite* lucky to have such a generous employer. This lady then looked at me disparagingly, as if I just wasn't getting her point. Then she said sarcastically that Robert would never get another opportunity like that one. I realized she was referring to his opportunity to siphon money from the firm without being caught.

Clearly this woman's narcissistic personality disorder was complicated by antisocial tendencies (Kernberg 1984). She was *proud* of his stealing money and getting away with it. She regretted his luck "running out" when he had been arrested. Didn't I understand that? She quickly decided that I was not important enough for her to speak to and asked to see the faculty person above me. Of course Robert went with her, but they did not stay long with that doctor either. I never found out what happened. I only hope that this tragic man finally saw therapy as a course that would explain his motivations and illuminate his ongoing need to pamper his wife. But at that point—as he may have intuited—she would probably leave him.

Cozolino (2010) has described patients like Robert as a type of narcissist: "pathological caretakers," persons who throw all their energy into meeting the needs of others, while abandoning their own. This behavior is rooted in that person's early requirement to accommodate to and serve their depressed, demanding parent, who had no resources with which to nurture a child. The parent realizes that she or he is helped by the day in, day out ministrations of the child, and a life-long pattern is begun.

> Narcissism is characterized by a two-sided existence: one reflecting an inflated sense of self-importance, the other mired in emptiness and despair. The origin of this formation of the self occurs when a child looking for love and attunement instead discovers the mother's own predicament (Miller 1981). The child, robbed of the possibility of self-discovery, compensates by caring for the parent under a real or imagined threat of abandonment. (Cozolino 2010, 296)

Robert is thus exhibiting more *masochistic* features (Wurmser 2007), which researchers identify as part of the diagnosis of pathological narcissism (Cooper 1998)—exhausting himself in the service of his insatiable wife. He was abandoning his own needs and risking his career. But Robert would have benefited from therapy, which would have nurtured his early self and helped him outgrow the compulsion to always put his wife first.

PROTECTING OURSELVES: HOW TO KNOW A NARCISSIST

We can do much to protect ourselves from narcissistic demands and neediness in those close to us or in the workplace. Narcissists do not distinguish between healthy traits like making you laugh and dressing in a very attractive way from damaging traits like embarrassing you or not respecting your schedule. If people call a narcissist annoying, he will enjoy that. If a prospective partner enjoys insulting people to get a laugh, that is an ominous sign. He will also enjoy upstaging people—that is, grabbing the spotlight. He will love being called attractive but enjoy just as much being called arrogant and impossible. It is the *conflation* of positive and negative traits that is our evidence. Narcissists push for adulation and attention *no matter who gets hurt.* In psychoanalytic parlance, they are both enticing and frustrating. When an entertainer on TV behaves this way, there is a button on the remote we can click. But if it is someone we are hoping will share our life, we must be wary. A handsome face will be hard to live with if that's all there is in the bargain.

Consider another narcissistic trait: a peculiar lack of continuity. To illustrate, if you were very angry with a narcissistic person yesterday, or she with you, she will not connect with it today. Again, like a little child, she lives very much in the present, and if today offers a new chance for fun and admiration, she is ready for it. Even if she stormed out of the door and you thought the relationship was over, she will reappear today if she wants something from you. There is no continuity between what happened yesterday and today, no responsibility for what she said yesterday and how you may have been affected by it, no accountability, no memory, it would seem, of yesterday. There is only today and its new opportunity for excitement and self-aggrandizement.

Actually we cannot say there is *no* memory. Should you remind her of what she said yesterday, she may remember it. But only long enough to berate you for bringing it up. "We were so happy," she will complain, "and now you have spoiled everything." That is her reaction when the issue concerns *her* behavior. When it concerns something she believes you have done to, or have not done for her, she can hold that grudge for a very long time.

To recap, here are the attitudes to be wary of:

1. An unrelenting self-interest and focus. It's "all about" him. He cannot talk about anything for long without boasting and recounting his achievements. These are usually exaggerated and overblown. Healthy personalities do not take themselves so seriously; they can laugh at themselves.

2. A thinly disguised expectation of future importance and glory. What sounds like confidence is usually hubris. There is an absence of tentativeness and doubt, which would show awareness and respect for the complexity of life and the rights of others. A healthy, confident person never loses sight of his responsibility to self and others, and his projects are often embedded in these.

3. An intolerance for competition. To a narcissistic person, competition is enraging. Right under the surface is a pervasive envy of anything or anyone thought to be superior or to have something he does not have. Often ambivalently welcome to healthy persons, competition is expected as the expression of other people's rights to offer alternatives and as respect for the complexity of a particular project.

4. An impatience with people and projects not considered by him important enough to associate with. The narcissist's grandiosity pushes him to seek people and settings that "make a splash." This is because he does not consider others his equals; they are valued according to their usefulness. If all this sounds Machiavellian, it is. And it is off-putting to normal people.

5. A blind spot for responsibility based on realistic values. Responsibility to others comes from a sense of mutual respect but it makes narcissists angry. Their focus is on power *over* others. They consider manipulation of others their right— what they are "good at."

6. An unrelenting need for adulation. The single most convincing difference between normal confidence and narcissism is this insistence on constant admiration. This is not the normal regard and recognition we all deserve for helping cook a holiday meal or doing well on an important exam. You feel this *weightiness* in a narcissist's presence of his endless neediness, a persistent blame that you are not doing enough for him. And his displeasure is your fault. So you redouble your effort to please him only to find that by the next day you are delinquent again. You are Sisyphus rolling the stone up the mountain. And you have the same fate.

Thus we have come full circle. The narcissist's arrest at an infantile stage of development *or* his permanent rage at never having had that stage guarantees that he will not progress—without a long course of therapy—to the ability for self-soothing and self-comforting, carrying *within himself* the emotional supplies that sustain more mature personalities. (Later psychoanalytic thinkers, notably Hans Loewald, have written that there is no conflict between the teachings of Kohut and Kernberg. *Both* positions are important explanations of narcissism [Loewald, 1973].) In a word, healthy confidence and self-esteem are an expression of *gratitude,* of the experience of "enough" that we have gleaned from our "good-enough" parent and our own hard work and talent. Narcissistic grandiosity is at base an expression of *frustration,* of "never enough," and of the narcissist's conviction that attention, support, and recognition *must come from others, from the outside.* His rage at you is because you have the power to withhold it (another parallel with the early mother–child relationship). And your exasperation with him is because his neediness seems a bottomless pit.

LOOKING AT RISK-TAKING IN A NEW LIGHT

This is an area full of more questions than answers. We discussed in previous chapters that tension-producing activities are worrisome. Anything that causes us chronic anxiety linked with helplessness damages our health, physically and emotionally. High self-esteem is correlated with low risk-taking and better health (Erol & Orth 2011). Yes, but it all becomes problematic when that activity is rewarding in the extreme and constitutes some of the most cherished human skills: Olympic sports, racing, mountain climbing, even ballet and other endeavors that require long arduous training.

The antithesis of our plea to preserve the peacefulness of childhood, all these vocations capture a child, early and totally, in a life of relentless training, supported by coaches and parents emotionally invested in the outcome. Such a child is caught in a trap she loves and hates, one that cancels the rest of childhood—friends, time to just talk and laugh. Instead, rigid schedules structure her day, from dawn to dusk, parceling out food and drink. And her body is the prize, with its narrower and narrower skills. Her mind is recruited as well, to govern her body through each tension-filled day.

How can all this be healthy? And yet we love the outcome—a "Firebird" who seems to lift off the stage, a skater who gracefully spins then skates backward and apparently upside-down, all this belying the enormous muscle strength it takes to do these things. These young people look like the picture of health. But are they emotionally healthy? Would you want their lives?

Sustaining this way of life is some degree of narcissism on the part of the star and her parents, coaches, and others. Adulation and admiration are their nutrients, and the hard-won ability to do these superhuman activities fulfills the very definition of narcissism—that is, exceptional, special, different, living by different rules, and loving the display of the body. With one difference: these talented young people can really do all these marvelous things. They do not just *think* they are different and exceptional; they truly are. Yes, it's narcissistic, but is it abnormal?

If we go back to our definition, that a behavior becomes abnormal at the point when it begins to hurt another person or oneself, we have part of the answer. The rigid restrictions hurt the star in that they regulate her every activity and constrain her life to one narrow path. It could even lead to physical injuries that shorten her life. But *if it is worth it to the star, whose business is it but hers?* (The dilemma is perhaps less so for a prima ballerina. They can dance until they feel they cannot perform the way they want. Then they can teach to great acclaim for the rest of their lives.)

It is when all this moves to another level, that of risk-taking, that the argument becomes more complicated. *When your skill requires that you regularly risk your life, the question becomes urgent.* Car racing, mountain climbing, repeatedly climbing rocks a goat would not attempt, camping on rock faces in freezing weather, activities that require life-threatening exposure and speeds, I must put in a different category. How does this advance human culture? And how much do they represent defiance, grandiosity, self-dramatization, and brinksmanship? These are much more a quest for personal glory, for accomplishing the seemingly impossible and beating the competition—a narcissistic goal. And, to be sure, many of these seekers after glory die in the attempt. There's the rub: *emotionally healthy people are self-protective and show low risk-taking behavior.* Any behavior that requires extreme risk and distorts our hold on reality needs to be questioned. (Recall the tragic death of John Kennedy Jr., his wife, and her sister. It is painful to think that better planning and a bit more realism would have saved them from his grandiosity.)

This will be an unpopular view, but the questions must be asked: Do extreme risk-takers care that their children could be fatherless or motherless? That the man or woman who loves them would be heartbroken? That parents who lose a child never transcend that? *At some point we must make a distinction between a skill we admire and a symptom that ignores the needs and rights of one's family, especially our children.* A dramatic example is the current reassessment of high school football in the light of recent data on the sequellae of concussion (Easterbrook 2013).

VULNERABILITY: THE CAPACITY FOR INTIMACY

The corollary of mutual respect, "vulnerability" refers to an openness and receptivity to others and to experience with them in general. In a love relationship, vulnerability represents a willingness to risk being hurt in order to be close. People who can be vulnerable feel that their opinions are important but that they are not the ultimate authority on anything. They do not take themselves too seriously; they can laugh at themselves. They recognize that they always have something to learn and that others have an equal right to offer a different view.

Vulnerability is not submission. It is based on the belief that you and the other person are equally deserving. That equality is exactly what is resented by narcissists. There is a strange two-dimensionality to their responses. As one narcissistic wife remarked during therapy, "I can't stand that you think I am *just like the next person.*" When we are open and vulnerable, we hold out our hand. If the other person takes it, we are glad. But if she does not, we do not punish her with anger and retaliation. We want our share but only our share, and we are happy with that. This wish for fairness leaves us vulnerable to the retaliation of those who want it all.

Some people say that narcissism among higher office-seekers is a given. Maybe so, but that doesn't mean we have to elect them. Entrusting our own and our children's welfare to glory-seekers has never been a good idea; much human tragedy stems from that mistake. Narcissists are not subtle. Their motives are out there for all to see. They are enticing but dangerous. Anyone astute enough to read this chapter can make the diagnosis. Their power-seeking and grandiosity are continuous with any tyrant you can think of and only differ in the amount of power they can garner. And that is the point; especially with politicians, they have no power unless we give it to them.

What we need to do instead is to take the reins ourselves. I encourage people in therapy to make a promise to themselves: "No more sick relationships." No more abusive people, no more "users." We ourselves are fair, and we must insist on being treated in a fair manner. We know what we need and what our families and communities need.

And now, overwhelmingly, we know what our planet needs (Pipher 2012). We must develop the global skills to understand and refuse pollution as well as the tyranny of business practices that support it. Taking care of our planet is part of taking care of our children.

IS PATHOLOGICAL NARCISSISM CURABLE?

A book edited by John S. Ogrodniczuk (2013), *Understanding and Treating Pathological Narcissism,* features over 30 experts who say yes. This book is a massive, modern, and mind-changing contribution to the field. Aaron L. Pincus outlines the dual nature of pathological narcissism—grandiosity and vulnerability to shame (96). Unexcelled for eloquence and clarity, Mardi Horowitz describes the "metabolism of shame" as a "dose by dose desensitization to experiences of embarrassment. Shame is accepted as part of the human predicament rather than a catastrophic feeling that the soul is being murdered by negative emotion" (90). We are reminded that while narcissists might be insufferable, they are still suffering people. They can experience a mixture of shame, fear, and rage. Still, they usually shun therapy with its potential for shame-inducing discussions. Therapy would also address the masochistic features in pathological narcissism, victimhood as a way of life (Cooper 1998).

In my experience, narcissists usually come to therapy at the request of an unhappy spouse, but grandiosity is the presenting picture. They do not care that their child is unhappy. They deny their spouse's complaints and make detailed counterallegations. They resist any recommendation from the therapist, or they will nominally accept it and then do nothing. If their motives are questioned, they often leave. While avoidance of shame may be their great need, it is this rigid resistance to being influenced that makes the question of change moot.

Nonetheless, some narcissistic persons do come to therapy and enjoy the opportunity of being the total focus of a dedicated therapist. Psychoanalytically oriented treatment "centers on the activation of the grandiose self and the need for helping the patient achieve full awareness of it in a neutral analytic situation" (Kernberg 1975, 286). This treatment requires that the therapist not retaliate when the patient criticizes and denounces the therapy. Narcissistic persons use primitive defenses like "splitting," seeing people and situations as all good or all bad (Perry & Bond 2005). Thus any interpretation that threatens their idealized self-image will be denounced or disowned. Careful, relentless attention to the effect of this defensiveness on interpersonal relationships can reorient the patient. Slowly, as a result of the therapist's interpretations, the narcissistic patient can realize the effects of his angry, destructive stance, as well as the exhaustion he may feel with its maintenance. His realistic needs for attention are met in the therapy; he begins to experience himself as a person among people, one of us, with all our vulnerabilities—not as a glorious exception.

This kind of methodical one-on-one therapy would be my approach, but there are other therapies that are perhaps more direct. Cognitive behavioral therapy seeks to address the patient's need to be more responsible. Experiential treatments like art and dance therapy work with body expression. Energy psychology might use the stimulation of certain acupuncture points at the same time a patient is describing her emotional struggles.

Dr. Simon Baron-Cohen, a Cambridge University professor of developmental psychopathology, sees narcissism as a failure of empathy. He has devised an empathy scale from 0 to 100, with 100 representing the most highly empathic persons. He finds narcissists ranking near 0, along with borderline personalities and psychopaths. According to Baron-Cohen (2011), the brain's empathy circuit, comprising 10 specific interacting regions including the mirror neuron system, is significantly unresponsive and underactive in these very disturbed people. Baron-Cohen makes a crucial point in identifying the deficit in empathic response as a result of early, documented abuse and neglect in the lives of those who score lowest on his empathy scale. A specialist in autism, Baron-Cohen has devised an intervention for sufferers of that spectrum that he suggests may be of help to other low scorers in empathy, including narcissists. This consists of educational software the person operates at the same time that oxytocin is inhaled through the nostrils. (Oxytocin is the hormone that facilitates bonding and empathy in humans; it is secreted, for instance, when a mother nurses her baby at the breast.) Baron-Cohen further suggested training in the identification of emotions, as well as role-playing.

The discussion of interventions must consider bullying. Who has not suffered as a vulnerable child at some point from bullying? Within the school system, identifying and curbing bullying is finally becoming more of a priority. Bullies show narcissistic traits like power seeking, excessive need for attention, and lack of empathy for others. To be fair, bullies might also be abused children who seek to discharge their anger on other, weaker children. Whatever their motives, bullying is a pernicious pattern that must be identified and corrected early and firmly by an astute faculty, by parent education, and by empowering all the children involved.

Also, families who have a narcissistic member can themselves learn through therapy how to limit the demands and intrusions of the narcissist. They can learn how to verbally respond and how to have time-limited meetings with him or her in neutral settings. Narcissists always *want* attention from their families. Many do want to keep their marriages. Often, they are more motivated for therapy by getting to know their grandchildren. All these are good motives for emotional growth. But realism must be our guide. The more destructive the narcissistic family member—for example, the evidence of children and grandchildren constantly in tears—the more that member must be limited. The price is loss of that parent or spouse and some loneliness, but sometimes it is the only way to be fair to everyone else.

Emotional growth out of early narcissism toward mutual respect and vulnerability is the most important maturational step for parents and teachers to encourage. It is a major antidote to the violence in our cities. It is the major hope we have in our quest for fairness in family life, for community welfare, and indeed in our striving toward democracy. Evolutionary biologist and professor of psychology David P. Barash (2013) cites a parable from Cherokee lore:

> A girl is troubled by a recurring dream in which two wolves fight viciously. Seeking an explanation, she goes to her grandfather, highly regarded for his wisdom, who explains that there are two forces within each of us, struggling for supremacy, one embodying peace and the other, war. At this, the girl is even more distressed and asks her grandfather who wins. His answer: "The one you feed." (12)

REFERENCES

Barash, D. P. (2013, September 29). "Are We Hard-Wired for War?" *New York Times Sunday Review*, 12.

Baron-Cohen, S. (2011). *The Science of Evil: On Empathy and the Origins of Cruelty*. New York: Basic Books.

Barry, C. (Ed.) (2010). *Narcissism and Machiavellianism in Youth*. Washington, DC: American Psychological Association.

Bloom, P. (2010, May 9). "The Moral Life of Babies." *The New York Times Magazine*, 45–65.

Christopher, T. B., Kerig, P. K., Stellwagen, K. K., et al. (Eds.) (2011). *Narcissism and Machiavellianism in Youth: Implications for the Development of Adaptive and Maladaptive Behavior*. Washington, DC: American Psychological Association.

Cooper, A. M. (1998). "Further Developments in the Clinical Diagnosis of Narcissistic Personality Disorder." In E. Ronningstam (Ed.), *Disorders of Narcissism: Diagnostic, Clinical, and Empirical Implications* (53–74). Washington, DC: American Psychological Association.

Cozolino, L. (2010). *The Neuroscience of Psychotherapy: Healing the Social Brain*. New York: W. W. Norton & Company, Inc.

Dingfelder, S. F. (2011, February). "Reflecting on Narcissism: Are Young People More Self-Obsessed Than Ever Before?" *Monitor on Psychology* 42(2): 64–69.

DSM IV R. (1994). Washington, DC: American Psychiatric Association.

Easterbrook, G. (2013). *The King of Sports: Football's Impact on America*. New York: Thomas Dunne Books.

Erol, R. Y. & Orth, U. (2011). "Self-Esteem Development from Age Fourteen to Thirty: A Longitudinal View." *Journal of Personality and Social Psychology* 10(3): 607–619.

Freud, S. (1938). "Three Contributions to the Theory of Sex." In A. A. Brill (Ed.), *The Basic Writings of Sigmund Freud*. New York: The Modern Library

Gazzaniga, M. (2011). *Who's in Charge? Free Will and the Science of the Brain*. New York: HarperCollins Publisher.

Horowitz, M. (2013). "Prototypical Formulation of Pathological Narcissism." In J. S. Ogrodniczuk (Ed.), *Understanding and Treating Pathological Narcissism*. Washington, DC: American Psychological Association.

Kernberg, O. (1975). *Borderline Conditions and Pathological Narcissism*. New York: Jason Aronson Inc.

Kernberg, O. F. (1984). *Severe Personality Disorders: Psychotherapeutic Strategies*. New Haven, CT: Yale University Press.

Kohut, H. (1971). *The Analysis of the Self*. New York: International Universities Press.

Loewald, H. W. (1973). "The Analysis of the Self. A Systematic Approach to the Psychoanalytic Treatment of Narcissistic Personality Disorder." *Psychoanalytic Quarterly* 42, 441–451.

Miller, A. (1981). *Prisoners of Childhood: The Drama of the Gifted Child and the Search for the True Self*. New York: Basic Books.

Murray, H. A. (1938). *Explorations in Personality*. New York: Oxford University Press.

Nelson, M. C. (Ed.). (1977). *The Narcissistic Condition: A Fact of Our Lives and Times*. New York: Human Sciences Press.

Ogrodniczuk, J. S. (Ed.). (2013). *Understanding and Treating Pathological Narcissism.* Washington, DC: American Psychological Association.

Ogrodniczuk, J. S., Piper, W. E., Joyce, A. S., et al. (2009). "Interpersonal Problems Associated with Narcissism among Psychiatric Outpatients." *Journal of Psychiatric Research,* 43, 837–842. doi:10.1016/jpsychires.2008.12.005

Orenstein, P. (2011). *Cinderella Ate My Daughter: Dispatches from the Front Lines of the New Girlie-Girl Culture.* New York: Harper/HarperCollins Publisher.

Perry, J. C. & Bond, M. (2005). "Defensive Functioning." In J. Oldham, A. E. Skodol & D. Bender (Eds.), *The American Psychiatric Publishing Textbook of Personality Disorders* (523–540). Washington, DC: American Psychiatric Press.

Piers, G. & Singer, M. B. (1971). *Shame and Guilt: A Psychoanalytic and Cultural Study.* New York: W. W. Norton & Company, Inc.

Pincus, A. L. (2013). "The Pathological Narcissism Inventory." In J. S. Ogrodniczuk (Ed.), *Understanding and Treating Pathological Narcissism* (93–110). Washington, DC: American Psychological Association.

Pipher, M. (2012). "Visions of a Sustainable Planet: We Need to Expand Our Moral Imagination." *Psychotherapy Networker* 26(5): 48–53.

Smith, E. E. & Aaker, J. L. (2013, December 1). "Millenial Searchers." *New York Times Sunday Review,* 1, 6.

Stinson, F. S., Dawson, D. A., Goldstein, R. B., et al. (2008). "Prevalence, Correlates, Disability and Co-Morbidity of DSM IV Narcissistic Personality Disorder: Results from the Wave 2 National Epidemiological Survey on Alcohol and Related Conditions." *Journal of Clinical Psychiatry* 69(7): 1033–1045.

Tucker, A. (2013, January). "Born to Be Mild: Are We Born Knowing Right from Wrong? New Research Offers Surprising Answers to the Age-Old Question of Where Morality Comes From." *Smithsonian Magazine* 43(9): 34–41, 76–77.

Twenge, J. M., Konrath, S., Foster, J. D., et al. (2008). "Ego-inflating over Time: A Cross-Temporal Meta-Analysis of the Narcissistic Personality Inventory." *Journal of Personality* 76(4): 875–901.

Waldinger, R. J. & Gunderson, J. G. (1987). *Effective Psychotherapy with Borderline Patients: Case Studies.* New York: Macmillan Publishing Company.

Winnicott, D. W. (1986). "The Mother's Contribution to Society." In Winnicott, C., Shepherd, R. & Davis, M. (Eds.), *Home Is Where We Start From: Essays by a Psychoanalyst.* New York: W. W. Norton & Company, Inc.

Wurmser, L. (2007). *Torment Me, but Don't Abandon Me.* Northvale, NJ: Jason Aronson Inc.

Chapter 11

Spirituality with Tolerance
Our Fitful Goal

Ah! Must Thou char the wood ere Thou canst limn with it?[*]
—Francis Thompson, *The Hound of Heaven*

Is it even possible, we well may ask, this idea of spirituality with tolerance? Spirituality is the assured part. As described later, it is part of our *biology*—a function of at least four specialized areas of our brain. But tolerance is a *learned* phenomenon, hard won, if at all. Tolerance is achieved with effort against our equally inherent wariness of strangers who do not behave or believe as we do, as well as our resentment of any interference with what we want to do. Disputes arise between us and our next-door neighbors over boundary rights or trees that can quickly rise to the boiling point, more real than any distant war. The project of tolerance is a challenge day by day, perhaps moment by moment.

And yet the will toward tolerance is an ancient aspiration. One of the earliest recorded is biblical. In his wonderful entreaty *Beyond Tolerance*, Gustav Niebuhr (2008) quotes the Hebrew Bible "in which God promises 'My house will be called a house of prayer for all peoples' " (194). Interfaith interest, cooperation, and support are the subject of Niebuhr's book, in which he documents that these were the stated goals of the founders of this great nation. But before reviewing

---

[*](Do we have to be raked over the coals before we "get it"?)

the psychology of tolerance, it is helpful to consider the *biology* of spirituality.

UNIQUELY HUMAN?

As convinced as I am of Darwinian evidence, I am still left with the question "Is that all?" We are genes; we are biochemistry; we are evolving physiology. But what else are we? "Survival of the fittest" explains our biology; does it explain Johann Sebastian Bach? Humans have musical, artistic, and mathematical abilities not explained by survival of the fittest. If evolution only wanted to assure survival and procreation, why do we want to name the stars? Why do we obsess over the structure of flowers?

The answer is that our marvelous neocortex, the new part of our brain involved in higher-order cognitive functions as well as the inhibition of impulses, wants ever more stimulation. Fascinated with complexity and hungry for problems to solve, our normal brain function creates connections and combinations of ideas that surprise and delight us. In the brains of certain unique individuals (Mozart complained that music played constantly in his mind, and he was relieved by writing it down), this brain activity reaches transcendent beauty. But if certain neurophysiologists are correct, even our spirituality is a function of uniquely human brain centers (Newberg, D'Aquili & Rause 2001). These researchers say that these specialized centers of our associative cortex explain why humans are incurably religious. Were we always religious?

A PRIMEVAL LONGING . . .

Our much-loved and read historian of religion, myth, and religious leaders, Karen Armstrong (2005) writes that when humans create religious ritual, they are responding to the question "What if?" (9). Because humans were afraid of life ending irrevocably in death, we boldly conjectured that we might go on to another reality. Armstrong describes Neanderthal grave sites wherein the deceased was put into a fetal position, as if anticipating a rebirth. We were playing with the possibility, she says, of other outcomes besides the unacceptable fact of biological death. Armstrong's impossible-to-summarize account follows the history of myth and ritual to the "Axial Age," c. 800–200 BCE, when the major religions arose. This "marks the beginning of religion as we know it. . . . Confucianism and Taoism in China; Buddhism and Hinduism in India; monotheism in the Middle East and Greek rationalism in Europe" (79).

This fear of the finality and ultimate disempowerment of death was what Freud (1961) saw as the reason humans needed religion. We were afraid to feel all alone in the dark, not knowing what could happen with the next dawn. More than frightening, it was disorganizing. We could be immobilized with terror; anticipatory anxiety is as disabling as an actual anxiety-provoking event. The belief that totems and rituals would reliably protect us relieved our primal anxiety. We could sleep. We could create culture.

Norman O. Brown (1959) went further and proposed that humans *compensate with competence*—with achievement, mastery, and excellence—for the desperate awareness of death. Brown, a scholar of history, philosophy, and morality, posited that the only way to overcome fear of death is for us to invest our talent and skills maximally in our work and in our love relationships such that we arrive at death, exhausted and grateful, because we have truly lived. Brown's book *Life against Death* provides the best exegesis of Freud for the general reader. Just as Winnicott applied psychoanalysis to the elucidation of the mother–child bond and deepened our understanding of infant experience, Brown explored the "psychoanalytic meaning of history" and the human predicament. Fear of death is our perennial struggle, he says, and the source of all creativity and human achievement. He does not mean this in a cynical way; it is a joyful, grateful-for-life stance he is describing.

A hallmark of healthy personality, spirituality is a longing to understand the universe and our place in it. It is the ultimate expression of our vulnerability. Spirituality refers to our conviction, shared by all human groups, of a reality beyond our senses, a reality greater than ourselves, not understood but felt. It includes what we call "intuition"—all the things that William James was referring to as "the reality of the unseen" (1961, title of chapter 3).

All human groups show certain common traits. All use language, spoken and often written. All create rituals to structure their interactions, with rules about ritual usage (Frazer 1993). And all human groups raise their faces to the sky and wonder. Can we say that wonder is an effect of evolution? Is evolution the final arbiter of our fate? Where does all this documented spirituality fit in? Now that evolution has secured our *survival*, what are we going to do with that?

GENETICS AND SPIRITUALITY: THE TWAIN MEET

Several years ago, when the human genome was first mapped, we were presented with the finding that we share 98.5 percent of our genes with the chimpanzee. On hearing this, I remember being depressed for about a week and a half until I decided that this could not be the whole story. What could possibly be in that 1.5 percent that could account for the cumulative and transmissible record of human culture? And what about the technological gulf between chimps and humans?

Human babies outsmart infant chimps by one year of age. And the reason for this clarifies the 1.5 percent question. In the embryonic chimp's brain, the genes that code for neuron-doubling stop the process at a certain point. In the *human* embryo, our genes for neuron-doubling keep the process going considerably longer, resulting in millions more neurons in the human embryo's brain:

> Any expansion in cerebral cortex means, up to a point, keeping as many cells in the neuroepithelium in their totipotent condition for as long as possible—squeezing proliferation power out of the neuroepithelium. The longer the population of totipotent progenitor cells can be maintained, the more cortical neurons will eventually be produced, and the more cortical expansion will be supported. (Taylor 2009, 53)

And not just *any* neurons. Our frontal cortex, an area rich in peptides (information molecules) and receptors (molecules that receive information) is uniquely human. It is our area for higher-order cognitive functions—decision making and planning for the future. Chimpanzees share 98.5 percent of our genes but lack a developed frontal cortex (Nelson 2011, 181; Pert 2003, 288), and human brains differ from those of other mammalian species in *organization,* not just in size (Gazzaniga 2008, 11). This was heartening. What else could be in that one-plus percent?

I learned that it's not that quantitative. For example, the *same* gene in chimps and in humans will *function differently* in each organism. That is, a gene for encoding a specific protein will make one protein in chimps and a different protein in humans. This is crucial because proteins—for example, enzymes and immunoglobulins—regulate our metabolism and immune systems respectively. Approximately 5,000 genes make us uniquely human (Taylor 2009, 70–89).

The one-plus percent difference was becoming less daunting. Could there then be specific human brain regions for spirituality?

According to medical researchers at the University of Pennsylvania, we have *four* "exclusively human" brain regions associated with religious feelings (Newberg et al. 2001). Their names for these four associative areas are "the visual association area . . . the orientation association area, the attention association area, and the verbal conceptual association area . . . the most complex neurological structures in the brain" (27–28, 32). In their brave new book, the researchers allege that these peculiarly human brain structures subserve religious and spiritual experience and show these to be part of our brain's *normal functioning.* The orientation association area, for example, supplies *two* experiences of the body, one creating the physical space in which the self can exist, and the other creating the brain's spatial sense of self (28). In reviewing a wealth of evidence, Newberg et al. show that the persistence of religious feelings in human cultures continues to be good for us, physically and emotionally. How that happened is one of their fascinating premises:

> [I]t's unlikely that the neurological machinery of transcendence [experiences beyond the limits of the physical body] evolved specifically for spiritual reasons. Still, we believe that evolution has *adopted this machinery,* and has favored the religious capabilities of the religious brain because religious beliefs and behaviors turn out to be good for us in profound and pragmatic ways. (129; emphasis added)

Neurologist Kevin Nelson (2011) disagrees. It may be natural for us to think that spiritual experiences reside in the cortex, the most recent, most advanced part of our brains. But "[o]ur spiritual experiences have instinctual qualities, originating in the most primitive parts of our brains. They appear intertwined with the brain's limbic structures, which produce feelings and emotions" (11). Nelson is a specialist on the science of near-death experience and reports that out-of-body experiences occur in 1 in 20 people (137).

> We have strong indications that much of our spirituality arises from arousal, limbic, and reward systems that evolved long before structures that made the brain capable of language and reasoning. Neurologically, mystical feelings may not be so much beyond language as *before* language. (258; emphasis his.)

Research on neuropeptides—molecules in the brain and nervous system that carry information—would support Nelson's allegation.

Peptide researcher Candace Pert (2003) reported that "core limbic brain structures, such as the amygdala, hippocampus and limbic cortex, believed by neuroscientists to be involved in emotional behavior contained a whopping 85 to 95% of the various neuropeptides we had studied"(133).

The neurological structures that allows us spiritual experiences—wherever they reside—may subserve another uniquely human trait, that of storytelling. English professor Jonathan Gottschall alleges that, for us, morality is taught through stories. Neuroscientists have established that our ability to project ourselves into the future allows us to try out different scenarios. We can rehearse potential outcomes and thus can judge their messages of danger or of opportunity. And through stories we can relate with empathy to a hero's good fortune and suffer when a villain wins. We have an inborn fairness meter; we want restitution. Gottschall's theory is that our fascination with stories—both writing and savoring them—is part of our biology, fostering pro-social behavior and encouraging cohesive societies. His message is that stories can thus be as important as genes and part of our evolution. They are also part of every religion and a major way that religions carry their messages.

RELIGIOUS BELIEF AND MENTAL HEALTH

People who have stable religious convictions live longer, have fewer strokes and heart attacks, lower blood pressure, and better immune systems when compared to the general population (Koenig 1999). Emotionally, being religious protects people from high rates of divorce, drug abuse, alcoholism, and suicide. For many people, a strong faith in God is protective against depression and anxiety. Moreover, practices such as meditation, mindfulness, and prayer are so effective in reducing stress that they are now incorporated in a number of clinical interventions including types of psychotherapy and physical rehabilitation (Holzel 2010).

Why should consenting to a set of rules and rituals be auspicious for the believers? It is the *believing*, to be sure. In the act of believing, we are investing those premises with trust and hope. But it's also the *belonging*, the identification with others who accept the same premises. We humans need personal validation to feel good about ourselves. (That is why shunning, or rejection, is one of the most painful punishments.) In belonging, there is a warm, collective feeling that tells us we are here, we are together, we belong together. Togetherness is as consoling as isolation is terrifying.

The therapeutic effects that psychotherapy and religious healing have in common were addressed by my friend and mentor, Jerome Frank, in his remarkable survey *Persuasion and Healing* (Frank & Frank 1991). Frank emphasized that wherever help was sought—from the shaman, priest, or personal or group therapy—the resolution of a person's quandary lay in the examination of her beliefs, especially her expectations. That such relief and healing can come from these diverse sources arises, I think, from the intense need of a suffering person for comfort, belonging, and feeling "blessed" by a much-trusted authority. Feeling understood, Frank says, produces relaxation and trust. In addition, the opportunity to confess and be forgiven is often a part of this experience.

The similarities are striking. No student of social history can ignore the survival benefits of religious feelings and beliefs. The difference I see is in *how* change occurs. The two processes—religious healing and psychotherapy—differ in at least one crucial aspect. In religious healing, one has only to ask for it, or pray for it, and it comes through grace or blessing. But in psychotherapy, a person may not be consciously *aware* of her guilt or grief, only that she finds herself inexplicably agitated or sad. A therapist then begins asking about the person's experience of her difficulty and listens for words that name certain feelings: anxious, depressed, angry, numb, hopeless. Then the task of systematically examining the person's defense patterns begins. It is hard work; it takes time and patience. In therapy, two intelligent people are meeting to examine what makes one of them suffer. That person flounders. Anxiety keeps much information out of consciousness until she becomes strong enough to realize the full extent of her conflict, anger, and ambivalence. At that point, the changes necessary for her future behavior become clearer, and at the same time she does not feel ready to execute them. It is an intellectual task before which the intellect quails. But the relief she eventually achieves is profound and durable. And it has been hard-won. It does not come by divine decree.

HOW BELIEVING HELPS

It was not just protection humans needed. It was help with the question of good and evil. All organized religions are structured to help with these ongoing dilemmas. What is meant by "evil"? What is "good"? Most of all, who has the right answers? One brave response is that it is *all* religions. "Interspirituality" is a concept offered by Wayne Teasdale (1999) to advance his notion that we benefit from considering all the varied forms of religious expression. Such respectful immersion into the spirit of all religion would have the effect of strengthening their commonalities and diminishing their differences. The fundament of religious feeling is the *personal longing for a connection to the divine.* All religions offer this connection, in diverse and original concepts and practices.

The appreciation of those diverse concepts and practices would seem to eliminate any need for tolerance. There would be nothing to tolerate if we could—with effort and commitment—teach each other about one another's faith and discuss the commonalities. "[W]ork across religious lines tends to worry some people ... who fear that conversation among believers in different traditions inevitably leads to a wearing down of important differences—the unique teachings that comprise Christianity or Judaism, for example. Yet the best of this work ... is not about erasing differences but trying to understand and allow for them. ... In dealing with religious differences, that's our charge. There's nothing easy about it" (Niebuhr 2008, xxiv–xxv).

Another view is that we need *no* religion. "Postmodern spirituality is characterized by individuals seeking personal growth and fulfillment through spiritual practices, without any scaffolding of traditional religious beliefs and without ties to formal communities of worship"(Griffith 2012, 319). This sentiment is extended by neurologists Newberg et al. (2001) when they say:

> All religions arise from and are maintained by transcendent experiences [experiences beyond the self which are caused by the activity of uniquely human brain associative centers], therefore, they all lead us, by different paths, toward the same goal of wholeness and unity, in which the specific claims of individual faiths converge into an absolute, undifferentiated whole. (166)

Is the implication that we need to be brave enough to leave the question of religious truth open, to live with the ambiguity the "big questions" instigate? To be comfortable with not knowing, but to continue our inquiry, recruiting all the disparate evidence we can find from every discipline? It would be a lonely, solitary venture. And that may be the point. We do not do well with loneliness.

Religions create communities that are cohesive and protective, providing greater social support and a deeper meaning to life for their members. We could go further and state the obvious: religious devotion has been a universal source of art, architecture, music, poetry, and literature. And its opposite—religious intolerance—has been the cause of bloodshed and destruction on a global scale. "Spiritual experiences bring out the best and the worst in us" (Nelson 2011, 255). In the name of one religion's being superior to another, we have had wars, crusades, exiles, massacres, inquisitions, pogroms, diasporas, and planes flying into skyscrapers. Not just because one religion is fervently held to be superior, but because no other religion but that one can be tolerated on the face of the earth.

Since the terrorist attacks of September 11, 2001, there has been an urgent interest in interfaith "cooperation circles," each consisting of members of at least three religions. They work on a variety of issues—for example, AIDS, environmental issues, and teaching children tolerance. By 2006, there were 320 such groups in 65 nations, as reported by Gustav Niebuhr (2008). These groups

> deliberately cross boundaries in an era in which religious differences are so explosive. Call it a quiet countertrend; it directly challenges violence in God's name, even if it does not replace it. At its heart, it's a grass-roots educational process in which the goal is to gain knowledge about individuals and their beliefs in a way that lessens fear. It's a new activity in the world, an entirely new phenomenon in our history. It is a social good, a basis for hope, and a tendency that ought to be nurtured and cultivated. (Niebuhr 2008, xix)

These interfaith education groups coexist, Niebuhr says, with religious fanatical groups in a "war of ideas." Religious intolerance is a play for *personal* preeminence. It sounds frighteningly familiar—continuous with the narcissistic pathology described in the last chapter. And like narcissism, religious intolerance is single-minded, self-dramatizing, and unempathic. It insists on a *personal* importance and identification with a given religion and is intolerant if not destructive toward all other religious positions. *Religious intolerance would seem to fit many of the criteria for pathological narcissism.*

"INHERITED" TOLERANCE

Empathy, self-awareness, and a concern for right and wrong appear for the first time in children between one and three years of age (Kagan & Lamb 1987). But decades of studies with babies and children yield a very mixed picture of children sharing toys and treats at one point and reacting aggressively in the next. And sometimes what looks like inborn intolerance is actually motivated by something else. "Three-month-olds like people of their own race more than others . . . and one-year-olds prefer native speakers to those of another tongue" (Tucker 2013). From the point of view of relational psychoanalysis, these behaviors may mean something quite different. They may well be part of the attachment process—the babies' bond with their mothers. Rather than assuming the beginnings of prejudice in babies, it is reasonable to think that an infant will feel *safer with familiar faces who look like her mother and family and who also sound like them.* Baron-Cohen (2011) writes that the capacity for empathy involves being able to take into consideration another person's point of view and compare it simultaneously with our own. This is a description of the positive effects of early attachment and may highlight the specific deficit in pathological narcissism—that there is no such complementarity.

Complicating all this is the finding that, aside from attachment or genetic issues, aggressive behavior in children has been linked to secondhand smoke. Linda Pagnani (2013) of the University of Montreal surveyed over 2,000 children from birth through 10 years of age. She collected reports from parents, teachers, and from the children themselves and found that children exposed to secondhand smoke in early childhood were more likely to become aggressive and antisocial. This was unrelated to a history of antisocial behavior in the parents. Pagnani reports that secondhand smoke is more toxic than inhaled smoke, especially while the brain is developing. The strong statistical correlations, she said, do predict aggressive and antisocial behavior in children. This constitutes one of the clearest instances of preventable aggression.

The deadly opposition between "my way or the highway" thinking, and a generous, patient, tolerant stance toward the beliefs of others, *might* be genetic, according to E. O. Wilson, the sociobiologist. In an interview in the *Atlantic* magazine (French 2011) Wilson described "eusocial" species—those which form societies with a division of labor—as the most successful creatures on earth. "Wilson posits two rival forces that drive human behavior: group selection and what he calls 'individual selection' ... with both operating simultaneously" (80–81). The group gene operates, Wilson says, for the greater good, while the "personal" gene [the narcissistic one?] seeks power and pre-eminence. Wilson (2012) says that answers to the ultimate questions will not come from organized religion but from science, especially genetics. The elegant patterns of evolution, as evidenced in the most minute species differences, are his revelations.

Categories of normal and abnormal behavior do not always over-lap categories of right and wrong, but it is tempting to put all this into psychological terms. Suppose the group gene does program for empathic and protective behavior, and the "personal" gene for nar-cissism and tyranny. In Wilson's (2012) model, he states that both these genes are operating simultaneously. And this is close to what we observe in daily life, people showing altruistic behavior one minute then aggressive behavior in another, sometimes in the same setting.

GENDER AND THE DIFFERENCE IT MAKES

One worries here that Wilson's model does not help with the prob-lem of gender differences. Violence is overwhelmingly perpetrated by males (Raine 2013). Most violence against women is caused by men. Men start wars of all types. Women almost never want war, although there are exceptions (Lower 2013; Zur & Morrison 1989). The popu-lations in prisons are still mainly male. Stephen Pinker (2011) is even more emphatic. He identifies

> the most fundamental empirical generalization about violence, that it is mainly committed by men. From the time they are boys, males play more violently than females, fantasize more about violence, consume more violent entertainment, commit the lion's share of violent crimes, take more delight in punishment and revenge, take more foolish risks in aggressive attacks, vote for more war-like policies and leaders, and plan and carry out almost all the wars and genocides. (684–685)

These data argue mightily for both genetic and social wellsprings. The genetic source is likely on the Y-chromosome, the mighty push of testosterone that changes the male baby's brain (Brizendine 2010) and instigates male-to-male combat with the goal of personal preem-inance (Dippel 2010). The social wellspring is rooted in the differ-ential socialization of boys and girls (Dinnerstein 1976, 1983), which crossculturally pushes children apart into narrowly prescribed categories. And educating girls is not a priority for those cultures that still seek to confine women in the home and limit their options. As Pinker (2011) also noted:

> Societies in which women get a better deal, both traditional and modern, tend to be societies that have less organized violence. [For example] among contemporary countries in the contrast between the low levels of political and judicial violence in the uber-feminist democracies of western Europe and the high levels in the genital-cutting, adulteress-stoning, burqa-cladding Sharia states of Islamic Africa and Asia. (686)

These clashing attitudes about raising children—different standards for girls and for boys—fill our world with polarized thinking, in which "ordinary women are too accustomed to deferring and ordinary men to prevailing" (Dinnerstein 1983, 306).

It is social and psychological development that is the crux of this issue, especially male adolescence, although we should remember, as Nicholas Kristof (2012, September 23) warns:

> that it is not just Muslims who periodically go berserk, but everybody—particularly in societies with large numbers of poorly educated young men. Upheavals are often more about demography than about religion: the best predictor of civil conflict is the share of a population that is aged 15 to 24. In the nineteenth century, when the United States brimmed with poorly educated young men, Protestants rioted against Catholics. (*New York Times Sunday Review*, SR13)

All this has been well described by psychologists, feminists, and others, and might sound out of date. It's not. Terrorist activities are still mainly carried out by young males—not only the 9/11 terrorist attack, but the ongoing Muslim attacks on both Americans and on other Muslims. On December 14, 2012, we were immobilized with grief at the slaughter of 20 first graders and six adults in Newtown, Connecticut, by a deranged 20-year-old male. The combination of out-of-control male rage and the availability of military assault weapons is by now formulaic: *both* are separate but equal contributors. With real and reliable gun control *and* early assessment plus ongoing treatment of troubled young men, we can interrupt that formula. This is not simple. A year after the Newtown shooting, Jeffrey Swanson, author of over 150 articles on mental illness, violence, and gun control, wrote:

New criteria and rules designed to identify the small number of seriously mentally ill people who are demonstrably dangerous and to prevent them from accessing firearms, now occupy center stage in the gun policy reforms emerging at the national and state levels. But the laws are both sensible and overreaching; lawmakers need to find the right balance between public safety and civil rights as they try to sort out one from the other. (Swanson 2013, 1,233)

Yet the *New York Times* (December 22, 2013) reported that, in one of Swanson's much-quoted studies, people with mental illness were found to have a *high* incidence of violence:

when substance abusers were excluded, 33 percent of people with a serious mental illness *reported* past violent behavior, compared with 15 percent of people without such a disorder. The study ... defined violent behavior as everything from taking part in more than one fist-fight as an adult to using a weapon in a fight. (Luo & McIntire, 28; emphasis added)

It does not help much to exhort the mentally ill to seek help, as was recommended by the American Psychological Association after the Newtown shooting and endorsed by President Obama (Clay 2013, 35). The most severely disturbed people will not seek treatment because they have no insight. Still, as reported in the *Monitor on Psychology*, (December 2013, 13), a Gallup poll taken after the Washington, D.C., Navy Yard shooting in September of 2013 found that 48 percent of Americans blame the mental health system for mass shootings.

What may have the greatest chance of making a difference is the recognition of schoolchildren who are perennial loners, who say "weird" or violent things, and seem sullen and angry much of the time. This is the type of student who is avoided by classmates, but alert teachers and school psychologists will identify them. *Then we must not lose track of them.* According to an American Psychological Association report (*National Psychologist* vol. 23, no.1), "establishing threat assessment teams of trained experts who can gather information to determine whether a person is on a path to violence is the most effective tool currently available to prevent episodes of mass violence" (8).

The Newtown shooting has to be the ultimate last straw for the majority of us who call ourselves "normal." In our dilemma about the proper balance between public safety and civil rights, it's time for the *civil rights of public safety*—the rights of 20 6-year-olds and their teachers, who could have been saved—perhaps—by a phone call from one of Adam Lanza's sane relatives who may have known more than we did about his condition. But lacking that, by effective gun legislation: Lanza's mother had multiple types of guns. Even a raging 20-year-old man could not have done much damage without them.

The urge for aggression is a genetic and hormonal component of male physiology, one of the fundamental differences between men's brains and women's:

> The amygdala is the brain center for fear, anger and aggression, and it is physically larger in men than in women, whereas the anger, fear and aggression *control center*—the prefrontal cortex—is relatively larger in women. . . . The male amygdala also has many testosterone receptors, which stimulate and heighten its response to anger, especially after the testosterone surges at puberty. That's why men whose testosterone levels are high, which includes younger men, have short fuses. . . . [A]s men age, their testosterone naturally declines, the amygdala becomes less responsive, the prefrontal cortex gains more control, and they don't get angry as fast. (Brizendine 2006, 129; italics added)

We are not, however, simply a bag of hormones and neurotransmitters. Unlike other mammals who cannot deviate from their genetic decree, humans perceive choices and make decisions. Without getting into the brouhaha about free will, it is clear that we add something simple and elegant to the wiring miracle of the brain. It is *attention*, the willful focusing of our minds, against a host of distractions, onto a single issue or feature of our present experience. It is not only a choice but a distinct *ability*. Professor of psychiatry Jeffrey M. Schwartz writes, "The act of focusing attention so that one thought, one possible action, prevails over all the other possible ones competing for dominance in consciousness. . . . It is this power of attention—to select one possibility over all others—that invests us with an efficacious will" (Schwartz & Begley 2002, 325). So it is the focusing of attention—what happens in socialization—that trains us to regulate and even override our impulses. The emotions instigated by hormones can be felt, identified, and *inhibited* by an act of will.

It would seem that if intolerance and violence are to be reduced, then something must be changed in children's socialization, especially the socialization of boys. Psychologists and other mental health specialists are recognizing this with new programs. One such program has been implemented by three culturally different psychologists on three themes: "intrapersonal awareness, interpersonal skill development and service to others" (Clay 2012, 54). William Seymour, Ramel I. Smith, and Hector Torres stress that influencing boys early in their development is crucial, especially in the areas of impulse control and taking the other person's point of view. They provide young boys with new role models who show that men can agree to disagree without becoming enemies—a brilliant definition of tolerance.

Poet, actor, and writer Carlos Andres Gomez has done the seemingly impossible—rewriting the formula young men in the modern era are taught. Aggression, Gomez says, dominates everything young men learn, particularly in the black and Latino neighborhoods where he grew up. A trained social worker, Gomez left this profession for an acting career and found a world of sensitivity and feeling that he had never known. Now he brings his message (Gomez 2012) to prisons and schools, telling men and boys that their cultivated toughness and arrogant attitude toward women are destructive of the women and of themselves. Caring and patience must be their salvation, or they will kill each other one by one. His remarkable message of tolerance, patience, and love could not be more timely.

Two notable texts describe in depressing detail that violence is committed by young men in armies, terrorist groups, or alone. Both books allege that men start wars because they are sexually frustrated and because they need to "re-assert" their masculinity (Dippel 2010; Potts & Hayden 2008). Moreover, "[a]ppetitive aggression, in which violent excesses are experienced as sensually pleasurable, may occur in war" (Weierstall, Schauer & Elbert, 2013, 47). But "fight-or-flight," we should remember, is a male pattern of coping (Cannon 1994), whereas "tend and befriend" is the female pattern. Female coping with stress is more characterized by

> nurturant activities designed to protect the self and offspring that promote safety and reduce distress; befriending is the creation and maintenance of social networks that may aid in this process . . . neuroendocrine evidence from animals and human studies suggest that oxytocin, in conjunction with female reproductive hormones and endogenous opioid peptide mechanisms, may be at its core. (Taylor et al. 2000, 411)

Additionally, women's morality is more about caring than justice (Brabeck 1983; Eagly, Eaton, Rose, Riger & McHugh 2012; Gilligan 1982; Takei 2012). If mirror neurons are involved in the experience of empathy, women have more such neurons (Orzhekhovskaia 2005). "In the female brain, the circuit for aggression is more closely linked to cognitive, emotional and verbal functions than is the male aggression pathway, which is more connected to brain areas for physical action" (Brizendine 2006, 42; see also Campbell 2005; Collaer & Hines 1995).

But do all these differences explain why men have to "reassert" their masculinity? Here is one dramatic historical instance in which women reacted differently, despite great frustration and fear. A colleague, a psychiatrist who grew up in postwar Europe, related the following experiences from when she was about four years old. Her country had lost over 50 percent of its men, she said, and women were struggling to survive and to feed their children. Women were running trains, farming, and using everything they could for food. Many of these women formed liaisons with other women; others struggled to nurture the older population and took in orphaned children. They did not start wars out of sexual frustration. They took care of each other, the children, and the wounded.

In the past, women have been the "outsiders" to history, its "court jester" (Dinnerstein 1983, 300–301). Now it is abundantly clear that empowering women as equal partners in industry and government, as well as influencing young boys away from aggression, are essential for our progress. Women "mentoring" men is the most innovative approach to this task (Takei 2012). Remember the Cherokee legend about the two fighting wolves, war and peace. The girl's grandfather told her that the one who wins is the one you feed. Do women feed one wolf and men another? Do both wolves eat the same food? Can the male need for dominance be redirected? We used to hear the phrase: If you want peace, work for justice. *New York Times* columnist Nicholas Kristof updates that plea: If you want justice, work for women's rights (Kristof & WuDunn 2010).

HUMANIZING NATURE

Community-wide education projects on mental health are being implemented:

> [T]here is evidence that a range of interventions can improve mental health literacy [awareness of the features and effects of mental illness] including whole-of-community campaigns, interventions in educational settings, Mental Health First Aid training, and information

websites. . . . Increasing the community's mental health literacy needs to be a focus for national policy and population monitoring so that the whole community is empowered to take action for better mental health. (Jorm 2012, 231)

The more information and training we have, the more capable we will be of definitive, responsible, and *timely* intervention. If Wilson's two-gene system operating simultaneously sounds simplistic, it is actually a fair explanation for the content of daily news reports: violence at one point, altruism the next. If Wilson is correct, both gene systems seem equally strong. But do genes or groups of genes that are responsible for such broad human *behaviors* operate "automatically"—the way we digest our food or secrete hormones? There is evidence that cognitive processes this advanced can have a biological basis.

Fairness itself and generosity, says psychologist Dacher Keltner (2009), light up our brains in areas identified as reward centers. He proposes a "jen ratio," which refers to our capacity to *elicit* generous behavior from others. He does not ignore our capacity for selfish behavior. He stresses generosity and altruism as deliberate and motivated behaviors. But he describes generous behavior as *part of our brain's reward system* and shows experimentally that caring behaviors light up these reward systems. This fits with more recent evidence that having an agreeable personality enhances the brain's production of pain-killing compounds when compared to persons with "angry hostility personality trait" (Pavius 2013). PET scan [positron emission tomography] subjects with agreeable personalities were shown to produce more "mu-opioids," the brain's natural painkillers (9). Altruism is good for us and makes us happy. It is an active choice and not necessarily a religious one.

A heartening example of this was reported by *New York Times* journalist Nicholas Kristof in the *New York Times Sunday Review*, November 6, 2011. The article featured John Wood, an American Microsoft marketing director, who, while working in Vietnam, saw that some schools had no books for the students. Wood decided to collect books for them and delivered hundreds of books to these schools. And here is the transformative event: The children wept with joy, clutching the books to their hearts as treasures. Wood reported that, upon seeing the children's gratitude, he felt such a powerful *exhilaration* that he quit Microsoft, started a foundation called Room to Read, and began traveling and raising funds for schools and libraries. By the time the *New York Times* article was published, Wood had established "12,000 of these libraries around the world, along with 1,500 schools" (Kristof 2011). His remarkable story is an example of Keltner's proposal: that altruism and generosity do indeed make us happy.

The other side of the argument can sound just as strong, writes evolutionary psychologist/biologist Robert Trivers. Biological opportunism is adaptive, and so are self-deception and deceit. We *don't* tell everyone our truth all the time; this simplifies life and protects our privacy. Children *are* notably sneaky to maximize their own advantage. While these things are true, on some level, Trivers's book feels reductionistic—like an expansion of the durable argument that we are deceitful and manipulative by evolutionary decree.

The *ability* to cheat *is* normal. It is part of the intelligence that secured our survival in times of food scarcity—part of our "Machiavellian Intelligence" (Byrne & Whiten 1989). And it is a place we can regress to. Viktor Frankl (1984) wrote poignantly about how civil and sophisticated people, within weeks of having been stripped of everything, could—without a glance backward—turn in their concentration camp-mates in order to save themselves. This desperate opportunism surfaces today in, for example, the publishing mills that many universities have become. "Much of the cheating in academia probably stems from concern over the potential demise of a career rather than the prestige of publication" (Fang & Casadevall 2013, 35). The same authors discuss how cheating can be contagious if people see that other cheaters are not caught (36).

Byrne and Comp (2004) connected the "rate" of cheating to cortical size in primates—the larger the cortex, the more cheating. Their findings, they said, are "consistent with the hypothesis that neocortical expansion has been driven by social challenges among the primates. Complex social manipulations such as deception are thought to be based upon rapid learning and extensive social knowledge; thus, learning in social contexts may be constrained by neocortical size" (1,693).

This is not to say that cheating is "normal" and we cannot help it, so there is no moral issue. That just because we have this fancy cortex and *can* cheat, we should sit back and enjoy it. If cheating continues to be part of our evolutionary biology, we should recognize that evolution was not always such a genius. What stops us is *caring* that our dishonesty hurts the people we care about and how ashamed this makes us feel. Further, how hurt we ourselves feel when we are deceived.

It is also difficult to respect the posture that psychopathic traits are variants of normal ones (Dutton 2013). Healthy people may be manipulative, but this motive is constrained by noting the effect on people we care about. And that is the point: psychopaths lack the bond. It is a difference in kind, not degree. Besides giving us the best metaphor for psychopaths—"sub-satanic"—Dutton is not convincing when he says that manipulation, dishonesty, and cruelty are simply dialed-up versions of normal behavior. These are instead primitive, "un-attached" behaviors.

Psychopaths lack caring and conscience, evidence of an earlier deficit in attachment (Celani 2010). That bond that sustains us throughout development is the source of conscience. There is no conscience without that bond. So psychopaths and some narcissists are not just cold-hearted and cruel; they lack the capacity to care that makes us human. Does this result from injury? "In tests of empathy and accuracy at judging other people's emotional states, criminal psychopaths show deficits that are similar to those of people with brain damage to the OFC [orbitofrontal cortex]" (Smoller 2012, 180). Whatever their source, these symptoms stem from the *failure to develop some normal parameter*, in this case, attachment to the parent. The process of evolution has been *amoral*. It has secured our survival and doubtless still operates, but now we must make our own decisions about what is fair and right.

THE PROJECT OF TOLERANCE

William Saletan (2012) speaks directly to this. We "do not have to believe in God" to believe in reason, he says:

> You just have to believe in evolution. Evolution itself has evolved: as humans became increasingly social, the struggle for survival, mating and progeny depended less on physical abilities and more on social abilities. In this way, a faculty produced by evolution—sociality—became the new engine of evolution. *Why can't reason do the same thing?* Why can't it emerge from its evolutionary origins as a spin doctor to become the new medium in which humans compete, cooperate and advance the fitness of their communities? Isn't that what we see all around us? Look at the global spread of media, debate and democracy. (12–13; italics added)

The traditional problems with religion are still with us. Why does each religion almost by definition reject all others as less "true"? *Does tolerance only work if everyone is tolerant?* Are we at that (some would say ineluctable) point when we recognize that our love for a religion rooted in our childhood culture *can* close our minds to the abuses within that religion? Is disillusioned Ireland a good example? (The Irish prime minister stated publicly to leaders of the Catholic Church that the Church has not served Ireland as promised and that Ireland was withdrawing its centuries-old trust [Lyall 2011].)

What will it take to resolve this dilemma? Perhaps Richard Dawkins's (2006) 21 cannons that leave no belief unchallenged. Religion gives people no choice as to what to believe, Dawkins says. Children are victims of parental indoctrination. Dawkins encourages us to be comfortably—even happily—atheists.

What Dawkins is leaving out, however, is what a psychologist might see as an important complication: the stability of the developed personality. Dawkins cannot expect that, upon reading his provocative volume, people will simply jump out of their historical skins and be the free thinkers he encourages. Personality is difficult to alter even in therapy, when people will identify such change as their deepest wish. Personality develops mainly in early childhood. Out of the combination of their genetic decree and the influences of their parental world, children build a cohesive sense of self. From the sights and sounds of their culture and their native language, they build an assumptive world, a stable set of expectations that help them to feel comfortable with themselves and with the expectations of their families. In addition, an important part of the world children take in is the family's faith and the ways in which it ritualizes and celebrates daily life. It becomes a part of the child's identification, providing stability and encouragement as the child grows, as well as rites of passage, like confirmation and bar and bat mitzvahs. Once personality is formed, its assumptions and motives operate broadly. It is not something a person can outgrow simply by reading a book.

Psychology respects this. Often in the process of therapy, a man or woman will question religious strictures along with other early constraints on their emotional growth, but this redefinition of the self is discovered by the person herself or himself. It is unfair to equate mental health with atheism as Dawkins has done. Wasn't his own journey a long process, I would ask. Some people today seem to worship technology. Is that better?

We are peculiarly in need of validation from others, from a community of like-minded people who will look out for one another. Religious longing, which we have learned arises naturally out of our normal brain functions, is often recruited into this community identi-fication. (If we could just expand its embrace to include all religions, as encouraged by Wayne Teasdale, 1999, and Gustav Niebuhr, 2008.) Disillusionment with religion is a personal stance. It takes unusual emotional stamina to endure high levels of ambiguity and uncertainty. Not all of us are ready to be so alone, "as on a darkling plain" (from Matthew Arnold's *Dover Beach*).

Tolerance *is* increasing, and violence is declining, says psycholo-gist Stephen Pinker (2011). With impressive charts and graphs, Pinker shows that war between developed countries has disappeared. Wars in the past, especially tribal warfare, were nine times more deadly than wars in the 20th century. During the Middle Ages, the murder rate was 30 times that of today. And, Pinker continues, because of the spread of government and increased literacy, we have come to understand the impulses that make us violent, like sadism and tribalism, as well as the "better angels of our nature," notably empathy and fairness, which help us resist violence. Pinker comes closest to our premise of spir-ituality with tolerance. He believes that human nature is compatible with a secular humanism he calls "enlightenment humanism"(180). Put simply, Pinker says that we do not need religion to be moral:

> Morality, then, is not a set of arbitrary regulations dictated by a venge-ful deity and written down in a book; nor is it the custom of a partic-ular culture or tribe. It is the consequence of the interchangeability of perspectives [being able to take another person's point of view] and the opportunity the world provides for positive-sum games [win-win situ-ations]. This foundation of morality may be seen in the many versions of the Golden Rule that have been discovered by the world's religions, and also in Spinoza's Viewpoint of Eternity, Kant's Categorical Impera-tive, Hobbes and Rousseau's Social Contract, and Locke and Jefferson's self-evident truth that all men are created equal. (Pinker 2011, 182)

Here then, if we are able to do it, is tolerance in its essence. If this eminently sensible teaching could spread in ever-widening circles of acceptance and understanding, it offers a way to have spirituality with-out violence and war, because we shall have outgrown them. Human-ism can confer tolerance, or make tolerance unnecessary. Humanism is the pinnacle of human striving, *the place where the projects of pac-ifism, concern for the environment and equality for women intersect. It is a sophisticated and emotionally mature position and, as Pinker doubtless knows, dependent on a high degree of universal education.*

But we can take first steps: for those groups that still want autocracy and over-control of their people, we can make efforts to reach out to their women. We can credit education and encouragement via the Internet and social media for demonstrations—finally—against the culture of rape in places like New Delhi, where an internationally denouncing of gang rape occurred in 2013. These abuses are thus exposed to world scrutiny. We can support groups like Woman to Woman.org, Change.org, and Heifer International.org. And we have the clear voices of reporters like Diane Rehm and Nicholas Kristof, who relentlessly analyze current events in terms of fairness and democratic ideals.

CHANGING THE WORLD WITH INFORMATION

Heartening new research describes attempts to offer young people in Middle Eastern countries "educational courses in Arabic, math and computer training . . . as well as art activities" (Kruglanski et al. 2013, 572). The authors stress alternatives to self-significance that ends in violence and death and offer the first evidence that young people can be "de-radicalized" through offering training in "carpentry, construction work, electronics as well as cosmetics and garment training for women" (selected by the participants themselves) (572). This research was conducted among incarcerated militants in Sri Lanka. (Note: The whole issue of *American Psychologist,* vol. 68, no. 7, is devoted to peace psychology. It features articles on scientific efforts for peace, intergroup conflict, problems with building peaceful societies, the issue of existential threat, and the contribution of positive psychology as well as the "de-radicalization" work just described.)

Humanism, as proposed by Pinker and others, represents an *ideal* of civilized citizenry, but we *can* spread the humanistic message. And we have those focused, responsible, and relentlessly analytical journalists; another is inspirational Bill Moyers. There is no substitute for doing their kind of thinking and negotiating. As more and more people achieve this level of sophistication and responsibility, humankind can rise to a new level of tolerance, Spinoza's notions of human perfectibility.

We have an even more penetrating—and quicker—ally in the Internet, from which an appeal can flash across the globe in milliseconds. Nicholas Kristof (*New York Times Sunday Review*, February 5, 2012) described a group of fourth graders who complained to Universal Studios that their studio's depiction of Dr. Seuss's Lorax did not include the "environmental themes." The children's complaint "went viral quickly gathering more than 57,000 signatures" (SR 11). The petition was successful, and Universal Studios *changed* their film to depict the Lorax as Dr. Seuss had intended. Fourth graders! (We also must credit careful, relentless environmental reporters on climate change like Mary Pipher 2012.) Kristof also featured Molly Katchpole, a 22-year-old who said she resented the five-dollar-a-month fee for debit cards planned by Bank of America, a practice sure to have been adopted by other banks. Molly wrote a petition and posted it on Change.org. The petition garnered 306,000 signatures in one month. The bank withdrew its plan for the fees.

Tolerance and empathy have been shown to increase in grade-school students who experience a half-day visit to an art museum. "We see the effects in significantly higher historical empathy and tolerance measures among students randomly assigned to a school tour of Crystal Bridges" (Bowen, Greene & Kisida 2013). The researchers saw a higher effect in students from disadvantaged areas.

What would be the aspects, or constituents, of tolerance?

Empathy—being able to feel what the other person is feeling;

Frustration Tolerance—patience when confronted with an impasse and the ability to endure the tension while working on a solution;

Support—the ability to reach out and sustain the other person, physically if necessary, but also psychologically; and lastly,

Constructive Self-Doubt and Flexibility—allowing the possibility that you are not always right or that you do not have all the facts in the case. This allows you to consider the other person's point of view until you understand it and/or can accept it. This also allows you to agree to disagree without becoming enraged.

THE "CULTIVATION" OF TOLERANCE

The proper attitude toward my own needs, the needs of my family and of those around me, as well as the urgent needs of the environment, is the nurturant stance of the gardener, whose responsibility it is to cultivate, to stay sensitive to delicate ecological interdependencies.

The gardener's task is to respond appropriately to the changing requirements of organic entities so far as she can understand them; it is to facil-
itate, to enable. Between humans, the skills this task requires are tact,
generous patience, imaginative empathy, [and] to relinquish the fantasy
of perfect power. (Dinnerstein 1983, 303)

Relinquishing the "fantasy of perfect power"—narcissism—is the
impediment. As Pinker, Dawkins, and others write, the antidote to
intolerance is education. It is heartening that, more and more, children in this country are taught progressive values. From their early
years in school to high school, there is an emphasis on conflict resolution, how to recognize and correct bullying, encouragement for
doing the fair and right thing each day, responsible sexuality and
sexual tolerance, respect for ethnic diversity, and an ongoing interest in each other's religious beliefs. Children in the classroom now
have access to psychologists via Skype (Schwark 2013). In addition,
children are being taught about the principles of organic gardening,
support for local agriculture, and the proper balance between con-
servation and investment. With the use of Twitter and the Internet,
especially sites like Change.org, thoughtful, concerned people can
confer a watchful eye on world events and can *impose* tolerance
when fairness and justice are threatened. Sometimes, as we saw with
the unfair bank fees, the solution takes a few thousand signatures.
Sadly, with other conflicts, like stopping an attack on citizens, it may
still take force.

Our fancy brains can do this. Whether or not mirror neurons allow
us to be empathic is disputed (Hickok 2009). But to be fair, mirror neurons and other brain mechanisms alleged to be involved with empathy
(Baron-Cohen 2011) are entities about which we do not know all we
will know. The brain does not operate from one region at a time but is
juggling many inputs; some are higher-order functions (thinking and
decision making), and some are "reptilian" brain impulses. Empathy
is not a simple system. It is broadly represented by at least two brain
systems, emotional and cognitive (Shamay-Tsoory, Aharon-Peretz &
Perry 2009).

And we are very much helped by gratitude, which seems to be a
wholly psychological achievement, the product of a broad, higher-
order assessment. Gratitude, in turn, is a major motivator for generosity and kindness. We are inspired to give back the good things we have
received. Even infants can be seen trying to feed the mother. Saying

grace before meals is a ritualized expression of gratitude. Then empathy, caretaking, and cooperation come more naturally.

But I have been arguing that what we need more desperately is tolerance. We do not need to empathize with other religions and other cultures so much as we need to tolerate their presence and way of life without wanting to annihilate them because they are different. Living in New York is a bit like this. Even if you are in a hurry, before you catch your bus, you will hear fragments of five different languages. Dishes from around the world are simmering in their special pots. People of different faiths sometimes reveal this in their clothing style. You may admire some of them and be annoyed by others, but you do not need to disparage them because they are different. It is a rich, stimulating mix. We might call this *living in tolerance.*

This tolerance can develop as an outcome of our freedom, a democratic achievement. "Freedom, however, is not the last word," writes Viktor Frankl (1984, 184). "Freedom is only part of the story and half the truth. . . . In fact, freedom is in danger of degenerating into mere arbitrariness unless it is lived in terms of responsibleness" (134). (The crisis over gun legislation comes to mind.) Frankl then offers the following quip, which makes us laugh but gives us pause: "I recommend that the Statue of Liberty on the East Coast be supplemented by a Statue of Responsibility on the West Coast" (134).

What Frankl is saying is that freedom is not enough. We cannot just take our freedoms and run with them. They *include* responsibility to others. I would add that emotional health is continuous with responsibility. A person cannot be emotionally healthy in a bubble. It is continuous with guarding our physical health, nurturing our relationships, especially with our children, and extends to the broader ideals of democracy. Fairness must come *from* us as well as to us. This may not require religion; it will always require spirited discussion.

REFERENCES

Armstrong, K. (2005). *A Short History of Myth.* Edinburgh: Canongate Books Ltd.

Baron-Cohen, S. (2011). *The Science of Evil: On Empathy and the Origins of Cruelty.* New York: Basic Books.

Bowen, D. H., Greene, J. P. & Kisida, B. (2013). "Learning to Think Critically. A Visual Art Experiment." *Educational Researcher,* 42(8). Published online November 12, 2013. doi:10:3102/0013189x13512675

Brabeck, M. (1983). "Moral Judgement: Theory and Research of Differences between Males and Females." *Developmental Review* 3(3): 274–91.

Brizendine, L. (2006). *The Female Brain.* New York: Three Rivers Press.

Brizendine, L. (2010). *The Male Brain.* New York: Broadway Books.

Brown, N. O. (1959). *Life against Death: The Psychoanalytic Meaning of History.* Middletown, CT: Wesleyan University Press.

Byrne, R. W. & Comp, N. (2004). "Neocortex Size Predicts Deception Rate in Primates." *Proceedings of the Royal Society of London,* 271, 1693–1699. doi:10.1098/rspb.2004.2780

Byrne, R. W. & Whiten, A. (1989). *Machiavellian Intelligence: Social Expertise and the Evolution of Intellect in Monkeys, Apes and Humans.* Oxford: Oxford University Press.

Campbell, A. (2005). "Aggression." In D. Buss (Ed.), *Handbook of Evolutionary Psychology,* 622–652. New York: Wiley.

Cannon, B. (1994). "Walter Bradford Cannon: Reflections on the Man and His Contributions." *International Journal of Stress Management* 1(2): 145–158.

Clay, R. A. (2012, June). "Redefining Masculinity: Three Psychologists Strive to Build A 'Better' Man." *Monitor on Psychology* 43(6): 52–54.

Clay, R. A. (2013, July–August). "Mental Health First Aid." *Monitor on Psychology* 44(7): 32–35.

Collaer, M. L. & Hines, M. (1995). "Human Behavioral Sex Differences: A Role for Gonadal Hormones during Early Development?" *Psychological Bulletin* 118(1): 55–107.

Dawkins, R. (2006). *The God Delusion.* Boston: Houghton Mifflin Company.

Dinnerstein, D. (1976). *The Mermaid and the Minotaur: Sexual Arrangements and Human Malaise.* New York: Harper and Row.

Dinnerstein, D. (1983). "Afterword: Toward a Mobilization of Eros." In M. Murray (Ed.), *Face to Face,* 293–309. Westport, CT: Greenwood Press.

Dippel, J. V. H. (2010). *War and Sex: A Brief History of Men's Urge for Battle.* Amhurst, NY: Prometheus Books.

Dutton, K. (2013). "Wisdom from Psychopaths? A Scientist Enters a High-Security Hospital to Extract Tips and Advice from a Crowd without a Conscience." *Scientific American Mind* 23(6): 36–43.

Eagly, A. H., Eaton, A., Rose, S. M., et al. (2012). "Feminism and Psychology: Analysis of a Half-Century of Research on Women and Gender." *American Psychologist* 67(3): 211–230.

Fang, F. C. & Casadevall, A. (2013, May–June). "Why We Cheat: Scientists Are Unravelling the Causes of Fraud and Dishonesty and Devising New Strategies for Rooting Them Out." *Scientific American Mind* 24(2): 30–37.

Frank, J. D. & Frank, J. B. (1991). *Persuasion and Healing: A Comparative Study of Psychotherapy,* 3rd ed. Baltimore: The Johns Hopkins University Press.

Frankl, V. (1984). *Man's Search for Meaning: An Introduction to Logo-therapy,* 3rd ed. New York: A Touchstone Book, Simon & Schuster.

Frazer, J. (1993). *The Golden Bough: A Study in Magic and Religion.* London: Wordsworth Editions Ltd.

French, H. W. (2011, November). "E. O. Wilson's Theory of Everything." *The Atlantic Magazine,* 70–82.

Freud, S. (1961). *The Future of an Illusion.* New York: Norton & Co., Inc.

Gazzaniga, M. (2008). *Human: The Science behind What Makes Us Unique.* New York: HarperCollins Publishers.

Gilligan, C. (1982). "In a Different Voice: Women's Conceptions of Self and Morality." *Harvard Educational Review* 47(4): 431–517.

Gomez, C. A. (2012). *Man Up: Cracking the Code of Modern Manhood.* New York: Penguin Books.

Gottschall, J. (2012). *The Story-telling Animal: How Stories Make Us Human.* New York: Houghton Mifflin Harcourt.

Griffith, J. L. (2012). "Psychotherapy, Religion and Spirituality." In R. D. Alarcon & J. B. Frank (Eds.), *The Psychotherapy of Hope: The Legacy of Persuasion and Healing,* 310–325. Baltimore: The Johns Hopkins University Press.

Hickok, G. (2009). "Eight Problems for the Mirror Neuron Theory of Action Understanding in Monkeys and Humans." *Journal of Cognitive Neuroscience,* 21, 1229–1243.

James, W. (1961). *The Varieties of Religious Experience: A Study in Human Nature.* New York: Collier Books.

Jorm, A. F. (2012). "Mental Health Literacy. Empowering the Community to Take Action for Better Mental Health." *American Psychologist* 67(3): 231–243.

Kagan, J. & Lamb, S. (Eds.). (1987). *The Emergence of Morality in Young Children.* Chicago: University of Chicago Press.

Keltner, D. (2009). *Born to Be Good: The Science of a Meaningful Life.* New York: W. W. Norton & Co.

Koenig, H. G. (1999). *The Healing Power of Faith.* New York: Simon and Schuster.

Kristof, N. D. (2011, November 6). "His Libraries, 12,000 So Far, Change Lives." *New York Times Sunday Review,* SR 11. (2012, February 5). "After Recess: Save the World." *New York Times Sunday Review,* SR11. (2012, September 23). "Exploiting the Prophet." *New York Times Sunday Review,* SR13.

Kristof, N. D. & WuDunn, S. (2010). *Half the Sky: Turning Oppression into Opportunity for Women Worldwide.* New York: Vintage Books.

Kruglanski, A. W., Belanger, J. J, Gelfand, M., et al. (2013). "Terrorism—A (Self)love Story: Redirecting the Significance Quest Can End Violence." *American Psychologist* 68(7): 559–575.

Lower, W. (2013). *Hitler's Furies: German Women in the Nazi Killing Fields.* New York: Houghton Mifflin.

Luo, M. & McIntire, M. (2013, December 22). "When Right to Bear Arms Includes the Mentally Ill." *New York Times,* 1, 28–29.

Lyall, S. (2011, September 18). "Rupture of Reverence for the Vatican Sets off a Transformation in Ireland." *New York Times,* A8.

Newberg, A., D'Aquili, E. & Rause, V. (2001). *Why God Won't Go Away: Brain Science and the Biology of Belief.* New York: Ballantine Books.

Niebuhr, G. (2008). *Beyond Tolerance: Searching for Interfaith Understanding in America.* New York: Viking Penguin.

Orzhekhovskaia, N. S. (2005). "[Sex Dimorphism of Neuron-Glia Correlations in the Frontal Area of the Human Brain]." *Morfologiia* 127(1): 7–9.

Pagnani, L. (2013). "Aggressive Behaviour Linked Specifically to Second-hand Smoke Exposure in Childhood." *Journal of Epidemiology and Community Health,* online May 21.

Pavius, J. (2013, March–April). "Placebos Work Better for Nice People: Agreeable People Produce More of the Brain's Natural Painkillers." *Scientific American Mind* 24(1): 9.

Pinker, S. (2011). *The Better Angels of Our Nature: Why Violence Is Declining.* New York: Viking.

Pipher, M. (2012). "Visions of a Sustainable Planet: We Need to Expand Our Moral Imagination." *Psychotherapy Networker* 36(5): 48–53.

Potts, M. & Hayden, T. (2008). *Sex and War: How Biology Explains Warfare and Terrorism and Offers a Path to a Safer World.* Dallas, Texas: Benbella.

Raine, A. (2013). *The Anatomy of Violence: The Biological Roots of Crime.* New York: Pantheon Books.

Saletan, W. (2012, March 25). "Why Won't They Listen? A Psychologist Argues That People Base Decisions on Moral Intuition, Not Reason." *New York Times Book Review,* 12–13.

Schwark, S. (2013, December). "APA Teams with Microsoft to Bring Mental Health into the Classroom." *Monitor on Psychology* 44(11): 12.

Schwartz, J. M. & Begley, S. (2002). *The Mind and the Brain: Neuroplasticity and the Power of Mental Force.* New York: Harper Perennial.

Shamay-Tsoory, S. G., Aharon-Peretz, J. & Perry, D. (2009). "Two Systems for Empathy: A Double Dissociation between Emotional and Cognitive Empathy in Inferior Frontal Gyrus versus Ventromedial Prefrontal Lesions." *Brain,* 132, part 3 (March 2009), 617–627.

Shorter, E. (1982). *A History of Women's Bodies.* New York: Basic Books, Inc.

Smoller, J. (2012). *The Other Side of Normal: How Biology Is Providing the Clues to Unlock the Secrets of Normal and Abnormal Behavior.* New York: William Morris.

Swanson, J. (2013). "Mental Illness and New Gun Law Reform: The Promise and Peril of Crisis-Driven Policy." *Journal of the American Medical Association,* 309, 1233–1234. doi:10.1001/jama.2013.1113

Takei, M. (2012). *She-Q: Why Women Should Mentor Men and Change the World.* Santa Barbara, CA: Praeger Publishing.

Taylor, J. (2009). *Not a Chimp: The Hunt to Find the Genes That Make Us Human.* New York: Oxford University Press Inc.

Taylor, S. E., Klein, L. C., Lewis, B. P., et al. (2000). "Behavioral Responses to Stress in Females: Tend-and-Befriend, Not Fight-or-Flight." *Psychological Review* 107(3): 411–429.

Teasdale, W. (1999). *The Mystic Heart: Discovering a Universal Spirituality in the World's Religions.* Novato, CA: New World Library.

Trivers, R. (2011). *The Folly of Fools: The Logic of Deceit and Self-Deception in Human Life.* New York: Basic Books.

Tucker, A. (2013, January). "Born to Be Mild: Are We Born Knowing Right from Wrong? New Research Offers Surprising Answers to the Age-Old Question of Where Morality Comes From." *Smithsonian Magazine* 43(9): 34–41, 76–77.

Weierstall, R., Schauer, M. & Elbert, T. (2013, May–June). "An Appetite for Aggression: The Peculiar Psychology of War Likely Holds Answers for Avoiding Future Atrocities." *Scientific American Mind* 24(2): 46-49.

Wilson, E. O. (2012). *The Social Conquest of the Earth.* New York: Liveright Publishing Corporation.

Zur, O. & Morrison, A. (1989). "Gender and War: Re-Examining Attitudes." *Journal of Orthopsychiatry* 59(4): 528–533.

Conclusion

Normal is worth saving.

—Allen Frances

It is presumptuous and perhaps disrespectful to the complexity of human life to attempt a "classification" of normal behavior when any so identified will swiftly veer off into some type of variation. And any such assessment by one writer will always be inadequate. But I feel it is better to have made the attempt and to keep the discussion ongoing about ethical, cultural, and historical variations. Throughout the book, I have stressed that "normal" is a broad range while symptoms are narrow and definable. These "essentials of healthy personality" can be thought of as benchmarks, educating and encouraging us. They remind us that, just as with diet and exercise, there is much we must do for ourselves. Like physical health, our emotional well-being is a personal responsibility. For example, learning to assert in a fair way takes the same discipline as making good food choices.

This thinking is timely. Many clinicians in this country are now rethinking the value of the DSM-5, the latest version of the American Psychiatric Association's Diagnostic and Statistical Manual. One major complaint is that the DSM-5 has added so many "new" symptoms that at this point, more than 50 percent of Americans can be diagnosed with a mental illness, particularly children. "The media will trumpet the release of the new D.S.M.," writes psychiatrist and author Sally Satel in the *New York Times* "Sunday Review" (May 12, 2013), "but practicing psychiatrists will largely regard it as a nonevent.

Unfortunately, the same cannot be said for other institutions—insurance companies, state and government agencies, and even the courts—which will continue to imbue the D.S.M. with a precision and an authority it does not have" (SR5).

The rest of the world is using the ICD, the World Health Organization's International Classification of Disease. The ICD combines mental illnesses and physical disorders into fewer categories that are much easier to use. This dilemma was summarized by Chris Hopwood, PhD, assistant professor of psychology at Michigan State University: "It's obviously inefficient to have two different systems for diagnosis—one for the United States and one for the rest of the world. One wonders whether there is really a need, frankly, for the DSM given the ICD" (quoted in Clay 2013, 27).

The purpose of this book has been to deepen the reader's understanding and appreciation for the parameters of emotional health. I wanted to initiate a discussion of the complex nature of "normal" that is more nuanced, practical, and humane. In this effort of many years, I feel validated by a new book by Allen Frances, MD, whose *Saving Normal* is a sobering critique of (as stated in his subtitle) "DSM-5, Big Pharma, and the medicalization of everyday life." Frances, one of the framers of the DSM-IV, became alarmed and disillusioned by what he calls "diagnostic inflation" in DSM-5. This, he says, has produced "fake epidemics" of autism, attention deficit disorder, and childhood bipolar disorder. Exaggerated diagnoses of depression now have record numbers of Americans on antidepressants and anxiolytic medications. As I have done in this book, Frances emphasizes that most human behavior is a variation of normal and that symptoms are narrow and definable. We need to have the information to know the difference between healthy behavior and a bona fide symptom. (Chronic anxiety is a red flag; being anxious before a big exam is not. Depression that keeps a person from going to work needs to be treated; a two- or three-day depression due to a disappointment needs only basic human caring and solace, not a drug.)

As I described in the introduction, this project began in the parking lot of a high school where I had just spent the day giving talks to the health classes. One of the students caught up with me at my car and asked a question she could not ask in class: "Why does my mother sleep 18 or 19 hours a day? She's done that for my whole life. *Is that normal?*" I was stunned by her question. I asked if her mother had ever been evaluated by a physician or other professional. She became tearful. That was her dilemma. Her father would never permit an evaluation. So she desperately needed an answer from me. I told her no, clearly it was not normal. I gave her my card and said she could call me at any time. She never did.

But her question stayed with me. I began thinking of the parameters of emotional behavior we could reliably call normal. Over a number of years, I collected some 22 such features—trust, fairness, reliability, concern for others, self-responsibility including concern for one's health, realism about one's capabilities and limitations, the capacity for intimacy, and protecting and nurturing ourselves and others. Then at one point, I combined them into pairs that could be discussed together: work and play; shame and guilt; love and sex. What emerged was a core outline for emotional health as coherent, I would argue, as some principles of physical health. For example, we all aspire to excellent heart health and blood pressure and to keeping our blood sugar low, although we achieve these imperfectly. But we are very clear about what we are reaching for because physicians *teach us*. This book is saying that emotional health is an entity, one that can be learned and taught and that can be a guide in therapy. It is an outline that can be added to, discussed, and differed with. And while a work in progress, it provides guidelines or principles so that we know what we are working toward. (A number of people in therapy have asked for such a book because, they said, there was too much to remember.)

I have also attempted a reversal of our usual emphasis on "improving depression" or "reducing anxiety." Like the teenager who started this project, people were reporting confusion about what constitutes emotional health. The extant wisdom is that nothing is normal and everything is normal. But that gets us neatly off the hook; no need to struggle for definitions of normal. I have come to think of emotional symptoms as the *failure* to achieve one or more of the parameters of emotional health. For example, not having developed the skill of self-soothing (the ability to steady ourselves with our own inner strength) leaves a person anxious, disorganized, and prone to seeking drugs, alcohol, or food. Similarly, not having learned and practiced mutual respect and openness to others during our development can foster narcissism and morbid self-absorption. Not having developed the skill of assertion requires a person to accept many situations he does not agree with or want.

Other writers see different parameters as essential to healthy personality. From his four decades of studying the brain's emotional capacities, neuroscientist Richard Davidson has derived a spectrum of six "emotional styles," including resilience and positive outlook (Winerman 2012). Sometimes what is considered normal comes out of the legal system's need for specificity (Mercado & Beattey 2012). And lately, there is an accumulation of data supporting the finding that our *life*—including our health, happiness, energy, and mood—is governed by the billions of microbes in our gut, known affectionately as our *microbiome* (Conniff 2013; Pollan 2013). All these are important, mind-stretching contributions to the understanding of normal, and there are many more. Our lives are richer for reading widely and considering all of them. My own view is that normal is more *relational*, more affected by our deliberate day-to-day decision making about relationships.

Defining "normal" takes into account our social world. The limitation of much psychological research is the belief that experimental findings will apply to complex human life as it is lived. This concern is shared by the accomplished researcher Jerome Kagan, who said in an interview: "[T]here are many studies in which a team of psychologists uses one procedure in one setting, gets a result and assumes that that result would hold no matter where you did the study, no matter what the procedure was and no matter what the population was" (Winerman 2012, 28). People are not interchangeable like hamsters and rats. College sophomores will never react the same as harried parents of toddlers. A contrived psychological game, contrasting an experimental group and a control group, even with impressive statistics, hardly represents real life with its messy, relentless variability. Believing too much in such "scientific" findings simply creates villages of cognitive elites who cite one another and whose view of life is very different from those of us who value *individual* experience. For example, one of my patients with bipolar disorder struggled to explain to me her subjective experience in the depressed phase. "You know how you feel when you first wake up," she said, "and you can't immediately get your thoughts together? That's how I feel all the time. *I can't get awake enough.*" Her statement told me more about the depressive phase of bipolar disorder than any controlled study. Each patient is an "n of 1."

We have had an almost phobic resistance to calling one behavior normal and another abnormal. But at some point, we have to make a decision between a behavior that is simply self-expressive and another that ends up being harmful to oneself or to others. Consider the controversial new data on concussion in childhood and its sequellae (Eisenberg et al. 2013; Halstead & Walter 2010). Physicians and other authorities are now reconsidering the methods in many contact sports. We cannot call "normal" any behavior that routinely damages our children's brains. And what of the teenager I described above? Her service to the family was "good"—keeping house and taking care of her younger siblings. But she was actually being *exploited* by her father while her mother slept 18 hours a day. Normal behavior is fair, and another word for "fair" is "responsible."

THINKING ABOUT THERAPY

This entire book has been a thinly disguised testimonial to the benefits of therapy. But even if a person is seriously considering it, finding a "good" therapist can be a daunting task. How will you know if a therapist's impressive training is accompanied by the things that cannot be taught—insight, dedication, and, most of all, caring? Will you be ready for what a good therapist will find and the recommendations he or she will make? The courage and realism that therapy requires is generated and maintained by the *relationship* between therapist and client. You are her focus and concern for the duration of your session and beyond. You and your issues engage all her skills and compassion, as well as—for me—a passion to *understand.* What are the private meanings, the deep longings that bring you to therapy? Some of them will be developmental, hidden in the experiential vault of early childhood, as we saw in the many stories in this book. What turned the trajectory of your development this way or that? Or stopped it? How does that happen? How can things that happened long ago have any bearing on the difficulties you are having today?

As we learned from the early chapters of this book, our beliefs, attitudes, and expectations derive from the time our parents and the other adults around us structured our world. Because little children are so vulnerable, their world is shaped between those who are nurturant and those who are unhelpful and even scary. Who is protective and who unpredictable? Children form passionate bonds with the people they need (the phenomenon called attachment), and from those bonds they develop patterns of behavior *shaped by the needs of their caretakers.* If the people responsible for the care of the baby's body (feeding, bathing, holding) are caring and allow that child's self-expression (even if that includes spitting out food), then all is well. But if the person the child needs also scares him, that is the horror chamber the child must live in. In this way, a child's personality forms from two major sources: a child's genetic—and epigenetic—capacities that she brings to the interaction with a given parent and the social world she inherits. (Of course, chance has an input—a fire, a war, financial reverses that can jettison a family from their home environment.)

But now that you are all grown up, can persistent emotional problems still derive from your parent's influence? It certainly can't be the parents you know today, at this point in your life. No. It is not your mother or your father *anymore. It is the whole* pattern *of responses you developed over the years to accommodate them or to react against them.* In your present life, those patterns may not be adaptive. But because of the stability of an already formed personality, you may continue to react "as if," not recognizing that your current situation is not the same or even similar to your historical one. Without insight, we will impose the same maladaptive interpretations onto the present situation. (Freud called this the "repetition compulsion"; we set up the old conflict in the here and now in order to correct and surmount it.) Or put another way, our expectations, and even more our fears, structure our present life, *because what we insistently expect, we will verily find.*

Personality is difficult to alter even in therapy, when people state this as their deepest wish. As Freud had predicted, the patient may resist the therapist at every turn, while protesting her wish to be different. This ambivalence, this multilayered conflict, is not amenable to logical argument because its roots are subconscious. They will be expressed in actions and in metaphors the therapist must understand and interpret. This is done by recruiting the intelligent person sitting before me. I think of therapy as the maturation of the entire personality, using the adult's stamina and skills to help him transcend his historical issues. "*Persuasion and Healing* [Frank & Frank 1991] linked psychology with neuroscience by emphasizing the importance of emotional arousal in rendering established beliefs open to change" (Viamontes & Beitman 2012, 34). Memories evoked in therapy are then amenable to interpretation that offers a new, more probable version of what had happened in one's life, this time with nowhere to hide. When those experiences are put back into memory—a process that requires new proteins to be made (the finding that earned Eric Kandel the 2000 Nobel Prize)—their angering or frightening effects have been neutralized by new facts and realism.

Developmental defenses are exposed as the subterfuges they are. For example, a person may have been using rationalization—reasoning to accommodate what she wants to believe. Or denial: It's not that bad; God is testing me; he or she doesn't mean it; or (the ultimate) he or she will change. Self-deception relents, and we then have the chance for new choices. Therapy is a course you take for a semester, a year, or longer. Like any course, each session is built on the one before. The learning and growing are cumulative. There is no substitute for doing the necessary thinking, discussing, and questioning. But with persistence, patience, humor, and the willingness to look inside, you will find new and liberating truths about yourself, your family, your partner, son, or daughter that will reform the relationship and allow you a way to move forward.

Don't be too impressed with "new" therapies; they are often superficial applications of established and proven therapies, without the depth. The revered Irvin Yalom, author of many books on pychotherapy, has a chastening view:

> The "new improvements" are neither original nor better. . . . We're not teaching our students the importance of relationships and how to work on them, what relational pathology consists of—how to examine your own conscience, how to enter your inner world, how to explore your dreams. All this, all the psychodynamic stuff, it's just not getting to students today. It's just too hard to teach. It's so much simpler to teach CBT [Cognitive Behavioral Therapy]. (Yalom quoted in Howes 2012, 69–70)

Therapy can be expensive, but like anything of value in your life, it is ultimately worth it. The insurance picture is changing. Enlightened companies see a great benefit from subsidizing their workers' health, physical and emotional. Alternatively, you may decide to cover the cost yourself. Using your insurance can mean that your diagnosis—depression, anxiety, etc.—will be on the insurance forms your company will see. (Many of my patients wanted to avoid that breach of confidentiality that is legal for insurance companies but no one else.) I have also had many patients whose families paid for their therapy. This happened with teens, college students, and newly married sons and daughters. Finally, some therapists have a "sliding scale" for fees. But if you agree you need therapy, it is at least as important as some of the electronic devices you pay for, and it will teach you much more. Remember, the Internet does not have a graduate degree and a clinical license.

REVIEWING THE CHAPTERS

In the introduction, I discussed the *evolution* of the definition of "normal." What is considered normal in one culture will not be seen as normal in others. This is a point for vigorous discussion, keeping the issue of fairness front and center. One example would be women's issues as they evolve in less democratic nations. Nicholas D. Kristof and Sheryl WuDunn (2010) offer a moving and inspiring education on this subject. Similarly, what is considered normal in one *era* may be different in another. Child labor laws had to be enacted because exploitation of children was considered normal by some employers.

Second, in the introduction, I described some of the first research supporting emotional health as a condition for human happiness and well-being. This theme—that emotional health and human happiness may be, at least in part, expressions of one another—is implied throughout the book and deserves more research. No one has said this better than Viktor Frankl (1984): "[H]appiness cannot be pursued. It must ensue, and it only does so as the unintended side-effect of one's personal dedication to a cause greater than oneself" (12).

In their impressive tome *Character Strengths and Virtues,* authors Christopher Peterson and Martin Seligman (2004) describe in detail the connections between "universal virtues" and human happiness and well-being. In their "lessons from history" (the entire first section of the book) the reader is treated to a heady tour of the history of wisdom, courage, humanity, justice, temperance, and transcendence, and an analysis of their attendant virtues. Written for researchers, clinicians, and other students of human behavior, this remarkable text is valuable for its brave and clear statements of our personal responsibility in creating our own happiness. Similarly, professor of psychology Sonja Lyubomirsky (2007) has documented that happy people have better work records, take better care of their health, have more self-confidence and better marriages. These are all features of emotionally healthy people. Is this a correlation, or does emotional health produce these outcomes? Are happy children more emotionally healthy than unhappy children? What is the relationship between emotional health and happiness? I have seen that when people leave therapy successfully, they do express relief and contentment. Symptoms—anxiety, depression—make us decidedly *un*happy.

Chapter One dramatized some of the classic (Freudian) defenses that we all may use for coping at various points in our lives. We may actually have evolved with psychological defenses (Varki & Brower 2013). So why are they abnormal? Because they distort reality (some defenses more so than others), preventing us from seeing the "big picture" and the real meaning of what is happening. But they *are* adaptive, and we all may need them at times. Actually, defenses like denial, rationalization, and projection distort reality *less* than do alcohol or other drugs. The defenses are accessible in psychological treatment.

Chapter Two describes self-esteem as the product of active self-expression, or what some researchers call "mastery." Successful experiences help a child feel happy with herself, and they accrue, earning the child more and more self-esteem. The point is that we cannot give a child self-esteem; it is earned through her own effort. In contrast, "self-worth," as defined by Nathaniel Brandon, is conferred on us by a loving parent, through the overvaluation given to a baby by the caring people around her. This overvaluation results in a life-long conviction of one's own "lovable-ness."

Chapter Three addressed the basic capacity to access all our feelings, happy or sad, curious or boring, scary or funny. Being fully spontaneous means that all our feelings are welcome and available to us, even if some of those feelings make us uncomfortable. Being open to all our feelings is part of being realistic.

In Chapter Four, work and play were explored as serious developmental, self-expressive, and even identity issues. The intellectual stimulation of work can be perennially satisfying. It alternates with and is interpenetrated by "play," defined as activities we engage in for no other reason than to enjoy them. Chapter Four highlighted the disruption of the capacity for work and play that is seen in depression and the subsequent reversal of depressive symptoms through careful and respectful examination of a person's lifestyle. Particular attention was focused on a depressed person's history and work schedule, diet, and hormonal status. A full physical exam was recommended. Most life changing, in my experience, is an examination of the person's capacity for play, with its many creative and self-expressive benefits.

Chapter Five described another hallmark of emotional health, the skill of steadying oneself before a challenge or after a disappointment. This skill is usually the outcome of the long period in early childhood when we were comforted by a protective parent, and it sustains us throughout life. Many writers stress the importance of gratitude. But gratitude cannot be felt by an ungratified person. Gratitude is the *result* of having been reliably comforted and protected in childhood or having learned that skill later in life, perhaps in therapy. Researchers have linked the deficit of early comforting to problems with substance abuse, overeating, self-loathing, morbid dependency, and alcoholism.

In Chapter Six, the main topic was couples therapy and the specific aspects of a healthy love relationship. They include valuing your partner's life and goals as you do your own, vulnerability (openness), reliability and trust, and emulation of your partner. Case histories of successful couples treatment were described, with attention to anger, jealousy, power struggles, low libido, and the problem of cybersex. At least one type of couple, those locked in a perennial power struggle, has a poor prognosis. Couples like this do stay together but miserably.

Chapter Seven addressed our early relationship with food and the ongoing use and abuse of food that women in particular show. Reasons for overeating were covered, as well as the particular family dynamics that might lead to anorexia. My research innovations for the treatment of hospitalized anorectics and bulimics were outlined. A significant case study showed how binging can follow sexual abuse.

Chapter Eight. Among the most painful feelings humans can feel, both shame and guilt are nonetheless normal emotions. I explained that shame and guilt derive from very different sources in the child, and they serve two very different functions. I described how shame represents a betrayal of our own inner values, while guilt is imposed on us by others who have their own agenda for our behavior. Both shame and guilt initially can cause a diminished sense of self and even painful self-hate. But both can be understood and resolved.

Chapter Nine. A great surprise to the couples I work with is that their anger is normal. Most significant in this chapter is the distinction between assertion and aggression. Aggression is described as the motive to *hurt*, which angers one's listener and destroys relationships. Conversely, assertion is the motive to *teach* others how you feel. A true assertion reassures the other person and preserves relationships. In addition, various types of aggression were described. And while that may seem boringly obvious, some forms of aggression, like sarcasm, are new to many couples.

Chapter Ten. When antisocial tendencies are also present, pathological narcissism is one of the most destructive of human tendencies. This sounds like an exaggeration until we consider that the features of pathological narcissism—power and attention seeking, a desperate need for admiration as a nutrient, rage and intolerance of any competition, and the need for more and more influence over others—are continuous with those of any tyrant in history. Because narcissistic persons avoid therapy and so do not develop any insight, there is often a poor prognosis for change. Teaching mutual respect and openness to children early on was suggested as a buffer against narcissism.

From the earliest period of my training, I have felt that therapists are often talking about morality. "It isn't easy to separate rationality from morality, for they are intimately connected" (Takei 2012, 97). Whenever we encourage a person or a couple to be fair, we are doing exactly that. I have stressed that the quintessential feature of healthy behavior is *fairness*—to others and to ourselves. It is the criterion that every child understands and insists on. Thus we may say that a major criterion for *ab*normal behavior is *exploitation*. This may sound reductionist, and it is, since psychoanalysis has shown that much of human motivation is subconscious. Nonetheless, I believe it is a powerful guideline. If we look for the exploitation, we will find the symptom. And narcissism, by definition, is among the most exploitative.

Chapter Eleven. Neurophysiologists at the University of Pennsylvania (Andrew Newberg, Eugene D'aquili & Vince Rause 2001) and neurologist Kevin Nelson (2011) have written that our brains are programmed to provide personal experience that transcends the body. I discussed their findings that spirituality is part of our *biology*. Religion is a feature of human groups everywhere, and so it is reasonable to say that the *longing* to connect with the ineffable is normal and can enrich our lives. That is a good thing, I contend, so long as religious feelings do not create an "us" and a "them"—a group who are perceived as different and thus are to be hated and discriminated against. I contend that tolerance is a learned skill and our only hope for living together harmoniously. The chapter continues with a discussion of gender differences as they bear on aggression. This is a theme made newly relevant by journalists and researchers. They document violence as emanating from cultures with large numbers of young, poorly educated males. These journalists are campaigning for more and better education as the modifier of such violence. I would ask if the violence against *women* in these cultures is not a significant complication. Would more fair attitudes toward women be part of the education of these young men? If not, where is the solution?

Some themes span several chapters. In Chapters 4, 6, 9, 10, and 11, self-responsibility is addressed as a hallmark of emotional health. This message can hardly be more timely. Examples of self-responsibility are inspirational. It was one woman border guard who stopped the twentieth hijacker in the 9/11 tragedy from entering the United States from Canada. And in the 1960s, one guardian of our FDA, Frances Oldham Kelsey, stopped thalidomide from being approved, preventing scores of short-limbed and no-limbed children from being born in the United States. Individual responsibility matters. Despite this emphasis, I do not expect that readers will hear this as a moralistic rant, but rather a wide-ranging explanation of why self-responsibility is a major feature of "normal."

Chapters Four and Seven waved a banner for alternative medicine with a strong emphasis on nutrition and bio-identical (human) hormone replacement. In Chapter Four I also cited arguments against pharmacotherapy. A wave of responsible criticism has emerged on this topic. David Healy's *Pharmageddon* (2012) exposes the astronomically inflated prices of drugs and other crimes by the drug companies. In *Saving Normal,* Allen Frances (2013) launches an informed and focused attack, long overdue, on the American Psychiatric Association's "inflated diagnoses" and "false epidemics." Frances's allegations dovetail nicely with my own view, as in his statement, "It remains reasonable to hold out some hope that common sense will eventually prevail. Who would have thought that Big Tobacco, once so seemingly invincible, could be taken down so quickly? . . . Big Pharma is clearly riding for the same fall—this emperor really does have no clothes" (282).

Yes. Then let's do the same for Big Fast Food. They consistently put profits before our children's health. Over the last 14 years, says a report in *Environmental Nutrition* (August 2013), the nutritional quality of fast food has increased only modestly. They are not even trying.

Over the years, I have used specific chapters to help people struggling in a particular area. A man suffering from guilt and shame would get Chapter Eight. A woman with self-esteem issues would read Chapter Two. Couples would get Chapter Six, Love and Sex, and bring their observations and questions into their therapy hour. Thus the chapters have grown by accretion, becoming more useful and relevant.

THE ALL-IMPORTANT DIFFERENCE: OUR CREATIVITY

So will we all be the same if we are emotionally normal? Hardly. Tolstoy famously wrote that happy families were all happy in the same way but that unhappy families were each unhappy in their own way (from the opening lines of *Anna Karenina*). He may have been noting that happy families show caring, enjoying one another's company and putting family needs before personal ones. If all humans behaved this way, we should not complain. Where we do differ significantly, whether happy or sad, is in our *creativity*. It begins early in our childhood preferences for special colors and favorite music. When we are older, creativity can move outdoors—swimming , tennis, hiking, canoeing. Or a fascination for things close to the earth—leaves, flowers, bugs. Then there is the discovery of a lifetime. A child makes a connection between some loved activity and his *future*—like a fascination with robots that leads to a career in prosthetics.

Many artists and other uniquely talented people have shown behaviors that seem quite abnormal; Lawrence Kubie (1969) discusses a number of them. My only point is that our uniqueness is in our creativity. Our musical, mathematical, and artistic abilities will always be individual expressions. Just as our genome is unique, so are our creations. Aristotle said that of all aspects of thinking, metaphor is the only one that cannot be taught. It comes out of our imagination. To tie this to the book's theme, we will not all be the same if we keep reaching for emotional health. Our originality will always make us unique.

SUMMARIZING THREE VIEWS OF "NORMAL"

Jordan Smoller (2012), the research psychiatrist and geneticist, stresses that normal refers to "a landscape of human possibilities" (324). "Variation," he says, "is part of its very definition" (334). "When I talk about the biology of normal, I'm referring to an understanding of what the brain and the mind are designed to do and how they function across the spectrum of human endeavor. We are now beginning to build that understanding through an unprecedented convergence of anthropology, genomics, psychology and neuroscience" (42).

Smoller highlights the work of professor of social work Jerome Wakefield (1992), who proposed a model of "harmful dysfunction" to help explain what makes a behavior abnormal. Disorders arise from "harmful failure of some internal mechanism to perform a function for which it was biologically designed" (Smoller 2012, 335). In a critique of the DSM-111-R, Wakefield (1992) wrote:

> I argue that disorder lies on the boundary between the given natural world and the constructed social world; a disorder exists when the

failure of a person's internal [homeostatic] mechanisms to perform their functions as designed by nature impinges harmfully on the person's well-being as defined by social values and meanings. The order that is disturbed when one has a disorder is thus simultaneously biological and social; neither alone is sufficient to justify the label *disorder*. (1992, 373; italics in original.)

This fits well with my notion that, for example, a *failure*, or dysfunction, to develop some *normal* parameter—for example, self-soothing and comforting—leaves people vulnerable to anxiety and drawn to drugs or alcohol. And failing to achieve spontaneity cuts a person off from information about our behavior that is obvious to others but not to oneself.

In Allen Frances's important, paradigm-shifting *Saving Normal* (2013), he also emphasizes the most notable feature of "normal"—its variability. All of us, he says, show a wide range of feelings and responses:

We can feel sadness, grief, worry, anger, disgust and terror because these are all adaptive. At times (especially in response to interpersonal, psychological, and practical stresses), our emotions may temporarily get out of hand and cause considerable distress or impairment. But homeostasis [the body's propensity to seek balance] and time are great natural healers, and most people resiliently right themselves and regain their normal balance. Psychiatric disorder consists of symptoms and behaviors that are *not self-correcting*—a breakdown in the normal homeostatic healing process. Diagnostic inflation occurs when we confuse the typical perturbations that are part of everyone's life with true psychiatric disorder (which is relatively uncommon, perhaps affecting 5 to 10 percent of the population at any given time). (31–32; emphasis added)

That is a generous and tolerant view, one that emphasizes individual experience. People do "right themselves" in time, but what of the damage that might have occurred while a person's emotions are out of control? Examples are all around us, but consider this hypothetical one: a man who periodically "blows up" at the supper table in a fit of profanity, terrifying his small children and driving his wife further from their intimate relationship. Is this kind of variability normal? I think not, because those "blowups" set the emotional tenor of this family's life. His children will be fearful at *every* suppertime in anticipation of their father's outburst, although it may only happen every three to four weeks. While *most of this man's behavior may be normal, his blowups are abnormal,* a form of aggression that consistently hurts others. Even if he is remorseful following his outbursts, he is essentially saying, "You have to put up with me. I need to blow up occasionally, and you have to be there for me to vent on." In a word, to be his built-in victims.

These outbursts are a *pattern,* one that will not resolve by itself. Neurosis can be defined as a learned pattern of maladaptive behavior developed in response to pressures against normal, autonomous growth. But now that this man is grown, he has a responsibility to understand and alter his behavior because of its effect on others. This change can be brought about by brave soul-searching, by talking with his family, or by speaking with a rabbi or minister. Or it may require the careful, sustained, and respectful analysis offered in therapy. How different this man's family life would be if he overcame his abusive tantrums. Following Allen Frances's reasoning, a person exhibiting one of these damaging behaviors may be essentially normal otherwise. I accept this, but I believe that person must take responsibility for the neurotic (abnormal) parts—understanding but not blaming the past and taking steps to change the present and the future.

My own view of "normal" is more relational than that of Smoller and Frances and somewhat closer to Wakefield, in that he insists on a social, interactional sphere. My professional views have been shaped by the *Object Relations* school of psychoanalysis, which teaches that a child's personality develops in the *interaction* with the parent in the unique individual responses between the two. This departure from Freud's *drive theory* was first proposed by W. R. D. Fairbairn (1952) and later expanded in the innovations of Donald Winnicott and others. (Drive theory assumed that all humans are dominated by two instincts, sex and aggression, and could only react according to those constraints.)

Much of psychoanalysis has progressed beyond this. Object Relations theory and therapy holds that the child is born innocent, helpless and deserving, and seeks attachment with the parent. The "new emphasis on the importance of interpersonally created meanings is the basis for the relational approach to psychoanalysis, a movement initiated by Fairbairn's insistence that the most important source of personality development is what actually happens between the child and his or her objects [parents]" (Celani 2010, 209–210). This position corrects the errors of drive theory while retaining Freud's valuable insights regarding psychological defenses and intrapsychic experience.

THE ESSENTIALS OF HEALTHY PERSONALITY

What have we learned about normality from these chapters that we can now *practice*? It is possible to derive some premises—we might even say *constructs*—about what is normal. Following the chapter format, we may say that:

(From Chapter One, Realism): We will try to focus on as many particulars of a situation as possible in our quest for objectivity, being aware that if we become anxious or angry, we are prone to denial, projection, rationalization, or any of the other classic Freudian defenses. We can think of "realism" as another word for "wisdom."

(From Chapter Two, Self-Esteem and Self-Confidence): We are aware that self-esteem comes from our own efforts and achievements and that no one can *give us* self-esteem. Conversely, self-worth, following Nathaniel Brandon, *is* given to us by loving parents and becomes our conviction of "lovable-ness." In turn, feeling loved and valued inspires us to achieve more, leading to greater self-esteem.

(From Chapter Three, Spontaneity): We accept all our feelings, even if they make us uncomfortable. We strive to understand those feelings without pushing them away because feelings enrich and inform our lives. This is how insight is developed.

(From Chapter Four, Work and Play): We appreciate that work and play derive from our creativity and often overlap and merge. We try to connect with work that is meaningful and fulfilling, but even lacking that, we continue the creative forms of play—painting, hiking, sewing, collecting, woodworking, singing, dance, gardening—that we loved as children. Childhood is full of clues to a happier life and sometimes teaches us what to avoid.

(From Chapter Five, Self-Soothing and Comforting): A healthy adult will be able to steady himself in disturbing situations without drugs or alcohol, calming the body and mind with humor and encouragement, breathing and exercise. This skill is normally learned as a toddler from a loving parent but it is effectively acquired later in life, often in therapy.

(From Chapter Six, Love and Sex): We strive for intimacy and sexual happiness, forming deep, long-lasting emotional bonds with others, especially partners, as well as caring about human welfare in general. We can communicate sexual frustrations and resolve them with the partner's help.

(From Chapter Seven, Food): We form a protective attitude toward our body, wanting clean and wholesome food for self and family, and we take a strong stance against polluters of our food supply—from banning pesticides as well as cheap, artery-clogging fast food and soda. Being thin is only part of the issue; being healthy in a healthy world is the rest (Pollan 2009).

(From Chapter Eight, Shame and Guilt): We will be aware that shame and guilt are normal emotions, that shame is a general "guardian" (Wurmser 1981) of our personal values. We know that the way to deal with shame is by fulfilling our outstanding responsibilities. *Chronic* shame or guilt, however, is a "red flag." It is evidence that a person cannot resolve his or her issues and would benefit from therapy.

(From Chapter Nine, Assertion versus Aggression): We understand the important difference between assertion and aggression—that is, that assertion is *teaching* the other person what you mean, whereas aggression is an attack. This skill follows the equation often used in negotiation: I don't want to hurt you, but I can't let you hurt me. Learning to assert builds self-esteem and self-responsibility, getting us more of what we want.

(From Chapter Ten, Mutual Respect, Vulnerability, and the Price of Narcissism): We will appreciate that mutual respect and narcissism are opposite motives. Mutual respect is based on the belief that the other person has the same rights and privileges we want for ourselves. Narcissism, except in early childhood, is destructive of relationships. Mutual respect and vulnerability must be cultivated and practiced for relationships to thrive. There is neurological evidence that practices such as mindfulness can increase the capacity for empathy (Holzel et al. 2011).

(From Chapter Eleven, Spirituality): We recognize spirituality as part of our *biology*, that our brains are wired for spiritual experiences (Nelson 2011; Newberg et al. 2001). We try to cultivate a high tolerance for ambiguity and will reform our views in the light of new evidence. While a very personal journey, an open curiosity and wonder about the universe and our place in it is good for our emotional and physical health. Atheism may close the door prematurely and can be rigid and unappreciative of the gifts of religion—for example, much of the world's art, architecture, and sacred music. But disillusionment with organized religion can be constructive and responsible; for example, abhorring sexual abuse of children by Catholic priests.

Do I dare to be even more concise and allow *three* premises/constructs? Could these three be a condensate of all the chapters above? Perhaps. All three are saying that "normal" means "self-responsible." Here is a trio that makes "normality" more specifiable:

1. Emotionally healthy adults *financially support themselves* (unless they are disabled or elderly, and even then they may contribute to their support). This one skill gathers many maturational points.
2. Emotionally healthy people *take responsibility for all their behavior, all four categories of behavior: words, feelings, thoughts, and actions.*
3. Emotionally healthy people *seek feedback from others about their behavior.* They don't just assume their behavior is fine; they pay attention to the effects of their behavior on others, especially children. *Then they reform their behavior to accommodate the legitimate needs of the other.*

These three tenets are offered as *goals*, not as weighty admonitions. They measure more our resolve to attain them than our day-to-day strength to do so. Like Michael Pollan's (2009) nine-word mantra "eat real food, not too much, mostly from plants," they will be imperfectly achieved. And like the "holy trinity" of the body—cardiovascular health, low blood pressure, and low blood sugar—they may be viewed as attainable only with superhuman effort.

Not so. The first—financially supporting oneself—is already very common. The second—taking full responsibility for all our behavior—is always a work in progress. (We get tired at times of all that responsibility and just want to sleep in. Or we get angry when we are the only one pulling our weight. And sometimes we get the flu.)

It is the third premise—seeking feedback from others and reforming our behavior accordingly—that reveals a truly thoughtful, flexible, sensitive, strong, and caring person. This third premise is the point where one's maturity, caring, and realism come together—maturity because it shows a person's ability to hold differing opinions in mind without becoming overwhelmed; caring because it comes from our emotional attachment rather than from cognition; and realism because it gives us the "big picture."

Again, the most defensive, rigid, unreachable people will not seek this kind of feedback from others, nor will they observe on their own the hurt and confusion their behavior causes in their spouse, their child, or their employee. In people this rigid, a fragile sense of self obliges them to resist the influence of others and maintain an inner conviction of superiority. Any criticism, however legitimate, will be met with cold silence or angry rejection. This morbid self-absorption—"my way or the highway" thinking—is the source of much human suffering.

The point at which a person's heart can curve back toward the other—the *heartcurve point?*—varies with one's ability to care. As we said above, it comes from emotional bonding rather than from cognition (although it is much helped by good thinking). This ability to care is in turn founded in a strong sense of self that is not threatened by the needs of others and allows that others are similarly deserving. This flexibility is a hallmark of normal functioning (Kubie 1969). There is a kind of *scale* that we perceive in others quite early on, their degree of openness—all the way from a reliably open demeanor to a usually closed attitude. More than anything else, this point determines the kind of relationship we can have with anyone.

A NORMAL PERSON

Gathered together into a concept, what does a "normal" person look and sound like? While the parameters are the same for men, I describe a woman (because it is mostly women who come for therapy) and a mother (because most of the women I have treated are mothers):

Because she can love deeply and work reliably, she fulfills Freud's two criteria for a normal life. And because she can play and enjoys it, she fulfills a whole set of capacities that are equally important. She becomes angry if people try to manipulate her, and she tells them so, without abusing them. She struggles with eating unhealthy foods, especially if she lets herself become too tired or too hungry.

Sometimes anger devolves into loud voices and hurt feelings. When this happens, she gives herself and the other person time, writing down the complaints each has made. Then they try again. She knows that sex is a good part of life, an important bond between her and her partner, but that the bond can be damaged if busy adults do not make time for sex.

She knows that to have one thing in life often means you have to give up another. She makes time for creativity, her own and others'. She is trustworthy and expects others to be the same. When they are not, she does not cooperate with them.

She cries because she cannot accomplish everything on her list every day. She laughs because she knows she puts all that on herself. Because she tries to be fair in all her interactions and makes amends when she is not; because she puts her best effort into all she does, and because she sees others as equally important as herself, she *is* normal.

Because her family's physical health is as important to her as their emotional health, because she takes responsibility for all her behavior and seeks feedback from others about how she is doing, and because she has a protective attitude toward her body as if she were her own child, *she is emotionally normal.* Her life may not be perfect, her health may not be perfect, but she *is* normal.

REFERENCES

Celani, D. P. (2010). *Fairbairn's Object Relations Theory in the Clinical Setting.* New York: Columbia University Press.

Clay, R. (2013 March). "The New DSM." *Monitor on Psychology* 44(3): 26–27.

Conniff, R. (2013 May). "The Body Eclectic." *Smithsonian Magazine,* 40–47.

Eisenberg, M. A., Andrea, J., Meehan, W., et al. (2013). "Time Interval between Concussions and Symptom Duration." *Pediatrics* 132(1): 8–17.

Fairbairn, W. R. D. (1952). *Psychoanalytic Studies of the Personality.* London: Routledge & Kegan Paul.

Frances, A. (2013). *Saving Normal: An Insider's Revolt against Out-of-Control Psychiatric Diagnosis, DSM-5, Big Pharma, and the Medicalization of Ordinary Life.* New York: HarperCollins.

Frank, J. D. & Frank, J. B. (1991). *Persuasion and Healing: A Comparative Study of Psychotherapy,* 3rd ed. Baltimore: The Johns Hopkins University Press.

Frankl, V. (1984). *Man's Search for Meaning: An Introduction to Logotherapy.* 3rd ed. New York: Touchstone.

Freud, A. (1966). *The Ego and the Mechanisms of Defense.* New York: International Universities Press.

Halstead, M. E. & Walter, K. D. (2010). "Sport-Related Concussion in Children and Adolescents." *Pediatrics* 126(3): 597–615.

Healy, D. (2012). *Pharmageddon.* Los Angeles: University of California Press.

Holzel, B. K. (2010). "Stress Reduction Correlates with Structural Changes in the Amygdale." *Social, Cognitive and Affective Neuroscience*, 5(1): 11–17.

Holzel, B. K., Carmody, J., Vangel, M., et al. (2011). "Mindfulness Practice Leads to Increases in Regional Brain Gray Matter Density." *Psychiatry Research* 191(1): 36–43.

Howes, R. (2012, July–August). "Looking Back to Move Forward: Irvin Yalom on Psychotherapy as Craft." *Psychotherapy Networker*, 69–70.

Kristof, N. D. & WuDunn, S. (2010). *Half the Sky: Turning Oppression into Opportunity for Women World-Wide.* New York: Vintage.

Lyubomirsky, S. (2007). *The How of Happiness: A New Approach to Getting the Life You Want.* New York: Penguin Press.

Mercado, C. C. & Beattey, R. A. (2012, November). "Is That a 'Normal' Behavior?" *Monitor on Psychology* 43(11): 25.

Nelson, K. (2011). *The Spiritual Doorway in the Brain: A Neurologist's Search for the God Experience.* New York: Dutton, Penguin Group Inc.

Newberg, A., D'Aquili, E. & Rause, V. (2001). *Why God Won't Go Away: Brain Science and the Biology of Belief.* New York: Ballantine Books.

Peterson, C. & Seligman, M. E. P. (2004). *Character Strengths and Virtues. A Handbook and Classification.* Washington, DC: American Psychological Association/Oxford University Press.

Pollan, M. (2009). *Food Rules: An Eater's Manual.* New York: Penguin Books.

Pollan, M. (2013, May). "Some of My Best Friends Are Bacteria." *New York Times Magazine*, May 19, 2013, 38–43, 50, 58–59.

Satel, S. (2013, May 12). "Why the Fuss Over the DSM-5?" *New York Times Sunday Review*, SR5.

Smoller, J. (2012). *The Other Side of Normal: How Biology Is Providing the Clues to Unlock the Secrets of Normal and Abnormal Behavior.* New York: William Morrow.

Takei, M. (2012). *She-Q: Why Women Should Mentor Men and Change the World.* Santa Barbara, CA: Praeger Publishers.

Varki, A. & Brower, D. (2013). *Denial: Self-Deception, False Beliefs and the Origins of the Human Mind.* New York: Twelve Press.

Viamontes, G. I. & Beitman, B. D. (2012). "Neural Substrates of Psychotherapy." In R. D. Alarcon & J. B. Frank, (Eds.), *The Psychotherapy of Hope. The Legacy of Persuasion and Healing.* Baltimore: The Johns Hopkins University Press.

Wakefield, J. C. (1992). "The Concept of Mental Disorder. On the Boundary between Biological Facts and Social Values." *American Psychologist* 47(3): 373–388.

Winerman, L. (2012, August). "Changing Our Brains, Changing Ourselves." *Monitor on Psychology* 43(8): 30–33.

Winerman, L. (2012, October). "The Ghost in the Lab." *Monitor on Psychology* 43(9): 28–31.

Wurmser, L. (1981). *The Mask of Shame*. Baltimore: The Johns Hopkins University Press.

Index

Page numbers in **bold** indicate main topics in the book.

About the Author

Camay Woodall, PhD, is currently working as a clinical psychologist in private practice. She was trained at the Johns Hopkins Hospital Department of Psychiatry and Behavioral Sciences, where she held a faculty position for six years.

Dr. Woodall holds a doctorate in psychology from Rutgers University, Newark, NJ. She worked in biochemistry research for 10 years while doing graduate work in psychology.

Dr. Woodall has published in the areas of eating disorders, personality disorders, and human sexuality.

Her publications include "Sexual Functioning of Female Eating Disordered Patients," with B. S. Rothschild, P. J. Fagan, & A. Andersen, in *International Journal of Eating Disorders* 10(4): 389–394, 1991; "The Use of Metaphor and Poetry Therapy in the Treatment of the Reticent Subgroup of Anorectic Patients," with A. Andersen, in L. M. Hornyak & E. K. Baker, *Experiential Therapies for Eating Disorders* (New York: Guilford Press, 1989); and "The Body as a Transitional Object in Bulimia: A Critique of the Concept," in *Adolescent Psychiatry*, vol. 14, 179–184, 1987.